An Annotated Anthology of Hymns

An Annotated Anthology of Hymns

edited with commentary by
J. R. WATSON

with a foreword by
TIMOTHY DUDLEY-SMITH

OXFORD
UNIVERSITY PRESS

OXFORD

UNIVERSITY PRESS

Great Clarendon Street, Oxford OX2 6DP

Oxford University Press is a department of the University of Oxford.
It furthers the University's objective of excellence in research, scholarship,
and education by publishing worldwide in

Oxford New York

Auckland Bangkok Bogotá Buenos Aires Cape Town Chennai
Dar es Salaam Delhi Hong Kong Istanbul Karachi Kolkata
Kuala Lumpur Madrid Melbourne Mexico City Mumbai Nairobi
São Paulo Shanghai Singapore Taipei Tokyo Toronto

and an associated company in Berlin

Oxford is a registered trade mark of Oxford University Press
in the UK and in certain other countries

Published in the United States
by Oxford University Press Inc., New York

© J. R. Watson 2002

The moral rights of the author have been asserted
Database right Oxford University Press (maker)

First published 2002

British Library Cataloguing in Publication Data

Data available

Library of Congress Cataloging in Publication Data

Data applied for

ISBN 0–19–826973–0

1 3 5 7 9 10 8 6 4 2

Typeset in Plantin
by Regent Typesetting, London
Printed in Great Britain
on acid-free paper by
T.J. International Ltd.,
Padstow, Cornwall

To
Kenneth and Margaret Trickett

Foreword

It is just a century, give or take a year or two, since *The Oxford Book of English Verse* was published under the same imprint as this present collection. Charles Cannan, a Fellow of Trinity and Secretary to the Clarendon Press, had entrusted the editorship to his close friend 'Q', Arthur Quiller-Couch, not yet forty and still some years away from his knighthood and his professorial chair. The book, according to Q's biographer, 'was received rather coldly at first but after a year or two came rapidly into favour and won recognition as the finest anthology of English verse that had ever been published'.

A few years later the Clarendon Press issued, in their still-familiar blue and gilt binding, *The Oxford Hymn Book*; and perhaps these two collections are the legitimate forebears of this book, even though the one is an anthology of verse rather than hymnody, and the latter contains both words and music for congregational use. Since then there have been three further editions of *The Oxford Book of English Verse*, the first a substantial revision by Q himself, the latest in 1999. In between came a whole range of Oxford anthologies of verse; and among their contributors are a number of names to be found among the authors of this present collection of hymns. In Q's original anthology of 1900, necessarily excluding all writers born after about 1860 or 1870, we find Addison and Alford; Blake, Bunyan, Bridges; and on to Watts and Whittier (no Wesley) making a total of some sixteen names also represented in the pages that follow. When we come to Lord David Cecil's *The Oxford Book of Christian Verse*, 1940, or Donald Davie's new edition of it in 1981, the total rises (as one would expect) to show about one in four of their chosen contributors to be represented here. Sometimes, indeed, they are generously represented: by the 1981 edition Isaac Watts and Charles Wesley account for eleven entries each, including a number of their hymns; and these two anthologies contain names now primarily associated with hymnody and remembered for their hymns rather than their verse. Such would include Samuel Crossman, Philip Doddridge, William Kethe, John Mason Neale, and James Montgomery. They demonstrate how in certain authors English poetry and English hymnody happily converge.

Three years after Lord David Cecil's 1940 anthology George Sampson, a London County Council Inspector of Schools and a lifelong enthusiast for the English language, was invited to give the British Academy Warton lecture, whose purpose is to present some aspect of English poetry. He chose to speak on hymns. The published version of his lecture entitled 'The Century of Divine Songs' (in his *Seven Essays*: Cambridge, 1947) is celebrated for his robust advocacy of the hymn as a literary form. So, describing Charles Wesley, he writes:

> He could express his great theme in forms so numerous that he became the most varied and audacious metrist of his time. We could spend a whole lecture in illustrating the fertility of his invention. Yet, is it not strange, the histories of prosody barely mention him? If his hymns had been addressed to Pan or Apollo or some other heathen figure, or if they were written in some foreign tongue, how loud the praise would be! But alas, he addressed the Christian Deity in English, and his poems are dismissed as mere hymns.

It is akin (though George Sampson was a lover rather than a writer of hymns) to Jane Austen's ironic defence of her art in *Northanger Abbey*. 'Oh! it is only a novel!' she writes,

> only some work in which the greatest powers of the mind are displayed, in which the most thorough knowledge of human nature, the happiest delineation of its varieties, the liveliest effusions of wit and humour are conveyed to the world in the best chosen language.

George Sampson gives similarly short shrift to those who would patronize or belittle the significance of hymnody, either in religion or as part of our literary heritage. 'The hymn is the ordinary man's theology,' he declares:

> The hymn echoes in the heart when the sermon is forgotten. Preachers may be feeble, and even foolish; but hymn does more than pulpit can to justify God's ways to man. It follows, therefore, that people should be given real hymns, and not deceptive imitations. Some people make a grave charge against hymns, and say that they are not poetry. I make a much graver charge, and say that many of them are not hymns. A hymn, like a ballad or a shanty, is a species of its own, and must be true to itself, and not spread itself out as a jelloid substance of blancmange consistency, flaccid, easily swallowed, and totally innutritious.

The pages that follow, illuminated by Professor Watson's notes and comments, offer just such real hymns, true to the genre and as effective, under God's good Spirit, in teaching and nourishing the soul as when they left their authors' hands.

Nearly half the hymn writers here represented were also included in *The Oxford Hymn Book* of 1908: real hymns are a lasting inheritance. They are supplemented by a range of writers belonging to the last hundred years, some still living (in spite of a widespread assumption that all hymn writers are dead) and writing for this twenty-first century; and by some earlier authors who had fallen out of fashion or who did not find favour with the editors, T. B. Strong, Dean of Christ Church, and William Sanday, Lady Margaret Professor of Divinity. In their 1908 book there is no Joachim Neander or Philipp Nicolai, no Ray Palmer or Dean Plumptre, no George Matheson or Horatius Bonar. It is a sign of their times that they included the work of very few women compared with this present collection: no Sarah Adams or Elizabeth Clephane; no Charlotte Elliott, Dora Greenwell, or Frances Ridley Havergal; no Anna Waring, Anne Steele, or Fanny Crosby. By contrast this book finds room for at least one hymn from each of these, together with later or even contemporary women writers: Mary Byrne, Elizabeth Cosnett, Frances Cox, Eleanor Farjeon, Julia Ward Howe, Eleanor Hull, and Joyce Placzek, better known as Jan Struther.

At their best, hymns lift the heart; and this collection, even when read rather than sung (and a quiet reading will often reveal what singers miss) is no exception. An earlier Professor of English, C. S. Lewis, wrote once of the Psalms what is true for all Christian hymnody:

What must be said, however, is that the Psalms are poems, and poems intended to be sung: not doctrinal treatises, nor even sermons. Those who talk of reading the Bible 'as literature' sometimes mean, I think, reading it without attending to the main thing it is about; like reading Burke with no interest in politics, or reading the *Aeneid* with no interest in Rome.

Not all the hymns that follow refer to our Lord Jesus Christ by name; but we can say of all truly Christian hymnody that He himself, implicitly where not explicitly, is 'the main thing it is about'. Wesley scholars are not totally agreed whether Charles Wesley's 'Christ the Friend of Sinners' is the hymn referred to in his journal which he began two days after his momentous conversion on Whitsunday 1738 'but was persuaded to break off, for fear of pride'. But without doubt it still poses the question to which, in one sense or another, every hymn in this collection is the reply:

> Where shall my wond'ring soul begin?
> How shall I all to heaven aspire?
> A slave redeemed from death and sin,
> A brand plucked from eternal fire,
> How shall I equal triumphs raise,
> Or sing my great Deliverer's praise?

Timothy Dudley-Smith

Ford, Salisbury
February 2001

Acknowledgements

I am grateful to the Council of the University of Durham for allowing me research leave in the Epiphany and Easter Terms of 1998 in order to begin work on this anthology. I would also like to thank the librarians of the University, especially of the Special Collections: this book would have been impossible without the resources of the Pratt Green Collection, which have made the Library such an important study centre for those who are interested in hymnology. The Trustees of the Fred Pratt Green Trust have been very supportive in the development of this Collection, and I am glad to record here a great debt to their imaginative and generous help.

The Introduction was read by Timothy Dudley-Smith, who made some valuable suggestions for its improvement: his scholarship, his wide knowledge of hymnody, and his feeling for language, have been an inspiration. His hymns have gladdened the hearts of many people over the years, and this book is greatly enriched by his graceful and dignified Foreword—so that he both begins and ends this book. I am deeply indebted to him.

My greatest debt, however, is recorded in the dedication: since we worked together on the *Companion to Hymns and Psalms* I have come to regard Kenneth Trickett as a scholar, critic and friend. He has seen almost every entry in this anthology, and his comments, criticisms, and corrections have been essential. Invariably, he has been encouraging, uncomplaining, and perceptive, and without his help this book would be much the poorer. Any errors that remain are, of course, my responsibility.

I should finally record my debt to Joyce Horn, for negotiating the copyrights and for being helpful far beyond the call of duty; and to Hilary O'Shea and the Oxford University Press for having faith in this project, and for being patient while it was being completed.

J. R. Watson

Durham
1 June 2001

Contents

Introduction   I

1. Ancient and Medieval Hymns   10

  1.   Hail, gladdening Light   11
  2.   Let all mortal flesh keep silence   12
  3.   The day of Resurrection   13
  4.   O happy band of pilgrims   15
  5.   The day is past and over   16
  6.   Of the Father's love begotten   18
  7.   We come with songs of blessing   20
  8.   Hark! a herald voice is calling   21
  9.   Blessed City, heavenly Salem   23
 10.   Sing, my tongue, the glorious battle   25
 11.   The royal banners forward go   28
 12.   *Hail thee, Festival Day*   30
 13.   Now that the daylight fills the sky   32
 14.   Before the ending of the day   33
 15.   O come, O come, Emmanuel   34
 16.   *All glory, laud, and honour*   36
 17.   Come, Holy Ghost, our souls inspire   38
 18.   Creator Spirit, by whose aid   39
 19.   Ye choirs of new Jerusalem   40
 20.   O what their joy and their glory must be   41
 21.   All creatures of our God and King   43
 22.   Jesus, the very thought of thee   44
 23.   Jesu, thou joy of loving hearts   46
 24.   Jerusalem the golden   47
 25.   Light's abode, celestial Salem   50
 26.   Day of wrath! O day of mourning!   52
 27.   To the Name of our Salvation   55
 28.   Ye sons and daughters of the King   57
 29.   The strife is o'er, the battle done   58
 30.   I bind unto myself today   60

31. Christ is the world's redeemer   63

2. The Reformation: England and Germany   65

32. All people that on earth do dwell   66
33. A safe stronghold our God is still   67
34. Out of the depths I cry to thee   69
35. Wake, O wake! with tidings thrilling   71
36. Ah, Holy Jesu, how hast thou offended   72
37. Now thank we all our God   73
38. The duteous day now closeth   75
39. All my heart this night rejoices   77
40. Praise to the Lord! the Almighty   79
41. All my hope on God is founded   81
42. Jerusalem, my happy home   83
43. My God, I love thee; not because   86
44. Let us, with a gladsome mind   87
45. The Lord will come and not be slow   89
46. The Lord's my shepherd, I'll not want   91

3. The Seventeenth Century: Anglicans and Puritans   93

47. Let all the world in every corner sing   94
48. King of glory, King of peace   95
49. Teach me, my God and King   97
50. The God of love my Shepherd is   99
51. My soul, there is a country   100
52. He wants not friends that hath thy love   102
53. Lord, it belongs not to my care   104
54. Ye holy angels bright   105
55. Who would true valour see   107
56. My song is love unknown   109
57. How shall I sing that majesty   111
58. Awake, my soul, and with the sun   113
59. Glory to thee, my God, this night   114
60. As pants the heart for cooling streams   116
61. Through all the changing scenes of life   117
62. While shepherds watched their flocks by night   119

4. Isaac Watts   121

63. Begin, my tongue, some heavenly theme   123
64. Awake our souls; away our fears   125
65. Come, let us join our cheerful songs   126
66. Come, we that love the Lord   127
67. There is a land of pure delight   130

68. We give immortal praise 132
69. Nature with open volume stands 133
70. When I survey the wondrous cross 135
71. Give me the wings of faith to rise 137
72. I sing the almighty power of God 138
73. God is the refuge of his saints 140
74. Jesus shall reign where'er the sun 142
75. O God, our help in ages past 143
76. I'll praise my Maker while I've breath 145

5. The Early Eighteenth Century 147

77. Jesus Christ is risen today 148
78. The Lord my pasture shall prepare 149
79. When all thy mercies, O my God 151
80. The spacious firmament on high 153
81. Hark the glad sound! the Saviour comes 154
82. O God of Bethel, by whose hand 156
83. See Israel's gentle shepherd stand 158
84. Ye servants of the Lord 159
85. Christians awake, salute the happy morn 160
86. Father of mercies, in thy word 162

6. Charles Wesley 164

87. And can it be, that I should gain 165
88. O for a thousand tongues to sing 167
89. Christ, whose glory fills the skies 169
90. Hark! the herald angels sing 170
91. Hail the day that sees him rise 172
92. Jesu, lover of my soul 174
93. Soldiers of Christ, arise 177
94. Gentle Jesus, meek and mild 180
95. Come, O thou Traveller unknown 182
96. Come, thou long-expected Jesus 186
97. Glory be to God on high 187
98. Ye servants of God 189
99. Father of everlasting grace 191
100. Rejoice, the Lord is King 193
101. Love Divine, all loves excelling 195
102. Lo! He comes with clouds descending 198
103. Let saints on earth in concert sing 200
104. Forth in thy name, O Lord, I go 202
105. O thou who camest from above 203

7. The Later Eighteenth Century 205

106.	The God of Abraham praise	207
107.	All hail the power of Jesu's name	210
108.	Rock of Ages, cleft for me	212
109.	Amazing grace! (how sweet the sound)	214
110.	Glorious things of thee are spoken	216
111.	How sweet the name of Jesus sounds	219
112.	God moves in a mysterious way	220
113.	Sometimes a light surprizes	222
114.	Hark, my soul! it is the Lord	224
115.	Where is this stupendous stranger	226
116.	Guide me, O thou great Jehovah	228
117.	Ride on, Jesu, all-victorious	229
118.	Behold the amazing gift of love	231
119.	Behold! the mountain of the Lord	232
120.	How bright these glorious spirits shine	233

8. The Romantic Movement and the Early Nineteenth Century 235

121.	And did those feet in ancient time	237
122.	Brightest and best of the sons of the morning	239
123.	By cool Siloam's shady rill	241
124.	From Greenland's icy mountains	242
125.	Holy, Holy, Holy! Lord God Almighty	244
126.	Ride on! ride on in majesty	245
127.	Angels from the realms of glory	247
128.	Hail to the Lord's Anointed	248
129.	Prayer is the soul's sincere desire	250
130.	For ever with the Lord	252
131.	New every morning is the love	253
132.	Blest are the pure in heart	255
133.	Sun of my soul, thou Saviour dear	257
134.	The head that once was crowned with thorns	258
135.	Lead us, heavenly Father, lead us	260
136.	In the cross of Christ I glory	261
137.	O worship the King	262
138.	Eternal Light! Eternal Light	265
139.	Lead, kindly Light	267
140.	Just as I am, without one plea	270
141.	Praise, my soul, the King of heaven	271
142.	Abide with me; fast falls the eventide	273
143.	I heard the voice of Jesus say	275

144. Jesus lives! thy terrors now   270
145. O come, all ye faithful   279
146. Nearer, my God, to thee   281
147. *All things bright and beautiful*   283
148. Once in royal David's city   285
149. There is a green hill far away   286

9. The High Victorian Period   288

150. Be thou my guardian and my guide   289
151. Firmly I believe and truly   290
152. Praise to the Holiest in the height   291
153. See amid the winter's snow   293
154. Souls of men! why will ye scatter   295
155. Hark! hark, my soul! Angelic songs are swelling   297
156. My God, how wonderful thou art   299
157. Lord, thy word abideth   300
158. Eternal Father, strong to save   302
159. As with gladness men of old   303
160. Forty days and forty nights   305
161. Come, ye thankful people, come   306
162. We plough the fields, and scatter   308
163. Alleluia, sing to Jesus   310
164. O praise ye the Lord   312
165. The King of love my Shepherd is   313
166. Crown him with many crowns   314
167. Now the day is over   316
168. Onward, Christian soldiers   317
169. Through the night of doubt and sorrow   319
170. O Jesus, I have promised   321
171. Fight the good fight with all thy might   323
172. O worship the Lord in the beauty of holiness   324
173. Beneath the Cross of Jesus   325
174. Lord speak to me, that I may speak   327
175. Take my life, and let it be   328
176. And art thou come with us to dwell   330
177. In heavenly love abiding   332
178. In the bleak mid-winter   333
179. Love came down at Christmas   335
180. For the beauty of the earth   336
181. The Church's one foundation   338
182. Saviour, again to thy dear name we raise   340
183. The day thou gavest, Lord, is ended   342
184. For all the saints   344

185. Lord, enthroned in heavenly splendour — 346
186. And now, O Father, mindful of the love — 348
187. Thy hand, O God, has guided — 350
188. O love that wilt not let me go — 352
189. God is working his purpose out — 353
190. *Lift high the Cross* — 354
191. Breathe on me, breath of God — 355
192. Hear us, O Lord, from heaven thy dwelling-place — 356

10. Nineteenth- and Early Twentieth-Century American Hymns — 358

193. Thou art the Way: to thee alone — 359
194. Take up thy cross, the Saviour said — 360
195. My faith looks up to thee — 361
196. Once to every man and nation — 362
197. It came upon the midnight clear — 364
198. Mine eyes have seen the glory — 365
199. Lord of all being, throned afar — 367
200. City of God, how broad and far — 368
201. Eternal ruler of the ceaseless round — 370
202. O little town of Bethlehem — 371
203. Dear Lord and Father of mankind — 373
204. Immortal Love, forever full — 375
205. To God be the glory — 376
206. Ho, my comrades! see the signal — 377
207. Thy kingdom come! on bended knee — 378
208. Where cross the crowded ways of life — 379

11. The Early Twentieth-Century — 381

209. Ye watchers and ye holy ones — 382
210. Judge eternal, throned in splendour — 383
211. O God of earth and altar — 385
212. I vow to thee, my country — 386
213. Be thou my vision, O Lord of my heart — 387
214. When through the whirl of wheels — 388
215. Awake, awake, to love and work — 390
216. Lord of all hopefulness, Lord of all joy — 391
217. Morning has broken — 392
218. In Christ there is no east or west — 393
219. Thine be the glory, risen, conquering Son — 394

12. The Mid-Twentieth Century, and the Hymn Explosion

12. The Mid-Twentieth Century, and the
    Hymn Explosion   396

220.   God of love and truth and beauty   397
221.   Lord of beauty, thine the splendour   398
222.   Good Christian men, rejoice and sing   399
223.   Ye that know the Lord is gracious   400
224.   Not far beyond the sea nor high   401
225.   By gracious powers so wonderfully sheltered   402
226.   O Lord of every shining constellation   404
227.   Lord, you have searched and known my ways   405
228.   I danced in the morning   406
229.   Born in the night   408
230.   Tell out, my soul, the greatness of the Lord   409
231.   Timeless love! we sing the story   410
232.   In Adam we have all been one   411
233.   Creator of the earth and skies   412
234.   We turn to you, O God of every nation   413
235.   God of freedom, God of justice   414
236.   We have a gospel to proclaim   415
237.   I come with joy, a child of God   416
238.   For the fruits of his creation   417
239.   When, in our music, God is glorified   418
240.   God in his love for us lent us this planet   419
241.   Give to me, Lord, a thankful heart   420
242.   Can we by searching find out God   421
243.   New songs of celebration render   423
244.   In praise of God meet duty and delight   424
245.   Hills of the North, rejoice   425
246.   Morning glory, starlit sky   427
247.   Lord Christ, we praise your sacrifice   428
248.   Like the murmur of the dove's song   430
249.   Christ triumphant, ever reigning   431
250.   The works of the Lord are created in wisdom   432
251.   All our days we will bless the Lord   433

Copyright Acknowledgements   435
Author Index   437
Index of Composers and Arrangers   440
Index of Hymns   443
Index of Tunes   447

Introduction

This is an anthology of two hundred and fifty hymns (plus one for good measure, and to make a point). They are hymns written in English, or translated into English from several languages—Greek, Latin, German, Danish, French, Welsh, Gaelic/Erse; they are a small representation of the vast number of hymns that have been used in worship over the centuries, and which have come down to us at the beginning of the twenty-first century as familiar and beloved. To these may be added the new hymns which, year by year, continue to enrich our experience.

Many people will remember hymns from their childhood, or from some special occasion, or because they have been part of a cultural tradition. They are remembered as lines of words and music, always existing somewhere deep in their inner selves. Many older people have them in their minds and hearts, a possession which they have kept long after other things have gone: it is common experience of those with elderly relatives that they can get them to sing hymns when they have forgotten almost everything else. The hymns are part of themselves, as ineradicable as the lines on their faces.

For some of them, hymns have been the only poetry that they have ever known. They have not, in many cases, been familiar with Shakespeare, or Milton, or Wordsworth, but the lines and verses that they have sung at school or on Sundays have satisfied their sense of rhythm and form, and the emotions and ideas of those familar hymns have given expression to some of their most deeply felt longings and aspirations. The hymn form has been their means of access to the beautiful, the hopeful, even the ineffable: it has spoken to them of the beauty of the created world; it has been their guide in moral thought, their instruction in theology, their comfort in grief. In the dry places of life, hymns have often been a well of living water, like the rain which filled the pools in the valley of Baca. And in times of joy, hymns have found the words which signify happiness, exultation, confidence, and hope.

Hymns are familiar, yet reverenced. I take that conjunction of ideas from Ruskin, whose mother made him learn chapters of the Bible as a child. He never regretted it: he said that those chapters became familiar 'in habitual music—yet in that familiarity reverenced, as transcending all thought, and ordaining all conduct'. We can apply his description to hymns: Ruskin saw, with an acute instinctual knowledge, that certain things could be simultaneously familiar and also reverenced. So it is that we greet certain verses like old friends:

> Jesus shall reign where'er the sun
> Doth his successive journeys run . . .

and yet we also know that they contain important precepts of conduct and of life:

> The trivial round, the common task,
> Will furnish all we ought to ask:
> Room to deny ourselves, a road
> To bring us daily nearer God.

Other hymns, of course, will remind us of more difficult times:

> Oft in danger, oft in woe,
> Onward, Christians, onward go;

or of the problems of temptation, of the evils of society, of greed and misery:

> We have not known you: to the skies
> Our monuments of folly soar . . .

These hymns—one from the early eighteenth century, two from the nineteenth, one from the twentieth—will serve to remind us of the great variety of the form. When Samuel Johnson said of Watts's devotional poetry that 'the paucity of its topics enforces perpetual repetition', he was clearly not aware that hymns could be quarried from any part of the Bible, and that they could encompass all the religious moods of the human soul. Hymns can contain systematic theology, Christian doctrine, praise, prayer, jubilation; they can express penitence and trust, and also faith, and hope, and love. When John Wesley was introducing his 'Large Hymn Book', the *Collection of Hymns for the Use of the People called Methodists* (1780), he described it as 'a little body of experimental and practical divinity', and the important words were 'experimental' and 'practical'. This was to be a hymn-book for those who *practised* religion; and it was to be an 'experimental' book, that is, tracing the patterns of religious *experience*. Hymns do this: they are full of information about Father, Son, and Holy Spirit, but they are concerned with the experience of these matters: the awareness of sinning against the Father, of mercy through the Son, of power through the Holy Spirit. And they have been written by those who write from the depths of their hearts: without that, a hymn would be the falsest of verse forms. But, as George Herbert put it:

The fineness which a hymn or psalm affords,
Is, when the soul unto the lines accords.

Hymns are rooted and grounded in the simplest of human emotions. The knowledge of wrongdoing, and the hope of forgiveness, are essential parts of the day-to-day life of most people. This is one of the reasons why hymns are universal: they satisfy deeply felt needs—a hunger for love, a need to feel 'right', a delight in a newly found hope that life can be meaningful and good. They satisfy, too, a need to recognize that which exists within us which we would rather not confront: as Charles Wesley put it, with a tender psychological understanding:

Show me, as my soul can bear
The depth of inbred sin.

They help us to understand ourselves and our place in the world, to 'find' ourselves: it is a great joy to find that someone has said in a hymn exactly what we have been struggling with in our own lives:

Lord, you have searched and known my ways,
And understood my thought from far;
How can I rightly sound your praise
Or tell how great your wonders are?

Hymns have been written, through the ages, for a purpose. They are written, first of all, in praise of God, Father, Son, and Holy Spirit. The greatest hymn of the early Church, the *Te Deum*, goes straight to the heart of the matter: 'We praise thee, O God: we acknowledge thee to be the Lord.' Any discussion of hymns should begin by understanding the way in which they are written to serve a particular need, and the way in which they belong to the Church for which they were written. They are intimately connected with the needs and occasions of that Church: the narrative of the Christian year, the great Festivals, the Saints' days. They are written, also, for those who are worshipping, for those who believe (in the words of the *Te Deum* again) in

The Father: of an infinite Majesty;
Thine honourable, true: and only Son;
Also the Holy Ghost: the Comforter.

Hymns speak to those who are united in a common belief. This means that they can assume some kind of acquiescence to what they are saying, and that they can appeal to the shared experience of a worshipping congregation. In turn, that congregation will be strengthened by the singing of hymns, by the rearticulation of its belief. In singing their thankfulness and praise, its various members go on their way together. But hymns are not only praise and the restatement of belief. They can be supplication, repentance, resolution, and prayer. They bring before God the problems of the human condition, the fears and hopes that are an inescapable part of the pilgrimage of life. It is not surprising that so many hymns make use of this pilgrimage metaphor, because it allows an examination of many things: weariness, courage, hope, rest, the coming to the journey's end. At times, on the journey, there are glimpses of another world, of a ladder which goes up from earth to heaven with the angels of God ascending and descending on it:

> Nearer, my God, to thee,
> Nearer to thee!

At other times, the way seems long and dreary, as each believer is a pilgrim through this barren land; while the Exodus narrative also serves as a resonant metaphor for freedom, and thus as a statement of human deliverance from a world of sin and death. Hymns celebrate that deliverance: they also reflect the moods and conditions of every day, of doubt and perplexity as well as faith and assurance, of the rough places as well as the smooth ones. In such a journey, prayer becomes an essential part of the Christian life; and hymns are like prayer, as George Herbert described it, 'God's breath in man returning to its birth'.

Hymns belong to the Church. They were given to the Church by those who wrote them, for the use of the faithful in worship. They encourage the practice of the presence of God, and the tricky business of human self-knowledge: they also help human beings to aspire to higher things. In the singing of hymns, men, women, and children give voice to hopes and aspirations that they would never normally hope to achieve:

> Praise, my soul, the King of heaven;
> To his feet thy tribute bring.
> Ransomed, healed, restored, forgiven,
> Who like me his praise should sing?

The four adjectival participles in the third line ring out with a confidence which drives the great hymn of praise. It is easy to doubt this unaccustomed assurance, but for many people it represents a self that is, for a moment, transformed in the singing of a hymn. The singers of hymns can, in their singing, become different from their ordinary selves: another way of putting it would be to say that they come into the presence of God.

Hymns belong to the Church, and speak of the soul. But because they are so rooted in human experience, they have an appeal which takes them beyond the Church for which they were written, or to the very edges of that Church. It is clear that for many people hymns are more attractive than teaching: as George Herbert put it:

> A verse may finde him, who a sermon flies,
> And turn delight into a sacrifice.

Benjamin Keach, the Baptist who is sometimes called 'a pioneer of congregational hymn-singing' because he introduced hymns into his Sunday
services in the 1660s, altered Herbert's verb to 'catch': 'a verse may catch
him, who a sermon flies'. Herbert's 'finde' is infinitely better: hymns do not
catch people, as if in some spiritual trap, but *find* them, seek for them, allow
something in the hymn to express their deepest feelings. In this sense, hymns
are the possession of everyone, believers, half-believers, and non-believers: a
hymn can be read by anyone, coming to it from almost every credal position,
or even from no position of belief at all. It is possible to see hymns as reaching out to all kinds of people, either because they sang them at school, or
because they express some necessary emotion—at Christmas, or Easter, or
on Remembrance Sunday—or just because they approve of the sense and
like the sound of them.

To 'like the sound of them' has to do with the hymn's particular relationship with music, words and tune fitting together. But that 'fitting' demonstrates the need for a particular craft and care in the writing. There are
several elements of this. In the first place, hymns must be absolutely regular
in form and metre, and must normally rhyme. I have come to think of these
things not as simple matters of word arrangement, or customary practice,
but as features which satisfy instincts that are more deep-seated and even
primitive. Just as folk songs and verse tales depend in part for their effect
upon a form that becomes spellbinding and incantatory, so hymns have a
regularity in metre that does more than just find words to fit a tune. Roman
Jakobson, in his essay on 'Linguistics and Poetics', described Serbian
reciters of folk poetry, who follow rules of versification and rhythm exactly.
Hymns are similarly bound, and in that binding they acquire at least some of
their force. Rhyme also is important: the strict following of rhyme satisfies
a need in the mind for shaping experience and language into form. The
second rhyme-word makes an echo, a similar sound to the first, which works
against the meaning of the words, setting up a lively pattern of closeness (in
sound) and apartness (in sense):

> Christ, whose glory fills the skies,
>   Christ, the true, the only Light,
> Sun of Righteousness, arise,
>   Triumph o'er the shades of night;
> Day-spring from on high, be near;
> Day-star, in my heart appear.

Such a rhyme pattern, repeated in verse after verse, holds together what is
being said in a formal word relationship that encloses the experience, shapes
it: and all lovers of hymns know, perhaps intuitively and almost unconsciously, that it is not just the thing said but the way of saying it that makes
the hymn. In what I think is the best essay on hymns ever written, his

introductory essay to *The Christian Psalmist* (1825), James Montgomery described each element of a hymn, lines and verses, as being 'like a rivulet':

> The syllables in every division ought to 'ripple like a rivulet', one producing another as its natural effect, while the rhythm of each line, falling into the general stream at the proper place, should cause the verse to flow in progressive melody, deepening and expanding like a river to the close; or, to change the figure, each stanza should be a poetical tune, played down to the last note.

This description is precise: the lines fit into the verses, and the verses into the whole hymn. A good hymn line is a beautiful thing in itself, with every syllable in its proper place, saying enough (and not too much), taking its place in the verse by relating, appropriately, to that which comes before and after it. The verse, too, has its own perfection; while a good hymn, like a Greek drama as described by Aristotle, has its own beginning, middle, and end. James Montgomery used Aristotle in his essay:

> A hymn must have a beginning, middle, and end. There should be a manifest gradation in the thoughts, and their mutual dependence should be so perceptible that they could not be transposed without injuring the unity of the piece; every line carrying forward the connection, and every verse adding a well-proportioned limb to a symmetrical body. The reader should know when the strain is complete, and be satisfied, as at the close of an air in music; while defects and superfluities should be felt by him as annoyances, in whatever part they might occur.

What Montgomery was drawing attention to here is the sense that a good hymn gives of saying just what it wants to say, and no more, with precision and economy. It is that 'rightness' of speech which is so important: a singer of hymns believes, when singing a good hymn, that it expresses and shapes a meaning which, without distractions and superfluities, corresponds to the movement of the inner spirit, and the pulses of the feeling heart.

Hymns can be used for private prayer, and often are: it used to be said, in former times, that if they had to go into hospital, an Anglican would take the *Book of Common Prayer* and a Methodist would take the *Methodist Hymn Book*. Hymns make fine texts for meditation and prayer, and can significantly deepen devotional and spiritual experience. But they are primarily texts for singing, and in that singing they come alive. To read 'The church's one foundation' is to engage with an impressive piece of Victorian ecclesiastical hymn-architecture: to sing it to AURELIA is to feel it quite differently. The music and the syllables go together: 'The church's one foun-*da*-tion' begins a verse in which the strong rhymes—'foundation/creation', 'sought her/bought her'—are brought out by the minims, double-strength among the crotchets. The same could be said of many tunes and many hymns: indeed, the fitting together of the two has been one of the masterly, at times almost magical, features of the hymn form. One of the great exponents of this art was William Henry Monk, the music editor of the first edition of *Hymns Ancient and Modern* in 1861; another was Arthur Sullivan, in *Church Hymns with Tunes* (1874); and another was Ralph Vaughan Williams, whose work on the *English Hymnal* brought into the repertoire a dazzling collection of his own and others' tunes.

The results are clear: 'O God, our help in ages past' to ST ANNE, 'Holy, holy, holy!' to NICAEA, and a thousand others. These are tunes and texts that have become inseparable, marriages of words and music that have become cultural artefacts, part of the religious experience for more than a century. Sometimes, too, tunes have carried their texts: in making this anthology, I have been struck again and again by the way in which a strong tune has preserved rather ordinary words. The result is a kind of utterance which is not simply a text on the page: it is sacred song, congregational praise. It is also a physical action: when a singer stands up to sing a hymn, he or she takes a breath, and begins. A hymn lives in the bodies and blood and lungs of the singers: it allows an *expression* (in more than one sense) of the mind and the body as well as the soul.

Congregations sing, moving together in this physical harmony: in their sound they are united, and whatever may be their private thoughts and interpretations of the words, by singing they surrender them to the unifying influence of congregational praise. We all know the scrupulous singer, who cannot bear to sing a particular verse, but for the most part the activity is a shared one, an experience which joins people together. Isaac Watts, following Revelation 7, saw the whole creation in such a way, united in the praise of God:

> The whole creation join in one
> To bless the sacred name
> Of him that sits upon the throne,
> And to adore the Lamb.

This anthology of hymns, therefore, is intended to celebrate an art form that I believe to be valuable, both as an aid to devotion and as an expression of the human soul. It contains information about each text, and the tunes to which it is sung, in the hope that this will lead to a greater appreciation of hymns in all their variety and beauty. It is divided into sections, beginning with translations of the early hymns of the Church written in Greek and Latin, and ending with the hymns of the last years of the twentieth century. I hope that it will show what hymns have said about innumerable examples of biblical teaching, and about countless elements of human experience. As Calvin said of the psalms, they are 'the Anatomy of all parts of the soul'. They speak to us in joy and in sorrow, in praise and in penitence, in hope and in faith. Above all, they speak to us in love, speaking the truth in love:

they were written by men and women who lived and died in faith and hope, and who also gave these hymns that, in later centuries, they might be loved by those who sang them; and every year, that great body of hymns is added to by those who know that tradition and want to add to it, in their own creative inspiration and energy. They know that, as T. S. Eliot pointed out, there is a relationship between tradition and the individual talent, so that they are adding their stones to the great cairn; and they know, too, that even in times of doubt

> The faithful few fought bravely
> To guard the nation's life.

The result is a precious inheritance, loved by those who use them in worship; loved, too, by others who no longer sing them but remember them from their past. It is this great possession, this collection of diverse and varied material which speaks to so many, that is the subject of this anthology. I hope that it will appeal to all who understand the beauty of words and music devoted to the understanding of the serious things of life.

A Note on Textual Procedure

I have taken the texts of the hymns from various sources, without feeling any need to stick to one particular book and its style. I have preferred the version in one hymn-book over another, either because the wording is more authentic, or because of the selection of verses, or (occasionally) because the version I have printed just happens to be the best known (sometimes, as in the case of 'Hark! the herald angels sing', this is different from the author's original text). I have tried to produce texts that are both sensible and interesting, and a commentary that helps understanding and appreciation. The selection reflects my own predilections, but it is also intended to be representative of hymns through the ages. I hope that it will provide the reader, whether churchgoing or not, with a collection of hymns that shows the genre at its best.

Most hymn-books are books for worship. This is not. This has allowed me to print hymns which some would consider unsuitable for worship at the beginning of the twenty-first century, but which have a place in the history of the Church and the development of religious thought (sometimes I have printed hymns *because* they have been forgotten, and do not deserve to be). It has also allowed me to print texts which do not have to conform to the sensitivities of many modern worshippers in matters such as the dislike of archaic language and the removal of non-inclusive gender-based terms. I can understand why each of these has been considered necessary and important: but I have preferred to print older hymns in the form in which they have customarily been known, retaining 'hath' and 'Thou', and (where necessary) 'men'. In the case of modern hymns, however, I have printed the text which has been approved by the author, often in a revised form.

There are strong arguments for modernizing worship, and they have been made, for example, by the editors of *Hymns for Today's Church*. But this anthology is not, in the first instance, compiled for the Church, although I hope that it is broadly in sympathy with it. It is primarily for anyone who is interested in hymns: it is a celebration of a literary form which I believe to be important in the history of ideas, in the formation of culture, and in the inner life of individual readers.

{1}

Ancient and Medieval Hymns

The first hymns in this chapter date from soon after the time of the life of Christ. By AD 64 St Paul was writing to the Ephesians and to the Colossians urging them to be filled with the Spirit: 'speaking to yourselves in psalms and hymns and spiritual songs'. In about AD 105 Pliny the Younger reported to the Emperor Trajan that the Christians were meeting early in the morning and singing hymns. It seems that some kind of hymn-singing took place in Christian worship from the very beginning; and one of the earliest hymns was probably 'Hail, gladdening light', which was spoken of by St Basil as 'ancient' sometime around the year 370.

Many hymns of the early Church were written in Greek, and this continued; meanwhile in Italy, Latin ones, under the influence of St Ambrose, Bishop of Milan from 374 to 397, began to be written: the great poets of Christian Latin hymnody, such as the Spanish lawyer Prudentius in the early fifth century and Venantius Fortunatus in the sixth, were succeeded by major figures in the Church such as Theodulph of Orleans (*c.*750–*c.*821) and St Fulbert of Chartres (*c.*960–1028); and then by monastic founders and teachers, such as St Bernard of Clairvaux, St Francis of Assisi, Peter Abelard, and, later in the Middle Ages, Bianco da Siena and Jean Tisserand. Their hymns were kept alive in the monasteries, and it was the tradition of singing the divine office which has led to many of them being preserved in breviaries.

The earliest of these hymns have a simplicity that is very touching: the medieval ones (from no. 19 onwards) become wonderfully imaginative presentations of such events as the Passion, or inspired longings for another and more beautiful world, where the blessed ones enjoy an eternal sabbath of peace and harmony. The old monks knew that here 'Brief life' was our portion, with 'brief sorrow, short-lived care', but believed that one day they would come to 'Jerusalem the golden', and stand before the Lord 'conjubilant with song'. Their ancient hymns were revived in the nineteenth century by scholars and translators such as John Mason Neale, and they have become a deeply loved link with the ancient traditions of the early Church.

The final hymns in this section are two early Celtic hymns, associated with St Patrick and with St Columba, from the far edges of the Roman empire.

I Hail, gladdening Light, of his pure glory poured
Who is the immortal Father, heavenly, blest,
Holiest of holies, Jesus Christ our Lord!

Now we are come to the sun's hour of rest;
The lights of evening round us shine;
We hymn the Father, Son, and Holy Spirit divine.

Worthiest art thou at all times to be sung
With undefilèd tongue,
Son of our God, giver of life, alone;
Therefore in all the world thy glories, Lord, they own.

Third-century Greek hymn,
tr. John Keble (1792–1866)

This Greek hymn, from the early years of the Church, is of unknown authorship. It dates probably from the third century, but may have been earlier: St Basil, who died in AD 379, referred to it as 'ancient'. It is found in some medieval manuscripts, and was printed in Archbishop Ussher's *De Symbolis* (1647).

Keble's translation was published in the *British Magazine* (1834) and later included in *Lyra Apostolica* (1836), the collection of verses by Keble and others who were part of the 'Oxford Movement', such as John Henry Newman, Isaac Williams, and Hurrell Froude. With its address to the 'Holiest of holies', and its interest in ancient ritual, this is a very characteristic hymn of the Oxford Movement: the hymn would have been valuable to Keble and his friends partly because it had been part of the Evening Service of the Orthodox Church for many centuries. It is sung (as its subtitle in later editions of *Hymns Ancient and Modern* indicates) 'at the lighting of the lamps'; and it celebrates the glory of God, and Christ the light of the world, against the background of early evening. The light is a symbol of the light that shined in the darkness, though without St John's comment that 'the darkness comprehended it not' (John 1: 5). Here the lights of evening are beautifully 'comprehended' as symbols of the divine, of the Son of God, 'giver of life, alone'.

Julian's *Dictionary of Hymnology* describes as the most remarkable characteristic of Greek hymnody 'its objectiveness, with which is closely connected its faculty of sustained praise . . . the attitude of the poet is always one of self-forgetful, rapt, or ecstatic contemplation.' The writer of this entry went on to contrast this with a feature of modern (i.e. nineteenth-century) hymnody, 'our self-regarding mode of praise'. His distinction between the two kinds of hymn suggests one reason why Keble (with his Oxford Movement love of 'reserve' in religious matters) would have been attracted to this simple but profound evening hymn. His translation is metrically irregular (as the original Greek text is), but it has an effective though unusual rhyme scheme, which helps to emphasize the art which coexists with the simplicity of the whole. However, the *English Hymnal* and *Songs of Praise* both preferred to print another translation of this text in a more regular metre, Robert Bridges's 'O gladsome light, O grace', from the *Yattendon Hymnal* (1899).

The best-known tune to these words is SEBASTE, by John Stainer (1840–1901), set to these words in the second edition of *Hymns Ancient and Modern* (1875). In the *Appendix* (1868) to the first edition, this hymn had been printed to a different tune by Sir Frederick Arthur Gore Ouseley; and there have been a number of attempts to set the words to music in different hymn-books. SEBASTE (the name given to the city of Samaria after the time of Herod the Great) has proved durable: it has some of the characteristics of Anglican chant, which allows it to carry the irregular rhythms without becoming too difficult or confusing.

2   Let all mortal flesh keep silence, and with fear and trembling stand;
     Ponder nothing earthly-minded, for with blessing in his hand
     Christ our God to earth descendeth, our full homage to demand.

     King of kings, yet born of Mary, as of old on earth he stood,
     Lord of lords, in human vesture—in the body and the blood—
     He will give to all the faithful his own self for heav'nly food.

     Rank on rank the host of heaven spreads its vanguard on the way,
     As the Light of light descendeth from the realms of endless day,
     That the powers of hell may vanish as the darkness clears away.

     At his feet the six-winged seraph; cherubim with sleepless eye
     Veil their faces to the Presence, as with ceaseless voice they cry—
     Alleluia, alleluia, alleluia, Lord most high!

                                    The Liturgy of St James,
                              tr. Gerard Moultrie (1829–85)

This hymn is based on the 'Prayer of the Cherubic Hymn' in the Liturgy of St James, which dates probably from the fourth century. A prose translation of some Eastern Liturgies, including this one, was printed in *Translations of the Primitive Liturgies*, edited by J. M. Neale and R. F. Littledale in 1869. Although his text dates from 1864, in *Lyra Eucharistica*, Moultrie may have known the prose version: it began 'Let all mortal flesh keep silence, and stand with fear and trembling, and ponder nothing earthly in itself'.

The hymn is a sublime command, and the invocation of silence adds emphasis to the awe-inspiring greatness of God which is signalled in this hymn. This is the opposite of those hymns which express the kindness and closeness of God ('What a friend we have in Jesus'): here God appears in majesty and light, accompanied by the glory of the heavenly host. The Eucharist is celebrated as an event in which this glory is given to the faithful.

Its first printing in *Lyra Eucharistica* was entirely appropriate. In the original Liturgy of St James, it was used as the bread and wine were brought into the sanctuary: it brings out the full drama of the occasion.

The tune, PICARDY, is from a folk-song book, *Chansons Populaires des Provinces de France*, published in Paris in 1860. It was called 'La Ballade de Jésus Christ' and began 'Jésus Christ s'habille en pauvre' ('Christ clothed himself in poverty'). The tune was one of many inspired choices for the *English Hymnal* of 1906 by Ralph Vaughan Williams, who set it to Moultrie's words. The combination of words and music is expressive of deep emotion and awe.

3   The day of Resurrection!
         Earth, tell it out abroad;
     The Passover of gladness,
         The Passover of God!
     From death to life eternal,
         From this world to the sky,
     Our Christ hath brought us over
         With hymns of victory.

     Our hearts be pure from evil,
         That we may see aright
     The Lord in rays eternal
         Of resurrection-light;
     And, listening to his accents,
         May hear so calm and plain
     His own '*All Hail*', and hearing,
         May raise the victor strain.

     Now let the heavens be joyful,
         And earth her song begin,
     The round world keep high triumph,
         And all that is therein;
     Let all things seen and unseen
         Their notes of gladness blend,
     For Christ the Lord hath risen,
         Our Joy that hath no end.

                          St John Damascene,
                 tr. John Mason Neale (1818–66)

From Neale's *Hymns of the Eastern Church* (1862). Neale described St John of Damascus (*c*.675–*c*.750) as 'The last but one of the Fathers of the Eastern Church, and the greatest of her poets'. He was given the name 'Chrysorrhoas' ('the golden speaker'). As a poet who was sensitive to the imaginative presentation of religious truths through image and symbol, he was known for supporting the veneration of icons in an iconoclastic age.

The hymn comes from the Golden Canon for Easter Day, sometimes known as 'The Queen of Canons', the special poem celebrating the Resurrection. Neale's original printing, with exclamation marks, and the brilliant interpolation of the sudden *'All Hail'* (so printed), captures wonderfully the excitement of the Eastern Church at the beginning of Easter Day. The reference is to Matthew 28: 9: 'behold, Jesus met them, saying, All hail.'

There is a skilful reference to the Passover as a type of salvation, in which 'the Lord passed over the houses of the children of Israel in Egypt, when he smote the Egyptians, and delivered our houses' (Exodus 12: 27); it is now 'the Passover of gladness', in which, by His death and Resurrection, Christ has 'brought us over' from death to life, as the children of Israel were brought over the Red Sea. Two events are telescoped here to make a pattern of deliverance.

Originally the hymn began ''Tis the day of resurrection'; the ''Tis' was dropped to make the hymn more suitable for congregational singing, with a strong metre of 7.6.7.6.D. Verse 3 originally ended:

> Let the round world keep triumph,
>   And all that is therein;
> Invisible and visible
>   Their notes let all things blend,
> For Christ the Lord hath risen,
>   Our joy that hath no end.

Amended versions appeared in *The Parish Hymn Book* of 1863, and in the *Appendix* (1868) to the first edition of *Hymns Ancient and Modern*.

The tune is usually ELLACOMBE, a German eighteenth-century tune from the Roman Catholic private chapel of the Duke of Würtemberg. It was brought into British use (with different words—'Come, sing with holy gladness') by the *Appendix* (1868) to the first edition of *Hymns Ancient and Modern*, and set to Neale's hymn in the *English Hymnal* of 1906. Since that time, it has been the customary tune for these words.

4   O happy band of pilgrims,
           If onward ye will tread
        With Jesus as your fellow
           To Jesus as your Head!

        O happy if ye labour
           As Jesus did for men;
        O happy if ye hunger
           As Jesus hungered then!

        The Cross that Jesus carried
           He carried as your due;
        The Crown that Jesus weareth,
           He weareth it for you.

        The faith by which ye see him,
           The hope in which ye yearn,
        The love that through all troubles
           To him alone will turn,

        What are they but forerunners
           To lead you to his sight?
        What are they save the effluence
           Of uncreated light?

        The trials that beset you,
           The sorrows ye endure,
         The manifold temptations
           That death alone can cure,

        What are they but his jewels
           Of right celestial worth?
        What are they but the ladder
           Set up to heaven on earth?

        O happy band of pilgrims,
           Look upward to the skies,
         Where such a light affliction
           Shall win you such a prize!

           John Mason Neale (1818–66)

This vigorous hymn of pilgrimage appeared in Neale's *Hymns of the Eastern Church* (1862), in a section devoted to the work of St Joseph of the Studium, entitled 'The Pilgrims of Jesus'. It was described as 'merely a Cento [or compilation of verses] from the Canon of SS. Chrysanthus and Daria (March 19)'. In the third edition of *Hymns of the Eastern Church* (1866), Neale promised that in future this hymn and two others would be relegated to an appendix because they contained so little from the Greek. It seems probable that Neale took the idea from a Greek hymn, but developed it in his own way. Verse 5 line 1 was originally the spectacular 'What are they, but vaunt-couriers . . .'.

The hymn is unusual for Neale in its powerful use of rhetoric. Its verses work by patterns of repetition and echo: 'O happy if ye labour . . . O happy if ye hunger', 'What are they . . . What are they'. These are reinforced by the strong parallels: Jesus is 'your fellow . . . your Head' and 'The Cross . . . The Crown' meet in verse 3. Verse 4 neatly versifies the Pauline triad of faith, hope, and love.

It is also unusual for Neale in the way in which on two occasions the sense is carried on from verse to verse, and in the number of rhetorical questions which are involved. Its subject matter, however, is characteristic of his work: the contrast is between the trials and hardships of earth on the one hand, and the joys of heaven on the other, so that trials and temptations become 'jewels' and a ladder to lead to heaven as it did for Jacob in his dream. They complement faith, hope, and love, which lead to the sight of Jesus in glory, and are themselves the effluence 'of uncreated Light'.

The customary tune for this hymn is KNECHT, so called after its composer, Justin Heinrich Knecht (1752–1817). He was a noted organist, who edited (with J. F. Christmann) *Vollständige Sammlung . . . Choralmelodien*, which included 97 of his own tunes. The best known of them is the forceful tune VIENNA, usually sung to 'They whose course on earth is o'er' or to 'Christ, from whom all blessings flow'.

5
> The day is past and over;
>   All thanks, O Lord, to thee;
> I pray thee that offenceless
>   The hours of dark may be:
> O Jesu, keep me in thy sight,
> And guard me through the coming night.
>
>   The joys of day are over;
>   I lift my heart to thee,
>   And call on thee that sinless
>   The hours of dark may be:
>   O Jesu, make their darkness light,
>   And guard me through the coming night.
>
>   The toils of day are over;
>   I raise the hymn to thee,
>   And ask that free from peril
>   The hours of dark may be:
>   O Jesu, keep me in thy sight,
>   And guard me through the coming night.

> Be thou my soul's preserver,
>   O God! for thou dost know
> How many are the perils
>   Through which I have to go.
> Lover of men! O hear my call,
> And guard and save me from them all.
>
> From the Greek,
> tr. John Mason Neale (1818–66)

From Neale's *Hymns of the Eastern Church* (1862): it was Neale's view that this hymn was by St Anatolius, Patriarch of Constantinople (*c.*400–58), but this is uncertain. It is ascribed to the sixth century in the *English Hymnal*.

Neale had a great affection for this hymn. He described it as 'a great favourite in the Greek Isles . . . It is to the scattered hamlets of Chios and Mitylene, what Bishop Ken's Evening Hymn is to the villages of our own land; and its melody is singularly plaintive and soothing.' His translation had a fourth verse, before the present one:

> Lighten mine eyes, O Saviour,
>   Or sleep in death shall I;
> And he, my doleful tempter,
>   Triumphantly shall cry:
> 'He could not make their darkness light,
> Nor guard them through the hours of night!'

There is another translation of these words by Robert Bridges, beginning 'Darkening night the land doth cover', and in a different metre (printed in the *BBC Hymn Book*, no. 509). It is a fine translation, but it does not have the sweet simplicity of Neale's verses.

The usual tune is HOMINUM AMATOR ('lover of mankind') by W. H. Ferguson (1874–1950); an earlier tune, ST ANATOLIUS is by A. H. Brown (1830–1926).

6   *Corde natus ex parentis*

Of the Father's love begotten
  Ere the worlds began to be,
He is Alpha and Omega,
  He the source, the ending he,
Of the things that are, that have been,
  And that future years shall see,
    Evermore and evermore.

At his word they were created;
  He commanded; it was done:
Heaven and earth and depths of ocean
  In their three-fold order one;
All that grows beneath the shining
  Of the light of moon and sun,
    Evermore and evermore.

O that birth for ever blessèd
  When the Virgin, full of grace,
By the Holy Ghost conceiving,
  Bare the Saviour of our race,
And the babe, the world's redeemer,
  First revealed his sacred face,
    Evermore and evermore.

O ye heights of heaven, adore him;
  Angel-hosts, his praises sing;
Powers, dominions bow before him,
  And extol our God and king:
Let no tongue on earth be silent,
  Every voice in concert ring,
    Evermore and evermore.

This is he whom seers and sages
  Sang of old with one accord;
Whom the writings of the prophets
  Promised in their faithful word;
Now he shines, the long-expected:
  Let creation praise its Lord,
    Evermore and evermore.

Christ, to thee, with God the Father,
  And, O Holy Ghost, to thee,
Hymn and chant with high thanksgiving
  And unwearied praises be,
Honour, glory, and dominion,
  And eternal victory,
    Evermore and evermore.

Aurelius Prudentius Clemens, known as Prudentius (348–c.413),
tr. John Mason Neale (1818–66) and Henry Williams Baker (1821–77)

This is a translation of part of a Latin hymn by Prudentius beginning 'Da puer plectrum', from his *Liber Cathemerinon*, or 'Book of the Christian Day'. Later the refrain 'Saeculorum saeculis' was added, giving rise to the translation's 'Evermore and evermore'. The Latin text is found in the Hereford and York rites during the Middle Ages, described as a 'hymnus omnis horae', a hymn for all hours.

Neale's translation, beginning 'Of the Father sole begotten' appeared in *The Hymnal Noted* Part 2 (1854). It was greatly altered by Baker, who produced verses of his own for the first edition of *Hymns Ancient and Modern* (1861).

Prudentius was a Spanish poet and successful lawyer, who retired into private life and wrote the poetry by which he is still known. His hymn is a magnificent celebration of God as both Creator and Christ-child, celebrating the presence on earth of the Incarnate Word who is also the Alpha and Omega (from Revelation 1: 8).

The tune is based upon a plainsong melody, found in medieval manuscripts in Italy and Germany with the words 'Divinum mysterium'. It was later included in Theodoric Petri's *Piae Cantiones* (1582), from which Thomas Helmore took it for *The Hymnal Noted*, Part 2 (1854). Helmore set it to the present hymn, and it has always been associated with these words. It is sung in unison, and carries the text with great vigour and energy. It is sometimes known as DIVINUM MYSTERIUM, from its medieval provenance, and sometimes given the title CORDE NATUS, from the first line of the Latin text.

7 *Te Deum laudamus*

We come with songs of blessing,
O Father, God Most High,
your Name on earth confessing
to whom the angels cry;
by all the hosts of heaven
continually adored,
to you all praise be given,
the everlasting Lord.

The heavens show your glory,
your greatness fills the earth;
the prophets tell your story,
apostles praise your worth.
The saints and martyrs name you
eternal Three-in-One,
and through the world acclaim you
as Father, Spirit, Son.

O King for ever glorious,
O Son for sinners slain,
O Christ who died victorious
to rise and rule and reign:
the hosts on high enthrone you
at God the Father's hand;
and wide, to those who own you,
the gates of heaven stand.

In mercy, Lord, behold us,
our God to whom we pray;
let Jesus' love enfold us
against that final day;
no tale of sin confound us
before the judgment throne;
his righteousness surround us,
who trust in God alone.

Timothy Dudley-Smith (1926–)

This is a modern version of the greatest of all Latin hymns, thought to have been written in the first half of the fifth century, and sometimes attributed to St Ambrose and St Augustine. It has appeared in many forms and been translated into many languages: the best known English version is that which is sung or said at Morning Prayer, 'We praise thee, O God: we acknowledge thee to be the Lord.'

It is, in the words of Julian's *Dictionary of Hymnology*, 'the most famous non-biblical hymn of the Western Church'. It is found in many breviaries, and was in use as a morning hymn for Sunday use ('omni Sabbato ad matutinos') at Arles sometime before AD 502. It is comprehensive in its references to the greatness and holiness of God, praised not only by the heavens and all the powers therein (angels, cherubin, seraphin) but also by apostles, prophets and martyrs. It then celebrates the Holy Trinity, Father, Son, and Holy Ghost (Dudley-Smith's verse 2), and the life of Christ—His birth, deliverance of man, and glory. By His death he opened the Kingdom of Heaven to all believers (verse 3), and will come to be our judge (verse 4); so that each person prays 'let me never be confounded' (verse 4).

Timothy Dudley-Smith's version, written in 1993, is that of a master craftsman: it includes all the essential elements of the original without ever becoming awkward or strained. There have been many previous attempts to make a modern hymn out of this ancient one, but perhaps only Charles Wesley's 'Infinite God, to thee we raise', now forgotten, is as accomplished.

The metre, 7.6.7.6.D is a common one, so there are a number of tunes which fit the words well. The author recommends OFFERTORIUM (used for 'Sometimes a light surprises'), or CRÜGER ('Hail to the Lord's Anointed'), or AURELIA ('The church's one foundation') or ST THEODULPH ('All glory, laud, and honour').

8   *Vox clara ecce intonat*

Hark! a herald voice is calling:
   'Christ is nigh' it seems to say;
'Cast away the dreams of darkness,
   O ye children of the day!'

Startled at the solemn warning,
   Let the earth-bound soul arise;
Christ, her Sun, all sloth dispelling,
   Shines upon the morning skies.

Lo! the Lamb, so long expected,
   Comes with pardon down from heaven;
Let us haste, with tears of sorrow,
   One and all to be forgiven;

So when next he comes in glory,
   Wrapping all the earth in fear,
May he then as our defender
   On the clouds of heaven appear.

Honour, glory, virtue, merit,
   To the Father and the Son,
With the co-eternal Spirit,
   While unending ages run.

School of St Ambrose (340–97),
tr. Edward Caswall (1814–78)

This hymn was once thought to be by St Ambrose, Bishop of Milan and great encourager of hymn singing, but it is probably by a follower of his. As an Advent hymn, it was appointed for daily use in a number of medieval breviaries. It was rewritten for the Roman Breviary of 1632, and it was this later version of the ancient monastic hymn that Edward Caswall translated for his *Lyra Catholica* of 1849.

Caswall began with 'Hark! an awful voice is sounding'. 'Awful' ought to be a perfectly acceptable word, as in 'Before Jehovah's awful throne'; but its other meaning (now its primary one) is so derogatory that it is not surprising that it has been altered. As early as 1861, the first edition of *Hymns Ancient and Modern* changed to 'thrilling'; other books, such as the *English Hymnal* and *Songs of Praise*, have preferred 'Hark! a herald voice is calling'. Julian's *Dictionary of Hymnology* prints a great many first lines of this great Advent hymn, including one of 1874 by a J. Wallace, beginning 'Hark, hark, the voice of chanticleer'.

The hymn is based on Romans 13: 11–12, later taken up into the Advent Collect in the *Book of Common Prayer*: 'Almighty God, give us grace that we may cast away the works of darkness, and put upon us the armour of light.' Its beautifully judged combination of warning and hope is characteristic of the Advent reminder that Christ, who 'came to visit us in great humility', will come again in His glorious Majesty to judge both the quick and the dead. It is interesting to note that Percy Dearmer, sensitive to the 'fear' expressed in verse 4, rewrote the verse between the first edition of *Songs of Praise* of 1925 and the 'Enlarged Edition' of 1931:

> So when love comes forth in judgment,
>   Debts and doubts and wrongs to clear,
> Faithful may he find his servants,
>   Watching till the dawn appear.

In *Songs of Praise Discussed*, Dearmer said that this had been done 'in the hope of bringing out that which is nearest the truth for thoughtful people in the present century'. It is fascinating to see an ancient and traditional hymn being reshaped in this way to suit 'thoughtful people' of the 1920s.

Perhaps because it recasts the Advent Collect so precisely, this hymn has been particularly associated with Church of England or Episcopal hymnbooks (including *The Hymnal 1982* in the USA); it is not often found in nonconformist books.

The tune most frequently used for these words is MERTON, by William Henry Monk (1823–89), first published in *The Parish Choir* (1850). As musical editor of *Hymns Ancient and Modern*, Monk set his own tune to these words, and it has become closely associated with them. It is a stately tune, climbing with some dignity in the first two lines, and then giving way to a very simple last line.

9   *Urbs beata Ierusalem/ Angularis fundamentum*

Blessed City, heavenly Salem,
    Vision dear of peace and love,
Who, of living stones upbuilded,
    Art the joy of heaven above,
And, with Angel cohorts circled,
    As a bride to earth dost move!

From celestial realms descending,
    Bridal glory round her shed,
To his presence, decked with jewels,
    By her Lord shall she be led:
All her streets, and all her bulwarks,
    Of pure gold are fashionèd.

Bright with pearls her portals glitter,
    They are open evermore;
And, by virtue of his merits,
    Thither faithful souls may soar,
Who for Christ's dear name, in this world
    Pain and tribulation bore.

Many a blow and biting sculpture
    Fashioned well those stones elect,
In their places now compacted
    By the heavenly Architect,
Who therewith hath willed for ever
    That his palace should be decked.

Laud and honour to the Father;
    Laud and honour to the Son;
Laud and honour to the Spirit;
    Ever Three, and ever One:
Consubstantial, co-eternal,
    While unending ages run. Amen.

———————

Christ is made the sure Foundation,
    And the precious Corner-stone,
Who, the two walls underlying,
    Bound in each, binds both in one,
Holy Sion's help for ever,
    And her confidence alone.

All that dedicated City,
    Dearly loved by God on high,
In exultant jubilation
    Pours perpetual melody:
God the One, and God the Trinal,
    Singing everlastingly.

To this temple, where we call thee,
　　Come, O Lord of Hosts, to-day;
With thy wonted loving-kindness
　　Hear thy people as they pray;
And thy fullest benediction
　　Shed within its walls for ay.

Here vouchsafe to all thy servants
　　What they ask of thee to gain;
Here to have and hold for ever
　　Those good things their prayers obtain,
And hereafter in thy glory
　　With thy blessed ones to reign.

Laud and honour to the Father;
　　Laud and honour to the Son;
Laud and honour to the Spirit;
　　Ever Three, and ever One:
Consubstantial, co-eternal,
　　While unending ages run. Amen.

　　　　　　Latin, sixth or seventh century,
　　　　　　tr. John Mason Neale (1818–66)

From Neale's *Mediaeval Hymns and Sequences* (1851), slightly altered for the second edition (1863). It is a translation of an early Latin hymn, originally intended to be sung at church dedications. The two-part hymn was originally one, going straight on from the end of verse 4 to 'Christ is made the sure Foundation'. Many different selections from the verses have been made.

Neale suggested that 'this hymn is intended to raise our thoughts from the material Church, the dedication of which we are assembled to keep, to that Church of the First-born, which is written in heaven: that "house not made with hands, eternal". The hymn is at least a thousand years old: at the dedication of how many thousand churches must it have been sung!'

Neale's love of tradition is clearly seen in this note. He was also concerned to point out a specific reference in line 2, 'Vision dear of peace and love'. At this point he made a distinction between Jerusalem and Sion: Jerusalem is 'Holy Sion's help for ever/ And her confidence alone': on the other hand, '*Sion* is generally understood of the Church militant, because the word means *expectation*; but *Jerusalem*, which signifies the *Vision of Peace*, is applied to the Church triumphant.' He also pointed out the appropriateness of the stone imagery: 'Each faithful soul is one of the stones which build up the heavenly temple'; and (with reference to verse 4) 'As stones are cut and chiselled into the right shape, before they can be built up together into a wall; so God's servants are tried by afflictions and sorrows in this world, that they may be made meet to be built up hereafter in His spiritual Temple.' Christ is the cornerstone (verse 6) who 'binds into one the Jews and Gentiles, once two, but united in Him'.

The source of much of this imagery is 1 Kings 8, the prayer of King Solomon at the dedication of the temple; but it also includes references to 1 Peter 2: 4–8, with the images of the living stones and the cornerstone; and the word 'tribulation' in verse 3 is a clear echo of Revelation 7: 14.

In the *English Hymnal* (1906) this hymn was set to a plainsong chant or to a nineteenth-century tune, URBS COELESTIS, by H. E. Hodson (1842–1917). It is now generally sung to WESTMINSTER ABBEY, a tune created from the 'Alleluias' at the end of Henry Purcell's anthem 'O God, thou art my God'. This tune was set to the present hymn by Sir Sydney Nicholson, who (like Purcell himself) had been organist of Westminster Abbey. It appeared in the shortened music edition of *Hymns Ancient and Modern* (1939), and subsequently in *Hymns Ancient and Modern Revised* (1950). It has been the preferred tune in most hymn-books since that time: its strong beat carries the full emphasis of Neale's trochaic lines (very different from 'Jerusalem the golden'). Its popularity was greatly assisted by its being chosen for the wedding of HRH Princess Margaret in 1960; it is certainly a magnificent tune for great occasions.

10   *Pange, lingua, gloriosi proelium certaminis*

Sing, my tongue, the glorious battle,
    Sing the ending of the fray;
Now above the Cross, the trophy,
    Sound the loud triumphant lay:
Tell how Christ, the world's Redeemer,
    As a Victim won the day.

God in pity saw man fallen,
    Shamed and sunk in misery,
When he fell on death by tasting
    Fruit of the forbidden tree;
Then another tree was chosen
    Which the world from death should free.

Thus the scheme of our salvation
    Was of old in order laid,
That the manifold deceiver's
    Art by art might be outweighed,
And the lure the foe put forward
    Into means of healing made.

Therefore when the appointed fullness
    Of the holy time was come,
He was sent who maketh all things
    Forth from God's eternal home;
Thus he came to earth, incarnate,
    Offspring of a maiden's womb.

———————

Thirty years among us dwelling,
    His appointed time fulfilled,
Born for this, he meets his Passion,
    For that this he freely willed,
On the Cross the Lamb is lifted
    Where his life-blood shall be spilled.

He endured the nails, the spitting,
    Vinegar, and spear, and reed;
From that holy Body broken
    Blood and water forth proceed:
Earth, and stars, and sky, and ocean
    By that flood from stain are freed.

Faithful Cross! above all other,
    One and only noble tree!
None in foliage, none in blossom,
    None in fruit thy peer may be;
Sweetest wood and sweetest iron!
    Sweetest weight is hung on thee.

Bend thy boughs, O Tree of Glory!
    Thy relaxing sinews bend;
For awhile the ancient rigour
    That thy birth bestowed, suspend;
And the King of heavenly beauty
    On thy bosom gently tend!

Thou alone wast counted worthy
    This world's ransom to uphold;
For a shipwreck'd race preparing
    Harbour, like the Ark of old;
With the sacred Blood anointed
    From the smitten Lamb that rolled.

———————

To the Trinity be glory
  Everlasting, as is meet;
Equal to the Father, equal
  To the Son, and Paraclete:
Trinal Unity, whose praises
  All created things repeat. Amen.

Venantius Fortunatus (c.530–609),
tr. Percy Dearmer (1867–1936)
and John Mason Neale (1818–66)

This is one of the great hymns of the medieval Church. It is said to have been written by Venantius Fortunatus in the year 569 when his friend Queen Rhadegunda, foundress of the Convent of the Holy Cross at Poitiers, received from the Holy Roman Emperor a fragment of the 'True Cross'. It is therefore connected with the *Vexilla Regis*, 'The royal banners forward go', which was written for the same occasion. It is usually divided into two parts, with the doxology appended to either part. The present text is that of the *English Hymnal* (1906), which uses Dearmer's translation (which is based on that of Neale) for the first part and Neale's (from *Mediaeval Hymns and Sequences*, 1851) for the second.

This hymn was found in many Breviaries and Missals of the Middle Ages. It is one of those fundamental hymns which depend on images that have become a part of Christian poetic thought: Christ as a victim who wins; the tree (the Cross) which provides the response to the other tree (the tree in the Garden of Eden); the coming to earth of the God who made the earth. In addition, there is in verse 3 an allusion to the 'art' of God, answering 'the lure the foe put forward' (the temptation of Eve) with another and finer art, in which the Fall is made into a means of healing: so that the Fall is a *felix culpa*, a 'Fortunate Fall'.

In the second part, the Passion of Christ is vividly described in the first two verses; the hymn then turns into a hymn of praise to the Cross itself, which becomes the most magnificent of all 'trees' because it bears the fruit of the Saviour. So it is, for us 'sweetest wood and sweetest iron', upholding the 'sweetest weight' of the body of God. Then, in a wonderful piece of imaginative sympathy, the poet pleads with the Cross to be gentle with the dying Christ; and the final verse sees it as 'preparing harbour', a means of salvation for a shipwrecked humanity, as Noah's ark was for him and his family.

The tune is a plainsong melody, from the Sarum Missal, in the Phrygian mode. It can be sung to a metrical harmonized tune such as ST THOMAS (*English Hymnal*: 31) but the plainsong tune is more appropriate for the medieval character of the words.

Vexilla regis prodeunt

The royal banners forward go;
The cross shines forth in mystic glow;
Where he in flesh, our flesh who made,
Our sentence bore, our ransom paid:

Where deep for us the spear was dyed,
Life's torrent rushing from his side,
To wash us in that precious flood,
Where mingled water flowed, and blood.

———————

Fulfilled is all that David told
In true prophetic song of old;
Amidst the nations, God, saith he,
Hath reigned and triumphed from the tree.

O tree of beauty, tree of light!
O tree with royal purple dight!
Elect on whose triumphal breast
Those holy limbs should find their rest:

On whose dear arms, so widely flung,
The weight of this world's ransom hung:
The price of humankind to pay,
And spoil the spoiler of his prey.

O cross, our one reliance, hail!
So may thy power with us avail
To give new virtue to the saint,
And pardon to the penitent.

To thee, eternal Three in One,
Let homage meet by all be done:
Whom by the cross thou dost restore,
Preserve and govern evermore.

Venantius Fortunatus (*c.*530–609),
tr. John Mason Neale (1818–66)

This ancient hymn is closely associated with 'Sing, my tongue, the glorious battle'; it is said to have been written on the same occasion as that hymn, to celebrate the procession of the fragment of the 'True Cross' in 569 to the Convent at Poitiers founded by Queen Rhadegunda.

The 'vexilla' were the standards of the Roman legions, which, after the conversion of the Emperor to Christianity, were surmounted by a cross (replacing the Roman eagle). In this hymn they become symbolic of the spiritual warfare which has been won by the Cross of Christ, so that the poem becomes an elaborate exposition of the significance of the Cross, here described as 'the tree' (perhaps referring to the ancient tradition that as the Fall came from an apple on a tree, so the Redemption came from another tree). It is the tree of the Old Testament ('that David told'), which was fore-told by the psalmist as allowing God to reign from the tree; it is the tree of beauty, of light, and of triumph; it is the tree on which the holy limbs (paradoxically) find rest, and on which the weight of the world's ransom hung. The hymn was therefore very appropriate to the occasion, allowing the fragment of the Cross to be venerated as it passed into the convent.

The reference to David is to Psalm 96: 10, in the 'Italic' version of the Psalm (the Latin text in use in Italy before the time of St Jerome and the Vulgate): 'Our God reigns from the tree'. The idea that Jesus is 'reigning' at the moment of His deepest suffering is typical of the unusual insights of this hymn.

It originally began:

> Vexilla regis prodeunt:
> Fulget crucis mysterium,
> Quo carne carnis conditor
> Suspensus est patibulo.

A 'patibulum' was a fork-shaped yoke, placed on the necks of criminals, to which their hands were tied. Here Christ (in flesh, the maker of our flesh) is suspended on the yoke: and on the yoke hung the weight of the world's ransom. The Cross is seen in the form of a Y, with the branches spread out, so that they become not only a yoke but a balance. On this balance, 'the ransom of the world was weighed' (Julian, *Dictionary of Hymnology*: 1220). In the translation in *Hymns Ancient and Modern*, this is made explicit:

> Upon its arms, like balance true,
> He weighed the price for sinners due,
> The price which none but he could pay,
> And spoiled the spoiler of his prey.

The last line of this verse (which is found in the text printed above, from the *English Hymnal*, 1906) is characteristic of the kind of imaginative and verbal leaps which have to be made in reading this hymn. Here there is an echo of Ephesians 4: 8: 'he led captivity captive'; but throughout Fortunatus allows his ingenious mind to play upon the various ways in which the 'tree', the 'true cross' can be made significant.

The traditional tune is a plainsong tune, called VEXILLA REGIS in *Hymns Ancient and Modern*. A fine twentieth-century tune, composed for the Latin text of this hymn, is GONFALON ROYAL, written by Percy Buck (1871–1947) when he was director of music at Harrow School and published in his *Fourteen Hymn Tunes* (1913). 'Gonfalon' is an Anglo-Norman word mean-ing 'banner'. It is a rousing unison tune, well suited to a school chapel, which has become happily associated with other long metre texts (such as 'Sing to the Lord a joyful song').

12   *Hail thee, Festival Day! blest day that art hallowed for ever;*
Day wherein God from heaven shone on the world with his grace.

Lo! in the likeness of fire, on them that await his appearing,
He whom the Lord foretold, suddenly, swiftly, descends.

Forth from the Father he comes with his sevenfold mystical dowry,
Pouring on human souls infinite riches of God.

Hark! in a hundred tongues Christ's own, his chosen Apostles,
Preach to a hundred tribes Christ and his wonderful works.

Praise to the Spirit of life, all praise to the Fount of our being,
Light that dost lighten all, Life that in all dost abide.

God, who art Giver of all good gifts and Lover of concord,
Pour thy balm on our souls, order our ways in thy peace.

God Almighty, who fillest the heaven, the earth and the ocean,
Guard us from harm without, cleanse us from evil within.

Kindle our lips with the live bright coal from the hands of the Seraph;
Shine in our minds with thy light; burn in our hearts with thy love.

Latin medieval hymn,
tr. George Gabriel Scott Gillett (1873–1948)

There are numerous versions of this hymn for the great festivals of the
Church which begin with the phrase 'Salve, festa dies' ('Hail, festival day').
Three were printed in the *English Hymnal*, by three different translators,
Maurice F. Bell, Percy Dearmer, and Gabriel Gillett, for Easter Day,
Ascension Day, and Whit Sunday respectively. The Latin text has its origin
in a hymn by Venantius Fortunatus (*c.*530–609) celebrating the conversion
of the Saxons by Felix, Bishop of Nantes, which began—

Tempora florigero rutilant distincta sereno
et maiore poli lumine porta patet

('The times glow with flower-bearing weather, and the doors of the heavens
are spread open with a greater light'). Fortunatus was celebrating the
coming of spring, literally and metaphorically, and some of the English
versions begin (after the first two lines):

Lo, the fair beauty of earth, from the death of the winter arising,
Every good gift of the year now with its Master returns.

Stanza 20 of Fortunatus' hymn began with the line 'Salve, festa dies, toto
venerabilis aevo' ('Hail, festival day, worthy of veneration in all ages'). This
section rapidly became popular, and various hymns were written from this
starting point. Gillett's translation is from a hymn used for the medieval
York processional.

The various versions of this hymn were probably popular in the later
Middle Ages. The Easter Day and Ascension Day texts, for example, were

used in the Sarum processionals. Thomas Cranmer translated one version, writing to Henry VIII in 1544: 'I have travailed to make the verses in English . . . only for a proof to see how English would do in song', which suggests that he was thinking of them as useful for worship, for people to sing in the vernacular. The nineteenth- and twentieth-century versions that have become well known were part of the revival of ancient hymnody inspired by such figures as John Mason Neale and Edward Caswall, and associated with the Oxford Movement (stanzas from this hymn may be found in Newman's *Hymni Ecclesiae*, 1838, 1865).

This particular version of the 'Salve, festa dies' text deals with the coming of the Holy Spirit, as told in Acts 2: 1–11. The 'sevenfold mystical dowry' of verse three refers to the seven gifts of the Holy Spirit, which are Wisdom, Understanding, Counsel, Fortitude, Knowledge, Piety, and Fear of the Lord. They come from Isaiah 11: 2, with piety added. Also from Isaiah is the image in the final verse of the Seraph with the 'live bright coal' (from Isaiah 6: 6–7). The combination of New Testament and Old Testament imagery is very effective, especially in this metre, with its full-lined couplets: the metre is basically that of Latin elegiacs (a hexameter line followed by a pentameter one), and it is predominantly dactylic (from the Greek word 'dactyl', a finger, signifying in this case three syllables that are long-short-short).

The Latin hymn would have had a plainsong tune, and it can still be sung to a plainsong chant. It is more often sung now to the modern tune, SALVE FESTA DIES, by Ralph Vaughan Williams, written for the *English Hymnal* of 1906: it is a unison tune which drives the long lines well in what Archibald Jacob (in the music notes to *Songs of Praise Discussed*) described as 'a genial, progressive rhythm'. A twentieth-century tune is here a fine accompaniment to words that are rich with ancient tradition and symbol.

13   *Iam lucis orto sidere*

Now that the daylight fills the sky,
We lift our hearts to God on high,
That he, in all we do or say,
Would keep us free from harm today.

May he restrain our tongues from strife,
And shield from anger's din our life,
And guard with watchful care our eyes
From earth's absorbing vanities.

O may our inmost hearts be pure,
From thoughts of folly kept secure,
And pride of sinful flesh subdued
Through sparing use of daily food.

So we, when this day's work is o'er,
And shades of night return once more,
Our path of trial safely trod,
Shall give the glory to our God.

All praise to God the Father be,
All praise, eternal Son, to thee,
Whom with the Spirit we adore
For ever and for evermore.

Latin, probably eighth century,
tr. John Mason Neale (1818–66) and others

This ancient morning hymn is found in eighth-century manuscripts, but may be older. It is found in many medieval breviaries, indicating its widespread use at prime in the daily office. Its simplicity and its dignity are well captured in Neale's translation, which was made for *The Hymnal Noted*, Part 1 (1852). It was much altered by the compilers of *Hymns Ancient and Modern*, where for many years (from the second edition of 1875 onwards) it was the first hymn in the book. Bishop Ken's 'Awake, my soul, and with the sun' has now returned to that place, as in 1861; but this hymn deserves to be remembered for its antiquity and for the simplicity with which it prays for a good and simple life, free from anger and tittle-tattle (both very dangerous in monastic communities), from worldly things, from foolishness, and from the lusts of the flesh (kept in check by the sparing use of food). Although these prayers may seem remote to modern readers, they are still important as elements of the Christian life.

It is usually sung to a plainsong tune, or to the tune used for its evening equivalent, 'Before the ending of the day', which is the triple-time version of PUER NOBIS NASCITUR, a medieval melody adapted by Michael Praetorius (1571–1621) and found in Theodoric Petri's *Piae Cantiones* (1582).

14   *Te lucis ante terminum*

Before the ending of the day,
Creator of the world, we pray
That with thy wonted favour, thou
Wouldst be our guard and keeper now.

From all ill dreams defend our eyes,
From nightly fears and fantasies;
Tread under foot our ghostly foe,
That no pollution we may know.

O Father, that we ask be done,
Through Jesus Christ thine only Son,
Who, with the Holy Ghost and Thee,
Doth live and reign eternally.

Latin, eighth century,
tr. John Mason Neale (1818–66)

Like the previous hymn, this ancient hymn is touching in its simplicity, and reverenced for its antiquity. It is found in a number of early monastic books in England and Germany from the eighth century onwards, and may have been written much earlier. It was used in the office of compline, and forms a beautiful prayer for the end of the day. It has been frequently translated, and is found in many versions. Neale's comes from *The Hymnal Noted*, Part 1 (1852), and is based on a version by Robert Campbell (1814–68), a lawyer and a member of the Scottish Episcopal Church, who published a collection of *Hymns and Anthems for Use in the Holy Services of the Church within the United Diocese of St Andrews, Dunkeld, and Dublane* (1850). This is also a source for no. 19.

A plainsong melody, TE LUCIS, is often used for these words. As with no. 13, the triple-time version of PUER NOBIS NASCITUR can also be used. It is found in *The Cowley Carol Book* (1902) , by G. R. Woodward and Charles Wood, and subsequently in the *English Hymnal* (1906), set to 'Come, thou Redeemer of the earth'. Its charming simplicity is well suited to the words.

15   *Veni, veni, Emmanuel*

O come, O come, Emmanuel,
And ransom captive Israel,
That mourns in lonely exile here,
Until the Son of God appear:
  Rejoice! Rejoice! Emmanuel
  Shall come to thee, O Israel.

O come, thou Rod of Jesse, free
Thine own from Satan's tyranny;
From depths of hell thy people save,
And give them victory o'er the grave:
  Rejoice! Rejoice! Emmanuel
  Shall come to thee, O Israel.

O come, thou Dayspring, come and cheer
Our spirits by thine advent here;
Disperse the gloomy clouds of night,
And death's dark shadows put to flight:
  Rejoice! Rejoice! Emmanuel
  Shall come to thee, O Israel.

O come, thou Key of David, come,
And open wide our heavenly home;
Make safe the way that leads on high,
And close the path to misery:
  Rejoice! Rejoice! Emmanuel
  Shall come to thee, O Israel.

O come, O come, thou Lord of Might,
Who to thy tribes on Sinai's height,
In ancient times didst give the law
In cloud and majesty and awe:
  Rejoice! Rejoice! Emmanuel
  Shall come to thee, O Israel.

Latin Advent antiphons,
tr. John Mason Neale (1818–66)

This Advent hymn comes from a translation by John Mason Neale of a text in a *Psalteriolum Cantionum Catholicarum*, printed in Cologne in 1710. But that printed text had its origins in the early monastic tradition, probably as far back as the eighth century, of singing 'antiphons' at vespers during the seven days before Christmas Eve.

The antiphons, sometimes called the 'O antiphons' or 'The Great O's', were designed to concentrate the mind on the coming Christmas, enriching the meaning of the Incarnation with a complex series of references from the Old and the New Testaments. They began as follows:

O Sapientia
O Adonai
O radix Jesse
O clavis David
O Oriens
O Rex gentium
O Emmanuel

The last of these is entirely appropriate, for it takes the sequence from a series of Old Testament images (Wisdom, Adonai, Stem of Jesse, Key of David, Day-spring, King) to the Old/New Testament 'Emmanuel' (from Isaiah 7: 14 to Matthew 1: 23). But the sequence is more ingenious than this: the first letter of the second word makes the acrostic SARCORE, which when read backwards is 'Ero cras', meaning 'I will be present tomorrow'. Thus the final antiphon, sung on 23 December, revealed the complete message on the night before Christmas Eve. The hymn, as it is usually printed, is a rare opportunity for modern congregations to be in touch with an ancient form of worship, rich in symbolic and imaginative reading, and dense with biblical references.

The eighteenth-century Latin text was reprinted in H. A. Daniel's *Thesaurus Hymnologicus*, published in Leipzig (1841–55), where it is headed 'De Adventu Domini'. It was translated by John Mason Neale as 'Draw nigh, draw nigh, Emmanuel', and published in his *Mediaeval Hymns and Sequences* (1851). Neale later revised his text, and the first line was altered for the first edition of *Hymns Ancient and Modern* of 1861. This has remained a standard text, although there have been many variations in other books, both in the wording and the order of verses.

The tune is invariably VENI IMMANUEL, contributed by Thomas Helmore to Neale's 'Draw nigh, draw nigh, Emmanuel' in *The Hymnal Noted*, Part 2 (1854), with the heading 'From a French Missal in the National Library, Lisbon'. The missal has never been identified; but the tune was discovered by Mother Thomas More (Dr Mary Berry) in a fifteenth-century 'Processional' in the Bibliothèque Nationale in Paris. It is effective as a plainsong tune, which is appropriate to its monastic origins, although the beginning of the refrain interrupts the movement in each verse.

16   *Gloria, laus, et honor*

All glory, laud, and honour
To thee, Redeemer, King,
To whom the lips of children
Made sweet hosannas ring.

Thou art the King of Israel,
Thou David's royal Son,
Who in the Lord's name comest,
The King and Blessed One.

The company of Angels
Are praising thee on high,
And mortal men and all things
Created make reply.

The people of the Hebrews
With palms before thee went;
Our praise and prayer and anthems
Before thee we present.

To thee before thy Passion
They sang their hymns of praise;
To thee now high exalted
Our melody we raise.

Thou didst accept their praises;
Accept the prayers we bring,
Who in all good delightest,
Thou good and gracious King.

All glory, laud, and honour
To thee, Redeemer, King,
To whom the lips of children
Made sweet hosannas ring.

St Theodulph (d. 821),
tr. John Mason Neale (1818–66)

Neale made two translations of 'Gloria, laus, et honor', this fine processional hymn for Palm Sunday. This, the better known of the two, was made for *The Hymnal Noted*, Part 2 (1854), with a fifth verse that was slightly different from the present version:

In hast'ning to Thy Passion,
They rais'd their hymns of praise:
In reigning 'midst Thy glory,
Our melody we raise.

In this edition the first line was 'Glory, and laud, and honour', which was altered to the present form by the compilers of *Hymns Ancient and Modern* in a trial edition of 1859; Neale acknowledged this (which makes for a more regular metre) as 'an improvement'. He also noted another verse which 'was usually sung, till the 17th century; at the pious quaintness of which we can scarce avoid a smile':

> Be Thou, O Lord, the Rider,
> And we the little ass;
> That to God's Holy City
> Together we may pass.

Another less peculiar verse followed:

> Receive, instead of palm-boughs,
> Our victory o'er the foe,
> That in the Conqueror's triumph
> This strain may ever flow:
>
> *All glory, laud, and honour . . .*

Neale's note to this hymn in *Mediaeval Hymns and Sequences* (1851, 1863), where it appears in a different metre, describes a picturesque event:

This processional Hymn for Palm Sunday is said to have been composed by St Theodulph at Metz, or as others will have it, at Angers, while imprisoned on a false accusation: and to have been sung by him from his dungeon window, or by choristers instructed by him, as the Emperor Louis and his Court were on their way to the Cathedral. The good Bishop was immediately liberated.

Theodulph became Archbishop of Orleans in 800. He was active at the court of Charlemagne, but under Charlemagne's successor, Louis I ('Louis the Pious', Emperor 814–40) he was accused in 817 of complicity in the rebellion of Bernard of Italy, and imprisoned. Modern scholars have cast doubt on the story of the release from prison, which would have appealed strongly to Neale (Louis did not visit Angers after 818, which was the date of Theodulph's imprisonment): Neale would have liked to think that a hymn could have had such a powerful effect.

This hymn is invariably sung to ST THEODULPH, a tune by Melchior Teschner (1584–1635), written for a German hymn, 'Valet will ich dir geben', and published in 1615. Bach used the tune in his *St John Passion*.

    Veni, Creator Spiritus

Come, Holy Ghost, our souls inspire,
And lighten with celestial fire;
Thou the anointing Spirit art,
Who dost thy sevenfold gifts impart:

Thy blessèd unction from above
Is comfort, life, and fire of love;
Enable with perpetual light
The dullness of our blinded sight;

Anoint and cheer our soilèd face
With the abundance of thy grace:
Keep far our foes, give peace at home;
Where thou art guide no ill can come.

Teach us to know the Father, Son,
And thee, of both, to be but One,
That through the ages all along
This may be our endless song,
    Praise to thy eternal merit,
    Father, Son, and Holy Spirit. Amen.

John Cosin (1594–1672)

This is a translation of a hymn attributed to Rhabanus Maurus (*c.*776–*c.*856), the Abbot of Fulda, in Germany, and later Archbishop of Mainz. It was a widely used hymn during the Middle Ages, especially at Whitsuntide and at ordination services. Dryden's paraphrase translation of the same hymn is 'Creator Spirit, by whose aid' (no. 18).

Cosin's translation was made for his *Collection of Private Devotions* (1627), a book which caused some controversy between Cosin and the Puritans because of its Laudian devotional practices. In the 1662 *Book of Common Prayer*, which was revised by Cosin (who became Bishop of Durham at the Restoration, having been in exile during the Commonwealth), this hymn was included in the service of ordination to the priesthood.

This is obviously very appropriate. The hymn begins with the fire which descended upon the disciples (Acts 2: 3), and continues with prayers for enlightenment, for inner holiness and cleanliness ('Anoint and cheer our soilèd face'), for peace, and for the imparting of the Holy Spirit itself, with its sevenfold gifts. These gifts (which also occur in Dryden's translation) are Wisdom, Understanding, Counsel, Fortitude, Knowledge, Piety, and the Fear of the Lord (see the note to Hymn no. 12).

The association of the words with the plainsong tune, VENI CREATOR, is of great antiquity. It seems to have become established in monastic services from the beginning: its easy melodic line, with its additional phrases for the two final lines, allow the combination of music and words (even in translation) to seem authentic.

18 *Veni, Creator Spiritus*

Creator Spirit, by whose aid
The world's foundations first were laid,
Come, visit every pious mind;
Come, pour thy joys on human kind;
From sin and sorrow set us free,
And make thy temples worthy thee.

O Source of uncreated light,
The Father's promised Paraclete,
Thrice holy Fount, thrice holy Fire,
Our hearts with heavenly love inspire;
Come, and thy sacred unction bring
To sanctify us while we sing.

Plenteous of grace, descend from high
Rich in thy sevenfold energy;
Make us eternal truths receive,
And practise all that we believe;
Give us thyself, that we may see
The Father and the Son by thee.

Immortal honour, endless fame,
Attend the almighty Father's name;
The Saviour Son be glorified,
Who for lost man's redemption died;
And equal adoration be,
Eternal Paraclete, to thee. Amen.

Latin, ninth century,
tr. John Dryden (1631–1701)

In Dryden's *Poetical Works* this is described as 'Veni, Creator Spiritus. Translated in Paraphrase', indicating that it is another (and freer) translation of the hymn used by John Cosin for 'Come, Holy Ghost, our souls inspire'. The present text, which is found in the *English Hymnal* and *Songs of Praise*, is a selection from Dryden's poem, published in his *Examen Poeticum* (1693). This was in heroic couplets, not divided into verses, and contained material which has usually been omitted in hymn-books.

One of the first to use it as a hymn was John Wesley, in his *Collection of Psalms and Hymns* of 1738. It has since become well known as a hymn which links the creative power of the Holy Spirit (from Genesis 1: 2—'and the Spirit of God moved upon the face of the waters') with the promise of the Holy Spirit as Comforter (John 14: 16). Its noble simplicity of diction, and its well-structured couplets, are characteristic of Dryden's poetic art.

The usual tune, VENI CREATOR (ATTWOOD), is by Thomas Attwood (1765–1838), organist of St Paul's Cathedral. It was written in 1831, at the request of the Bishop of London, for a hymn-anthem (based on Cosin's words rather than Dryden's) to be used at an ordination service. Attwood is said to have finished it on the way to the Cathedral. With the adoption of the plain-song tune for Cosin's hymn, this tune has been nicely transferred to Dryden's words.

19   *Chorus novae Ierusalem*

Ye choirs of new Jerusalem,
     Your sweetest notes employ,
The Paschal victory to hymn
     In strains of holy joy.

How Judah's Lion burst his chains,
     And crushed the serpent's head;
And brought with him, from death's domains,
     The long-imprisoned dead.

From hell's devouring jaws the prey
     Alone our Leader bore;
His ransomed hosts pursue their way
     Where he hath gone before.

Triumphant in his glory now
     His sceptre ruleth all,
Earth, heaven, and hell before him bow,
     And at his footstool fall.

While joyful thus his praise we sing,
     His mercy we implore,
Into his palace bright to bring
     And keep us evermore.

All glory to the Father be,
     All glory to the Son,
All glory, Holy Ghost, to thee,
     While endless ages run. Alleluya! Amen.

                    St Fulbert of Chartres (*c*.960–1028),
                       tr. Robert Campbell (1814–68)

This hymn is from Robert Campbell's *Hymns and Anthems for Use in the Holy Services of the Church within the United Diocese of St Andrews, Dunkeld, and Dunblane*, published in Edinburgh in 1850. Campbell was a Roman Catholic convert, and his hymn gathers up elements of a long tradition: not only is it full of allusions (such as 'crushed the serpent's head', from Genesis 3: 15), but it also draws on medieval legends of the harrowing of hell. Christ as the deliverer of the prisoners from the chains of hell is found in Revelation 5, which also describes Him as the Lion of Judah: 'Behold the Lion of the tribe of Judah, the Root of David, hath prevailed to open the book, and to loose the seven seals thereof' (verse 5). This is itself an allusion to many references to the Lion of Judah in the Old Testament. The hymn thus explores many kinds of traditional imagery to describe the triumph of Christ in the 'Paschal victory' over sin, death, and hell. It concludes fittingly, with prayer: that as we celebrate His victory, so we implore His mercy to bring us, like the redeemed souls at the harrowing of hell, into paradise.

St Fulbert was Bishop of Chartres, where he inaugurated the rebuilding of the cathedral after the fire of 1020. His hymn was a late addition to the cycle of office hymns, used for vespers from Low Sunday (the Sunday after Easter Day) to Ascension Day.

The customary tune, ST FULBERT, is by Henry Gauntlett (1805–76), set to these words in the first edition of *Hymns Ancient and Modern* in 1861, and associated with them since that time.

20   *O quanta qualia sunt illa Sabbata*

O what their joy and their glory must be,
Those endless Sabbaths the blessed ones see!
Crown for the valiant; to weary ones rest;
God shall be all, and in all ever blest.

What are the Monarch, his court, and his throne?
What are the peace and the joy that they own?
Tell us, ye blest ones, that in it have share,
If what ye feel ye can fully declare.

Truly 'Jerusalem' name we that shore,
'Vision of peace', that brings joy evermore;
Wish and fulfilment can severed be ne'er,
Nor the thing prayed for come short of the prayer.

We, where no trouble distraction can bring,
Safely the anthems of Sion shall sing;
While for thy grace, Lord, their voices of praise
Thy blessed people shall evermore raise.

There dawns no Sabbath, no Sabbath is o'er,
Those Sabbath-keepers have one and no more;
One and unending is that triumph-song
Which to the Angels and us shall belong.

Now in the meanwhile, with hearts raised on high,
We for that country must yearn and must sigh,
Seeking Jerusalem, dear native land,
Through our long exile on Babylon's strand.

Low before him with our praises we fall,
Of whom, and in whom, and through whom are all;
Of whom, the Father; and in whom, the Son;
Through whom, the Spirit, with these ever One. Amen.

Peter Abelard (1079–1142),
tr. John Mason Neale (1818–66)

This translation of Peter Abelard's hymn on the joys and glories of paradise was first published in *The Hymnal Noted*, Part 2 (1854), by Thomas Helmore and John Mason Neale. The translation follows the Latin metre, as Neale liked to do, and the result is a hymn in which the long couplets allow the thought to develop in extended sections. In the last verse, for example, Neale italicized the prepositions to emphasize the multiple nature of God:

> Low before Him with our praises we fall,
> *Of* Whom, and *in* Whom, and *through* Whom are all:

It makes a very distinctive hymn experience, in which the longing of those on earth is expressed by their address to the blessed ones. The situation on earth is likened to the Babylonian captivity, from which the children of Israel returned to Jerusalem: here Jerusalem is the 'vision of peace' (see Neale's note to 'Blessed City, heavenly Salem'), where wish and fulfilment are the same, and where prayers are always answered, for the thing prayed for cannot come short of the prayer. There are abundant images for heaven: the court, the throne, the monarch, the shore, the place of safety and the place of song. All these are gathered up into the idea of an endless Sabbath, a holy day that has no beginning and no end.

Peter Abelard, the great teacher, philosopher, and theologian, lived from 1079–1142. His tragic love for Heloise, daughter of a canon of Notre Dame in Paris, was the most distressing event in his controversial and troubled life (see Helen Waddell, *Peter Abelard, a novel*, London, 1933). It is possible that one surviving text of this hymn was written for the abbey of the Paraclete where Heloise was the abbess. If this is so, then the lines gain an additional poignancy, in their representation of the joys of heaven in contrast to the pain of earth.

Many translations have been made of Abelard's hymn. A fine modern one, by Alan Gaunt, is printed in *Rejoice and Sing* (no. 659).

The tune is REGNATOR ORBIS, from a Paris antiphoner of 1681. It conveys the medieval resonance of the hymn very well, having affinities with plainchant. Indeed, one place where the tune is found is in François la Feillée's *Méthode du plain-chant* of 1808.

21
All creatures of our God and King
Lift up your voice and with us sing
  Alleluia, alleluia!
Thou burning sun with golden beam,
Thou silver moon with softer gleam,
  O praise him, O praise him,
  Alleluia, alleluia, alleluia.

Thou rushing wind that art so strong,
Ye clouds that sail in heaven along,
  O praise him, alleluia!
Thou rising morn, in praise rejoice,
Ye lights of evening, find a voice:

Thou flowing water, pure and clear,
Make music for thy Lord to hear,
  Alleluia, alleluia!
Thou fire so masterful and bright,
That givest man both warmth and light:

Dear mother earth, who day by day
Unfoldest blessings on our way,
  O praise him, alleluia!
The flowers and fruits that in thee grow,
Let them his glory also show:

And all ye men of tender heart,
Forgiving others, take your part,
  O sing ye, alleluia!
Ye who long pain and sorrow bear,
Praise God and on him cast your care:

And thou, most kind and gentle death,
Waiting to hush our latest breath,
  O praise him, alleluia!
Thou leadest home the child of God,
And Christ our Lord the way hath trod:

Let all things their Creator bless,
And worship him in humbleness;
  O praise him, alleluia!
Praise, praise the Father, praise the Son,
And praise the Spirit, Three in One:
  O praise him, O praise him,
  Alleluia, alleluia, alleluia.

St Francis of Assisi (1182–1226),
tr. William Henry Draper (1855–1933)

This is based on the 'Cantico di fratre sole' (the 'Canticle of brother Sun'), attributed to St Francis, said to have been written in vernacular Italian in the last year of his life, but perhaps composed over a period of years. In the original the saint gives each element, such as fire and water, a human gender, so that they become 'brother' and 'sister'. This remains in the appellation of 'Dear mother earth' in verse 4, and is suggested by the personification of death as 'kind and gentle' in verse 6. These elements in the hymn make it seem tender as well as grand. It is based in part upon Psalm 148.

This version of the canticle (it is too free to be called a translation) was made by William Henry Draper when he was vicar of Adel, near Leeds, for a children's Whitsuntide procession: it was written between 1906 and 1919 (when it appeared in *The Public School Hymn Book*), but Draper said that he could not remember exactly when.

The hymn has deservedly become very popular, in part because of the splendid tune, LASST UNS ERFREUEN ('Let us rejoice') first found in a German Catholic book of 1623, *Ausserlesene, Catholische, Geistliche Kirchengesäng*, published in Cologne. This had the 'alleluias' in a different order, but a revised form of the tune appeared in a sequel published in Cologne in 1625. This was used by Vaughan Williams in the *English Hymnal* (1906) for Athelstan Riley's new hymn, 'Ye watchers and ye holy ones'. Draper seems to have seen the possibilities of setting a version of St Francis' text to this freshly recovered tune: tune and words were first published together in *The Public School Hymn Book* of 1919.

22   *Jesu, dulcis memoria*

Jesu, the very thought of thee
    With sweetness fills my breast;
But sweeter far thy face to see,
    And in thy presence rest.

Nor voice can sing, nor heart can frame,
    Nor can the memory find,
A sweeter sound than thy blest name,
    O Saviour of mankind!

O hope of every contrite heart,
    O joy of all the meek,
To those who fall, how kind thou art!
    How good to those who seek!

But what to those who find? Ah! this
    Nor tongue nor pen can show;
The love of Jesus! what it is,
    None but his loved ones know.

Jesu, our only joy be thou,
    As thou our prize wilt be;
Jesu, be thou our glory now,
    And through eternity.

                    Edward Caswall (1814–78)

Edward Caswall was an Anglican clergyman who resigned his living in 1846 to follow Newman into the Roman Catholic Church. This is his translation from a Latin text, perhaps written by an anonymous Cistercian monk of the eleventh or twelfth century, added to by various hands and at various dates, and perhaps written in England (the best account of it is by F. J. E. Raby, in the *Bulletin of the Hymn Society*, 33, October 1945). This simple and graceful hymn appeared in Caswall's *Lyra Catholica* of 1849, a book containing the first fruits of his conversion to Roman Catholicism. It appears among the Breviary hymns, Part II, 'Hymns belonging to the Proper of the Season' for the 'Feast of the Most Holy Name of Jesus, the Second Sunday after Epiphany'. The hymn is very properly about seeking after Jesus, and about the practice of the presence of God, which is the prize (Philippians 3: 14) of the final verse.

This first part of the hymn is for Vespers, with an appropriate emphasis on 'rest': the word is beautifully placed at the end of the first verse. The second part, 'O Jesu! King most wonderful!' ('Jesu, Rex admirabilis'), is for Matins, with the contrasting 'truth begins to shine', as the night gives way to the morning.

Many tunes have been used for this hymn. J. B. Dykes's plangent ST AGNES, which fits the words well, was one of the Victorian tunes to escape Vaughan Williams's blue pencil in the *English Hymnal* of 1906, though it was relegated to an Appendix in 1933, and replaced by Gordon Slater's ST BOTOLPH (now used for 'I come with joy'). The lively and purposeful METZLER'S REDHEAD (so called because of its composer, Richard Redhead, and his publisher, Metzler) was used for *Hymns Ancient and Modern* and for many other books. *Hymns and Psalms* (1983) used the American folk tune LAND OF REST as an alternative tune, and the *BBC Hymn Book* (1951) used an English folk tune, MENDIP. A German tune, NUN DANKET ALL, is found in *Rejoice and Sing*.

23

Jesu, thou joy of loving hearts,
    Thou fount of life, thou light of men;
From the best bliss that earth imparts
    We turn unfilled to thee again.

Thy truth unchanged hath ever stood;
    Thou savest those that on thee call;
To them that seek thee thou art good,
    To them that find thee, all in all.

We taste thee, O thou living bread,
    And long to feast upon thee still;
We drink of thee, the fountain-head,
    And thirst our souls from thee to fill.

Our restless spirits yearn for thee,
    Where'er our changeful lot is cast,
Glad when thy gracious smile we see,
    Blest when our faith can hold thee fast.

O Jesu, ever with us stay,
    Make all our moments calm and bright;
Chase the dark night of sin away,
    Shed o'er the world thy holy light.

Latin twelfth century,
freely tr. Ray Palmer (1808–87)

This is a free version, rather than a strict translation, of some verses beginning 'Jesu, dulcedo cordium'. They come from a poem entitled 'Iubilus rhythmicus de Nomine Jesu' ('Poetic celebration of the name of Jesus'), beginning 'Jesu, dulcis memoria' (from which comes Edward Caswall's 'Jesu, the very thought of thee', no. 22). The Latin original was at one time thought to be by St Bernard of Clairvaux, but it is now thought to be of English origin, perhaps by a Cistercian monk. Another of Caswall's translations, 'O Jesus, King most wonderful', is from the same hymn.

Palmer, who was an eminent Congregational minister in Maine and in New York State, wrote this version in 1858, calling it 'Jesus the Beloved'. It was published in the *Sabbath Hymn Book* (Andover, USA, 1858). The reference to the living bread (John 6: 51) makes the hymn suitable for Holy Communion, but the allusion to living water (John 4: 10 ff.) suggests a wider application. Palmer's beautiful handling of the verse form, as in his 'My faith looks up to thee' (no. 195, written much earlier), is shown in the numerous parallels, which are nicely varied with other lines. Thus in line 2, Jesus is 'fount' and 'light'; in verse 2, 'To them that seek thee' is paralleled by 'To them that find thee'; and in verse 3, 'we taste . . . and long', 'we drink . . . and thirst'. The result is a hymn which rapidly became popular on both sides of the Atlantic.

In *Hymns Ancient and Modern* it was set to a rather dull tune called EALING by Sir Herbert Oakeley (1830–1903); but since it is written in long metre, many tunes can be used for it. The most popular seem to be ST SEPULCHRE, by George Cooper (1820–76) used in *Hymns Ancient and Modern New Standard* (see 'And art thou come with us to dwell', no. 176); and WAREHAM, by William Knapp (1698–1768), to which it is well suited.

24   *Urbs Sion aurea*

Jerusalem the golden,
    With milk and honey blest,
Beneath thy contemplation
    Sink heart and voice opprest.
I know not, O I know not,
    What social joys are there,
What radiancy of glory,
    What light beyond compare.

They stand, those halls of Sion,
    Conjubilant with song,
And bright with many an Angel,
    And all the Martyr throng:
The Prince is ever in them,
    The daylight is serene,
The pastures of the blessed
    Are decked in glorious sheen.

There is the throne of David,
    And there, from care released,
The song of them that triumph,
    The shout of them that feast;
And they who, with their Leader,
    Have conquered in the fight,
For ever and for ever
    Are clad in robes of white.

O sweet and blessed country,
    Shall I ever see thy face?
O sweet and blessed country,
    Shall I ever win thy grace?
Exult, O dust and ashes!
    The Lord shall be thy part:
His only, his for ever,
    Thou shalt be, and thou art!

Bernard of Cluny (twelfth century),
tr. John Mason Neale (1818–66)

In his *Mediaeval Hymns and Sequences* (1851), Neale translated part of Bernard's 3,000–line poem *De Contemptu Mundi*, which he later expanded. It began 'Brief life is here our portion' ('Hic breve vivitur'), which itself has often been used as a hymn.

Bernard's poem had been brought to Neale's attention when selections from it were printed by Richard Chenevix Trench, Dean of Westminster, in his *Sacred Latin Poetry, Chiefly Lyrical* of 1849. Bernard of Cluny (referred to by Neale as Bernard of Morlaix, from his birthplace in Brittany) was a monk at Cluny in the twelfth century. His poem is dated *c.*1140: as its title implies, it is an attack on earthly pleasures; but it begins with a contrasting description of the peace and beauty of heaven. The antithesis is between the brief life which is 'here our portion' and the everlasting life which is '*there*' (italicized in the original, and in some editions capitalized). Neale said that 'I have no hesitation in saying that I look upon these verses of Bernard as the most lovely, in the same way that the *Dies Irae* is the most sublime, and the *Stabat Mater* the most pathetic, of mediaeval poems.'

The section which is concerned with the joys of heaven, as opposed to the troubles of earth, naturally became the most popular, partly because of its subject matter (for it is more agreeable to contemplate the joyful than to dwell on the miserable). In the second edition the lines used for the first three verses of this hymn were given further prominence by being capitalized, and Neale added a note referring to them:

It would be most unthankful, did I not express my gratitude to God, for the favour He has given some of the centos made from the poem: but especially '*Jerusalem the Golden*'. It has found a place in some twenty hymnals; and for the last two years [i.e. after the publication of *Hymns Ancient and Modern* in 1861] it has hardly been possible to read any newspaper which gives prominence to ecclesiastical news, without seeing its employment chronicled at some dedication or other festival. It is also a great favourite with dissenters, and has obtained admission in Roman Catholic services.

The great strength of the hymn is its masterly combination of metre and imagery. For this translation, Neale departed from his usual custom of following the metre of the original, 'because our language, if it could be tortured to any distant resemblance of its rhythm, would utterly fail to give any idea of the majestic sweetness which invests it in Latin'. Bernard's metre was a dactylic hexameter, divided into three parts, with internal rhyming as well as end-rhymes:

> Tunc nova gloria ‖ pectora sobria ‖ clarificabit:
> Solvit enigmata ‖ veraque sabbata ‖ continuabit.

Neale's chosen metre, 7.6.7.6., with its heavy iambic stresses, succeeds remarkably in conveying what he calls the 'majestic sweetness': the images are held firmly in place in the line, and the whole hymn has a visionary quality that is akin to the language of Revelation (especially chapters 5 and 7) but which also includes the Old Testament reference to Canaan as a land flowing with milk and honey (Exodus 3: 8, 17).

Hymns Ancient and Modern added a doxology in place of the last four lines, which Neale (in a note of 1865) approved of, suggesting that it might be used to conclude any selection made from these verses:

> Jesu, in mercy bring us
> To that dear land of rest
> Who art, with God the Father
> And Spirit, ever blest.

In addition, *Hymns Ancient and Modern*, uneasy with polysyllabic words, sadly altered 'Conjubilant' to 'All jubilant' (rectified at last in its most recent edition, *Common Praise*, 2000). Neale himself altered verse 2 line 6 to 'The daylight is serene' (1863) from the rather artificial 'The light is aye serene' (1851).

The hymn is a magnificent vision, capturing in its first three verses the hope of eternal life in imagery which is both traditional and assured, and in the fourth verse answering the inevitable question—'Shall I ever see thy face?'—with a resounding affirmative. But something of its success must be the result of the conjunction of Neale's rhythmical verse with the strong tune EWING, composed by Alexander Ewing (1830–95) for 'For thee, O dear, dear country', another hymn made from Neale's translation of Bernard's *De Contemptu Mundi*. The tune written for these words by Samuel Sebastian Wesley (1810–76), AURELIA (the title comes from the 'golden' of Neale's first line), has somehow become associated with 'The Church's one foundation' (no. 181).

25   *Jerusalem luminosa*

Light's abode, celestial Salem,
    Vision dear whence peace doth spring,
Brighter than the heart can fancy,
    Mansion of the highest King;
O, how glorious are the praises
    Which of thee the prophets sing!

There for ever and for ever
    Alleluya is outpoured;
For unending, for unbroken
    Is the feast-day of the Lord;
All is pure and all is holy
    That within thy walls is stored.

There no cloud nor passing vapour
    Dims the brightness of the air;
Endless noon-day, glorious noon-day,
    From the Sun of suns is there;
There no night brings rest from labour,
    There unknown are toil and care.

O how glorious and resplendent,
    Fragile body, shalt thou be,
When endued with so much beauty,
    Full of health, and strong, and free,
Full of vigour, full of pleasure
    That shall last eternally!

Now with gladness, now with courage,
    Bear the burden on thee laid,
That hereafter these thy labours
    May with endless gifts be paid,
And in everlasting glory
    Thou with joy may'st be arrayed.

Laud and honour to the Father;
    Laud and honour to the Son;
Laud and honour to the Spirit,
    Ever Three and ever One;
Consubstantial, co-eternal,
    While unending ages run. Amen.

Ascribed to St Thomas à Kempis (*c.*1380–1471),
            tr. John Mason Neale (1818–66)

From Neale's *Joys and Glories of Paradise* (1865). It is a translation of a hymn
by Thomas à Kempis, or one of his followers, on the subject 'Of the Glory
of the Heavenly Jerusalem, so far as concerneth the Glorified Body'. It had
twelve verses. It was paralleled by a similar hymn 'as concerning the

Endowments of the Glorified Soul', which celebrated the mind and the higher senses:

> Every sense in every fibre
>   There, beholding God, shall thrill;
> All the intellectual vigour
>   Clearly comprehend Him still;
> Whom, embracing unitively,
>   Thou shalt love with perfect will.

The present hymn on the Glorified Body has become much better known than the one on the Soul, perhaps because Neale was often concerned about sickness and death: he published *Hymns for the Sick* in 1843, at a time when he thought that he was going to die of consumption. His celebration is part of a pattern in which the body is pure and healthy, and it is always spring and summer in nature. This is the original verse 5, of the original twelve verses:

> There the everlasting spring-tide
>   Sheds its dewy, green repose;
> There the summer, in its glory,
>   Cloudless and eternal glows;
> For that country never knoweth
>   Autumn's storms nor winter's snows.

The body is always youthful, yet also free from the lusts of the flesh, as in the original verses 7 and 8:

> Youth with all its freshest vigour
>   Into age there cannot wane,
> There the old man shall not sorrow
>   For departed years again:
> Nothing past, and nothing future,—
>   Time doth present still remain.

> Animal and carnal passion
>   Nevermore can weary there;
> The new flesh made spiritual
>   Then the spirit's yoke shall bear;
> Sensual vigour, perfect reason,
>   Both one common law shall share.

Neale's imagery describes perfection in terms of physical health (as he does elsewhere) in a way that movingly underlines the pain and suffering which many had to endure on earth. The hymn is one of those that celebrates the promise of perfection, which Neale is able to describe, not only in traditional imagery but also in a strong trochaic rhythm, which gives to the lines their springy forward movement, and their fine assurance.

The strong rhythms of Neale's lines are finely articulated by the tune to which this hymn is usually sung, REGENT SQUARE, by Henry Smart (1813–79). Smart was organist of the nearby St Philip's Church, Regent Street, London, from 1839 to 1844. It is sometimes used for 'Praise, my soul, the King of Heaven', and many other hymns.

26   *Dies irae, dies illa*

Day of wrath! O day of mourning!
See fulfilled the prophet's warning:
Heaven and earth in ashes burning!

Oh! what fear man's bosom rendeth,
When from heaven the Judge descendeth,
On whose sentence all dependeth!

Wondrous sound the trumpet flingeth,
Through earth's sepulchres it ringeth,
All before the throne it bringeth.

Lo! the Book, exactly worded,
Wherein all hath been recorded;
Thence shall judgment be awarded.

When the Judge his seat attaineth
And each hidden deed arraigneth,
Nothing unavenged remaineth.

What shall I, frail man, be pleading,
Who for me be interceding,
When the just are mercy needing?

King of majesty tremendous,
Who dost free salvation send us,
Fount of pity, then befriend us!

Faint and weary thou hast sought me,
On the cross of suffering bought me;
Shall such grace be vainly brought me?

Guilty, now I pour my moaning,
All my shame with anguish owning:
Spare, O God, thy suppliant groaning.

Low I kneel, with heart submission;
See, like ashes, my contrition;
Help me in my last condition.

Ah, that day of tears and mourning!
From the dust of earth returning,
Man for judgment must prepare him;
Spare, O God, in mercy spare him.
Lord, all pitying, Jesu blest,
Grant them thine eternal rest.

Attributed to Thomas of Celano (thirteenth century),
tr. W. J. Irons (1812–83)

This hymn has been described as 'the most majestic of medieval Sequences' (a 'Sequence' was a composition said or sung between the Gradual and the Gospel). It is thought to have been originally a hymn for Advent, but it is now always associated with the Mass for the Dead. In its Latin form in the Requiem Mass, it forms a text that has been set to intense and thrilling music by composers such as Verdi and Britten. The triple rhyme in the Latin text, which is preserved in the translation, was described by H. A. Daniel (in his *Thesaurus Hymnologicus*, 1841–55) as being 'verba tot pondera, immo tonitrua' ('words so weighty, like thunder'). Richard Chenevix Trench (see no. 24) said that they were like 'blow following blow of the hammer on the anvil' (*Sacred Latin Poetry*, 1849).

There have been many translations. Scott used part of it in *The Lay of the Last Minstrel* (1805), and Goethe used it in *Faust*. Irons wrote his version after hearing the *Dies Irae* sung at a Requiem Mass for the Archbishop of Paris in the cathedral of Notre Dame. The Archbishop had been shot during the revolution of 1848, and his Requiem Mass was an occasion of deep mourning in a city which was tense with political unrest. The hymn was printed in a pamphlet for use at the season of Advent at Margaret Street chapel (now All Saints', Margaret Street), and subsequently in Irons's *Psalms and Hymns*, enlarged edition (1873).

There have also been many variations in the text. The Latin original of the second line, 'Teste David cum Sibylla' appears in some of them as 'David's word with Sibyl's blending' (as in the *English Hymnal*). This is explained by Trench as involving ancient prophetic texts, Jew and Gentile joining to bear testimony. A fuller version of the text above appeared in the second edition of *Hymns Ancient and Modern* (1875), in six-line verses, with material which is not in the above text, such as three lines from Matthew 25: 33:

With thy favoured sheep O place me,
Nor among the goats abase me,
But to thy right hand up-raise me.

Whatever version is used, the hymn has a tremendous force in its description of the Day of Judgement, and its portrayal of the frailty of humankind. The whole of nature seems to be called before the awesome Judge, and the only possible plea is 'spare me', a plea justified solely by the contrition of the sinner and the grace of the Cross. As another verse puts it:

> Through the sinful woman shriven,
> Through the dying thief forgiven,
> Thou to me a hope hast given.

The hymn is generally thought to have been written by Thomas of Celano, a Franciscan who was the friend and biographer of St Francis. His original source was from Zephaniah 1: 15: the Vulgate, or Latin text, provided the opening for 'Dies irae, dies illa'. In the English Authorized Version text it is: 'That day [the great day of the Lord, verse 14] is a day of wrath, a day of trouble and distress, a day of wasteness and desolation, a day of darkness and gloominess, a day of clouds and thick darkness.'

The hymn has tended to disappear from modern hymn-books. This is part of the general emphasis on the love of God rather than the wrath of God: but it is right at times to be reminded of the awe which human beings should feel in His presence, and at the prospect of the Day of Judgement. If we add to that the hymn's long history, its poetic assembling of powerful images, and its rhythmical assurance, there can be no doubt that it is one of the great hymns of the Western world.

It is usually sung to a plainsong melody, but *Hymns Ancient and Modern* printed a tune by John Bacchus Dykes (1823–76) called DIES IRAE. But in this case the tune seems less important than the words.

27 *Gloriosi salvatoris nominis praeconia*

To the Name of our Salvation
  Laud and honour let us pay,
Which for many a generation
  Hid in God's foreknowledge lay,
But with holy exultation
  We may sing aloud today.

Jesus is the name we treasure,
  Name beyond what words can tell;
Name of gladness, name of pleasure,
  Ear and heart delighting well;
Name of sweetness passing measure,
  Saving us from sin and hell.

'Tis the name for adoration,
  Name for songs of victory,
Name for holy meditation
  In this vale of misery,
Name for joyful veneration
  By the citizens on high.

'Tis the name that whoso preacheth
  Speaks like music to the ear;
Who in prayer this name beseecheth
  Sweetest comfort findeth near;
Who its perfect wisdom reacheth
  Heavenly joy possesseth here.

Jesus is the name exalted
  Over every other name;
In this name, whene'er assaulted,
  We can put our foes to shame:
Strength to them who else had halted,
  Eyes to blind, and feet to lame.

Therefore we in love adoring
  This most blessed name revere,
Holy Jesu, thee imploring
  So to write it in us here,
That hereafter heavenward soaring
  We may sing with angels there.

Fifteenth century,
tr. John Mason Neale (1818–66), altered by others

Neale called this hymn a 'German Hymn in imitation of the Pange Lingua' in his *Mediaeval Hymns and Sequences* (1851), where it first appeared. In the same way that St Thomas Aquinas wrote a hymn, 'Sing, my tongue, the Saviour's glory', in imitation of Venantius Fortunatus's 'Sing, my tongue, the glorious battle' (no. 10), so Neale saw this hymn as a later imitation (found in an Antwerp breviary of the fifteenth century), in the same metre, 87.87.87. The present hymn is concerned with a different topic, however: whereas the first two were concerned with the Cross and with the life of Jesus, this hymn was written during the fifteenth-century cult of devotion to the Holy Name. Although this was found earlier in the Middle Ages, as in 'Jesu, dulcis memoria' (no. 23), the devotion to the Holy Name was encouraged by St Bernardino of Siena and became a strong devotional impulse in the sixteenth century. Joan of Arc, for example, had a standard with the icon of the Holy Name.

The Holy Name of Jesus is found throughout the New Testament, especially in Philippians 2, where God 'also hath highly exalted him, and given him a name which is above every name: That at the name of Jesus every knee should bow, . . .'. It is significant that this was a favourite chapter of Charles Wesley, who wrote of 'Jesus, the Name that charms our fears' (in 'O for a thousand tongues to sing', no. 88). Neale's hymn also resembles Wesley's practice in the way in which it conducts the reader from earth to heaven in the final verse; but it also has a stately trochaic rhythm which is unlike Wesley's practice. Its regularity is entirely suitable for the idea of a steady veneration.

The tune to which this is most frequently set is ORIEL, by Caspar Ett (1788–1847), a Bavarian musician and organist at Munich, who published *Cantica Sacra in usum Studiosae juventutis* in 1840. A descant was written for it by Alan Gray (1855–1935), which livens up the rather dull melody. More attractive as a setting is GRAFTON, a French nineteenth-century tune brought to Britain in *The Oxford Hymn Book* (1908) and given the name GRAFTON in *Songs of Praise* (1925, where it was set to 'Lord, behold us with thy blessing'). It may also be sung to Henry Smart's splendid REGENT SQUARE.

28 *O filii et filiae*

Alleluya! Alleluya! Alleluya!
Ye sons and daughters of the King,
Whom heavenly hosts in glory sing,
To-day the grave hath lost its sting.
Alleluya!

On that first morning of the week,
Before the day began to break,
The Marys went their Lord to seek.
Alleluya!

An angel bade their sorrow flee,
For thus he spake unto the three:
'Your Lord is gone to Galilee.'
Alleluya!

That night the apostles met in fear,
Amidst them came their Lord most dear,
And said: 'Peace be unto you here!'
Alleluya!

When Thomas afterwards had heard
That Jesus had fulfilled his word,
He doubted if it were the Lord.
Alleluya!

'Thomas, behold my side,' saith he,
'My hands, my feet, my body see;
'And doubt not, but believe in me.'
Alleluya!

No longer Thomas then denied;
He saw the feet, the hands, the side;
'Thou art my Lord and God,' he cried.
Alleluya!

Blessèd are they that have not seen,
And yet whose faith hath constant been,
In life eternal they shall reign.
Alleluya!

On this most holy day of days,
To God your hearts and voices raise
In laud, and jubilee, and praise.
Alleluya!

And we with Holy Church unite,
As evermore is just and right,
In glory to the King of Light.
Alleluya!

Jean Tisserand (d. 1494),
tr. John Mason Neale (1818–66)

This great Easter hymn is attributed to Tisserand, a Franciscan monk. It appears in an untitled book with the title 'L'aleluya du jour des Pasques' ('The Alleluia for Easter Day') printed between 1518 and 1536, and again in *L'Office de la Semaine Sainte*, published in Paris in 1674. Neale's translation appeared in his *Mediaeval Hymns and Sequences* (1851), and was made popular by an altered version beginning 'O sons and daughters, let us sing' in the first edition of *Hymns Ancient and Modern* (1861). The present text is that of the *English Hymnal*, which went back to Neale's original.

This hymn was used to salute the Blessed Sacrament on the evening of Easter Day. It retells the story of the first Easter, but is unusual in its inclusion of St Thomas and his doubt (from John 20: 19–29). It incorporates that doubt in a more general celebration of Easter, providing an account of a very human story .

The tune is called after the Latin hymn, O FILII ET FILIAE ('O sons and daughters'). It was set to these words in *Airs sur les hymnes sacrez* (Paris, 1623), and has always been used for them, though with different harmonizations in different books. There is a fine version by Elizabeth Poston in *The Cambridge Hymnal* (1967).

29   *Finita iam sunt praelia*

The strife is o'er, the battle done;
Now is the victor's triumph won;
O let the song of praise be sung:
              Alleluia!

Death's mightiest powers have done their worst,
And Jesus hath his foes dispersed;
Let shouts of praise and joy outburst:
              Alleluia!

On the third morn he rose again
Glorious in majesty to reign;
O let us swell the joyful strain:
              Alleluia!

He brake the age-bound chains of hell;
The bars from heaven's high portals fell;
Let hymns of praise his triumph tell:
              Alleluia!

Lord, by the stripes which wounded thee,
From death's dread sting thy servants free,
That we may live, and sing to thee:
              Alleluia!

                    Seventeenth-century (?) Latin hymn,
                      tr. Francis Pott (1832–1909)

This Latin hymn is of unknown origin. John Mason Neale, who printed it in his *Hymni Ecclesiae* (1851) and translated it for his *Mediaeval Hymns and Sequences* (1851), thought that it was from the twelfth century; but the earliest version that we have is from a Jesuit book, *Symphonia Sirenum Selectarum*, printed in Cologne in 1695. The text begins:

Alleluia! Alleluia!
Finita iam sunt praelia,
Est parta iam victoria!
Gaudeamus, et canamus: Alleluia!

Neale's translation, which begins 'Finished is the battle now' has largely been eclipsed by Pott's translation, which was published in his *Hymns fitted to the Order of Common Prayer* (1861). Pott (part-author of 'Forty days and forty nights', no. 160), though under the age of thirty, was a member of the committee which produced the first edition of *Hymns Ancient and Modern*. He must have shown it to the committee before publishing it in his own book, because it appeared in the 1861 edition, though with a slightly altered text. The *English Hymnal* (1906) returned to Pott's original version, which is printed here.

The hymn is simple yet grand, a plain statement of the Easter message that uses the three-line rhyming verses to great effect: the rhymes come like successive hammer blows, giving the lines a robust force that is both triumphant and convincing. The last line of the hymn is particularly climactic: 'That we may live' refers to our being given life by the Resurrection of Jesus Christ from the dead, and it is in that life that we are able to sing.

There are two principal tunes to these words, each extremely effective in its own way. *Hymns Ancient and Modern*, and many subsequent hymn-books, use VICTORY, written by William Henry Monk (1823–89) for these words, adapting a theme from Palestrina's *Magnificat Tertii Toni* of 1591. The tune is remarkable for the number of repeated notes in the melody, especially in the second line. The other tune, VULPIUS, is ascribed to Melchior Vulpius (*c.*1560–1615) and found in his *Ein schön geistlich Gesangbuch* (Jena, 1609), where is was set to a hymn by Michael Weisse beginning 'Gelobt sei Gott' (which became an alternative name for the tune). It occurs in *Songs of Praise* (1925): C. A. Alington later wrote 'Good Christian men, rejoice and sing' for it in the enlarged edition of 1931.

30 I bind unto myself today
    The strong name of the Trinity,
By invocation of the same,
    The Three in One, and One in Three.

I bind this day to me for ever,
    By power of faith, Christ's incarnation;
His baptism in the Jordan river;
    His death on cross for my salvation;
His bursting from the spicèd tomb;
    His riding up the heavenly way;
His coming at the day of doom;
    I bind unto myself today.

I bind unto myself the power
    Of the great love of cherubim;
The sweet 'well done' in judgement hour;
    The service of the seraphim,
Confessors' faith, apostles' word,
    The patriarchs' prayers, the prophets' scrolls,
All good deeds done unto the Lord,
    And purity of virgin souls.

I bind unto myself today
    The virtues of the star-lit heaven,
The glorious sun's life-giving ray,
    The whiteness of the moon at even,
The flashing of the lightning free,
    The whirling wind's tempestuous shocks,
The stable earth, the deep salt sea
    Around the old eternal rocks.

I bind unto myself today
    The power of God to hold and lead,
His eye to watch, his might to stay,
    His ear to hearken to my need;
The wisdom of my God to teach,
    His hand to guide, his shield to ward,
The word of God to give me speech,
    His heavenly host to be my guard.

Christ be with me, Christ within me,
    Christ behind me, Christ before me,
Christ beside me, Christ to win me,
    Christ to comfort and restore me,
Christ beneath me, Christ above me,
    Christ in quiet, Christ in danger,
Christ in hearts of all that love me,
    Christ in mouth of friend and stranger.

I bind unto myself the name,
　　The strong name of the Trinity,
By invocation of the same,
　　The Three in One, and One in Three;
Of whom all nature hath creation,
　　Eternal Father, Spirit, Word:
Praise to the Lord of my salvation,
　　Salvation is of Christ the Lord.

　　　　Attributed to St Patrick (c.386–460),
　　　　tr. Cecil Frances Alexander (1818–95)

These words are of great antiquity, and are thought to have been by St Patrick, patron saint and converter of Ireland. They are found in two eleventh-century manuscripts, and include two other verses not printed here. The name 'St Patrick's Breastplate' comes from the tradition that it was sung by a Christian soldier putting on a *lorica* or breastplate while praying before battle. By a natural transition, it became a hymn about the Christian life 'for the protection of body and soul against demons and men and vices':

when any person shall recite it daily with pious meditation on God, demons shall not dare to face him, it shall be a protection to him against all poison and envy, it shall be a guard to him against sudden death, it shall be a lorica for his soul after his decease [from the preface to the printed manuscripts].

Legend has it that the hymn was also known as 'The Deer's Cry', and that it was made in the time of the Irish king Loegaire mac Neill, who opposed Patrick and his followers when they were going to Tara (in County Meath, north-west of Dublin, the seat of the high kings of Ireland):

Patrick sang it when the ambuscades were laid for him by Loegaire, in order that he should not go to Tara to sow the faith, so that on that occasion they were seen before those who were lying in ambush as if they were wild deer having behind them a fawn; and 'Deer's Cry' is its name.

This hymn comes out of the twilight world of such legends, and out of its early Christian origins, to speak with great force and truth about the battles of the soul and the body. The various episodes of Christ's own life become 'armour', and so does the splendour of creation; although the greatest and most enduring armour is the Holy Trinity itself. The verse beginning 'Christ be with me' is a moving prayer which complements the power of the 'binding' verses: it has been likened to the ornaments on Celtic crosses or other art forms (by David Adam, quoted in the *Companion to the Hymnal 1982*): it is 'a weaving of the Presence around our lives like the Celtic patterns on stones and in the illuminated Gospels: Christ moves in and out, over and under' (*The Edge of Glory; Prayers in the Celtic Tradition*, 1988).

The hymn is very suitable for the baptism of the newly converted, for confirmation and for ordination, as well as for the commemoration of St Patrick on 17 March. It is interesting to note, however, that there have been different reactions to it, and even some unease. Percy Dearmer, who printed a shorter version in *Songs of Praise* (without what he called 'the traces of white magic'—found, perhaps, in the verses not printed above) described it as 'at once a war-song, an incantation, and a creed'. He dismissed the attribution to St Patrick, and clearly found the hymn uncongenial to his early twentieth-century progressive mind: 'one does not need to be too near to the incantations of the Dark Ages' (*Songs of Praise Discussed*: 279–80). Erik Routley, more sympathetically, noted 'a very primitive blending of supernatural faith and natural experience':

the sea and rocks and sun and moon are treated on equal terms with the articles of the Faith. Since Christian faith is not least a matter of coming to proper terms with the created world, there is nothing theologically improper in this; on the contrary, the hymn in a way not found elsewhere brings heaven and earth together.   (*A Panorama of Christian Hymnody*: 131)

Routley's description suggests that he felt that the hymn still needed justifying in the 1970s; the revival of interest in Celtic Christianity and spirituality since then has given further emphasis to the value of this hymn as an expression of faith and courage.

Cecil Frances Alexander's translation was written for the commemoration of St Patrick's day in 1889. It was included in the Appendix to the *Irish Church Hymnal* (1891), and printed as a Saint's Day hymn in the *English Hymnal* (1906).

The tune is called ST PATRICK, said to be 'From an Ancient Irish Hymn Melody'. It was taken from *The Complete Collection of Ancient Irish Music, Part II* (1902). The tune to verse 6 is usually DEIRDRE, named after the heroine of Irish legend; it was found in Edward Bunting's *Ancient Music of Ireland* (1841) and used in *The English Hymnal*. An alternative tune for this verse is CLONMACNOISE, another ancient Irish melody, used in *Songs of Praise* with the name MORLEY, and used by Sir Richard Runciman Terry for the Roman Catholic *Westminster Hymnal* of 1912. Another is GARTAN, used from 1916 onwards in *Hymns Ancient and Modern*.

31

Christ is the world's redeemer,
The lover of the pure,
The fount of heavenly wisdom,
Our trust and hope secure;
The armour of his soldiers,
The Lord of earth and sky;
Our health while we are living,
Our life when we shall die.

Christ has our host surrounded
With clouds of martyrs bright,
Who wave their palms in triumph,
And fire us for the fight.
Christ the red Cross ascended
To save a world undone,
And, suffering for the sinful,
Our full redemption won.

Down in the realm of darkness
He lay a captive bound,
But at the hour appointed
He rose, a victor crowned;
And now, to heaven ascended,
He sits upon the throne,
In glorious dominion,
His Father's and his own.

All glory to the Father,
The unbegotten One;
All honour be to Jesus,
His sole-begotten Son;
And to the Holy Spirit,
The perfect Trinity.
Let all the worlds give answer:
Amen: so let it be!

Ascribed to St Columba (521–97),
tr. Duncan MacGregor (1854–1923)

This is a translation of part of a hymn, 'In Te Christe credentium misererais omnium', part 2 of which is thought to have been written by St Columba. It is said that St Gregory, having seen another poem by him, 'Altus Prosator vetustus dierum', commented that it neglected the Holy Trinity; the present hymn was written in response.

MacGregor's translation was made for the celebrations in honour of St Columba held on Iona, 9 June 1897, to commemorate the 1,300th anniversary of his death. It was published in his *St Columba, a Record and a Tribute*, published in 1898. It has long been popular in Scottish and Irish hymnbooks, which is appropriate in view of its ancient Celtic origins. In the

Revised Church Hymnary (1927) the line 'In glorious dominion' was used to replace the original 'Whence he had ne'er departed' (translating Columba's 'ubi nunquam defuerat'), which, while expressing the full divinity of Christ, seems to ignore the full implications of the Incarnation.

The hymn is notable for its inclusiveness: Christ, in the tradition of Celtic Christianity, is 'the Lord of earth and sky', but also the redeemer, the lover, the fount of wisdom; He is also our trust and hope, our armour, our health, and our life. All these attributes are found in the densely packed first verse, and expanded in the following two, which are then followed by a doxology. It is a hymn which seems filled with the joyful spirit that sent St Columba to Iona, and inspired his disciples to convert Scotland and the north of England.

The customary tune is MOVILLE, a traditional Irish melody found in *The Complete Collection of Ancient Irish Music as noted by George Petrie* (1902). The name refers to a monastic school in Ireland attended by Columba. An alternative tune is WOLVERCOTE (one of the tunes for 'O Jesus, I have promised', no. 170); another, STOKESAY CASTLE, by Eric Thiman (1900–75), is in *Rejoice and Sing* (1991).

{2}

The Reformation: England and Germany

The monastic hymns, used for centuries, disappeared in Britain at the
Reformation, along with the monasteries themselves. In English and
Scottish worship they were replaced by the metrical psalms. These were
beloved of Calvin in Geneva and by the English Protestant exiles who had
fled the country during the reign of Mary Tudor (1553–8). The accession of
Elizabeth I in 1558 brought these exiles back in force, carrying their psalm-
books with them: the result was *The Whole Booke of Psalmes* of 1562, containing versions by Thomas Sternhold, John Hopkins, William Kethe, and
others, and the *Scottish Psalter* of 1564. In England 'Sternhold and Hopkins'
was the main psalm-book for over a hundred years, but the only one of its
versions which has survived in general use is William Kethe's version of the
hundredth psalm. At the end of this section, however, are included three
other famous psalm versions, two by John Milton and the third from the
Scottish Psalter of 1650.

Calvin's exclusive reliance on metrical psalms contrasted with Luther's
love of hymns. The Lutheran church in Germany began a tradition of hymn-
singing and hymn-writing that was, in the words of Catherine Winkworth
(describing Luther's hymns) 'full of fire and strength, of clear Christian
faith, and brave joyful trust in God'. These hymns were translated in the
nineteenth century by German scholars such as Winkworth herself, Frances
Elizabeth Cox, Richard Massie, and others, including Thomas Carlyle.
They are incorporated here, because they were written by German poets in
the full tide of the Reformation.

At the same time, there were Roman Catholic resistances to the Reformation. One of the great hymns of the period is 'Jerusalem, my happy home',
perhaps written by an imprisoned priest; and the Counter-Reformation is
represented by a hymn sometimes attributed to St Francis Xavier.

32

All people that on earth do dwell,
    Sing to the Lord with cheerful voice;
Him serve with fear, his praise forth tell,
    Come ye before him, and rejoice.

The Lord, ye know, is God indeed,
    Without our aid he did us make;
We are his folk, he doth us feed,
    And for his sheep he doth us take.

O enter then his gates with praise,
    Approach with joy his courts unto;
Praise, laud, and bless his name always,
    For it is seemly so to do.

For why? the Lord our God is good:
    His mercy is for ever sure;
His truth at all times firmly stood,
    And shall from age to age endure.

To Father, Son, and Holy Ghost,
    The God whom heaven and earth adore,
From men and from the angel-host
    Be praise and glory evermore. Amen.

William Kethe (died *c*.1594)

The first four verses of this rendering of Psalm 100 appeared in John Daye's *Psalter* (1560–1), and in the *Anglo-Genevan Psalter* of 1560.

Metrical psalms were an important feature of Reformation worship, especially in Geneva under the influence of John Calvin. They allowed believers to sing, while avoiding what Calvin saw as the dangerous freedom and latitude of hymns. Psalms were therefore produced in metrical versions, both in French and in English: the English versions were used by the Protestant exiles in Geneva and elsewhere. One of them was William Kethe, who lived at first at Frankfurt and then moved to Geneva: his authorship of this psalm is not certain, but is based on the letters 'W. Ke.' in some editions.

Some versions of this psalm, notably in the *Scottish Psalter*, print some variants: verse 1 line 3 is 'Him serve with mirth', which chimes with 'rejoice' (based on 'serve the Lord with gladness, and come before his presence with a song'), but which is now an odd word ('mirth' has connotations of unseemly laughter). Verse 2 line 3 has 'We are his flock', perhaps based on the work of a printer who transposed 'o' and 'l'. 'Flock' is quite acceptable, connecting as it does with 'feed' and 'sheep'; but perhaps it makes the metaphor too insistent. Another Scottish reading is the splendid imperative (verse 2 line 1) 'Know that the Lord is God indeed', which invokes awe.

The present version (with the exception of 'folk' for 'flock') is the one which appeared in *The Whole Booke of Psalmes*, also known as the 'Old Version' or as 'Sternhold and Hopkins' after its major contributors. To the four verses was added the doxology which is printed here as a fifth verse. It was by John Mason Neale, based on the later metrical psalm book, the 'New Version' of Tate and Brady (1696), and it appeared in the first edition of *Hymns Ancient and Modern* in 1861.

The survival of this psalm, when so many others have been forgotten, except in Scotland, is probably owing to the combination of the words with the tune, which carries them with dignity and grandeur. The tune, known as the OLD HUNDREDTH, is so called because it was set to these words in the *Anglo-Genevan Psalter* of 1560 (although it was first written for another long metre metrical psalm, 134). It has been in continuous use since the Reformation, and it was the invariable tune of the 'Old Version' of this psalm. It was probably written by Louis Bourgeois, who edited and composed many of the tunes for the French Protestant psalter, which were then taken over and used by the English writers. It is very fitting for what John Julian, in his *Dictionary of Hymnology*, called 'the solidity, the breadth' of the English psalter: it helps to make the psalm heroic, a moving expression of the spirit of the Reformation.

33
A safe stronghold our God is still,
 A trusty shield and weapon;
He'll help us clear from all the ill
 That hath us now o'ertaken.
  The ancient Prince of Hell
  Hath risen with purpose fell;
  Strong mail of Craft and Power
  He weareth in this hour,
  On Earth is not his fellow.

With force of arms we nothing can,
 Full soon were we down-ridden;
But for us fights the proper Man,
 Whom God himself hath bidden.
  Ask ye, Who is this same?
  Christ Jesus is his name,
  The Lord Zebaoth's Son,
  He and no other one
  Shall conquer in the battle.

> And were this world all Devils o'er,
>   And watching to devour us,
> We lay it not to heart so sore,
>   Not they can overpower us.
>   And let the Prince of Ill
>   Look grim as e'er he will,
>   He harms us not a whit:
>   For why? His doom is writ,
>   A word shall quickly slay him.
>
> God's Word, for all their craft and force,
>   One moment will not linger,
> But spite of Hell, shall have its course,
>   'Tis written by his finger.
>   And though they take our life,
>   Goods, honour, children, wife,
>   Yet is their profit small;
>   These things shall vanish all,
>   The City of God remaineth.

Martin Luther (1483–1546),
tr. Thomas Carlyle (1795–1881)

Luther's great paraphrase of Psalm 46 ('God is our refuge and strength') was first printed in 1529, and became popular throughout Germany. Its strength can be appreciated, even by non-German speakers, by reading the first line—'Ein' feste Burg ist unser Gott'. It was translated by Thomas Carlyle, who published it in an essay in *Fraser's Magazine* in 1831, entitled 'Luther's Psalm'. In that essay Carlyle, who admired Luther's courage (and later wrote about it in *Heroes and Hero-Worship*), concentrated on Luther as a poet, although his poetry was seen as part of his bravery. He was a prophet-poet, in Carlyle's eyes:

not only permitted to enter the sphere of Poetry, but to dwell in the purest centre thereof: perhaps the most inspired of all Teachers since the first Apostles of his faith; and thus not a Poet only, but a Prophet and God-ordained Priest, which is the highest form of that dignity, and of all dignity.

Luther's paraphrase is the work of a man who changed the world, and it may be that it should be judged differently from other hymns. Carlyle certainly saw it as grander and more sublime:

The following, for example, jars upon our ears: yet there is something in it like the sound of Alpine avalanches, or the first murmur of earthquakes; in the very vastness of which dissonance a higher unison is revealed to us.

His own translation preserves something of that distinctive roughness. The imagery of battle is employed with energy and force, and the lines are often full of violent twists of syntax, with unexpected inversions, suspensions, and questionings. It is an unashamedly warlike hymn, with descriptions of medieval fighting, of being clad in strong mail and being down-ridden. It is therefore purposeless to complain that the hymn is too warlike to sing, or that it is too exclusively masculine (most notably in the mention of 'wife' in the last verse); that is what the hymn is—a rough, masculine, violent experience, written by a powerful man and translated by a man who responded to that power. It was, and still is, possible to admire the hymn as an expression of trust in the strength of God when surrounded by a wicked and cruel world.

Heinrich Heine, the German poet, called it 'A battle hymn', in a romantic description:

... this defiant song, with which he [Luther] and his comrades entered Worms. The old cathedral trembled at these new notes, and the ravens were startled in their hidden nests in the towers. This hymn, the Marseillaise Hymn of the Reformation, has preserved its potent spell even to our days . . .

The tune, EIN' FESTE BURG, was composed by Luther for his own hymn, and has invariably been associated with it.

34
Out of the depths I cry to thee,
    Lord God! O hear my prayer!
Incline a gracious ear to me,
    And bid me not despair:
If thou rememberest each misdeed,
If each should have its rightful meed,
    Lord, who shall stand before thee?

'Tis through thy love alone we gain
    The pardon of our sin;
The strictest life is but in vain,
    Our works can nothing win;
That none should boast himself of aught,
But own in fear thy grace hath wrought
    What in him seemeth righteous.

Wherefore my hope is in the Lord,
    My works I count but dust;
I build not there, but on his word,
    And in his goodness trust.
Up to his care myself I yield,
He is my tower, my rock, my shield,
    And for his help I tarry.

> And though it linger till the night,
>   And round again till morn,
> My heart shall ne'er mistrust thy might,
>   Nor count itself forlorn.
> Do thus, O ye of Israel's seed,
> Ye of the Spirit born indeed,
>   Wait for your God's appearing.
>
> Though great our sins and sore our wounds,
>   And deep and dark our fall,
> His helping mercy hath no bounds,
>   His love surpasseth all:
> Our trusty loving Shepherd, he
> Who shall at last set Israel free
> From all their sin and sorrow.
>
> > Martin Luther (1483–1546),
> > tr. Catherine Winkworth (1827–78)

This is Martin Luther's rendering of Psalm 130, beginning 'Aus tiefer Noth schrei ich zu dir', written in 1523 and published in 1524. It therefore comes between Luther's courageous stand at the Diet of Worms (1521) and his marriage (1525). It adapts Psalm 130—'Out of the depths have I cried unto Thee, O Lord'—and gives it a particularly Protestant interpretation, emphasizing the saving love of God rather than any attempt to win salvation through works alone. It was a hymn that Luther particularly loved, and it was sung at his funeral.

Catherine Winkworth, who translated it, wrote of Luther's hymns in her book, *The Christian Singers of Germany* (1869):

Luther throws into them all his own fervent faith and deep devotion. The style is plain, often rugged and quaint, but genuinely popular. So, too, was their cheerful trust and noble courage; their clear, vigorous spirit, that sprang from steadfast faith in a Redeemer. All the many conflicts, inward and outward, of Luther's life, had only deepened his experience; they had by no means damped his courage or his power of enjoyment.

Winkworth did two translations. This one is taken from *Lyra Germanica* (1855). She later published one in *The Chorale Book for England* (1863), preserving Luther's original metre. It began:

> Out of the depths I cry to Thee,
> Lord, hear me, I implore Thee

Because it preserves Luther's metre of 8.6.8.6.88.7, it can be sung to the original tune, COBURG, used by J.S. Bach in his Cantata 'Aus tiefer Noth'. The tune for the present version is usually ST MARTIN, by James Hallett Sheppard (1835–79).

35   Wake, O wake! with tidings thrilling
The watchmen all the air are filling,
    Arise, Jerusalem, arise!
Midnight strikes! no more delaying,
'The hour has come!' we hear them saying,
    'Where are ye all, ye virgins wise?
      The Bridegroom comes in sight,
      Raise high your torches bright!'
        Alleluia!
    The wedding song
    Swells loud and strong:
Go forth and join the festal throng.

Sion hears the watchmen shouting,
Her heart leaps up with joy undoubting,
    She stands and waits with eager eyes;
See her Friend from heaven descending,
Adorned with truth and grace unending!
    Her light burns clear, her star doth rise.
      Now come, thou precious Crown,
      Lord Jesu, God's own Son!
        Hosanna!
    Let us prepare
    To follow there,
Where in thy supper we may share.

Every soul in thee rejoices;
From men and from angelic voices
    Be glory given to thee alone!
Now the gates of pearl receive us,
Thy presence never more shall leave us,
    We stand with angels round thy throne.
      Earth cannot give below
      The bliss thou dost bestow.
        Alleluia!
    Grant us to raise,
    To length of days,
The triumph-chorus of thy praise.

                Philipp Nicolai (1556–1608),
      tr. Francis Crawford Burkitt (1864–1935)

This was first published in Philipp Nicolai's *Frewden-Spiegel des ewigen Lebens* ('The Joyous Mirror of Life Eternal') in 1599, together with its tune. It was entitled 'Of the Voice at Midnight, and the Wise Virgins who meet their Heavenly Bridegroom. Matt. 25'. It is said to have been written in 1597, during a terrible plague at Unna in Westphalia (where Nicolai was the pastor), suggesting a wonderful faith in adversity. It is based on the story of the wise and foolish virgins in Matthew 25: 1–13, but also on the great mystery of the marriage supper of the Lamb in Revelation 19: 6–9. The watchman who summons the children of light, evoked so dramatically here, is from Isaiah 52: 8 and Ezekiel 3: 17.

The translation, by the Norrisian Professor of Divinity at Cambridge, was made for the *English Hymnal* (1906). It makes a very grand, even spectacular hymn for Advent, or for the expectation of Christ's coming in glory. Burkitt's translation has come to be preferred to Catherine Winkworth's version, 'Wake, awake, for night is flying', although that also is very fine.

The tune, WACHET AUF, takes its name from the first line of Nicolai's text, 'Wachet auf! ruft uns die Stimme'. It appeared with the words in 1599, and is thought to have been composed by Nicolai himself. Bach used it magnificently in Cantata no. 140, and Mendelssohn also included it in his oratorio *St Paul*.

36   Ah, Holy Jesu, how hast thou offended,
That man to judge thee hath in hate pretended?
By foes derided, by thine own rejected,
      O most afflicted.

Who was the guilty? Who brought this upon thee?
Alas, my treason, Jesu, hath undone thee.
'Twas I, Lord Jesu, I it was denied thee:
      I crucified thee.

Lo, the good Shepherd for the sheep is offered;
The slave hath sinnèd, and the Son hath suffered;
For man's atonement, while he nothing heedeth,
      God intercedeth.

For me, kind Jesu, was thy incarnation,
Thy mortal sorrow, and thy life's oblation;
Thy death of anguish and thy bitter Passion,
      For my salvation.

Therefore, kind Jesu, since I cannot pay thee,
I do adore thee, and will ever pray thee,
Think on thy pity and thy love unswerving,
      Not my deserving.

Johann Heermann (1585–1647),
freely tr. Robert Bridges (1844–1930)

This moving hymn on the sufferings of Christ is based on Johann Heermann's 'Herliebster Jesu, was hast du verbrochen', published in his *Devoti Musica Cordis* (1630). This German hymn was in turn based on a Latin meditation once thought to be by St Augustine, but now known to have been written by Jean de Fécamp (d. 1078), Abbot of Fécamp in Normandy. Bridges's translation was published in his *Yattendon Hymnal*

(1899): he used only some of Heermann's fifteen verses, and had in mind the Latin text as well as the German.

The hymn sets up questions in the first part, which allow revealing answers, stressing the individual's response to the events of the Passion: it was 'my treason', and (countering this in verse 4) 'my salvation'. The hymn thus provides a commentary which becomes severely personal, and in the process very demanding, as each person has to recognize that his or her sins are a copy of the the sins of those who crucified Christ.

The words are also wonderfully suited to the tune, which carries the sacred meditation with gravity and solemnity. It is called HERZLIEBSTER JESU, after the German original. A version of it is found in Johann Crüger's *Neues vollkömliches Gesangbuch Augsburgischer Confession*, published in Berlin in 1640. It was made famous by Bach, who used it three times in the *St Matthew Passion* and twice in the *St John Passion*.

37
    Now thank we all our God,
        With heart and hands and voices,
    Who wondrous things hath done,
        In whom his world rejoices;
    Who from our mothers' arms
        Hath blessed us on our way
    With countless gifts of love,
        And still is ours to-day.

    Oh may this bounteous God
        Through all our life be near us,
    With ever joyful hearts
        And blessed peace to cheer us;
    And keep us in his grace,
        And guide us when perplexed,
    And free us from all ills
        In this world and the next.

    All praise and thanks to God
        The Father, now be given,
    The Son, and Him who reigns
        With them in highest heaven,
    The One eternal God,
        Whom earth and heaven adore,
    For thus it was, is now,
        And shall be evermore!

        Martin Rinkart (1586–1649),
      tr. Catherine Winkworth (1827–78)

This is a translation of Rinkart's 'Nun danket alle Gott', probably first published in his *Jesu Herz-Büchlein* of 1636 (no copies are known to exist). The earliest surviving text is that of Johann Crüger's *Praxis Pietatis Melica* of 1647. In the 1663 edition of Rinkart's book, which has survived, it is entitled 'Tisch-Gebetlein' ('Short Dinner-Table Prayer'), pointing to its origin as a grace before a meal.

The translation is from Catherine Winkworth's *Lyra Germanica*, Second Series (1858), where it is entitled 'The Chorus of God's Thankful Children'. In line 2, Winkworth's 'heart' is frequently altered to 'hearts' in modern editions.

The first two verses are based on Ecclesiasticus 50: 22–4:

Now therefore bless ye the God of all, which only doeth wondrous things every where, which exalteth our days from the womb, and dealeth with us according to his mercy. He grant us joyfulness of heart, and that peace may be in our days in Israel for ever: That he would confirm his mercy with us, and deliver us at his time!

The third verse is a paraphrase of the *Gloria Patri*. Together the three verses, which began as a simple grace before a meal, have become a magnificent hymn on the grand scale, suitable for great occasions and large public gatherings. They are sometimes thought of as a German *Te Deum*, and were used by Bach for his Cantata 192. They gain in force, as Wesley Milgate has pointed out, from the circumstances in which Rinkart found himself: he was pastor at Eilenburg, in Saxony, during the Thirty Years War, during which he ministered to the people in times of famine, plague, and death (including the death of his first wife). Milgate writes: 'The thought of this faithful pastor, frail in physique but heroic in service, ministering to such distress and courageously facing lawless bands, gives great poignancy and resonance to his famous hymn' (*Songs of the People of God*: 27).

The hymn has always been sung to its original tune in Johann Crüger's *Praxis Pietatis Melica* of 1647, usually entitled NUN DANKET. It is thought to be by Crüger himself, for it is marked with his initials in a later book, Christoff Runge's *Geistliche Lieder und Psalmen* (1653). Mendelssohn regularized the original rather free rhythm, and set it for six parts in 1840 in his *Lobgesang* or 'Hymn of Praise' (the 'Symphony-Cantata', Opus 52). Modern hymn-books use a four-part reduction of this; it is a tune which not only has its history to commend it, but which also carries the words with a dignity and majesty which are entirely appropriate for big occasions.

A modern tune, sung in unison and in a different mode, is entitled GRACIAS. It is by Geoffrey Beaumont (1903–70), and was published in his *Twentieth-Century Folk Mass* of 1957. Boldly and even defiantly, it sets syncopated rhythms working against the steady regularity of Winkworth's lines; and it has been taken up by hymn-book compilers who seek a catchy alternative to the original Germanic grandeur, beginning with the *Baptist Hymn Book* of 1962.

38
The duteous day now closeth,
Each flower and tree reposeth,
   Shade creeps o'er wild and wood:
Let us, as night is falling,
On God our maker calling,
   Give thanks to him, the giver good.

Now all the heavenly splendour
Breaks forth in starlight tender
   From myriad worlds unknown;
And man, the marvel seeing,
Forgets his selfish being,
   For joy of beauty not his own.

His care he drowneth yonder,
Lost in the abyss of wonder;
   To heaven his soul doth steal;
This life he disesteemeth,
The day it is that dreameth,
   That doth from truth his vision seal.

Awhile his mortal blindness
May miss God's loving-kindness,
   And grope in faithless strife:
But when life's day is over
Shall death's fair night discover
   The fields of everlasting life.

Paul Gerhardt (1607–76),
tr. Robert Bridges (1844–1930)

Gerhardt's evening hymn begins 'Nun ruhen alle Wälder' ('Now all the woods are sleeping'). It was first published in Johann Crüger's *Praxis Pietatis Melica* in the third edition of 1648, in nine stanzas of six lines each. Although a great favourite in Germany, it was (according to Percy Dearmer in *Songs of Praise Discussed*: 36) despised by Frederick the Great, who described it as 'foolish and stupid stuff' ('töricht und dummes Zeug'). Frederick's antipathy to the nature poetry of the romantic period was not shared by others: the hymn was much admired by Schiller, for example.

Bridges's hymn begins as a free translation of the first two of these stanzas, and then continues with Bridges's own poetry. It was published in *Hymns in Four Parts with English Words for Singing in Churches, Part IV* (1899) and (in the same year) in the *Yattendon Hymnal*. A much closer translation of the original, by Catherine Winkworth, was published in *Lyra Germanica* (1855), beginning:

> Now all the woods are sleeping,
> And night and stillness creeping
> O'er city, man and beast;
> But thou, my heart, awake thee,
> To prayer awhile betake thee,
> And praise thy Maker ere thou rest.

Bridges's hymn perhaps shows the influence of his friend Gerard Manley Hopkins, whose poem, 'The Starlight Night' anticipates verse 2, and whose attitude to nature as evidence of God may inform verses 2 and 3. The present text is a most unusual hymn, concentrating as it does on human self-forgetfulness rather than on praise and adoration. As with Bridges's other translations, such as 'All my hope on God is founded', the language is openly archaic and convoluted, as if Bridges was deliberately aiming to detach his writing from the cadences of everyday speech. This is particularly obvious in verse 3, with lines such as 'This life he disesteemeth', and the tendency to place verbs at the end of the sentence. The result is a hymn with a very deliberate language of its own, dignified and distinctive: it succeeds because of the very simple natural beauty of Gerhardt's vision of the sleeping woods and the starlit sky, which come through the sophisticated syntax and the elaborate vocabulary with a loveliness that Bridges seems to respect when he writes about it with such care.

The tune is called INNSBRUCK, from the Austrian town: it is a German traditional melody, first found in a manuscript of 1505 and thought to have been arranged by one Heinrich Isaak. At one time it was set to a poem beginning 'Innsbruck, ich muss dich lassen' ('Innsbruck, I must leave thee'), which was then given a religious slant by changing Innsbruck into the world ('O Welt, ich muss dich lassen'). It was harmonized by J. S. Bach and used in the *St Matthew Passion*. It is set to this hymn, in Catherine Winkworth's translation, in *The Chorale Book for England* (1863).

39

All my heart this night rejoices,
    As I hear,
    Far and near,
Sweetest angel voices;
'Christ is born', their choirs are singing,
    Till the air
    Everywhere
Now with joy is ringing.

For it dawns,—the promised morrow
    Of His birth
    Who the earth
Rescues from her sorrow.
God to wear our form descendeth,
    Of His grace
    To our race
Here His Son He lendeth:

Yea, so truly for us careth,
    That His Son
    All we've done
As our offering beareth;
As our Lamb who, dying for us,
    Bears our load,
    And to God
Doth in peace restore us.

Hark! a voice from yonder manger,
    Soft and sweet,
    Doth entreat,
'Flee from woe and danger;
Brethren come, from all doth grieve you
    You are freed,
    All you need
I will surely give you.'

Come then, let us hasten yonder;
    Here let all,
    Great and small,
Kneel in awe and wonder.
Love Him who with love is yearning;
    Hail the Star
    That from far
Bright with hope is burning!

Blessed Saviour, let me find Thee!
Keep Thou me
Close to Thee,
Cast me not behind Thee!
Life of life, my heart Thou stillest,
Calm I rest
On Thy breast,
All this void Thou fillest.

Thee, dear Lord, with heed I'll cherish,
Live to Thee,
And with Thee
Dying, shall not perish;
But shall dwell with Thee for ever,
Far on high,
In the joy
That can alter never.

Paul Gerhardt (1607–76),
tr. Catherine Winkworth (1827–78)

The German original of this Christmas hymn begins 'Fröhlich soll mein Herze springen' ('Gladly shall my heart leap'); it was first published in the 1656 edition of Johann Crüger's *Praxis Pietatis Melica*, with fifteen stanzas. Catherine Winkworth's translation of ten of these was published in her *Lyra Germanica*, Second Series (1858), a successor to her first volume with that title of 1855. Winkworth and her sister Susanna (translator of German mystical prose under the title *Theologia Germanica*, 1854) were brilliant young scholars, and Catherine's two volumes, eagerly taken up by the compilers of *Hymns Ancient and Modern*, did much to popularize German hymns.

Gerhardt's hymn was described by E. E. Koch as 'a glorious series of Christmas thoughts, laid as a garland on the manger at Bethlehem'. Winkworth's free translation, seven verses of which are printed here, adds a touching title to this Christmas hymn: 'A Song of Joy at Dawn'. Her ten stanzas are usually reduced to four for congregational singing, but the selections vary, and it is useful to see more than four because the hymn partly depends upon its accumulation of beautiful thoughts and images, and the gentle succession of unusually shaped verses. The rhymes are especially important in this hymn, the short lines chiming within the longer ones, and the whole making a bell-like verbal music. In verse 4 'Brethren come' is now often printed as 'Come, O come', to avoid the exclusive language.

Paul [us] Gerhardt was a Lutheran pastor near Berlin, who is described in Julian's *Dictionary of Hymnology* as ranking next to Luther as the most gifted hymn-writer of the Lutheran church. The entry quotes a German literary historian: 'With a firm grasp of the objective realities of the Christian Faith, and a loyal adherence to the doctrinal standpoint of the Lutheran Church, Gerhardt is yet genuinely human; he takes a fresh, healthful view both of nature and of mankind.'

In its first printing of 1656, this hymn had a tune set to it; but it has become inseparably linked to a very charming and lyrical tune by J. G. Ebeling (1637–76), published in 1666. It was set to another Gerhardt text, 'Warum sollt ich mich denn grämen' ('Why should I then grieve myself'). It was transferred to the present words by Arthur Sullivan, the music editor of *Church Hymns with Tunes* (1874), and given the name BONN. Surprisingly, Sullivan's inspired initiative did not make the hymn very popular: it was not found in *Hymns Ancient and Modern* (until *Common Praise*, 2000) or the *English Hymnal*. It has been left to Nonconformist books to keep it alive, and it deserves to be better known.

40   Praise to the Lord! the Almighty, the King of Creation!
O my soul, praise Him, for He is thy health and salvation!
     All ye who hear,
     Now to his temple draw near,
Join me in glad adoration!

Praise to the Lord! who o'er all things so wondrously reigneth,
Shelters thee under His wings, yea so gently sustaineth;
     Hast thou not seen
     How thy desires have been
Granted in what he ordaineth?

Praise to the Lord! who doth prosper thy work and defend thee,
Surely his goodness and mercy here daily attend thee;
     Ponder anew
     What the Almighty can do,
If with His love He befriend thee!

Praise to the Lord! Oh let all that is in me adore Him!
All that hath life and breath, come now with praises before Him!
     Let the Amen
     Sound from His people again,
Gladly for ay we adore Him!

                Joachim Neander (1650–80),
             tr. Catherine Winkworth (1827–78)

Neander's words, beginning 'Lobe den Herren, den mächtigen König der Ehren', were first published in *Glaub- und Liebesübung: Aufgemuntert durch Einfältige Bundes-Lieder und Danck-Psalmen* (Bremen, 1680). There were five stanzas in the hymn, of which Winkworth translated four, quite freely but following Neander's metre.

The hymn is justly famous as a hymn of adoration and praise. It is based on many passages from the Psalms, most notably Psalm 103: 1–6 and Psalm 150. Julian's *Dictionary of Hymnology* describes it as 'a magnificent hymn of praise to God, perhaps the finest production of its author, and of the first rank in its class'. The *Dictionary* also notes that it was the favourite hymn of Kaiser Friedrich Wilhelm III of Prussia, who heard it sung while visiting the mines at Waldenburg in 1800.

Catherine Winkworth's translation was first published in *The Chorale Book for England* (1863), which she produced with two musicians, William Sterndale Bennett (Professor of Music at Cambridge) and Otto Goldschmidt (husband of the singer Jenny Lind). *The Chorale Book*, as its title implies, was intended to introduce the German tunes to the British public, set to the texts of the two volumes of *Lyra Germanica* (1855, 1858). The 'Translator's Preface' said: '*The Lyra Germanica* was intended chiefly for use as a work of private devotion; *The Chorale Book for England* is intended primarily for use in united worship in the church and family, and in meetings for the practice of church music.'

The text printed above is Winkworth's original. It has often been altered, especially in verse 1, line 5, where 'Join me' is usually printed as 'Praise Him'. This is defensible, because the translation is quite free with the last three lines of Neander's verse:

> Kommet zuhauf,
> Psalter und Harfe, wacht auf,
> lasset die Musicam hören!

Another common change is in verse 2, line 4, where 'desires' becomes 'heart's wishes', which makes a better accord with the music.

Many hymn-books have added their own verses. The most blatant example of this is in the *English Hymnal*, where no less than three verses (perhaps the work of Percy Dearmer) occur before the last one:

> Praise to the Lord, who, when tempests their warfare are waging,
> Who, when the elements madly around thee are raging,
> > Biddeth them cease,
> > Turneth their fury to peace,
> Whirlwinds and waters assuaging.

> Praise to the Lord, who when sickness with terror uniting,
> Deaf to entreaties of mortals, its victims is smiting,
> > Pestilence quells,
> > Sickness and fever dispels,
> Grateful thanksgiving inviting.

Praise to the Lord, who when darkness of sin is abounding,
Who, when the godless do triumph, all virtue confounding,
  Sheddeth his light,
  Chaseth the horrors of night,
Saints with his mercy surrounding.

The first and last of these are often found in other hymn-books, usually sandwiched between verses 3 and 4 of Winkworth's text.

The vigorous tune, LOBE DEN HERREN, which may have originated as a folk song, was first printed in 1665, and was set to these words in *A und O: Joachimi Neandri Glaub- und Liebesübung* (Bremen, 1680). It is a tune which carries the long lines well, and which allows for the powerful rhythmic contrast between the long lines and the short ones. The result is a combination of words and tune which is joyful and exciting.

41   All my hope on God is founded;
             He doth still my trust renew.
           Me through change and chance he guideth,
             Only good and only true.
                God unknown,
                He alone
             Calls my heart to be his own.

           Pride of man and earthly glory,
             Sword and crown betray his trust;
           What with care and toil he buildeth,
             Tower and temple, fall to dust.
                But God's power,
                Hour by hour,
             Is my temple and my tower.

           God's great goodness aye endureth:
             Deep his wisdom passing thought;
           Splendour, light, and life attend him,
             Beauty springeth out of naught.
                Evermore
                From his store
             New-born worlds rise and adore.

           Daily doth the almighty giver
             Bounteous gifts on us bestow;
           His desire our soul delighteth,
             Pleasure leads us where we go.
                Love doth stand
                At his hand;
             Joy doth wait on his command.

Still from man to God eternal
Sacrifice of praise be done,
High above all praises praising
For the gift of Christ his Son.
Christ doth call
One and all:
Ye who follow shall not fall.

Joachim Neander (1650–80),
tr. Robert Bridges (1844–1930)

This is a free translation of Neander's 'Meine Hoffnung stehet feste', printed (like 'Praise to the Lord! the Almighty, the King of Creation!') in *Glaub- und Liebesübung: Aufgemuntert durch Einfältige Bundes-Lieder und Danck-Psalmen* (Bremen, 1680), and then (with its tune) in *A und O: Joachimi Neandri Glaub- und Liebesübung* (Bremen, 1680). Bridges' translation appeared in his *Yattendon Hymnal* of 1899.

Neander's hymn is based on 1 Timothy 6: 17: 'Charge them that are rich in this world, that they be not high-minded, nor trust in uncertain riches, but in the living God, who giveth us richly all things to enjoy.' As in many of the psalms, it sets the transience of human life and the instability of earthly achievement against the enduring power and goodness of God.

Bridges's translation is remarkable for its rhythmical firmness (Bridges was an expert on prosody) and for its elaborate Miltonic syntax, with inversion and suspension everywhere. A good example is the inversion of 'Me through change and chance he guideth', and the postponement of the verb in 'Daily doth the almighty giver/ Bounteous gifts on us bestow'. The text is about as removed from ordinary speech as it is possible to get, and yet it works magnificently: the grandeur of the theme, and the compelling rhythm of the lines, produce a hymn of celebratory splendour.

Another translation, by Fred Pratt Green, beginning 'All my hope is firmly grounded' is less archaic but also less memorable. It is printed in America in *The United Methodist Hymnal* (1989).

For many years, the tune for this hymn was the fine German tune known as MEINE HOFFNUNG, from *A und O: Joachimi Neandri Glaub- und Liebesübung*. It was harmonized in *The Chorale Book for England* (1863), the book which contained Catherine Winkworth's translations of German texts set to Chorale tunes (see under 'Praise to the Lord! the Almighty, the King of Creation!', no. 40). Bridges used this tune in the *Yattendon Hymnal*. It has been challenged as a primary tune for this hymn by Herbert Howells's MICHAEL, written about 1930 at the request of the Director of Music at Charterhouse School, Dr Thomas Fielden. Howells is said to have written it at the breakfast table: it has a stirring and characteristic Howellsian opening on high notes, and carries the words with precision and splendour. It is named after the composer's son, who died in childhood. Some American and Canadian books have dropped MEINE HOFFNUNG, and use MICHAEL exclusively (the Canadian *Voices United* has both texts, by Bridges and by Pratt Green, but only MICHAEL as tune). *Common Praise* (2000) also uses MICHAEL. A further tune, GROESWEN, is a nineteenth-century Welsh tune, which has been used for this hymn in Scotland, in the *Revised Church Hymnary* of 1927 and in the *Church Hymnary, Third Edition* of 1973.

42   Jerusalem, my happy home,
              When shall I come to thee?
          When shall my sorrows have an end?
              Thy joys when shall I see?

          O happy harbour of the saints!
              O sweet and pleasant soil!
          In thee no sorrow may be found,
              No grief, no care, no toil.

          In thee no sickness may be seen,
              No hurt, no ache, no sore;
          In thee there is no dread of death,
              But life for evermore.

          No dampish mist is seen in thee,
              No cold nor darksome night;
          There every soul shines as the sun;
              There God himself gives light.

          There lust and lucre cannot dwell;
              There envy bears no sway;
          There is no hunger, heat, nor cold,
              But pleasure every way.

          Jerusalem, Jerusalem,
              God grant I once may see
          Thy endless joys, and of the same
              Partaker ay may be!

          Thy walls are made of precious stones,
              Thy bulwarks diamonds square;
          Thy gates are of right orient pearl;
              Exceeding rich and rare.

          Ah, my sweet home, Jerusalem,
              Would God I were in thee!
          Would God my woes were at an end,
              Thy joys that I might see!

          Thy saints are crowned with glory great;
              They see God face to face;
          They triumph still, they still rejoice;
              Most happy is their case.

We that are here in banishment,
    Continually do mourn;
We sigh and sob, we weep and wail,
    Perpetually we groan.

Our sweet is mixed with bitter gall,
    Our pleasure is but pain,
Our joys scarce last the looking on,
    Our sorrows still remain.

But there they live in such delight,
    Such pleasure and such play,
As that to them a thousand years
    Doth seem as yesterday.

Quite through the streets with silver sound
    The flood of life doth flow,
Upon whose banks on every side
    The wood of life doth grow.

There trees for evermore bear fruit,
    And evermore do spring;
There evermore the angels sit,
    And evermore do sing;

There David stands with harp in hand
    As master of the choir:
Ten thousand times that man were blest
    That might this music hear.

Our Lady sings Magnificat
    With tune surpassing sweet;
And all the virgins bear their parts,
    Sitting about her feet.

Te Deum doth Saint Ambrose sing,
    Saint Austin doth the like;
Old Simeon and Zachary
    Have not their songs to seek.

There Magdalene hath left her moan,
    And cheerfully doth sing
With blessèd saints, whose harmony
    In every street doth ring.

Jerusalem, my happy home,
    Would God I were in thee!
Would God my woes were at an end
    Thy joys that I might see!

                        'F. B. P' (c.1580).

This is part of a hymn of twenty-six verses found in a manuscript book in the British Museum, beginning 'A Song Made by F. B. P'. The full text is printed in the *English Hymnal*: the selection above omits the starred verses. It is based on a passage from the *Liber Meditationem*, or *The Meditations of St Augustine*, a popular text in the later Middle Ages. Another version of it, by one W. Prid, was printed in 1585, and there have been many subsequent imitations.

One theory about the authorship is that the initials 'F. B. P' stand for 'Francis Baker Pater', and that the lines were by a Roman Catholic priest, who was imprisoned for his faith. This would certainly account for the intensity of feeling which is apparent in these verses. In his imprisonment, he sees God as light, and heaven as a place where there is no grief and hurt, and no 'dampish mist' of imprisonment either. Instead of the walls of the Tower of London, the walls of Jerusalem are of precious stones, with clear windows and golden tiles. To the inhabitants of a heaven, time does not hang heavily (as it does for those in prison) but a thousand years seem 'as yesterday' (from Psalm 90: 4).

The final part of the hymn contains the charming vision of David as master of the choir, of the Blessed Virgin Mary singing the Magnificat, and St Ambrose and St Augustine singing the *Te Deum*. Simeon sings the *Nunc Dimittis* (from Luke 2: 29–32) and Zacharias the *Benedictus* (Luke 1: 68–79). Joining them are St Mary Magdalen, who has 'left her moan' (bathing Christ's feet with her tears) and the whole company of the blessed saints. The whole hymn is a vision of the most affecting kind, almost primitive in its simplicity, but speaking very movingly of the contrast between the woes of earth and the joys of heaven.

In the original manuscript, the hymn is prefaced by 'to the tune of Diana'. It is in common metre, so may be sung to a number of tunes: indeed, the *English Hymnal* prints four of them, all from English Traditional melodies: ST AUSTIN, SOUTHILL, STALHAM, and DUNSTAN.

43
My God, I love thee; not because
    I hope for heaven thereby,
Nor yet because who love thee not
    Are lost eternally.

Thou, O my Jesus, thou didst me
    Upon the cross embrace;
For me didst bear the nails and spear,
    And manifold disgrace,

And griefs and torments numberless,
    And sweat of agony;
E'en death itself; and all for one
    Who was thine enemy.

Then why, O blessèd Jesu Christ,
    Should I not love thee well,
Not for the sake of winning heaven,
    Or of escaping hell;

Not with the hope of gaining aught,
    Not seeking a reward;
But as thyself hast lovèd me,
    O ever-loving Lord!

E'en so I love thee, and will love,
    And in thy praise will sing,
Solely because thou art my God,
    And my eternal King.

Seventeenth-century Latin hymn,
tr. Edward Caswall (1814–78)

This translation was first published in Caswall's *Lyra Catholica* (1849), containing the first-fruits of his love for Roman Catholicism. The Latin original is found in two texts by members of the Society of Jesus, and it is clearly a product of the Counter-Reformation. The Latin text is itself a translation of a Spanish poem, 'No me mueve, mi Dios', which at one time was attributed to the founder of the Jesuits, St Francis Xavier.

The Spanish poem was translated into Latin by Johannes Nadasi in *Pretiosae Occupationes Morientium* (1657), and a different version, 'O Deus ego amo te' (the text used by Caswall) is found in W. Nakatenus's *Coeleste Palmetum* (Cologne, 1669). It begins:

O Deus ego amo te,
nec amo te ut salves me,
aut quia non amantes te
aeterno punis igne.

The last line, with its reference to 'igne' ('in fire') explains why Caswall's translation ended its first verse 'Nor because they who love thee not/ Must burn eternally'. The Spanish original is now thought not to have been written by St Francis Xavier, but Caswall was writing in an age which thought that it was (which added an air of romance and sanctity to the poem): he had no doubts about the authorship, calling his translation 'Hymn of St Francis Xavier'. It is based principally on 1 John 4: 7–8, 18–19:

Beloved, let us love one another: for love is of God; and every one that loveth is born of God, and knoweth God. He that loveth not knoweth not God; for God is love . . . There is no fear in love; but perfect love casteth out fear: because fear hath torment. He that feareth is not made perfect in love. We love him, because he first loved us.

One tune to this hymn is ST FRANCIS XAVIER, by John Stainer (1840–1901), which was written for these words in the second edition of *Hymns Ancient and Modern* (1875). It has also been set to SONG 67, one of the tunes in George Wither's *Hymns and Songs of the Church* (1623). The melody is found earlier, in a Welsh psalm book, Edmund Prys's *Llyfr y Psalmau* (1621), but in Wither's book the bass part was supplied by Orlando Gibbons and set to the 67th Song, a rendering of the account of St Matthias in Acts 1 (the tune is sometimes called ST MATTHIAS). Alternatively, the hymn is sung to James Turle's WESTMINSTER (used for Faber's 'My God, how wonderful thou art'), or to the *Scottish Psalter* tune CULROSS.

44
    Let us, with a gladsome mind,
    Praise the Lord, for he is kind:
      For his mercies ay endure,
      Ever faithful, ever sure.

    Let us blaze his name abroad,
    For of gods he is the God:
      For his mercies ay endure,
      Ever faithful, ever sure.

    He with all-commanding might
    Filled the new-made world with light:
      For his mercies ay endure,
      Ever faithful, ever sure.

    He the golden-tressèd sun
    Caused all day his course to run:
      For his mercies ay endure,
      Ever faithful, ever sure.

    The hornèd moon to shine by night,
    'Mid her spangled sisters bright:
      For his mercies ay endure,
      Ever faithful, ever sure.

> All things living he doth feed,
> His full hand supplies their need:
> *For his mercies ay endure,*
> *Ever faithful, ever sure.*
>
> Let us, with a gladsome mind,
> Praise the Lord, for he is kind:
> *For his mercies ay endure,*
> *Ever faithful, ever sure.*
>
> John Milton (1608–74)

This is the *Songs of Praise* text of Milton's paraphrase of Psalm 136 ('O give thanks unto the Lord, for he is good; for his mercy endureth for ever'). It was first published in *Poems of Mr John Milton, both English and Latin, Compos'd at several times* (1645). In that edition, this and another paraphrase (of Psalm 114) were described as 'don by the Author at fifteen years old'. This dates them at 1624, or just possibly 1623 (Milton's birthday was 9 December).

Milton's lines suggest a youthful exuberance, but they have had to be regularized in metre; and many of his twenty-four verses have been omitted, such as the one referring to 'large lim'd [limbed] Og' (from Deuteronomy 3: 11). The justification for this is that the psalm does two things: it gives glory and praise to God as the creator, but also goes on to celebrate His mighty acts in the history of the people of Israel. In words that are still often printed (for example in *Hymns and Psalms*): 'He his chosen race did bless/ In the wasteful wilderness:' in this historical process He shows himself to be the 'God of gods'. This is ingeniously connected with the verses about the sun and the moon: Milton uses a common Renaissance motif, which would have been instantly perceived by his readers, contrasting the Christian God with the classical deities. The hornèd moon represents Diana, and the golden-tressèd sun is Apollo. In Milton's appropriation of the psalm, the classical deities are controlled by the God who is greater than them all. Similarly, in 'On the Morning of Christ's Nativity', he sees the Incarnation as causing the heathen gods to flee ('Peor, and Baalim,/ Forsake their Temples dim').

The hymn which remains shows unmistakable signs of Milton's genius, in the choice and placing of words such as 'blaze', and the lovely verse about the moon. It has survived into modern hymn-books, therefore, in spite of the obvious archaisms, such as 'ay endure', and the need to omit certain verses, such as the penultimate one:

> Let us therefore warble forth
> His mighty Majesty and worth.

'Ay endure' has sometimes, less euphonically, been changed to 'still endure'; and the whole version has been subject to alterations of many kinds, including complete rewriting. Thus Sir Henry Williams Baker (1821–77) turned it into a harvest hymn, beginning 'Praise, O praise our God and

King', for the first edition of *Hymns Ancient and Modern*. He used Milton's verse on the moon, which was (according to Percy Dearmer's scathing comment) 'reduced to the libretto level':

> And the silver moon by night
> Shining with her gentle light.

Another version, by Michael Saward, beginning 'Let us gladly with one mind', is in *Hymns for Today's Church* (1982).

The customary tune for these words, which rises and falls in a way which led Archibald Jacob (in *Songs of Praise Discussed*) to describe it as 'naive', is MONKLAND, by John Antes (1740–1811), a Moravian minister and composer. It was printed in *Hymn Tunes of the Church of the Brethren* (Manchester, 1824). It was given the name MONKLAND and set to Baker's 'Praise, O praise our God and King' in *Hymns Ancient and Modern* (1861). Monkland is the name of the Herefordshire village where Baker was squire and parson, and the arrangement of the tune in 1861 is sometimes attributed to John Wilkes, who was organist at the village church. Another serviceable tune, no longer much in use, was EVER FAITHFUL, EVER SURE by Arthur Sullivan, for his *Church Hymns with Tunes* of 1874. That book was more faithful than some to Milton's irregular versification, and it is not surprising to find the metre as marked '7.7.7.7. (Peculiar)'.

45   The Lord will come and not be slow,
    His footsteps cannot err;
   Before him righteousness shall go,
    His royal harbinger.

   Truth from the earth, like to a flower,
    Shall bud and blossom then;
   And justice, from her heavenly bower,
    Look down on mortal men.

   Rise, God, judge thou the earth in might,
    This wicked earth redress;
   For thou art he who shalt by right
    The nations all possess.

   The nations all, whom thou hast made
    Shall come, and all shall frame
   To bow them low before thee, Lord,
    And glorify thy name.

   For great thou art, and wonders great
    By thy strong hand are done:
   Thou in thy everlasting seat
    Remainest God alone.

      John Milton (1608–74)

Milton wrote three sets of metrical psalms, the first as a young man of fifteen (including the exuberant 'Let us with a gladsome mind', no. 44), the others in 1648 and 1653. The present hymn is a cento, or selection of verses, from the 1648 rendering of Psalms 80 to 88, 'wherein all but what is in a different Character [i.e. in italics], are the very words of the Text, translated from the Original'.

The psalms were very important to the Protestants of the Reformation, and to the seventeenth-century Puritans. They were seen as the work of 'holy David', writing under inspiration from the Holy Spirit, and therefore it was important not only to use them in worship (hence the importance of Sternhold and Hopkins's *The Whole Booke of Psalmes*, or 'Old Version' as it came to be known) but also to translate them faithfully, and with as little deviation from the text as possible. Milton's solution was to stick to the text wherever possible, but to indicate his own additions by printing them in italics.

Verse 1 in the hymn is from Psalm 85: 13, which Milton wrote as follows:

> Before him Righteousness shall go
> *His Royal Harbinger,*
> Then will he come, and not be slow
> His footsteps cannot err.

The line-order changes were made for the *New Congregational Hymn Book* of 1859, and have become universally accepted. The printing of the verse shows how Milton added the most impressive line, with its reference to the royalty of God, and the fine three-syllabled 'Harbinger'. A harbinger was one who went before a king or a lord to prepare his lodging, and here it is not only impressive and exotic, but absolutely precise.

The second verse is also from Psalm 85 (which is the psalm sung on Christmas Day, and therefore appropriate for 'The Lord shall come', although this coming is the Second Coming); the third, with its magnificent prayer-imperative ('Rise, God') from Psalm 82: 8. The last two verses are from Psalm 86: 9, 10. Every verse shows Milton's mastery of tone and rhythm, with his additions subtly improving the original phrases without losing their sense. Thus in 'Truth from the earth, like to a flower', Milton adds the simile to Coverdale's 'Truth shall flourish out of the earth' to give the sense of beauty in the natural world and in spring. 'The Lord will come' like the spring ('the dayspring from on high').

Some books add other verses:

> Surely to such as do him fear
> Salvation is at hand;
> And glory shall ere long appear
> To dwell within our land.

Mercy and truth that long were missed,
    Now joyfully are met;
Sweet peace and righteousness have kissed,
    And hand-in-hand are set.

(Psalm 85: 9, 10)

The usual tune for this hymn is ST STEPHEN, sometimes called NEWING-TON, by William Jones (1726–1800) of Nayland in Suffolk, and published in his *Ten Church Pieces for the Organ* (1789). Another tune, noble but not so lively, which used to be associated with it, is GRÄFENBERG, from Johann Crüger's *Praxis Pietatis Melica* of 1653.

46

The Lord's my shepherd, I'll not want;
    He makes me down to lie
In pastures green; he leadeth me
    The quiet waters by.

My soul he doth restore again,
    And me to walk doth make
Within the paths of righteousness,
    Ev'n for his own name's sake.

Yea, though I walk in death's dark vale,
    Yet will I fear no ill;
For thou art with me, and thy rod
    And staff me comfort still.

My table thou hast furnishèd
    In presence of my foes;
My head thou dost with oil anoint,
    And my cup overflows.

Goodness and mercy all my life
    Shall surely follow me,
And in God's house for evermore
    My dwelling-place shall be.

Scottish Psalter (1650).

This is the best-known and most popular metrical version of the twenty-third Psalm, first published in this version in the *Psalter* of 1650 (with the words 'none ill' in verse 3, which are still sometimes used in Scotland). Its use at funerals is an indication of its power to comfort the bereaved, with its images of green pastures and quiet waters, and its clear expression in verse 3 of the presence of God in the valley of the shadow of death. Nature imagery unites with biblical imagery to soothe the afflicted mind, and this is followed by images of sitting at table and dwelling in the house of the Lord which are similarly comforting. It is one of those psalms which can speak to all sorts and conditions, to people of many different shades of belief and half-belief.

It is odd, however, that this rendering of a psalm which has been so frequently and beautifully versified should have acquired such pre-eminence: it is a relatively recent phenomenon, and is probably owing to its association with the tune CRIMOND, and the use of that tune on two great royal occasions.

CRIMOND was printed in the *Scottish Psalter* of 1929, although it was not associated with any particular psalm. The tunes given for Psalm 23 were WILTSHIRE and MARTYRDOM. CRIMOND became famous during the early years of broadcasting, when it was frequently sung by the Glasgow Orpheus Choir under Sir Hugh Roberton. Perhaps because of this dissemination on 'the wireless', it was chosen for the Wedding of Princess Elizabeth to Prince Philip in November 1947, and for the Silver Wedding celebrations of King George VI and Queen Elizabeth in April 1948.

There has been some doubt concerning the authorship of the tune. In many books it has been ascribed to Jessie Seymour Irvine (1836–87), daughter of the minister of Crimond (a parish in Aberdeenshire), on the evidence of a letter from her sister Anna. But in *The Northern Psalter* of 1872 it was credited to a less romantic figure, David Grant, an Aberdeen tobacconist. It now seems likely that this is correct. The matter is discussed by Sir Ronald Johnson in a definitive article in the *Bulletin* of the Hymn Society of Great Britain and Ireland (no. 176, 1988: 38–42). Johnson's findings destroy an affecting legend concerning the daughter of the manse (and the foundations of a small tourist industry in Crimond) but give credit where it seems to be due.

{3}

The Seventeenth Century:
Anglicans and Puritans

The seventeenth century was a time of great turbulence and conflict in both Church and State. The consequences of the Reformation were the Thirty Years War in Europe, and the continuous tension between Anglicans and Puritans in England and Scotland. Religious conflicts became entangled with political struggles, as Parliament and King fought for supremacy throughout the century, most dramatically in the Civil War.

The hymns of the century reflect the conditions in which they were written, and the positions of their authors. Those by Herbert and Vaughan were poems rather than hymns, although Herbert's paraphrase of the twenty-third Psalm was written in the traditional common metre, as if to be sung. Other Anglican writers included Samuel Crossman, who became Dean of Bristol, John Mason, an eccentric parish priest, and Thomas Ken, the saintly and incorruptible Bishop of Bath and Wells. Their work stands beside that of the true moderate, Richard Baxter, who was one of those ejected from his living in 1662 under the Act of Uniformity; and the courageous dissenter John Bunyan, who was imprisoned for his beliefs in Bedford jail.

At the end of the century came *A New Version of the Psalms of David, Fitted to the Tunes used in Churches*, by Nahum Tate and Nicholas Brady. It reflected the new plainness of the English language encouraged by the philosophers (i.e. scientists) of the Royal Society, and became a widely accepted successor to *The Whole Booke of Psalmes*, which thereafter became known as the 'Old Version'. Tate and Brady's psalms, with some of their paraphrases added (including 'While shepherds watched their flocks by night') continued in use until well into the nineteenth century.

47   Let all the world in every corner sing,
                    My God and King!
                The heavens are not too high,
                His praise may thither fly;
                The earth is not too low,
                His praises there may grow.
            Let all the world in every corner sing,
                    My God and King!

            Let all the world in every corner sing,
                    My God and King!
                The Church with psalms must shout,
                No door can keep them out;
                But, above all, the heart
                Must bear the longest part.
            Let all the world in every corner sing,
                    My God and King!

                    George Herbert (1593–1633)

This is taken from *The Temple*, Herbert's collection of religious poems published in 1633, shortly after his death (see 'King of glory, King of peace', no. 48), where it is entitled 'Antiphon (I)'. An antiphon, as its name implies, was 'a composition in verse or prose, consisting of verses or passages sung alternately by two choirs in worship' (*Oxford English Dictionary*), or by the Decani and Cantoris side of a choir alternately. In the original text the first two lines were designated 'Cho.' (Chorus) and the short lines 'Vers.' (Versicle). A versicle was 'one of a series of short sentences, usually taken from the psalms and of a precatory nature, said or sung antiphonally in divine service' (*OED*).

In *The Temple* there is only one 'Let all the world . . .' between the two sets of six-syllable lines. The poem is printed 'Cho. . . . Vers. . . . Cho. . . . Vers. . . . Cho': the extra Chorus alters the pattern to allow it to be sung in its present two-verse form as a hymn. It was first printed in this way in *Church Hymns with Tunes* (1874).

It is notable for the simplicity of the phrase, 'My God and King', which Herbert used often, and for the rhymes of the first verse, in which 'high/fly' contrasts with 'low/grow'. Also characteristic of Herbert is his emphasis on the importance of the heart: although the Church sings (or 'shouts') psalms, it is the heart which must 'bear the longest part', continue the praise even longer than the Church does. It is consistent with Herbert's idea (in 'King of glory, King of peace') that 'Seven whole days, not one in seven/ I will praise thee'.

Various tunes were tried in the nineteenth century to make Herbert's words singable. *Church Hymns with Tunes* printed UNDIQUE GLORIA, by Sir George Job Elvey (1816–93), organist of St George's Chapel, Windsor; the

1889 Supplement to the 1875 edition of *Hymns Ancient and Modern* set a tune by William Henry Monk (1823–89) called HERBERT. These were superseded by the splendid LUCKINGTON, by Basil Harwood (1859–1949), a prolific composer of vigorous tunes, from the *Oxford Hymn Book* of 1908; it is named after a village near Malmesbury in Wiltshire. An alternative is Erik Routley's AUGUSTINE, which allows the poem to be sung in its original form, with 'Let all the world . . .' only once in the middle. *Songs of Praise* printed a tune by Martin Shaw, HIGH ROAD.

48

King of glory, King of peace,
   I will love thee;
And that love may never cease,
   I will move thee.
Thou hast granted my request,
   Thou hast heard me;
Thou didst note my working breast,
   Thou hast spared me.

Wherefore with my utmost art
   I will sing thee,
And the cream of all my heart
   I will bring thee.
Though my sins against me cried,
   Thou didst clear me;
And alone, when they replied,
   Thou didst hear me.

Seven whole days, not one in seven,
   I will praise thee;
In my heart, though not in heaven,
   I can raise thee.
Small it is, in this poor sort
   To enrol thee:
E'en eternity's too short
   To extol thee.

George Herbert (1593–1633)

From *The Temple*, Herbert's collection of religious poems published in 1633, shortly after his death at the age of thirty-nine. On his deathbed, he gave the manuscript to a friend to take to Nicholas Ferrar, of the Anglican community at Little Gidding, with the words:

Tell him, he shall find in it a picture of the many spiritual Conflicts that have past betwixt God and my soul, before I could subject mine to the will of *Jesus my Master*: in whose service I have now found perfect freedom; desire him to read it: and then, if he can think it may turn to the advantage of any dejected poor Soul, let it be made publick: if not, let him burn it: for *I and it, are less than the least of God's mercies.*

Seldom can a book which has become a classic of Christian spirituality, and helped so many people, have been introduced with such self-effacement and diffidence. In *The Temple*, this poem is entitled 'Praise (II)'. It has echoes of many praise psalms, especially 111, 113, and 116. It was first used as a hymn by Robert Bridges, in the *Yattendon Hymnal* (1899). In the original it was in four-line stanzas.

In Herbert's development of the theme, he praises God especially because he has been forgiven. His penitence and anguish ('my working breast') have been noted, and he has been 'cleared' of the sins that cried against him. This is made even clearer in the verse from *The Temple* that is customarily omitted (partly because it is almost impossible to sing, and partly because it makes a poem of seven four-line verses, which cannot be fitted to the tune):

> Thou grew'st soft and moist with tears,
>   Thou relentedst:
> And when Justice call'd for fears,
>   Thou dissentedst.

The verses, with their alternating long and short lines, provide a series of contrasting movements. So do the verses themselves, which change from 'I . . . I' (verse 1) to 'Thou . . . Thou' (verse 2, now the second half of the eight-line stanza). The 'I' prays to God ('I will move thee') to ensure that his love will continue ('Because he hath inclined his ear unto me, therefore will I call upon him as long as I live', Psalm 116: 2). This pattern of prayer and forgiveness is repeated throughout, giving the 'I' figure cause for thankfulness and praise, so that, in a daring image, he will bring to God 'the cream' of his heart, the richest part.

The reference to 'King of peace' illustrates the neat complexity of Herbert's mind. Hebrews 7: 2 describes Melchisidec, the priest-king, who was 'King of righteousness' but also 'King of Salem, which is, King of peace'. As Rosamond Tuve pointed out (*A Reading of George Herbert*: 71), Melchisidec prefigured Christ in the Eucharist when he gave bread and wine to Abraham: his action 'is the Old Testament type of Christ's feeding of His Church, and Christ is the God who nourishes, the Priest who officiates, the King, and the sacrifice'. As she says, 'this is a Holy Communion poem'. Herbert's use of the phrase 'King of peace' is therefore a strong signal, inaugurating the pattern of forgiveness and praise that is highly appropriate to the Holy Communion.

The hymn is also notable for its spectacular use of language and rhythm, using rhetoric and rhyme in significant ways. 'Seven whole days, not one in seven' is an example of the Renaissance figure of *Epanalepsis*, when 'ye make one word both beginne and end your verse'; and the rhymes work by changing one or two letters, to chime their meaning—'clear me/ hear me', 'praise thee/ raise thee'. The striking images and words carry on the element of surprise which is found in the metre, reaching a climax in the final verse. There 'this poor sort' (in such a poor way) is a small way to celebrate you ('to enrol thee'), but that is not surprising, for even eternity is too short for your praise. The paradox that even eternity (which has no end, by definition) can be too short for God's praise is one of the witty ways in which Herbert celebrates God, who is unending even beyond that which is unending.

The hymn is usually sung to GWALCHMAI, a Welsh tune by J. D. Jones, first published in 1868. It was set to these words in the *English Hymnal* (1906), and has formed a beautiful setting for them ever since.

49
Teach me, my God and King,
In all things thee to see;
And what I do in any thing
To do it as for thee.

A man that looks on glass,
On it may stay his eye;
Or if he pleaseth, through it pass,
And then the heaven espy.

All may of thee partake;
Nothing can be so mean,
Which with this tincture, 'for thy sake',
Will not grow bright and clean.

A servant with this clause
Makes drudgery divine;
Who sweeps a room, as for thy laws,
Makes that and the action fine.

This is the famous stone
That turneth all to gold;
For that which God doth touch and own
Cannot for less be told.

George Herbert (1593–1633)

From *The Temple*, published in 1633 (see under 'King of glory, King of peace'). Its title in that book is 'The Elixir', which identifies Herbert's pervasive use in this poem of the ideas found in the medieval practice of alchemy. Alchemists sought the elixir, or 'philosopher's stone', because it was thought that it would turn ordinary metals into gold. Herbert appropriates the idea, and transforms it into a Christian metaphor: to see God in all things, and to do all things for God, is to find the secret which will turn an ordinary life into a blessed (golden) one.

The important processes are those of 'seeing' God and working for God. Seeing God involves not only looking at the material world but seeing beyond it, as a man can look not only on glass but through it at the sky. Working for God means doing a task properly, 'for his sake': this will make drudgery divine, and the meanest object bright and clean. The zeugma at the end of verse 4, 'Makes that and the action fine', is a neat statement of this, and typical of Herbert: it suggests a simultaneous and twofold process. Armed with the clause, 'for thy sake', the servant (and we are all servants of God) makes the action fine as well as the room.

'For thy sake' is a tincture, a compound which is used for cleaning. But 'tincture' was also a term from alchemy, which refers back to the poem's title. The elixir was sometimes known as the 'universal tincture' (OED, sense 6), so that here the tincture is the transforming element, the secret compound (in alchemy, 'a supposed spiritual principle or immaterial substance' OED) that can transform the soul and make it into spiritual gold. Centuries of searching for the philosopher's stone (says Herbert in the final verse) end in this, because the life that is touched by God is truly golden. To 'touch', in this verse, adds yet another word from alchemy: it meant to test with a touchstone. As Herbert's editor, F. E. Hutchinson, notes, 'What God has "touched" and approved as gold, no one may rightly reckon *for less.*'

The original poem had (in one manuscript) a second verse that is invariably omitted from hymn-books:

> Not rudely, as a beast
> To runne into an action;
> But still to make thee prepossest,
> And give it his perfection.

To run into an action rudely, like a beast, is to do something without thought, especially without the thought of God (as opposed to the first verse's 'to do it as for thee'). The Christian approach to work is therefore to make God 'prepossest', that is in occupation of the mind and body before beginning something. If that is done, then the action will be given 'his perfection' ('his' means 'its' at this point). This additional verse, awkward though it seems, is in keeping with the rest of the poem.

Although some of the language is difficult, and the alchemical significance is now obscure, the general meaning of this hymn is clear. The hymn has a neat and pointed sharpness which allows it to be sung successfully, in spite of the twists and turns of the argument and the difficult imagery. Its inclusion in the *English Hymnal* must have been something of an experiment, but it has proved surprisingly popular and durable.

The tune associated with these words is SANDYS, found in William Sandys's *Christmas Carols Ancient and Modern* (1833), set to 'A child this day is born'. The *Oxford Book of Carols* (1928) says that it was from the west of England. It was set to this hymn and harmonized by Ralph Vaughan Williams for the *English Hymnal*.

50   The God of love my Shepherd is,
          And he that doth me feed;
      While he is mine and I am his,
          What can I want or need?

      He leads me to the tender grass,
          Where I both feed and rest;
      Then to the streams that gently pass:
          In both I have the best.

      Or if I stray, he doth convert
          And bring my mind in frame:
      And all this not for my desert,
          But for his holy name.

      Yea, in death's shady black abode
          Well may I walk, not fear;
      For thou art with me, and thy rod
          To guide, thy staff to bear.

      Surely thy sweet and wondrous love
          Shall measure all my days;
      And as it never shall remove,
          So neither shall my praise.

                    George Herbert (1593–1633)

This metrical version of the twenty-third Psalm is from *The Temple* (1633), where it has one more verse, usually omitted:

      Nay, thou dost make me sit and dine,
          Ev'n in my enemies sight:
      My head with oyl, my cup with wine
          Runnes over day and night.

Interestingly, it is the only version of a psalm in the book, probably because the twenty-third Psalm so perfectly expressed Herbert's sense of the providence of God and of his own trust in Him. He had in his mind the earlier version from *The Whole Booke of Psalmes*, written by William Whittingham, one of the Protestant exiles during the reign of Mary Tudor, which began:

      The Lord is only my support,
          And he that doth me feed,
      How can I then lack any thing
          Whereof I stand in need?

Although Herbert takes over the second line without alteration, it is significant that he transforms Whittingham's opening by adding the words 'of love': he also goes back to the *Book of Common Prayer* for the image of the shepherd, whereas Whittingham was translating from the Vulgate, 'Dominus regit me'.

What is most characteristic of Herbert, however, is the unobtrusive rhetoric of the verse. Again and again, he links two things together: 'all this not for my desert,/ But for his holy name'; 'My head with oyl, my cup with wine/ Runnes over'. The figure is that of zeugma, or a yoke, in which two things depend on one verb: the final example is that of God's love and human praise never ceasing:

> And as it never shall remove,
> So neither shall my praise.

Here both human and divine depend upon the verb 'never shall remove': Herbert provides a beautiful series of interconnections, all depending on the relationship between the poet and God: 'While he is mine, and I am his'. The result is a version of the psalm which quietly strengthens its most important feature, the sense of human dependence upon God's providence and love.

The tune most frequently used is UNIVERSITY, by Charles Collignon (1725–85), Professor of Anatomy at the University of Cambridge. It was published in 1793, and was used for Herbert's poem when it first appeared in modern hymn-books, in the *English Hymnal* of 1906. It is a good example (as with nos. 48 and 49) of Vaughan Williams's genius for finding a lively and singable tune to make Herbert's (sometimes difficult) words accessible.

51

My soul, there is a country
   Afar beyond the stars,
Where stands a wingèd sentry
   All skilful in the wars.

There, above noise, and danger,
   Sweet peace sits, crowned with smiles,
And One born in a manger
   Commands the beauteous files.

He is thy gracious friend,
   And—O my soul, awake!—
Did in pure love descend
   To die here for thy sake.

If thou canst get but thither,
   There grows the flower of peace,
The rose that cannot wither,
   Thy fortress and thy ease:

Leave then thy foolish ranges;
   For none can thee secure,
But one, who never changes,
   Thy God, thy life, thy cure.

Henry Vaughan (1622–95)

This is from *Silex Scintillans: or Sacred Poems and Private Ejaculations* (1650), Vaughan's collection of religious poems published at a difficult time (Vaughan had probably fought on the Royalist side in the Civil War, and the King had been executed in 1649). Vaughan gives the poems the title 'Silex scintillans' or 'Sparkling flint', suggesting their origins in his own hard experience.

This poem, entitled 'Peace', was first used as a hymn in the nineteenth century, when it was printed in Godfrey Thring's *The Church of England Hymn Book* of 1882. In the second line, Vaughan's 'Far beyond' is sometimes printed as 'Afar', to assist the metre, and bring the line up to the normal six syllables.

Percy Dearmer called it 'this exquisite lyric': it stretches the mind wonderfully with its portrayal of the sentry standing guard over a heaven of peace and love. At the centre is 'one, who never changes': the implied contrast is with earth, where the roses wither, and human beings engage in 'foolish ranges' (living their lives without purpose or direction). In the heavenly country, by contrast, 'sweet peace sits crowned with smiles': Vaughan's experience in the Civil War must have made him more aware than most people of the precious value of peace.

He also practised as a country doctor in Breconshire, and had an interest in what today would be called 'holistic medicine' (he translated a work entitled *Hermetical Physick*). So in this poem God is 'thy life, thy cure', the remedy for those diseases which hurt the body and torment the soul. God is always there: He is the 'one, who never changes'. The phrase is echoed by Henry Francis Lyte, who was partly responsible for a revival of Vaughan's work in the nineteenth century, in 'Abide with me' (no. 142)—'O thou who changest not, abide with me'. God is constant, whereas human nature is fragile and fickle, ranging about in a vain search for peace. That peace is the attribute of God, a God who 'did in pure love descend/ To die here for thy sake'. That great gesture is the ultimate source of our peace: the heavenly country is thus a fortress and an ease, a place where the soul can feel secure.

The tune is CHRISTUS DER IST MEIN LEBEN, by Melchior Vulpius (*c*.1560–1615) from his *Ein schön geistlich Gesangbuch* (1609). It was harmonized by Bach in his *Choralgesänge* (1769). Archibald Jacob, in *Songs of Praise Discussed*, described it as 'a simple but lovely tune, permeated with a feeling of gentle serenity, yet with a deep undercurrent of emotional significance.' It is sometimes called VULPIUS, or PASTOR, or BREMEN. The hymn is also frequently sung as an anthem, to the fine setting by C. H. H. Parry.

52

He wants not friends that hath thy love,
    And may converse and walk with thee,
And with thy saints here and above,
    With whom for ever I must be.

In the communion of saints
    Is wisdom, safety and delight;
And when my heart declines and faints,
    It's raisèd by their heat and light.

As for my friends, they are not lost;
    The several vessels of thy fleet,
Though parted now, by tempests tossed,
    Shall safely in the haven meet.

Still we are centred all in thee,
    Members, though distant, of one head;
In the same family we be,
    By the same faith and spirit led.

Before thy throne we daily meet
    As joint-petitioners to thee;
In spirit we each other greet,
    And shall again each other see.

The heavenly hosts, world without end,
    Shall be my company above;
And thou, my best and surest friend,
    Who shall divide me from thy love?

               Richard Baxter (1615–91)

These verses are taken from a poem entitled 'The Resolution. *Psalm* 119.96. Written when I was Silenced and cast out, &c.' It was written in 1663, not long after Baxter had become one of the ejected clergy after the Act of Uniformity of 1662. In it Baxter movingly finds consolation in the idea that in the communion of saints he will be reunited with the fellow-believers from whom he has become separated, and with the other ejected clergy ('the several vessels of thy fleet'). Baxter's ecumenical spirit is eloquently shown here: he once described himself as 'an Episcopal-Presbyterian-Independent', which was an impossible thing to be in the contentious seventeenth century. Isaac Watts wrote of him that he had 'wrought hard for an end of controversies, and laboured with much zeal for the conversion of souls, though with much more success in the last than in the first'.

The quotation from Psalm 119 is 'I have seen an end of all perfection: but thy commandment is exceeding broad.' This clearly refers to the end of Baxter's hopes for religious toleration following the Restoration, and for his plans of a 'holy commonwealth'; while the title of the poem, 'The Resolution', could refer to the way in which matters had been resolved (with many clergy leaving their churches on 'Black Bartholomew's Day', St

Bartholomew's Day in 1662), or to the poet's own 'resolution', his determination to do what he thought right.

Although the title quotes Psalm 119, the chief inspiration of this poem is Ephesians 2: 19: 'Now therefore ye are no more strangers and foreigners, but fellow-citizens with the saints, and of the household of God.' From the idea of the 'household' comes the homely verse 4; while at other points there are references to the journey to Emmaus (verse 1, from Luke 24: 32), to coming in to harbour (verse 3, from Psalm 107), and to the unity with Christ on earth and in heaven (Romans 8).

It was published in Baxter's *Poetical Fragments* (1681), described on the title page as 'Heart-Imployment with God and It Self' and 'The Concordant Discord of a Broken healed Heart'. It was signed and dated: 'London. At the door of Eternity. Rich. Baxter Aug. 7. 1681.'

The emphasis on the human heart, and the ever-present sense of eternity, are two reasons why Baxter's poems are still so moving. The present one was extracted from 'The Resolution' and made into a hymn by the editors of the *English Hymnal* (1906), one of their many remarkable contributions to twentieth-century worship. It appeared in *Songs of Praise*, and in many hymn-books after that, sometimes altered (*Rejoice and Sing*, for example, altered the first line to 'They lack not friends who have thy love' to avoid the slightly archaic—and the undoubtedly masculine—'He wants not friends').

No really strong tune has been accepted as inevitable for these words, which is why they are not as frequently sung as they deserve to be. The *English Hymnal* and *Songs of Praise* both used the Scottish CAMERONIAN MIDNIGHT HYMN; *Hymns and Psalms* uses an Australian tune, VERMONT, by A. E. Floyd (1877–1974), and a seventeenth-century tune, WHITEHALL, by Henry Lawes (1596–1662); *Rejoice and Sing* uses a slightly later tune, ILLSLEY, by John Bishop (1665–1737). *Common Praise* (2000), the new *Hymns Ancient and Modern*, prints Jeremiah Clarke's UFFINGHAM as a first tune, together with CAMERONIAN MIDNIGHT HYMN.

53   Lord, it belongs not to my care
              Whether I die or live;
              To love and serve thee is my share,
              And this thy grace must give.

              If life be long, I will be glad
              That I may long obey;
              If short, yet why should I be sad
              To end my little day?

              Christ leads me through no darker rooms
              Than he went through before;
              He that into God's kingdom comes
              Must enter by this door.

              Come, Lord, when grace hath made me meet
              Thy blessed face to see:
              For if thy work on earth be sweet,
              What will thy glory be!

              Then I shall end my sad complaints
              And weary, sinful days,
              And join with the triumphant saints
              That sing my Saviour's praise.

              My knowledge of that life is small,
              The eye of faith is dim;
              But 'tis enough that Christ knows all,
              And I shall be with him.

                              Richard Baxter (1615–91)

These verses are from a poem entitled 'The Covenant and Confidence of
Faith'; in the original these lines began 'Now it belongs not'. Originally verse
2 ended with the awkward line 'That shall have the same pay', referring to
the parable of the workers who received the same money for working fewer
hours in the vineyard (Matthew 20). It is often amended to 'To soar to endless day' (the version above is from the *English Hymnal*). In its original form,
it reinforced the idea of either a long life (a long 'day' of life) or a short one:
the reward in Christ is the same.

The hymn is one of trust, based on the idea of Covenant theology, which
was very popular with the Puritans of the seventeenth century. God's grace
'must give' an opportunity for the Christian to 'love and serve': in this way
both sides keep to the bargain—God gives grace and life, the poet loves and
serves. The idea of 'the gift of life' is fundamental to this poem: and there is
a sad addition in the original, 'This Covenant my Dear Wife in her former
Sickness subscribed with a cheerful will.'

The hymn meditates upon life and death in a way that is both touching
and profound. The poet passes to God the great decisions about life or
death: if he is allowed to live, he will love and serve; if he dies, he will not be

sad because he will be with Christ. On earth, Christ went through the dark rooms of the house of life: and the poet knows that he may have to follow Him before coming to the glory that shall be. What that glory will consist of, he does not know, because his knowledge of it is small and the sight which faith gives ('the eye of faith') is a dim sight; but he ends in trust ("'tis enough') that Christ knows all, and is all. The thought is based on Philippians 1: 20–3:

According to my earnest expectation and my hope, that in nothing I shall be ashamed, but that with all boldness, as always, so now also Christ shall be magnified in my body, whether it be by life, or by death. For to me to live is Christ, and to die is gain. But if I live in the flesh, this is the fruit of my labour: yet what I shall choose I wot not. For I am in a strait betwixt two, having a desire to depart, and to be with Christ; which is far better.

Baxter takes this passage and turns it into a hymn of trust and hope, while acknowledging the limits of his human understanding. It is about uncertainty and certainty: uncertainty about what the future may bring, but ultimately a certainty that 'Christ knows all,/ And I shall be with him.'

There are a number of tunes to this hymn. The most commonly used is ST HUGH, by E. J. Hopkins (1818–1901), organist of the Temple Church for over fifty years. A lovely alternative is HARESFIELD, by John Dykes Bower (1905–81).

54

Ye holy angels bright,
　Who wait at God's right hand,
Or through the realms of light
　Fly at your Lord's command,
　　Assist our song,
　　　Or else the theme
　　　Too high doth seem
　　For mortal tongue.

Ye blessed souls at rest,
　Who ran this earthly race,
And now, from sin released,
　Behold the Saviour's face,
　　God's praises sound,
　　　As in his sight
　　　With sweet delight
　　Ye do abound.

Ye saints, who toil below,
Adore your heavenly King,
And onward as ye go
Some joyful anthem sing;
Take what he gives
And praise him still,
Through good or ill,
Who ever lives.

My soul, bear thou thy part,
Triumph in God above,
And with a well-tuned heart
Sing thou the songs of love;
Let all thy days
Till life shall end,
Whate'er he send,
Be filled with praise.

Richard Baxter (1615–91) and others

Much of this hymn comes from Baxter's *The Poor Man's Family Book* of 1672, where it was part of a sixteen-verse poem entitled 'A Psalm of Praise to the tune of Psalm 148'. The 'tune of Psalm 148' refers to the 6.6.6.6. 44.44. metre of that psalm in the 'Old Version' of the Metrical Psalms (used also for 'My song is love unknown', no. 56). The springy short lines contribute greatly to the vigorous effect of this hymn.

Baxter's text has undergone much amendment from its original version, and verse 3 was not by him at all. It was the work of John Hampden Gurney (1802–62), Rector of St Mary's, Marylebone, and a great meddler with other people's hymns. In this case, however, his addition is effective, linking the worship of the blessed souls in heaven with that of the saints on earth. The hymn is thus a celebration of the Communion of Saints as well as a command to praise, 'through good or ill' and 'whate'er he send'. Baxter's own life, with his ejection from his living in 1662, and the title of his book, 'The *Poor Man's* Family Book' give a sharp edge to these phrases.

One tune is DARWALL'S 148th, by John Darwall (1731–89), vicar of St Matthew's, Walsall, who wrote a tune for every one of the metrical psalms. This is the only one which survives in common use. It has an effective pause at the end of line 5, which means that it cannot be used for hymns in the similar metre of 6.6.6.6.8.8. Another is CROFT'S 136th, by William Croft (1678–1727), found in Henry Playford's *The Divine Companion* (1707).

55

Who would true valour see,
   Let him come hither;
One here will constant be,
   Come wind, come weather.
There's no discouragement
Shall make him once relent
His first avowed intent
   To be a pilgrim.

Whoso beset him round
   With dismal stories,
Do but themselves confound,
   His strength the more is.
No lion can him fright,
He'll with a giant fight,
But he will have a right
   To be a pilgrim.

Hobgoblin, nor foul fiend,
   Can daunt his spirit:
He knows he at the end
   Shall life inherit.
Then, fancies, fly away,
He'll fear not what men say,
He'll labour night and day
   To be a pilgrim.

John Bunyan (1628–88)

This hymn is a fine representative of the seventeenth-century Puritan tradition, by one who was imprisoned for his beliefs. In Part I of *The Pilgrim's Progress* Bunyan tells the story of Christian's difficult journey from the City of Destruction to the Celestial City, and in Part II Christian's wife and children journey in his footsteps with their friends, under the guidance of Mr Greatheart. Near the end they meet Mr Valiant-for-Truth, 'with his sword drawn, and his face all bloody'. He has been fighting three men, Wildhead, Inconsiderate, and Pragmatick, and won the victory over them, and over others who would have discouraged him. He then sings this song.

It was (perhaps not surprisingly) not thought of as a hymn until 1873, when it appeared in *Our Hymn Book*, edited by E. Paxton Hood. For the *English Hymnal* (1906), the committee had Vaughan Williams's tune MONK'S GATE available for it, but chose for a text to prefer a modern imitation of Bunyan's words, Percy Dearmer's 'He who would valiant be'. Dearmer's later note in *Songs of Praise Discussed* is instructive, because it is typical of Dearmer's early twentieth-century approach to anything that looked like superstition:

To include the hobgoblins would have been to ensure disaster; to ask the congregation of St Ignotus, Erewhon Park [i.e. Nowhere Park], to invite all to come and look at them, if they wished to see true valour, would have been difficult. But when with the help of the marvellous folk-tune which Vaughan Williams had discovered, we had made a great hymn, it became easy for our imitators to complain that we had altered the words. We felt that we had done rightly; and that no one would have been more distressed than Bunyan himself to have people singing about hobgoblins in church. He had not written it for a hymn, and it was not suitable as a hymn without adaptation.

Dearmer's early modernism sounds curiously old-fashioned now. Congregations have apparently found no difficulty in using Bunyan's robust language to express their own feelings about spiritual courage, and even the hobgoblins are back in most texts. In its present form, the hymn has become widely known, and has been adopted by every denomination. Bunyan's ideas of valour and virtue, and of the need not to be discouraged, have meant that the hymn has transcended its dissenting origins: it has some claim to be thought of as the most non-denominational hymn in the language, a treasure for every believer. The pilgrim metaphor is common to all who are engaged on the journey of life.

Poetically the language is direct and forceful: but the chief glory of the hymn's language is its rhyming. The first half of each verse has awkward two-syllable rhymes, indicative of effort—'hither/weather', 'stories/more is', 'spirit/inherit'; but after the pause in mid-verse, the triple rhymes are much easier, leading the singer on to the final line with its unrhymed word 'pilgrim', the most important word in the hymn.

The tune is almost invariably MONK'S GATE, adapted by Ralph Vaughan Williams (1872–1958) from a tune which he heard at Monk's Gate near Horsham in Sussex. It had been used for a traditional sea song beginning 'Our captain calls all hands on board tomorrow'. It carries the awkward, effort-ful rhythms of Bunyan's verse with great skill.

56

My song is love unknown,
  My Saviour's love to me,
Love to the loveless shown,
  That they might lovely be.
    O who am I,
      That for my sake
      My Lord should take
    Frail flesh and die?

He came from his blest throne,
  Salvation to bestow,
But men made strange, and none
  The longed-for Christ would know.
    But O my friend,
      My friend indeed,
      Who at my need
    His life did spend!

Sometimes they strew his way,
  And his sweet praises sing,
Resounding all the day
  Hosannas to their King.
    Then 'Crucify!'
      Is all their breath,
      And for his death
    They thirst and cry.

Why, what hath my Lord done?
  What makes this rage and spite?
He made the lame to run,
  He gave the blind their sight.
    Sweet injuries!
      Yet they at these
      Themselves displease,
    And 'gainst him rise.

They rise, and needs will have
  My dear Lord made away;
A murderer they save,
  The Prince of Life they slay.
    Yet cheerful he
      To suffering goes,
      That he his foes
    From thence might free.

In life no house, no home,
My Lord on earth might have;
In death no friendly tomb
But what a stranger gave.
What may I say?
Heaven was his home;
But mine the tomb
Wherein he lay.

Here might I stay and sing,
No story so divine:
Never was love, dear King,
Never was grief like thine!
This is my friend,
In whose sweet praise
I all my days
Could gladly spend.

Samuel Crossman (1624–84)

This moving meditation on the Passion of Christ was first published in
Crossman's *The Young Man's Meditation* (1664). This short book of poems
was reprinted in 1863, which no doubt was responsible for this text's being
used as a hymn in the *Anglican Hymn Book* of 1868. It was taken up by other
hymn-books, and has since become one of the best-known hymns for
Passiontide.

Crossman, an Anglican divine (he became Dean of Bristol) was like other
seventeenth-century hymn-writers in that he wrote in the shadow of George
Herbert's *The Temple*: the phrase 'Never was grief like thine' is an echo of
Herbert's poem 'The Sacrifice'. Like Herbert, Crossman uses paradox and
irony in this hymn: it is 'the Prince of Life' who is slain, and Christ is not
only the 'dear Lord' but the 'dear King' who becomes the powerless victim.
The verses tell the story and comment on it at the same time: at one point
the speaker reminds us, with pointed irony, that the only thing that the Lord
has done is heal the sick (verse 4): it is for making the lame run and the blind
see that He is attacked, and if the people think that He has somehow done
them an injury, then these are 'sweet injuries' indeed. Similarly, the first
verse plays upon the suffixes to the word 'love': it is a 'love unknown'
(unprecedented, unparalleled) that is shown to the love-less so that they
might become love-ly. On two occasions, before this love, the speaker is at a
loss: 'O who am I?', he cries in verse 1, searching for his own identity and
conscious of his own lack of worth; and 'What may I say?', he exclaims in
verse 6, as though no words can express the wonder of what has happened.
At the end, astonishment, paradox, irony, exclamation, all turn to praise at
the extraordinary events that the hymn recalls.

In most early printings of this hymn, the tune was Henry Lawes's PSALM 47; but John Ireland (1879–1962) wrote the beautiful LOVE UNKNOWN for *The Public School Hymn Book* (1919). Perhaps because it was written for these words, it has become a much-loved setting for them, and is now used almost universally.

57
How shall I sing that majesty
    Which angels do admire?
Let dust in dust and silence lie;
    Sing, sing, ye heavenly choir.
Thousands of thousands stand around
    Thy throne, O God most high:
Ten thousand times ten thousand sound
    Thy praise; but who am I?

Thy brightness unto them appears,
    Whilst I thy footsteps trace;
A sound of God comes to my ears,
    But they behold thy face.
They sing because thou art their sun,
    Lord, send a beam on me;
For where heaven is but once begun
    There alleluias be.

Enlighten with faith's light my heart,
    Inflame it with love's fire;
Then shall I sing and bear a part
    With that celestial choir.
I shall, I fear, be dark and cold,
    With all my fire and light;
Yet when thou dost accept their gold,
    Lord, treasure up my mite.

How great a being, Lord, is thine,
    Which doth all beings keep!
Thy knowledge is the only line
    To sound so vast a deep.
Thou art a sea without a shore,
    A sun without a sphere;
Thy time is now and evermore,
    Thy place is everywhere.

John Mason (*c.*1645–94)

John Mason, Crossman's younger contemporary and a more obscure figure, asks the same questions as those of 'My song is love unknown': 'How shall I sing?' (echoing 'What may I say?') and 'Who am I?'.

This was the first hymn in Mason's *Spiritual Songs; or, Songs of Praise to*

Almighty God upon Several Occasions (1683). It was part of a longer hymn of praise, which is based partly upon Psalm 104, celebrating God:

O Lord my God, thou art very great; thou art clothed with honour and majesty.
Who coverest thyself with light as with a garment: who stretchest out the
    heavens like a curtain:
Who layeth the beams of his chambers in the waters: who maketh the clouds
    his chariot: who walketh upon the wings of the wind: . . .

and partly upon Psalm 139: 1–18, which relates this magnificence to the human condition:

O Lord, thou hast searched me, and known me.
Thou knowest my downsitting and mine uprising, thou understandest my
    thought afar off . . .
Such knowledge is too wonderful for me; it is high, I cannot attain unto it.

Whether or not Mason had these psalms particularly in mind, they represent the way in which his hymn is particularly effective in charting the greatness of God and the smallness of humanity. God is admired by thousands of angels, so how can human beings hope to add to their hymns of praise? or, as Mason succinctly puts it, 'Who am I?' His answer is that with faith and love he can become a part of the celestial choir, even if he is a dark and cold one, and he has only a 'mite' (remembering the story of the widow's mite, from Mark 12: 42). The final verse returns to the magnificence of God, the sea without a shore, the sun without a sphere (God has no boundaries: His time is evermore, and His place is everywhere). It is an attempt to describe the essence of God's being, the reality of its splendour, as opposed to the dimness of earth: Mason's hymn has something in common with the thinking of his contemporaries who were neo-Platonists, such as Henry More and Ralph Cudworth. Julian's *Dictionary of Hymnology* describes Mason's diction as having an 'ancient quaintness', but it also notes that 'his familiarity with the Platonic school of divinity, and one or two classical quotations, point to a scholarly training.' Mason was, in fact, an enthusiast who became an eccentric: vicar of Water Stratford (near Stowe, in Buckinghamshire), he promised his parishioners that the Second Coming would be in their village, thus encouraging all kinds of strange people to invade it and disturb the peace.

Mason encouraged the singing of hymns, as opposed to metrical psalms, and this may have been one of them (its metre, double common metre, would make this easy). Its first modern appearance was in the *English Hymnal* (1906), where it was set to a psalm tune, OLD 137th, of 1563; it is more usually set to SOLL'S SEIN (used by the *English Hymnal* for 'The summer days are come again' by Samuel Longfellow). SOLL'S SEIN ('It shall be') is a seventeenth-century German tune, first published in 1649, to a hymn beginning with those words. A fine modern tune is COE FEN, by Kenneth Naylor (1931–91), formerly music master at the Leys School, Cambridge, which is used in *Rejoice and Sing* (1991) and *Common Praise* (2000).

58   Awake, my soul, and with the sun
Thy daily stage of duty run;
Shake off dull sloth, and joyful rise
To pay thy morning sacrifice.

Redeem thy mis-spent time that's past,
And live this day as if thy last;
Improve thy talent with due care;
For the great day thyself prepare.

Let all thy converse be sincere,
Thy conscience as the noon-day clear;
Think how all-seeing God thy ways
And all thy secret thoughts surveys.

Wake, and lift up thyself, my heart,
And with the angels bear thy part,
Who all night long unwearied sing
High praise to the eternal King.

———————

Glory to thee, who safe hast kept,
And hast refreshed me whilst I slept;
Grant, Lord, when I from death shall wake,
I may of endless light partake.

Lord, I my vows to thee renew;
Scatter my sins as morning dew;
Guard my first springs of thought and will,
And with thyself my spirit fill.

Direct, control, suggest, this day
All I design, or do, or say,
That all my powers, with all their might,
In thy sole glory may unite.

Praise God, from whom all blessings flow,
Praise him, all creatures here below;
Praise him above, angelic host,
Praise Father, Son, and Holy Ghost.

       Thomas Ken (1637–1711)

This morning hymn was probably written before 1674, and appeared in an unauthorized publication in 1692. It was printed as a pamphlet (authorized) in 1694, and then printed in an Appendix to *A Manual of Prayers for the Use of the Scholars of Winchester College* (1695). Ken, who became Bishop of Bath and Wells, was educated at Winchester, and was a prebendary of the cathedral there from 1680 to 1685.

A revised version of the text, probably by Ken himself, appeared in a later edition (1709) of *A Manual of Prayers*. There are thus many variations in wording, as well as in the selection of verses from the original fourteen, and hymn-books have printed many different texts. The present one is from *Hymns Ancient and Modern New Standard* (1983).

Ken was writing for schoolboys, but the subtitle of *A Manual of Prayers* is *For the Use of the Scholars of Winchester College. And all other Devout Christians*. It is a hymn which has become universally known and loved for its plain speaking and neat versification: it is able to sum up the daily discipline of the Christian life with a high sense of purpose and yet with humanity. It also sets this earthly life in the context of the greater life that is to come, in which the angels 'unwearied sing' their praises to God.

The tune in some early editions of *Hymns Ancient and Modern* was COMMANDMENTS, a tune from the Genevan Psalter of 1556; but this has been generally superseded by MORNING HYMN, composed for these words by François Barthélémon (1741–1808), a French-born violinist and composer who lived in London from 1764 onwards. He composed the tune at the request of the chaplain to an orphanage for girls; it was published in 1789.

59

Glory to thee, my God, this night
For all the blessings of the light;
Keep me, O keep me, King of kings,
Beneath thy own almighty wings.

Forgive me, Lord, for thy dear Son,
The ill that I this day have done,
That with the world, myself, and thee,
I, ere I sleep, at peace may be.

Teach me to live, that I may dread
The grave as little as my bed;
Teach me to die, that so I may
Rise glorious at the aweful day.

O may my soul on thee repose,
And may sweet sleep mine eyelids close,
Sleep that may me more vigorous make
To serve my God when I awake.

When in the night I sleepless lie,
My soul with heavenly thoughts supply;
Let no ill dreams disturb my rest,
No powers of darkness me molest.

Praise God, from whom all blessings flow,
Praise him, all creatures here below,
Praise him above, angelic host,
Praise Father, Son, and Holy Ghost.

Thomas Ken (1637–1711)

This is a companion hymn to 'Awake, my soul', with the same kind of history: it was probably written before 1674, and was printed in the Appendix to *A Manual of Prayers for the Use of the Scholars of Winchester College* in 1695. It was similarly revised in 1709, and there are many different versions of the text. The present one is that of *Hymns Ancient and Modern New Standard* (1983).

It has the same virtues as the Morning Hymn, but they are perhaps even lovelier here. The rhymes are particularly noticeable as holding the simple thoughts in a strong verse form: they allow the singer to express a trust in God (with a most delicate repetition, 'Keep me, O keep me'), to make a confession, and to lie down in peace of mind. The peace comes from living the kind of life that makes the grave as harmless as the bed: the rhyme 'dread/bed' is particularly effective here. Ken may have had in mind the ending of Psalm 4: 'I will lay me down in peace, and take my rest: for it is thou, Lord, only, that makest me dwell in safety.' If the singer is sleepless, then there is a prayer for heavenly thoughts, and to be guarded against the powers of darkness, which echoes the Third Collect at Evening Prayer: 'Lighten our darkness, we beseech thee, O Lord; and by thy great mercy defend us from all perils and dangers of this night; . . .'.

The traditional tune is TALLIS' CANON, sometimes called EVENING HYMN, by Thomas Tallis (*c.*1505–85), first published as a setting for Psalm 67 in Matthew Parker's *The Whole Psalter translated into English Metre*, published between 1561 and 1567. It is a canon, as the title of the tune implies, with the tenor part following the melody after four beats. It has been associated with these words since the eighteenth century.

60   As pants the hart for cooling streams
              When heated in the chase,
          So longs my soul, O God, for thee,
              And thy refreshing grace.

          For thee my God, the living God,
              My thirsty soul doth pine:
          O when shall I behold thy face,
              Thou majesty divine?

          God of my strength, how long shall I,
              Like one forgotten, mourn—
          Forlorn, forsaken, and exposed
              To my oppressor's scorn?

          Why restless, why cast down, my soul?
              Hope still, and thou shalt sing
          The praise of him who is thy God,
              Thy health's eternal spring.

          To Father, Son, and Holy Ghost,
              The God whom we adore,
          Be glory, as it was, is now,
              And shall be evermore.

                    Nahum Tate (1652–1715)
              and Nicholas Brady (1659–1726)

This metrical version of Psalm 42 is from *A New Version of the Psalms of David* (1696), slightly altered as in the second edition of 1698. Tate and Brady's was the first successful psalm book to dislodge Sternhold and Hopkins's *The Whole Booke of Psalmes* of 1562, which became known in consequence as the 'Old Version'. It was this 'new' version that Thomas Hardy remembered singing in 'Afternoon Service at Mellstock', midway through the nineteenth century:

          On afternoons of drowsy calm
              We stood in the panelled pew,
          Singing one-voiced a Tate-and-Brady psalm
              To the tune of 'Cambridge New'.

The text printed here (from *Hymns and Psalms*) is taken from verses 1, 2, 10 and 12 of the original, adding Tate and Brady's *Gloria Patri* from the end of their book. It captures well the psalmist's theme of the soul under pressure: 'I will say unto God my rock, Why hast thou forgotten me? why go I mourning because of the oppression of the enemy?'

Tate and Brady paraphrase this with skill and eloquence, and their rendering is throughout much more mellifluous than that of the 'Old Version'. The boldness of opening a hymn with a simile is justified not only by the original text but also by the sustained iambic rhythm, which gives the verse a flowing and natural quality. A comparison with Hopkins's earlier version will demonstrate this. Hopkins writes:

> Like as the hart doth pant and bray
> The well-springs to obtain,
> So doth my soul desire alway
> With thee, Lord, to remain.

The first stress falls on 'as', and the 'and bray' (not in the 1611 text, nor in that of the *Book of Common Prayer*) seems to have been put in to rhyme with 'alway'. Tate and Brady were sometimes too smooth and soothing in their versification, but on this occasion their poetic skill was admirable.

Since the *Appendix* (1868) to the first edition of *Hymns Ancient and Modern*, this hymn has always been associated with the plangent Scottish tune MARTYRDOM, by Hugh Wilson (1764–1824). Wilson was born at Fenwick, near Kilmarnock, and the tune was at one time written in common time with the name FENWICK. It was printed in triple time, as it now usually is, and given its present name, in R. A. Smith's *Sacred Music*, published in Edinburgh in 1825. Both forms are effective, and are printed in *The Scottish Psalter* of 1929 (84, 85) but the triple-time version has a spring which the four-beat version lacks.

61 Through all the changing scenes of life,
    In trouble and in joy,
  The praises of my God shall still
    My heart and tongue employ.

  O magnify the Lord with me,
    With me exalt his name;
  When in distress to him I called,
    He to my rescue came.

  The hosts of God encamp around
    The dwellings of the just;
  Deliverance he affords to all
    Who on his succour trust.

  O make but trial of his love:
    Experience will decide
  How blest are they, and only they,
    Who in his truth confide.

  Fear him, ye saints, and you will then
    Have nothing else to fear;
  Make you his service your delight,
    Your wants shall be his care.

To Father, Son, and Holy Ghost,
The God whom we adore,
Be glory, as it was, is now,
And shall be evermore.

Nahum Tate (1652–1715)
and Nicholas Brady (1659–1726)

This metrical version of the first part of Psalm 34 (verses 1–10) is from *A New Version of the Psalms of David* (1696), incorporating changes made for the second edition of 1698, and adding Tate and Brady's *Gloria Patri* from the end of their book. This makes a much better ending than the original, which paraphrases 'The young lions do lack, and suffer hunger; but they that seek the Lord shall not want any good thing':

While hungry lions lack their prey,
The Lord will food provide
For such, as put their trust in him,
And see their wants supply'd.

The opening verse shows how Tate and Brady could take liberties with the original in order to produce mellifluous and effective verse. The *Book of Common Prayer* version is 'I will alway give thanks unto the Lord: his praise shall ever be in my mouth.' By invoking the 'changing scenes', and by remembering that human life is often 'in trouble and in joy', the versifiers have provided a hymn that is a comfort to all those who suffer a time of unhappiness. Its message is the counsel of 'experience', the 'experimental religion' which the seventeenth-century writers were so fond of recommending, a religion based upon individual commitment and personal behaviour. It was this religion that John Wesley was referring to when he called his 1780 *Collection of Hymns for the Use of the People called Methodists* 'a little body of experimental and practical divinity'. In its present context, however, it seems to suggest a comfort which is based not on some instant conversion but on the steady contemplation of accumulated experience.

The hymn is associated with the tune WILTSHIRE, which carries the words with a strong and sweet melodic line. It is by Sir George Thomas Smart (1776–1867), an organist of the Chapel Royal and a friend of Weber (who died in Smart's house in London in 1826). It first appeared in Smart's nicely named *Divine Amusement: Being a Selection of the most admired Psalms, Hymns, and Anthems used in St James's Chapel* (c.1795), and it was set to these words in his *Collection of Sacred Music* of 1863.

62   While shepherds watched their flocks by night,
      All seated on the ground,
      The angel of the Lord came down,
      And glory shone around.

      'Fear not', said he (for mighty dread
      Had seized their troubled mind),
      'Glad tidings of great joy I bring
      To you and all mankind.

      To you in David's town this day
      Is born of David's line
      A Saviour, who is Christ the Lord;
      And this shall be the sign:

      The heavenly babe you there shall find
      To human view displayed,
      All meanly wrapped in swathing bands,
      And in a manger laid.'

      Thus spake the seraph; and forthwith
      Appeared a shining throng
      Of angels praising God, and thus
      Addressed their joyful song:

      'All glory be to God on high,
      And to the earth be peace;
      Good will henceforth from heaven to men
      Begin and never cease.'

                        Nahum Tate (1652–1715)

This paraphrase of Luke 2: 8–14 was first printed in *A Supplement to the New Version of Psalms by Dr Brady and Mr Tate*, published in 1700, which contained this hymn for Christmas, and others for Easter and for Holy Communion. It has become very well known, and can be relied upon as one of the familiar landmarks of a Christmas service. It is unusual for a hymn in its combination of narrative and direct speech; but Tate's regular verse carries the story with unobtrusive strength and a grand simplicity.

The Scottish paraphrases have a version which is substantially the same except for the beginning and the end. The first verse is:

      While humble shepherds watch'd their flocks
      In Bethleh'm's plains by night,
      An angel sent from heav'n appear'd,
      And fill'd the plains with light.

Much of the remainder of the text is the same as the English version, but the last two lines are:

      Good-will is shown by Heav'n to men,
      And never more shall cease.

A more politically correct version of the final verse has been engineered by the editors of *Rejoice and Sing*:

> 'All glory be to God on high,
> and to the world be peace!
> Goodwill henceforth from heaven to earth
> begin and never cease!'

The best-known tune for these words is WINCHESTER OLD, from Thomas Este's The Whole Booke of Psalmes: with their wonted tunes of 1592. It was used for the present hymn in the first edition of *Hymns Ancient and Modern* (1861), and has been closely associated with it since that time. The strong beats of the tune enhance the grandeur of Tate's regular rhythm. Some hymn-books print a version with the melody in the tenor line. It also has a fine descant.

An entirely different experience is gained from singing the words to a 'repeating' tune. One is NORTHROP, by Abraham Northrop (1863–1938), which was written for these words by a Methodist organist from West Hartlepool; it requires the last line of each verse to be sung three times. In some parts of England, especially in Lancashire, carol services are often enlivened by singing this hymn to LYNGHAM, by Thomas Jarman (1776–1861), which requires the second line of each verse to be repeated, and then has a complicated setting of the fourth line, which is sung four times by the tenors and basses, and three times by the sopranos and altos. The effect is astonishing (and invigorating).

{4}

Isaac Watts

During the seventeenth century, hymn-writing developed slowly and with difficulty. Many of the hymns which are still used today were poems, individual expressions of belief and personal holiness. Metrical psalms were still the dominant form, and they continued to appear in different versions, such as those of Francis Rous (1579–1659) and William Barton (c.1603–78), as well as in the official *Scottish Psalter* of 1650. Barton was one of those who wrote hymns as well as psalms; so was George Wither (1588–1667), who wrote 'Come, O come in pious lays', and Benjamin Keach (1640–1704).

Keach, a Baptist minister, introduced hymn-singing into his services, and wrote hymns himself. They were clumsy attempts at versifying obvious ideas, and are now forgotten. Similarly, Barton's voluminous work has disappeared. It was probably Barton's work that offended the young Isaac Watts, who is said to have complained to his father about the hymns that were sung at the chapel in Southampton. His father challenged him to do better, and a great hymn-writer was born.

Watts, who was born in 1674, came on to the scene at exactly the right moment. He took the struggling and experimental hymn form, and transformed it by a combination of poetic energy and high devotional seriousness. His poetry in *Horae Lyricae* (1706, 1709) shows his love of inspirational verse, written with passion and excitement; and his hymn-writing shows his ability to discipline himself to write in a few well-known metres, and with a purposeful clarity.

He was the son of a man who, like Bunyan, had been to prison for his dissenting beliefs. But he was very well educated at a dissenting academy, and his wide interests included language, philosophy, and science. His love of the beauty of the created world is part of his interest in science, but it is related to his theology also. His hymns show the mind of a poet applied with skill and dedication to the expression of his belief: they have a measured dignity about them which is instantly recognizable as the work of an assured hand. That assurance came not only from his craft as a poet, but also from his clarity of belief, and his unwavering pursuit of the truth of revealed religion. He believed in the importance of human reason, but knew also that beyond that, there were the great mysteries of faith and hope.

Some of his hymns, especially such great ones as 'When I survey the wondrous cross', have never been surpassed; and his version of the psalms, in which he gave New Testament interpretations of Old Testament texts, contains such masterpieces as 'O God, our help in ages past'. They set the standard for a century and more, and were an inspiration to those who came after, so that Watts has been rightly seen as the first really great hymn-writer in English.

63

Begin, my tongue, some heavenly theme,
    Awake, my voice, and sing
The mighty works, or mightier name,
    Of our eternal King.

Tell of his wondrous faithfulness,
    And sound his power abroad,
Sing the sweet promise of his grace,
    And the fulfilling God.

Proclaim salvation from the Lord
    For wretched dying men;
His hand has writ the sacred word
    With an immortal pen.

Engraved as in eternal brass
    The mighty promise shines,
Nor can the powers of darkness rase
    Those everlasting lines.

His every word of grace is strong
    As that which built the skies;
The voice that rolls the stars along
    Speaks all the promises.

O might I hear thine heavenly Tongue
    But whisper, Thou art Mine,
Those gentle Words should raise my Song
    To Notes almost divine.

Now shall my leaping heart rejoice
    To know thy favour sure:
I trust the all-creating voice,
    And faith desires no more.

            Isaac Watts (1674–1748)

This hymn is characteristic of Watts's plain speaking. It comes from *Hymns and Spiritual Songs* (1707), from Book II, *Compos'd on Divine Subjects*, and is entitled 'The Faithfulness of God in his Promises'.

The language of this hymn has been altered in places: verse 2 line 4 was 'And the performing God', which is hard to sing now because it suggests a performance; and verse 4 line 4 was 'The record of the skies', which gave more point to 'rase' ('erase'), but which was also suggestive of keeping a book (Watts changed it himself for the second edition of *Hymns and Spiritual Songs* of 1709). The final verse began:

    How would my Leaping Heart rejoyce,
    And think my Heaven secure!

Two of the original nine verses (5 and 7) are usually omitted in modern printings of the hymn:

> He that can dash whole Worlds to Death,
>   And make them when he please,
> He speaks, and that Almighty Breath
>   Fulfils his great Decrees . . . .

> He said, Let the wide Heav'n be spread,
>   And Heav'n was stretch'd abroad;
> Abrah'm, I'll be thy God, he said,
>   And he was Abrah'm's God.

Augustus Montague Toplady, in his *Psalms and Hymns for Public and Private Worship* (1776) altered 'Begin, my tongue' to 'Begin my soul', not realizing that the whole point of this hymn is the government and use of the tongue (for human beings) and the creative and promising spoken word (for God): the first three verses include verbs such as 'sing', 'tell', 'sound abroad', and 'proclaim'. In the second part of the hymn 'He speaks', and

> The voice that rolls the stars along
> Speaks all the promises.

God promises, and it comes to pass, as it did to Abraham, because God is the 'performing' (or 'fulfilling') God, who ensures that what He decrees will happen. And the final use is to whisper to the individual, so that the hymn ends with the singer being promised 'Thou art mine' and feeling that his heaven is secure.

It is entirely characteristic of Charles Wesley's enthusiasm that he should have multiplied Watts's image a thousand-fold: 'O for a thousand tongues to sing/ My great Redeemer's praise' (from *Hymns and Sacred Poems*, 1740).

One tune for this hymn is ST MAGNUS, probably by Jeremiah Clarke (*c*.1673–1707), also set to 'The head that once was crowned with thorns'. For both sets of words it is a rousing tune, with a fine climax at the end of the second line, followed by a nicely developed second half. Another tune, used in *Congregational Praise* and in *Rejoice and Sing*, is STROUDWATER, by Matthew Wilkins, and printed in *A Book of Psalmody . . . by Matthew Wilkins of Great Milton, near Thame in Oxfordshire*, published about 1730. It became popular as a psalm tune in Scotland, and was no. 128 in *The Psalter in Metre* of 1899. Its haunting melody makes it very suitable for a Scottish metrical psalm, and it was set to no less than three of them in *Church Hymnary*, third edition (1973). Percy Dearmer, who used it for another hymn in *Songs of Praise*, noted 'the rather unusual melodic progression at the beginning of the 1st line, and at the end of the 3rd'. He also thought it was 'an excellent tune', which 'should rapidly become very popular'.

64   Awake our souls; away our fears;
                    Let every trembling thought be gone;
                Awake and run the heavenly race,
                    And put a cheerful courage on.

                True, 'tis a strait and thorny road,
                    And mortal spirits tire and faint;
                But they forget the mighty God
                    That feeds the strength of every saint.

                Thee mighty God! whose matchless power
                    Is ever new and ever young,
                And firm endures, while endless years
                    Their everlasting circles run.

                From thee, the overflowing spring,
                    Our souls shall drink a fresh supply,
                While such as trust their native strength
                    Shall melt away, and droop, and die.

                Swift as the eagle cuts the air,
                    We'll mount aloft to thine abode;
                On wings of love our souls shall fly,
                    Nor tire amidst the heavenly road.

                        Isaac Watts (1674–1748)

From *Hymns and Spiritual Songs*, Book I, *Collected from the Scriptures*. It is entitled 'The Christian Race, Isa. 40. 28, 29, 30, 31'.

The passage from Isaiah reminds the reader (verse 28) that 'the everlasting God, the Lord, the Creator of the ends of the earth, fainteth not, neither is weary . . .':

He giveth power to the faint; and to them that have no might he increaseth strength. Even the youths shall faint and be weary, and the young men shall utterly fall: But they that wait upon the Lord shall renew their strength; they shall mount up with wings as eagles; they shall run, and not be weary; and they shall walk, and not faint.

Watts versifies this passage with typical economy and energy, giving it life by the very strong iambic rhythms—'A*wake* our *souls*; a*way* our *fears*'. As in 'O God our help in ages past', there is an emphasis on the power and enduring nature of God: in a telling image, God is firm (and central) while the years go round in circles, suggesting a lack of direction and a pointlessness. In this whirl of time, those who trust in God 'shall renew their strength'; and they have a direction, which is towards heaven, mounting there with the swiftness of eagles and on the wings of love.

It is interesting to compare this hymn with Thomas Ken's 'Awake, my soul, and with the sun', which is contemporary with it. Ken's graceful couplets contrast with Watts's energetic quatrains, and Watts's stress on 'every saint' (as opposed to those 'who trust their native strength') is a characteristic Puritan and Dissenting emphasis.

The customary tune, which suits the strong iambic rhythm of the words, is SAMSON, adapted from Handel's oratorio of that name written in 1742. It is taken from the chorus 'Then round about the starry throne', and was adapted for hymn-singing in *The Bristol Tune Book* of 1863.

65
Come, let us join our cheerful songs
With angels round the throne;
Ten thousand thousand are their tongues,
But all their joys are one.

'Worthy the Lamb that died,' they cry,
'To be exalted thus!'
'Worthy the Lamb!' our lips reply,
'For he was slain for us.'

Jesus is worthy to receive
Honour and power divine;
And blessings more than we can give
Be, Lord, for ever thine.

Let all that dwell above the sky,
And air, and earth, and seas,
Conspire to lift thy glories high,
And speak thine endless praise.

The whole creation join in one
To bless the sacred name
Of him that sits upon the throne,
And to adore the Lamb.

Isaac Watts (1674–1748)

From *Hymns and Spiritual Songs*, Book I, *Collected from the Scriptures*, and entitled 'Christ Jesus the Lamb of God, worshipped by all the Creation, Rev. 5. 11, 12, 13.'

The versification of this celebrated passage from Chapter 5 of Revelation is done with consummate skill. Watts takes 'Worthy is the Lamb that was slain' from verse 12, and slices it neatly into the common metre form, using 'they cry' to finish the line before allowing the sentence to fill the next line with neatness and precision. That precision, which is the hallmark of Watts's work, is beautifully seen throughout: the pauses and line breaks are perfectly judged.

But the hymn transforms the sublime vision of Revelation by allowing human beings to join the ten thousand thousand: the word 'cheerful' in the first line sounds a very human note, as if the whole process is one of good cheer (as indeed it should be). As Watts said elsewhere, 'Religion never was designed / To make our pleasures less'. Here the human joy of praising God is clearly suggested, but it is also joined with the sublimity of angelic contemplation of the Lamb that was slain; so that the hymn starts on earth and ends in heaven.

The tune which is usually used for these words is NATIVITY, by Henry Lahee (1826–1912), first published in 1855. It was called by this name because it was first set to a Christmas hymn by Philip Doddridge, 'High let us swell our tuneful notes'. Its rising first line, with its strong rhythm, starts each verse with an energy that is entirely suitable for the words. The second half of each verse is more difficult to sing with a straight face after reading Nicholas Temperley's *The Music of the English Parish Church*, in which he points out that Lahee's melody is the same as that of the nursery rhyme 'Mary, Mary, quite contrary'. The only way to conceal this is to give each of the six notes of the last line its full weight, which produces a different effect from the tripping 'And pretty maids all in a row'. If this is done, the tune is a splendid accompaniment to the words, as it has been ever since they were brought together in the second edition (1875) of *Hymns Ancient and Modern*. Alternatively, LYNGHAM can be used (see no. 62), as in Baptist hymn-books from 1933 onwards.

66   Come, we that love the Lord,
           And let our joys be known;
    Join in a Song with sweet Accord,
           And thus surround the Throne.

        The Sorrows of the Mind
           Be banish'd from the Place!
    Religion never was design'd
           To make our Pleasures less.

        Let those refuse to sing
           That never knew our God,
    But Fav'rites of the heavenly King,
           May speak their Joys abroad.

        The God that rules on high,
           And thunders when he please,
    That rides upon the stormy Sky,
           And manages the Seas,

        This awful God is ours,
           Our Father and our Love,
    He shall send down his heav'nly Pow'rs
           To carry us above.

There we shall see his Face,
And never, never sin;
There from the Rivers of his Grace
Drink endless Pleasures in.

Yea, and before we rise
To that immortal State,
The Thoughts of such amazing Bliss
Should constant Joys create.

The Men of Grace have found
Glory begun below,
Celestial Fruits on earthly Ground
From Faith and Hope may grow.

The Hill of Zion yields
A Thousand sacred Sweets,
Before we reach the heav'nly Fields,
Or walk the golden Streets.

Then let our Songs abound,
And ev'ry Tear be dry;
We're marching thro' Immanuel's Ground
To fairer Worlds on high.

Isaac Watts (1674–1748)

First published in *Hymns and Spiritual Songs* (1707), from Book II, entitled *Compos'd on Divine Subjects* and entitled 'Heavenly Joy on Earth'. This hymn has been changed and adapted in many ways, most notably in John Wesley's abbreviation for his 1780 *Collection of Hymns for the Use of the People called Methodists*, which began 'Come, ye that love the Lord' and was printed in four eight-line verses. This version survived in Methodist books until *Hymns and Psalms* (1983), which reverted to the four-line stanza and printed an odd selection of verses, losing the magnificent ending.

This is Isaac Watts in the mood of a seventeenth-century Puritan, journeying with his friends ('Come, we') towards the Celestial City, as Bunyan had described it shortly before in *The Pilgrim's Progress*. Watts conveys the sense of this as a joyful pilgrimage, more suited to Part II of *The Pilgrim's Progress* than to the arduous adventures of Part I. Christiana and her companions, under the tutelage of Mr Greatheart and Mr Valiant-for-Truth, are also recalled in the initial 'Come we'. The unexpected word, which occurs on two occasions, is 'pleasure': it suggests a joy in the religious life which is entirely in keeping with Watts's theology, in which 'glory' is begun below through the offices of faith and hope. The world is not the desert of so many pilgrimage hymns, but a place where celestial fruits may grow, if only because it is 'Immanuel's ground', the place in which the Christian can walk knowing that it belongs to the God who was Immanuel, 'God with us'. In its celebration of the pleasures of religion, it looks forward to the 'fairer worlds' which will continue those joys in heaven. The last spectacular verse, with its reference to songs that are to abound, unites that image with the idea that God shall wipe away all tears from their eyes (from Revelation 21: 4), and has echoes of the magnificent Chapter 35 of Isaiah:

And the ransomed of the Lord shall return, and come to Zion with songs and everlasting joy upon their heads: they shall obtain joy and gladness, and sorrow and sighing shall flee away.

No single tune has become firmly associated with this hymn, though American and Canadian books frequently use ST THOMAS, by Aaron Williams, from *The New Universal Psalmodist* of 1770. *Rejoice and Sing* uses WINDERMERE, by Arthur Somervell, and *Hymns and Psalms* uses an old favourite, MOUNT EPHRAIM. Wesley's eight-line version may be sung either to RIDGE, a fine but difficult tune by Samuel Wesley, or to Henry Gauntlett's ASCENSION. In some American and Canadian books (and in some British books such as *The Salvation Army Tune Book*), Watts's text is frequently printed with a refrain by the nineteenth-century evangelist Robert Lowry, and the whole mixture is sung to a rousing march entitled MARCHING TO ZION. The refrain takes Watts's last image of marching through Immanuel's ground, and makes the most of it:

> We're marching to Zion,
> Beautiful, beautiful Zion;
> We're marching upward to Zion,
> The beautiful city of God.

67   There is a land of pure delight
          Where saints immortal reign;
      Infinite day excludes the night,
          And pleasures banish pain.

      There everlasting spring abides,
          And never-withering flowers;
      Death, like a narrow sea, divides
          This heavenly land from ours.

      Sweet fields beyond the swelling flood
          Stand dressed in living green;
      So to the Jews old Canaan stood,
          While Jordan rolled between.

      But timorous mortals start and shrink
          To cross this narrow sea,
      And linger shivering on the brink,
          And fear to launch away.

      O could we make our doubts remove,
          Those gloomy doubts that rise,
      And see the Canaan that we love
          With unbeclouded eyes!

      Could we but climb where Moses stood,
          And view the landscape o'er,
      Not Jordan's stream, nor death's cold flood,
          Should fright us from the shore!

                          Isaac Watts (1674–1748)

This hymn, perhaps the most beautiful of all Watts's hymns, was delightfully entitled 'A Prospect of Heaven makes Death easy'. It was first printed in Book II of Watts's *Hymns and Spiritual Songs* (1707). Some modern books, possibly uncomfortable with the word 'doubts' in a hymn, amend verse 5 line 2 to 'gloomy thoughts'.

The hymn is, of course, the reverse of gloomy. Part of its charm is its use of the 'prospect' that occurs in the title, which allows the singer to catch a glimpse of heaven from a distance, as Moses saw the promised land from Mount Pisgah before his death (Deuteronomy 34: 1–5). That land is so beautiful—sweet fields beyond the swelling flood—that if we could see it clearly we would not be afraid of death. There it is always spring: Watts is probably influenced by Milton at this point, for Milton saw one consequence of the Fall as the unwelcome changes of climate:

                    else had the Spring
        Perpetual smil'd on earth with vernant Flours,
                          (*Paradise Lost*, X. 678–9)

The other seventeenth-century writer to whom Watts was indebted is (once again) Bunyan. Part I of *The Pilgrim's Progress* finds Christian and Hopeful, after many adventures, entering the country of Beulah, where 'they heard continually the singing of birds, and saw every day the flowers appear in the earth . . .'. They were 'beyond the valley of the Shadow of Death, and also out of the reach of Giant Despair, neither could they from this place so much as see Doubting Castle. Here they were within sight of the city they were going to . . .'.

These references are part of Watts's Puritan inheritance, in which writers such as Milton and Bunyan show the soul in pilgrimage (Doubting Castle may have suggested the 'doubts' in verse 5): they blend with the Old Testament account of Moses, and the vision of the new Jerusalem in Revelation 21 and 22. But these ideas are also embodied in a metaphor from the local landscape: Watts's sight of the sweet fields and the living green is said to have been inspired by the view across Southampton Water. He loved clarity in speech and thought, and the beauty of the landscape on a fine day is a fitting emblem for a state of mind that he continually strove for, one in which all is bright and clear, as an emblem of Christian hope. In such a state of mind, a prospect of heaven makes death easy.

There are two tunes which are particularly associated with this hymn. The first is MENDIP, one of the English traditional melodies used by Ralph Vaughan Williams for the *English Hymnal*: it was collected by Cecil Sharp in Somerset in 1903, and given the Somerset name by Vaughan Williams. The other is BEULAH, used in the 1889 *Supplement* to the 1875 edition of *Hymns Ancient and Modern*: the name appropriately picks up the Bunyan reference.

68   We give immortal praise
                  To God the Father's love,
               For all our comforts here,
                  And better hopes above.
               He sent his own eternal Son
               To die for sins that man had done.

               To God the Son belongs
                  Immortal glory too,
               Who bought us with his blood
                  From everlasting woe:
               And now he lives, and now he reigns,
               And sees the fruit of all his pains.

               To God the Spirit's name
                  Immortal worship give,
               Whose new-creating power
                  Makes the dead sinner live:
               His work completes the great design,
               And fills the soul with joy divine.

               Almighty God, to thee
                  Be endless honours done,
               The undivided Three,
                  And the mysterious One:
               Where reason fails with all her powers,
               There faith prevails, and love adores.

                     Isaac Watts (1674–1748)

This great hymn of praise is from *Hymns and Spiritual Songs* (1709), the enlarged version of Watts's earlier book of the same title, published in 1707. It was entitled 'A Song of Praise to the Blessed Trinity', and is written in the traditional metre which the metrical psalmists used for Psalm 148— 6.6.6.6.44.44. This was a psalm which Watts greatly loved, with its repeated exhortation to praise the Lord for his goodness: here Watts gives the psalm a Christian content. As he said, he wished to make David and Asaph 'always speak the common sense of a Christian'. Originally the hymn began in the first person, with 'I give immortal praise': its transference to the plural makes it suitable for congregational singing, in a communal activity of praise. Other hymns of Watts, such as 'When I survey the wondrous cross', remain more private, and allow the individual singer to express his own devotion.

The alteration from 'I' to 'we' was made in the eighteenth century, probably by George Whitefield. It suits the character of the hymn, which is a general expression of worship, invoking God as Father, Son and Holy Spirit, and ending with a verse celebrating the Holy Trinity itself, the undivided Three and the mysterious One. 'Mysterious' is used very precisely here, to mean not only something which is hard to comprehend, but also (from its old meaning) something which is holy and awe-inspiring.

The tune is CROFT'S 136th, by William Croft (1678–1727), published in 1707, so that it is contemporary with Watts's hymn. It was called '136th' because it was originally set to that psalm in Henry Playford's *The Divine Companion, or David's Harp New Tun'd*. It later became closely associated with these words, and is sometimes called 'CROFT'S 148th' for that reason.

69   Nature with open volume stands
           To spread her Maker's praise abroad,
       And every labour of his hands
           Shows something worthy of a God.

       But in the grace that rescued man
           His brightest form of glory shines;
       Here on the cross 'tis fairest drawn
           In precious blood and crimson lines.

       Here his whole name appears complete;
           Nor wit can guess, nor reason prove,
       Which of the letters best is writ,
           The power, the wisdom, or the love.

       O the sweet wonders of that cross
           Where God the Saviour loved and died!
       Her noblest life my spirit draws
           From his dear wounds and bleeding side.

       I would for ever speak his name
           In sounds to mortal ears unknown,
       With angels join to praise the Lamb,
           And worship at his Father's throne.

                       Isaac Watts (1674–1748)

From *Hymns and Spiritual Songs* (1707), Book III, *Prepared for the Holy Ordinance of the Lord's Supper*, which suggests that this, like 'When I survey the wondrous cross', was intended as a hymn for Holy Communion. It was entitled 'Christ Crucify'd; The Wisdom and Power of God'. It is very characteristic of Watts's theology: the mind can learn much from nature (and modern science was one of Watts's delights), but the greatest truth is that of revealed religion in the person and death of Jesus Christ.

There was an original verse 4, which drew attention to the most difficult aspect of the Atonement, the idea that the Crucifixion shows God's vengeance as well as His grace:

> Here I behold his inmost heart
>   Where grace and vengeance strangely join,
> Piercing his Son with sharpest smart
>   To make the purchased pleasures mine.

The 'purchased pleasures' are those of the redeemed soul, but it is difficult to imagine God as piercing the heart of Jesus in vengeance for the Fall. It is a daring image to describe the wounds in the side of Christ, which do not just pierce His side but enter His heart. The verse has to be seen as part of the cosmic pattern which Watts is celebrating here: God can be found in nature, as the first verse indicates, but more wonderfully on the Cross, 'where God the Saviour loved and died'. Even as He pierces the heart of Christ, He is piercing His own heart. The complexity is considerable here, illustrated especially when the 'letters' (words) appear: as grace and vengeance 'strangely join', so now the reader looks at the words and cannot decide which is the most important ('best is writ'). Ordinary ways of reading collapse before the wonder of the crucified God. This is the most significant entry in the 'open volume' of nature, the crucified God/Christ, drawn in blood and crimson lines.

Watts may have remembered a verse from Richard Baxter's poem, 'The Resolution':

> The World's thy Book: There I can read
>   Thy Power, Wisdom, and thy Love:
> And thence ascend by Faith, and feed
>   Upon the better things above.

But Watts takes the argument further by making the Cross the centre of the book, its central and most memorable illustration.

The hymn has obvious affinities with 'When I survey the wondrous cross', but it concentrates more on the theology of the Atonement and less on the individual response to it. It is a brilliant development of the common 'book' metaphor for nature, the *liber naturae* in which God's power and love can be read. Here the world of nature itself has the Crucifixion as its central and pivotal moment. Erik Routley, who was probably responsible for reintroducing this hymn into modern use in *Congregational Praise* (1951), described it as 'the greatest of all hymns on the Atonement written since the Reformation' (*Hymns Today and Tomorrow*: 68).

There is no single tune which has become identified with these words, which is another reason why they are not so well known as those of 'When I survey'. *Congregational Praise* used ELTHAM, an eighteenth-century tune from Nathaniel Gawthorn's *Harmonia Perfecta* (1730); *Hymns and Psalms* uses NÜRNBERG, a melody by Bach, harmonized by John Wilson, or ELTHAM. *Rejoice and Sing* prints TUGWOOD, by Nicholas Gatty (1874–1946).

70   When I survey the wondrous cross,
           On which the Prince of Glory died,
        My richest gain I count but loss,
           And pour contempt on all my pride.

        Forbid it, Lord, that I should boast
           Save in the death of Christ my God;
        All the vain things that charm me most,
           I sacrifice them to his blood.

        See from his head, his hands, his feet,
           Sorrow and love flow mingled down;
        Did e'er such love and sorrow meet,
           Or thorns compose so rich a crown?

        His dying crimson, like a robe,
           Spreads o'er his body on the tree;
        Then am I dead to all the globe,
           And all the globe is dead to me.

        Were the whole realm of nature mine,
           That were a present far too small;
        Love so amazing, so divine,
           Demands my soul, my life, my all.

                    Isaac Watts (1674–1748)

From *Hymns and Spiritual Songs* (1707), Book III, *Prepared for the Holy Ordinance of Lord's Supper*, which indicates that, like 'Nature with open volume stands', it was a hymn for Holy Communion. It was entitled 'Crucifixion to the World by the Cross of Christ, Gal. vi. 14.' The verse of Galatians is: 'But God forbid that I should glory, save in the cross of our Lord Jesus Christ, by whom the world is crucified unto me, and I unto the world.'

Watts takes this text, and produces from it a profound meditation on the sufferings and death of Jesus Christ, discussing its effect on the individual believer. It is a very complex hymn, drawing on traditions of contemplative thought that go back to the Middle Ages, and which have affinities with Counter-Reformation theology, as found in the *Spiritual Exercises* of St Ignatius Loyola. St Ignatius exhorts his readers 'Represent to yourself Christ crucified', and that is precisely what Watts does. His tradition of Protestant thought and practice is subsumed into this more ancient and traditional mode of approaching the great mystery of the Passion.

The opening verse sounds assured, with its magisterial 'When I survey'; but the poise of that beginning quickly breaks down as the third line is reached, when gain becomes loss (an echo of Philippians 3: 8), and pride becomes a reason for contempt. It is as though the sight of the Crucifixion overwhelms the reader/singer, and forces a revision of his or her normal ways of seeing things. So, in the second verse, the only boast can be in the death of Christ, and all the vain things of this world are sacrificed.

The third verse redirects attention away from the self and back to the figure on the Cross: 'See . . .'. There are the two great features of the Crucifixion, sorrow and love, love and sorrow. The rhetorical figure is one of chiasmus, a crossing over in the manner of the Greek letter chi: it is found again in the great fourth verse, which takes up the idea from Galatians 6: 14:

> Then am I dead to all the globe,
> And all the globe is dead to me.

The reader or singer sees the vivid splash of colour, 'his dying crimson', spreading over the body of the crucified Christ, flowing down like the love and sorrow: the result is that the world ('the globe') now seems dead, of no account, and he/she seems to be no longer a part of it. But if the whole of the natural world were available, it would be too small a present for the one whose amazing love can only be requited with 'my soul, my life, my all'.

Such a summary of the meaning is an attempt to draw out the salient features of Watts's extraordinary verse. But it cannot capture the astonishing blend of emotion which this hymn produces in the reader or singer: the initial assurance giving way to a total surrender of the self and the world in the contemplation of divine love. The long metre lines carry this with dignity and splendour, usually in units of two lines, the second half of each verse answering or amplifying the first; while the chiasmus pattern ensures a movement of the mind between two things, love and sorrow, sorrow and love, the self and the globe, the globe and the self. These are part of the greater pattern which the hymn develops, the interaction between the self and the Cross, and the Cross and the self.

In the first edition of 1707, the second line was 'Where the young Prince of Glory died'. Watts changed this for the second edition of 1709, partly for metrical reasons (to avoid the stress on 'the' in the iambic metre), and partly because its spectacular vision of the Christ figure interferes with the strenuous simplicity of the remainder of the hymn. Throughout it is now a chaste, reflective, meditative work, rich with the decorum of its grave and simple lines. It demonstrates, in a particularly fine manner, Donald Davie's remarks about Calvinist worship, where 'art is measure, is exclusion; is therefore simplicity (hard-earned), is sobriety, tense with all the extravagances that it has been tempted by and has denied itself' (*A Gathered Church*: 25–6). Matthew Arnold, who sang this hymn at a service on the morning of his death, thought that 'When I survey' was the greatest hymn in the language.

The customary tune is ROCKINGHAM, a tune which is both lyrical and dignified, especially when taken at a steady pace. It was adapted by Edward Miller (1735–1807) from an eighteenth-century tune used in evangelical chapels to hymns in a different metre. It was printed by Miller in *The Psalms of David for the use of Parish Churches* (1790), and given the title 'Rockingham. L. M. Part of the Melody taken from a Hymn Tune'. The Marquis of Rockingham was Miller's friend and patron.

It was set to this hymn in *Hymns Ancient and Modern* (1861), and in some books before then. It has become the accepted tune, although the most recent edition of *Hymns Ancient and Modern, Common Praise* (2000) strikingly added the English traditional melody O WALY WALY as an alternative; and JOB, by the Methodist William Arnold (1768–1832), is used in some parts of the north of England. JOB is a plangent tune, which requires the first half of the fourth line of each verse to be repeated; it can be very effective ('And pour contempt . . . And pour contempt on all my pride').

71   Give me the wings of faith to rise
               Within the veil, and see
           The saints above, how great their joys,
               How bright their glories be.

           Once they were mourners here below,
               And poured out sighs and tears;
           They wrestled hard, as we do now,
               With sins, and doubts, and fears.

           I ask them whence their victory came;
               They, with united breath,
           Ascribe their conquest to the Lamb,
               Their triumph to his death.

           They marked the footsteps that he trod,
               His zeal inspired their breast;
           And, following their incarnate God,
               Possess the promised rest.

           Our glorious Leader claims our praise
               For his own pattern given;
           While the long cloud of witnesses
               Show the same path to heaven.

                        Isaac Watts (1674–1748)

This is from *Hymns and Spiritual Songs* (1709), entitled 'The Examples of Christ and the Saints'. It is a striking hymn from the very beginning, when the prayer for the 'wings of faith' is almost an imperative—'Give me'. Watts is (almost) demanding to be shown the joys and glories of heaven: this is in keeping with his most inspired and energetic poetry, in which he relishes the inspired and prophetic role of the poet. Alterations to 'Give us' weaken this intensity.

In this hymn, Watts hopes to penetrate the veil which hides heaven from our eyes. The image is from Hebrews 6: 19–20:

Which hope we have as an anchor of the soul, both sure and stedfast, and which entereth into that within the veil; Whither the forerunner is for us entered, even Jesus . . . .

Watts recognizes the hard lot of saints on this earth (in the original verse 2 'they were mourning here below,/ And wet their couch with tears'), but this earthly trouble leads to the great reward in heaven, as it does in Revelation 7: 14:

These are they which came out of great tribulation, and have washed their robes, and made them white in the blood of the Lamb.

These are the 'cloud of witnesses' (Hebrews 12: 1–2), which he finds so inspiring, and which leads him to reflect on their zeal and their trust in Christ. Watts's Puritan background (which included his father's imprisonment) is clearly seen in the pattern of Christian experience which underpins this hymn: tribulation, following in the footsteps of Christ, zeal, and triumph, are the elements of life which the hymn represents.

The metre is common metre, which allows the hymn to be sung to many tunes. The most frequently used ones seem to be SONG 67, from E. Prys's *Psalms* of 1621, and the springy MYLON, attributed to Johann Gottlieb Naumann (1741–1801). A modern tune, SAN ROCCO, by Derek Williams (born 1945) was composed for this hymn.

72   I sing the almighty power of God
                          That made the mountains rise,
                       That spread the flowing seas abroad,
                          And built the lofty skies.

                       I sing the wisdom that ordained
                          The sun to rule the day;
                       The moon shines full at his command,
                          And all the stars obey.

                       I sing the goodness of the Lord,
                          That filled the earth with food;
                       He formed the creatures with his word,
                          And then pronounced them good.

                       Lord, how thy wonders are displayed
                          Where'er I turn mine eye,
                       If I survey the ground I tread,
                          Or gaze upon the sky;

> There's not a plant or flower below
> But makes thy glories known,
> And clouds arise and tempests blow
> By order from thy throne.
>
> God's hand is my perpetual guard,
> He guides me with his eye;
> Why should I then forget the Lord,
> Whose love is ever nigh?

Isaac Watts (1674–1748)

This is the only hymn to have survived in common use from Watts's *Divine Songs Attempted in easy Language for the Use of Children*, published in 1715. It was entitled 'Praise for Creation and Providence'. Its survival is probably owing to its fine simplicity in its rendering of the created world, borrowing ideas and phrases from the account of creation in Genesis 1, and admiration from the psalms. The tempests of verse 5, for example, are from two of Watts's favourite psalms, 107 and 148—'stormy wind fulfilling his word', verse 8 (it was foolish of *Hymns and Psalms* to omit verse 5, on the grounds that some Christians do not like the idea of God sending tempests).

Watts's *Divine Songs* were once very popular, and they went through hundreds of editions. They present an image of the child as unnaturally good and pious, and they were recommended as suitable guidelines for children by generations of well-meaning adults. But they also work by fear, and encourage the child to repress natural instincts such as play. They contain threats of hell, even in this hymn, where the good child is made to sing (in verses that are now omitted):

> Creatures (as num'rous as they be)
> Are subject to thy care;
> There's not a place where we can flee
> But God is present there.
>
> In heaven he shines with beams of love,
> With wrath in hell beneath!
> 'Tis on his earth I stand or move,
> And 'tis his air I breathe.

The child's love for God here seems to be based on the fact that he or she is in debt to God, and also that he or she is unable to escape from Him.

Divine Songs contained such poems as 'How doth the little busy bee', and ''Tis the voice of the sluggard', which became famous through parody. William Blake's *Songs of Innocence and of Experience* (1789–94), with its emphasis on play and freedom, was the most famous and remarkable response to Watts's view of children.

This hymn, in its abbreviated form, shows the best side of Watts's book, and has become a simple response to the created world that allows both admiration and gratitude, together with an admonition not to forget God. It is the best kind of children's hymn, written with simplicity and also with dignity, so that it can be sung without embarrassment by adults.

Because this hymn is in common metre, it can be sung to many tunes. *Rejoice and Sing* uses two metrical psalm tunes of Scottish origin, MONTROSE and LONDON NEW; Methodist books use MONTROSE, but also ST SAVIOUR by F. G. Baker (1840–1919), named after a church in the Isle of Wight where he was organist.

73
> God is the refuge of his saints,
>   When storms of sharp distress invade;
> Ere we can offer our complaints,
>   Behold him present with his aid.
>
> Let mountains from their seats be hurled
>   Down to the deep, and buried there,
> Convulsions shake the solid world,
>   Our faith shall never yield to fear.
>
> Loud may the troubled ocean roar,
>   In sacred peace our souls abide;
> While every nation, every shore,
>   Trembles and dreads the swelling tide.
>
> There is a stream, whose gentle flow
>   Makes glad the city of our God,
> Life, love, and joy still gliding through,
>   And watering our divine abode.
>
> This sacred stream, thy vital word,
>   Thus all our raging fear controls;
> Sweet peace thy promises afford,
>   And give new strength to fainting souls.
>
> Zion enjoys her monarch's love,
>   Secure against the threatening hour;
> Nor can her firm foundation move,
>   Built on his faithfulness and power.

Isaac Watts (1674–1748)

From *The Psalms of David, Imitated in the Language of the New Testament* (1719), a metrical version of Psalm 46, first part, entitled 'The Church's Safety, and Triumph among national Desolations'. Watts thought that his versification of the psalms was his greatest achievement: he was proposing, he said, 'to accommodate the book of Psalms to Christian worship', and he wanted to make David and Asaph 'always speak the common sense of a

Christian'. His intention was revealed by the full title of the book, which continued '*And Applied to the Christian State and Worship*'.

It is interesting to compare this hymn with another version of Psalm 46, 'A safe stronghold our God is still' (no. 33), which uses the idea of a stronghold to emphasize the fight between Christ and the forces of evil (perhaps inspired by verse 6 of the psalm, 'The heathen raged . . .').

Watts's version is still a grand one, using the eight-syllabled long metre lines to create a sense of power, often by allowing the stressed syllables to fall on the important words:

> *God* is the *refuge* of his *saints*

But the significant alteration which he makes to the psalm is to give his own interpretation to verses 4 and 5 of the original:

There is a river, the streams whereof shall make glad the city of God, the holy place of the tabernacles of the most High;
God is in the midst of her; she shall not be moved: God shall help her, and that right early.

Watts turns this into a stream of 'life, love and joy', that turns out to be 'thy vital word', which controls fear. The promises of God give new strength, perhaps with the suggestion of the promise of the Messiah; certainly, life, love, and joy are all words which Watts associated with the New Testament, as in 'Joy to the world, the Lord is come'.

There is no generally accepted tune for this hymn, and perhaps for that reason it is not as well known as it should be. It did not appear, for example, in *Hymns Ancient and Modern* until *Common Praise* (2000), and it is not in the *English Hymnal*. *Common Praise* uses the same tunes as Methodist books, LASUS by Arthur Henry Mann (1850–1929) from the *Methodist Hymn Book*, and CANNOCK by Walter Stanton (1891–1978) from *Hymns and Psalms*. *Congregational Praise* used BOURTON by Eric Thiman (1900–75).

74   Jesus shall reign where'er the sun
                      Doth his successive journeys run;
                      His kingdom stretch from shore to shore
                      Till moons shall wax and wane no more.

                      For him shall endless prayer be made,
                      And praises throng to crown his head;
                      His name like sweet perfume shall rise
                      With every morning sacrifice.

                      People and realms of every tongue
                      Dwell on his love with sweetest song;
                      And infant voices shall proclaim
                      Their early blessings on his name.

                      Blessings abound where'er he reigns;
                      The prisoner leaps to lose his chains;
                      The weary find eternal rest,
                      And all the sons of want are blest.

                      Let every creature rise and bring
                      Peculiar honours to our King;
                      Angels descend with songs again,
                      And earth repeat the loud Amen.

                              Isaac Watts (1674–1748)

This is also from *The Psalms of David* (1719). This is Watts's version of Psalm 72: it shows very clearly his 'Christianizing' of the psalms. It was entitled 'Christ's Kingdom among the Gentiles', and transforms some of the verses from the psalm: 'They shall fear thee as long as the sun and moon endure, throughout all generations'; 'The kings of Tarshish and of the isles shall bring presents'. This is seen even more clearly in two verses which are normally omitted:

                      Behold the Islands with their kings,
                      And Europe her best tribute brings:
                      From North to South the princes meet
                      To pay their homage at his feet.

                      There Persia, glorious to behold,
                      There India shines in eastern gold,
                      And barbarous nations at his word
                      Submit and bow and own their Lord.

A further verse recalls Milton's *Paradise Lost*, with its portrayal of the Fall as a 'fortunate fall', because it was followed by the Redemption:

                      Where he displays his healing power,
                      Death and the curse are known no more;
                      In him the tribes of Adam boast
                      More blessings than their father lost.

The best-known tune for these words is the vigorous TRURO, an anonymous tune published in Thomas Williams's *Psalmodia Evangelica* (1789). It is also frequently sung to GALILEE, by Philip Armes (1836–1908), organist of Durham Cathedral, the tune set in the second edition of *Hymns Ancient and Modern* (1875).

75
O God, our help in ages past,
    Our hope for years to come,
Our shelter from the stormy blast,
    And our eternal home:

Under the shadow of thy throne
    Thy saints have dwelt secure;
Sufficient is thine arm alone,
    And our defence is sure.

Before the hills in order stood,
    Or earth received her frame,
From everlasting thou art God,
    To endless years the same.

A thousand ages in thy sight
    Are like an evening gone,
Short as the watch that ends the night
    Before the rising sun.

The busy tribes of flesh and blood,
    With all their cares and fears,
Are carried downward by the flood,
    And lost in following years.

Time, like an ever-rolling stream,
    Bears all its sons away;
They fly forgotten, as a dream
    Dies at the opening day.

O God, our help in ages past,
    Our hope for years to come,
Be thou our guard while troubles last,
    And our eternal home.

        Isaac Watts (1674–1748)

This is another hymn from *The Psalms of David* (1719), entitled 'Psalm 90 v. 1–5. First Part (C. M.)', with the subtitle 'Man frail, and God eternal'.

This is one of Watts's greatest hymns on the human condition, setting the shortness of life and the littleness of human beings against the timeless greatness of God, who was God before the hills, and who has been our help (in the past) and hope (in the future). The stress on '*our* help' was even stronger in the original version, which began 'Our God, our help'. This was the natural language for Watts, writing in the Puritan and Dissenting tradition, which saw God as the covenant God of a chosen people, so that He became 'our God', and the righteous became his 'saints', who in this hymn dwell secure under the shadow of His throne. To them, God is the 'eternal home', the place where the soul feels 'at home' and the place to return to, the permanent resting place as opposed to the unstable life of the busy tribes, who are swept away and lost in the swift movement of time.

'Our God' was altered to 'O God' by John Wesley, in his *Collection of Psalms and Hymns* of 1738, the first hymn-book which he published in Britain. The other principal change from Watts's original text is the customary omission of two verses:

> Thy word commands our flesh to dust,
>   'Return, ye sons of men':
> All nations rose from earth at first,
>   And turn to earth again . . . .
>
> Like flowery fields the nations stand
>   Pleas'd with the morning light;
> The flowers beneath the mower's hand
>   Lie withering e'er 'tis night.

As with another great hymn, 'Abide with me', the shortening has improved the final work. These verses, good though they are, weaken what Percy Dearmer, in *Songs of Praise Discussed*, referred to as 'the grandly sustained flow of thought' of this hymn. He quoted F. J. Gillman, in *The Evolution of the English Hymn*, writing of 'its simple strength, its transparency, its hold upon the common mind, its straightforwardness, its accentual and punctuative perfection, and its faithfulness to Scripture.' Gillman was right, especially in praising 'the accentual and punctuative perfection': Watts shows himself a master at using the common metre stanza and the evenly paced lines to reinforce the power of a statement such as 'Thy saints have dwelt secure' or the grandeur of

> Before the hills in order stood,
>   Or earth received her frame,

in which the stresses and pauses are exactly right to convey the sense of a cosmic solidity, which is only surpassed by the power of God Himself, 'from everlasting . . . to endless years the same'. Similarly, the transience of human beings is brilliantly evoked by the contrast between 'a thousand ages' and the homely image of 'an evening gone'.

This hymn has become a traditional part of Remembrance Day services, which is entirely appropriate; but it would be a pity if it became too closely identified with one great national occasion, because it deserves to be sung at many times and seasons. If the psalm itself is magnificent, these verses enhance it.

The tune to which it is always sung is ST ANNE, probably by William Croft (1678–1727), organist of Westminster Abbey, and at one time organist of St Anne's Church, Soho, from which the name is taken. It appeared anonymously in the sixth edition of *A Supplement to the New Version of Psalms by Dr Brady and Mr Tate*, published in 1708. It was set to these words in the first edition of *Hymns Ancient and Modern* (1861) by the musical editor, William Henry Monk, and it has proved to be an inspired setting, allowing the words to reverberate, and carrying the ideas with a steady pace and with great dignity.

76   I'll praise my Maker while I've breath,
      And when my voice is lost in death
          Praise shall employ my nobler powers:
      My days of praise shall ne'er be past
      While life, and thought, and being last,
          Or immortality endures.

      Happy the man whose hopes rely
      On Israel's God: he made the sky,
          And earth and seas, with all their train;
      His truth for ever stands secure;
      He saves th'oppressed, he feeds the poor,
          And none shall find his promise vain.

      The Lord pours eye-sight on the blind;
      The Lord supports the fainting mind;
          He send the labouring conscience peace:
      He helps the stranger in distress,
      The widow, and the fatherless,
          And grants the prisoner sweet release.

      I'll praise him while he lends me breath,
      And when my voice is lost in death
          Praise shall employ my nobler powers:
      My days of praise shall ne'er be past
      While life, and thought, and being last,
          Or immortality endures.

                    Isaac Watts (1674–1748)

From *The Psalms of David* (1719), on Psalm 146, entitled 'Praise to God for his Goodness and Truth'. The present version is Watts's original adapted by John Wesley: originally the first line read 'I'll praise my Maker with my breath', and there were two other stanzas which Wesley omitted when he printed the hymn in his first hymn-book, the Charlestown *Collection of Psalms and Hymns* of 1737. The first, the original verse 2, was one of those stanzas which expressed Watts's sense of human frailty:

> Why should I make a man my trust?
> Princes must die and turn to dust;
>   Vain is the help of flesh and blood:
> Their breath departs, their pomp and power,
> And thoughts all vanish in an hour,
>   Nor can they make their promise good.

After this, the present verse 2 forms a telling contrast:

> Happy the man whose hopes rely
> On Israel's God: . . .

The original verse 5 holds out a spectacular promise of judgement, and it is interesting that Watts sees this as another justification for praising God:

> He loves his saints; he knows them well,
> But turns the wicked down to hell;
>   Thy God, O Zion, ever reigns:
> Let every tongue, let every age,
> In this exalted work engage:
>   Praise him in everlasting strains.

The first of these verses expands verse 3 of the psalm: 'Put not your trust in princes, nor in the son of man, in whom there is no help.' The second one is from verse 9: 'but the way of the wicked he turneth upside down.' Watts's version 'turns' them, not just upside down, but down to hell.

In its shortened and less threatening form, this hymn was greatly loved by John Wesley, who died singing it.

The original printing of this psalm describes it as being 'As the 113th Psalm', in other words written to the metre of that psalm. In American and Canadian books it is sung to a tune by Matthäus Greiter (originally set to his paraphrase from Psalm 119) which was set to Psalm 113 in the Anglo-Genevan psalter, and so the tune came to be known as THE 113th PSALM TUNE. This is the tune which John Wesley is thought to have sung. British books tend to use a tune by a Swiss composer, Johann Schmidlin (1722–72), called variously DRESDEN or LUCERNE; or a rousing tune, MONMOUTH, by Gabriel Davis (died 1824), from his *Sacred Music* (*c*.1800), which is notable for the number of notes which are used for some syllables ('Or i -i-i-mmortality endures').

{5}

The Early Eighteenth Century

By the time of Watts's death in 1748, he had become famous: his influence is clearly seen in other nonconformist writers of the first half of the eighteenth century such as Philip Doddridge and Anne Steele. Steele's hymns, published under the name of 'Theodosia' ('gift of God') made her the first woman hymn-writer to be widely anthologized. Although her hymns are largely forgotten, 'Father of mercies, in thy word' survives in some books, and deserves to do so.

This was the age of science, the great period of the Royal Society, culminating in the work of Boyle and Newton. Newtonian physics was behind Addison's wonderful celebration of the sky in 'The spacious firmament on high'; and science, reason, and religion became important interrelated topics in the literature of the period. Reason was evidently wonderful, and the works of nature were thought to be clear evidence of the benevolence of God, but writers such as Swift and Pope satirized the misuse of reason and its tendency to encourage human pride.

In religious and Church matters, the intensity of the seventeenth century gave way to a broad and tolerant Christianity, sometimes called Latitudinarian: *The Spectator*, from which Addison's hymns came, was representative of a certain kind of religious and moral culture, reasonable, benevolent, and interested in science. The fact that this culture was also associated with an age of mercantile prosperity meant that there were social and political problems which were largely untouched, and it was this question which became the concern of the early Methodists.

The hymns of the period reflect a tolerance, a view of Divine Providence as benign, and a genuine encouragement to Christian believers on their journey: they include two of the great hymns on Christian festivals, 'Jesus Christ is risen today', and John Byrom's jolly 'Christians, awake, salute the happy morn', together with one of the great hymns for Advent, Doddridge's 'Hark the glad sound! the Saviour comes'.

77   *Surrexit Christus hodie*

Jesus Christ is risen today, *Alleluia.*
Our triumphant holy day, *Alleluia.*
Who did once, upon the cross, *Alleluia.*
Suffer to redeem our loss: *Alleluia.*

Hymns of praise then let us sing, *Alleluia.*
Unto Christ, our heavenly King, *Alleluia.*
Who endured the cross and grave, *Alleluia.*
Sinners to redeem and save: *Alleluia.*

But the pains which he endured, *Alleluia.*
Our salvation have procured, *Alleluia.*
Now above the sky he's King, *Alleluia.*
Where the angels ever sing: *Alleluia.*

Lyra Davidica (1708), and other books

This hymn could have appeared under 'Ancient and Medieval Hymns', but it is printed here because it was one of the first of them to appear in a post-Reformation hymn-book. This text, by an unknown translator, is from an anonymous Latin hymn, 'De Resurrectione Domini', found in a Munich manuscript of the fourteenth century, and in a Breslau manuscript of the fifteenth century. The first English version appeared in *Lyra Davidica, or a Collection of Divine Songs and Hymns, partly new composed, partly translated from the High German and Latin Hymns; and set to easy and pleasant tunes.* London: J. Walsh, 1708. The Latin version began:

Surrexit Christus hodie
Humano pro solamine.
Alleluia.

Two of the verses (one in the Breslau MS only) were:

Mulieres o tremulae
In Galilaeam pergite!

Discipulis hoc dicite,
Quod surrexit rex gloriae.

This becomes in 1708:

Haste ye females from your fright
Take to Galilee your flight
To his sad disciples say
Jesus Christ is risen to day.

The 1708 text was altered in John Arnold's *Compleat Psalmodist* of 1749, where verses 2 and 3 have no reference to the Latin original, and are close to the present text. Even closer (the exception is 'hath' for the modern 'have' in verse 3) is the printing in a Supplement of 1816 to Tate and Brady's *A New Version of the Psalms of David.*

The three verses have sometimes had a doxology added to make a fourth; but the florid 'Alleluias' at the end of each line make a much longer hymn to sing than appears on the page. In the form given above, it has become a necessary part of Easter Day services in many churches, especially in the Church of England (Methodist and United Reformed Church books use Charles Wesley's more complex and allusive 'Christ the Lord is risen today', sung to the same tune). Its simplicity of idea and expression makes it instantly accessible, and the contrast between the credal statement of each line and the resounding 'Alleluia' which follows is very effective. As Wesley Milgate points out (*Songs of the People of God*: 124), the medieval church forbade the use of 'Alleluia' from the Saturday before Septuagesima until Easter; the continued repetition in this hymn is thus a powerful expression of joy at the Resurrection.

Archibald Jacob, in *Songs of Praise Discussed*, described the tune, EASTER HYMN, as 'one of the most famous of all hymn-tunes'. It appeared in *Lyra Davidica* in 1708; the composer is unknown. Jacob remarked 'the prevalent rising movement throughout', and continued: 'The melody fully bears out the remark in the preface to the above book [*Lyra Davidica*], "there is a desire for a little freer air than the grand movement of the psalm-tunes." '. Milgate (p. 125) notes that the 'Alleluias' after the third and fourth lines are begun on notes successively higher than the first setting of the word, 'since each repetition of the *Alleluia* in the medieval Easter vigil was a tone higher than the one preceding'.

78

The Lord my pasture shall prepare,
And feed me with a shepherd's care:
His presence shall my wants supply,
And guard me with a watchful eye;
My noon-day walks he shall attend,
And all my midnight hours defend.

When in the sultry glebe I faint,
Or on the thirsty mountain pant,
To fertile vales and dewy meads
My weary wandering steps he leads;
Where peaceful rivers, soft and slow,
Amid the verdant landscape flow.

Though in a bare and rugged way,
Through devious lonely wilds I stray,
Thy bounty shall my pains beguile;
The barren wilderness shall smile
With sudden greens and herbage crowned,
And streams shall murmur all around.

Though in the paths of death I tread,
With gloomy horrors over-spread,
My steadfast heart shall fear no ill,
For thou, O Lord, art with me still;
Thy friendly crook shall give me aid,
And guide me through the dreadful shade.

Joseph Addison (1672–1719)

This stately paraphrase of Psalm 23 is found in *The Spectator*, No. 441, Saturday, 26 July 1712. The essay begins 'Man, considered in himself, is a very helpless and a very wretched Being', but it goes on to qualify this bleak assessment of human life: 'At the same time that he reflects upon his own Weakness and Imperfection, he comforts himself with the Contemplation of those Divine Attributes, which are employed for his Safety and his Welfare.' Addison is advocating a trust in God, and reflects that 'David has very beautifully represented this steady Reliance on God Almighty in his twenty-third Psalm, which is a kind of Pastoral Hymn, and filled with those Allusions which are usual in that kind of writing.' The essay concludes with the psalm itself, in this rendering.

Addison notes the 'steady Reliance' on God, and one of the most remarkable features of this version is its unhurried and steady metre, which conveys the sense of trust and tranquillity. The 'pastoral' note which Addison had observed is found in the original psalm, with 'The Lord is my shepherd', but here the idea is sustained throughout the hymn: as sheep need pasture and guidance, so the shepherd ('pastor') with his crook will guard and keep him, even in 'the Paths of Death'; and the 'goodness and mercy' of the psalm becomes 'bounty', as the wilderness is made green and watered (perhaps from Isaiah 35).

Addison has transposed the psalm into an eighteenth-century mode: this paraphrase is one in which the good landscape is that of peaceful rivers and fertile vales, much like the paintings of Claude Lorrain which were so popular at the time. The uncomfortable landscape is that of the thirsty mountain and the bare and rugged ways: wildness, later so prized by poets and artists, is for Addison something to be avoided. His idea of God's loving care is to be set down in a green place, with streams that murmur all around (not unlike the river walks of his college at Oxford, Magdalen).

It is interesting to compare the language of this paraphrase, with words such as 'pasture', and its 'noon-day walks', with George Herbert's simpler 'The God of love my shepherd is'. Addison's diction is urbane and dignified, part of the way in which this rendering of the twenty-third Psalm becomes a delight in its calm precision. It is simple, with rhymes that give a feeling of assurance, and with a decorum that is sustained from the first verse to the last.

The usual tune is SURREY, by Henry Carey (1687–1743), which was composed for these words, and published *c.*1723 in John Church's *An Introduction to Psalmody* with the words 'Psalm the 23rd, Paraphrased by Mr. Addison, set to Musick by Mr. Henry Carey'. It has remained as the tune since that time: it succeeds very well in capturing the steadiness and balance of the text.

79
    When all thy mercies, O my God,
      My rising soul surveys,
    Transported with the view, I'm lost
      In wonder, love, and praise.

    Unnumbered comforts to my soul
      Thy tender care bestowed,
    Before my infant heart conceived
      From whom those comforts flowed.

    When in the slippery paths of youth
      With heedless steps I ran,
    Thine arm unseen conveyed me safe
      And led me up to man.

    Through hidden dangers, toils, and deaths,
      It gently cleared my way,
    And through the pleasing snares of vice,
      More to be feared than they.

    When worn with sickness oft hast thou
      With health renewed my face,
    And when in sins and sorrows sunk
      Revived my soul with grace.

    Ten thousand thousand precious gifts
      My daily thanks employ,
    Nor is the least a thankful heart,
      That tastes those gifts with joy.

    Through every period of my life
      Thy goodness I'll pursue,
    And after death in distant worlds
      The glorious theme renew.

    Through all eternity to thee
      A joyful song I'll raise;
    For oh! eternity's too short
      To utter all thy praise.

             Joseph Addison (1672–1719)

This hymn is from *The Spectator*, No. 453, Saturday, 9 August 1712, after an essay which begins 'There is not a more pleasing Exercise of the Mind than Gratitude'. Addison discusses examples of gratitude in pagan worship, and in the Old Testament, where 'The Jews . . . have set the Christian World an Example how they ought to employ this Divine Talent of which I am speaking.' The principal theme of the discourse is summed up in the first sentence of the second paragraph: 'If Gratitude is due from Man to Man, how much more from Man to his Maker?'

The hymn which follows has thirteen verses. Selections have been made from them in various ways, and the eight verses above are rarely found together in one book, although the first two and the last two verses are common to most. It was a popular hymn in collections of the eighteenth century: John Wesley included some verses, much altered, in his first hymnbook, the Charlestown *Collection of Psalms and Hymns* (1737).

The first verse employs the metaphor of climbing a hill to see a 'prospect', in this case the spectacle of God's merciful guidance and blessing. Addison 'surveys' the landscape of his life, and is lost 'in wonder, love, and praise' (Charles Wesley thought highly enough of this line to borrow it, bringing 'lost' to the beginning of the line, in 'Love divine, all loves excelling'). Addison recalls (in a verse usually omitted) the providence of God

> When in the silent Womb I lay
> And hung upon the Breast

and (in verses 2 and 3 above) he remembers infancy and youth, where the 'slippery paths' are especially memorable. As a response, he undertakes to 'pursue' the goodness of God through every period of his life, and through eternity too: the end of the hymn borrows the witty idea from George Herbert ('King of glory, king of peace') that eternity will be too short for the praise and thanks which are due to God.

A tune often used for these words is BELGRAVE, by William Horsley (1774–1858), organist of Belgrave Chapel, London, and composer of the tune to 'There is a green hill far away'. Others include CONTEMPLATION, by Sir Frederick Arthur Gore Ouseley (1825–89), written for these words and used in the 1889 *Supplement* to the second edition of *Hymns Ancient and Modern* (1875); and HARINGTON, by Henry Harington (1727–1816), well known in Scotland as a tune for Psalm 84 'How lovely is thy dwelling place'.

80   The spacious firmament on high,
      With all the blue ethereal sky,
          And spangled heavens, a shining frame,
          Their great Original proclaim.
      The unwearied sun, from day to day,
      Does his Creator's power display,
          And publishes to every land
          The work of an almighty hand.

      Soon as the evening shades prevail,
      The moon takes up the wondrous tale,
          And nightly to the listening earth
          Repeats the story of her birth;
      Whilst all the stars that round her burn,
      And all the planets in their turn,
          Confirm the tidings as they roll,
          And spread the truth from pole to pole.

      What though in solemn silence all
      Move round the dark terrestrial ball;
          What though nor real voice nor sound
          Amid their radiant orbs be found:
      In reason's ear they all rejoice,
      And utter forth a glorious voice,
          For ever singing as they shine,
          'The hand that made us is divine.'

                Joseph Addison (1672–1719)

This hymn is found in *The Spectator*, No. 465, Saturday, 23 August 1712. It concludes a discussion on strengthening and confirming faith. Addison recommends a number of practices, including 'an habitual Adoration of the Supreme Being, as well in constant Acts of Mental Worship, as in outward Forms', and 'Frequent Retirement from the World, accompanied with religious Meditation'. Those who take time to attend to religious matters, he argues, will be impressed by the way in which the world has been created: the 'Supreme Being'

has made the best Arguments for his own Existence, in the Formation of the Heavens and the Earth, and these are arguments which a Man of Sense cannot forbear attending to, who is out of the Noise and Hurry of Human Affairs.

The essay then quotes the first four verses of Psalm 19, in the version from the *Book of Common Prayer* ('The Heavens declare the glory of God: And the Firmament sheweth his handy Work'), followed by the 'Ode', as Addison calls it.

Although first published in a periodical as an Ode, this text was rapidly taken over and used as a hymn. It appeared in many anthologies and compilations of the eighteenth century, and continued to be popular thereafter.

It is perhaps the greatest hymn of an age of Newtonian mathematics and physics (the *Opticks* had been published in 1704, and the *Arithmetica Universalis* in 1707). It is significant, therefore, that Addison can claim that 'In reason's ear' the planets all rejoice: he lived in an age which discovered the workings of creation and attributed them to God.

The certainty of the age is demonstrated in the unhurried majesty of the lines, beginning with the astonishing words 'spacious' and 'firmament', which mean 'the firmament of space' (in which Newton discovered the movement of the planets) but also suggests 'spacious space', a magnificent part of the divine creation which contains the sun, the stars, and the circling planets. The planets, says Addison, do not really sing: they move in solemn silence. But that movement is itself a proclamation of the Creator's power, and thus (in its way) a 'song' to those who listen with the ears of reason. Science and religion join in worship, in the celebration of 'the work of an almighty hand'.

The principal tune is called LONDON, or sometimes KETTERING or ADDISON'S (the last in *Songs of Praise*). It is by John Sheeles (1688–1761), and was published in 1740. More recently Walford Davies (1869–1941) wrote FIRMAMENT for these words, which has since become widely accepted. However, the metre allows any suitable long metre tune to be used, and Benjamin Britten produced a dramatic effect by setting this hymn to TALLIS' CANON at the end of *Noye's Fludde*.

81   Hark the glad sound! the Saviour comes,
           The Saviour promised long;
       Let every heart prepare a throne,
           And every voice a song.

       He comes the prisoners to release,
           In Satan's bondage held;
       The gates of brass before him burst,
           The iron fetters yield.

       He comes the broken heart to bind,
           The bleeding soul to cure,
       And with the treasures of his grace
           To enrich the humble poor.

       Our glad hosannas, Prince of Peace,
           Thy welcome shall proclaim,
       And heaven's eternal arches ring
           With thy beloved name.

                   Philip Doddridge (1702–51)

These are four verses from a seven-verse hymn in Doddridge's *Hymns founded on Various Texts in the Holy Scriptures* (1755) published after his death by his friend Job Orton. It was entitled 'Christ's message. Luke iv. 18, 19'. It is dated in the manuscript 28 December 1735.

The passage to which Doddridge was referring concerns the preaching of Christ in the synagogues of Galilee: 'The Spirit of the Lord is upon me, because he hath anointed me to preach the gospel to the poor; he hath sent me to heal the broken-hearted, to preach deliverance to the captives, and recovering of sight to the blind, to set at liberty them that are bruised, to preach the acceptable year of the Lord.'

This text is even more comprehensively illustrated by the verses (2, 4, 6) which are customarily omitted. The first is a fine description of Christ the inspired preacher:

> On him the Spirit largely pour'd
> Exerts its sacred Fire;
> Wisdom and Might, and Zeal and Love
> His holy Breast inspire.

The second (verse 4 of the original) uses sight and blindness both metaphorically and literally:

> He comes from the thick Films of Vice
> To clear the mental Ray,
> And on the Eye-Balls of the Blind
> To pour celestial Day.

Verse 6 of the original is concerned with the last phrase of the Biblical text, 'the acceptable year of the Lord':

> His Silver Trumpets publish loud
> The Jub'lee of the Lord;
> Our Debts are all remitted now,
> Our Heritage restor'd.

A note to the second line directs attention to Leviticus 25 (God addressing Moses), which calculates seven times seven years from the arrival in Canaan, and proclaims the following fiftieth year as the year of jubilee.

The hymn was also influenced by Alexander Pope's Sacred Eclogue, *Messiah* (1712), which was itself based on passages from Isaiah and on Virgil's Fourth Eclogue, especially lines 29–30, 37–40:

> Hark! a glad voice the lonely desart chears;
> Prepare the way! a God, a God appears: . . .
> The Saviour comes! by ancient bards foretold:
> Hear him, ye deaf, and all ye blind, behold!
> He from thick films shall purge the visual ray,
> And on the sightless eye-ball pour the day: . . .

This hymn is almost exclusively used during Advent, even though *Songs of Praise* prints a hopeful note 'Other occasions also'. It shows a very skilful use of the common metre stanza, with the two halves of each verse balancing each other, and sometimes a neat parallelism within the half-verse.

In the Scottish tradition it was considerably altered by William Cameron for the *Translations and Paraphrases* of 1781, after which it became very popular. Julian's *Dictionary of Hymnology* quotes Lord Selborne in the *York Church Congress Report* of 1866 as saying 'a more sweet, vigorous, and perfect composition is not to be found even in the whole body of ancient hymns.'

The hymn is usually sung to BRISTOL, from Thomas Ravenscroft's *Whole Booke of Psalmes* of 1621. It was set to this tune in *Hymns Ancient and Modern* (1861), and has remained associated with it since that time; in the Canadian book, *Voices United*, however, it is set to RICHMOND.

82   O God of Bethel, by whose hand
                        Thy people still are fed,
                    Who through this weary pilgrimage
                        Hast all our fathers led:

                    Our vows, our prayers, we now present
                        Before thy throne of grace;
                    God of our fathers, be the God
                        Of their succeeding race.

                    Through each perplexing path of life
                        Our wandering footsteps guide;
                    Give us each day our daily bread,
                        And raiment fit provide.

                    O spread thy covering wings around,
                        Till all our wanderings cease,
                    And at our father's loved abode
                        Our souls arrive in peace.

                        Philip Doddridge (1702–51)

This is part of a five-verse hymn, beginning 'O God of Jacob, by whose hand', published in Doddridge's *Hymns founded on Various Texts in the Holy Scriptures* (1755). Doddridge first wrote 'O God of Bethel' in the manuscript, dated 1736 or 1737, and this has always been preferred to Orton's amended version. It was entitled 'Jacob's Vow: from Genesis 28: 20–22'.

In its original form, the hymn is a revealing exercise in Puritan Covenant theology. Doddridge's last three verses make a bargain with God—if He will preserve and protect us, then we will make Him our God:

If thou thro' each perplexing Path
  Wilt be our constant Guide;
If thou wilt daily Bread supply
  And Raiment wilt provide;

If thou wilt spread thy Shield around
  Till these our Wand'rings cease,
And at our Father's lov'd Abode
  Our Souls arrive in Peace:

To thee as to our Covenant-God
  We'll our whole selves resign;
And count that not our Tenth alone,
  But all we have is Thine.

Early in its life the hymn was taken into the Scottish tradition, and it was then much altered for the *Scottish Translations and Paraphrases* of 1781. The Scottish version became widely known and very popular: it was frequently used, for example, in the celebrations in 1960 to mark the four-hundredth anniversary of the Reformation in Scotland.

The alterations include the provision of the present verse 2, which nicely links the present-day pilgrimage with the tradition of those who have trod the same path before. In Scotland, with the example of the Covenanters and of the persecuted church (whose emblem is a burning bush, with the motto *Nec tamen consumebatur*, 'And yet it was not consumed'), such a link with history forms a powerful element of the hymn. That power contrasts well with the simplicity and humility of the prayer for guidance and preservation.

There are several good tunes to this hymn. The one which is usually set is SALZBURG, by Johann Michael Haydn (1737–1806), younger brother of the great composer, and organist of the cathedral at Salzburg. In the Scottish church it is often sung to ST PAUL (ABERDEEN), and *Hymns Ancient and Modern* uses MARTYRDOM. All are familiar tunes for these words.

83   See Israel's gentle shepherd stand
            With all-engaging charms;
          Hark how he calls the tender lambs,
            And folds them in his arms!

          Permit them to approach, he cries,
            Nor scorn their humble name;
          For 'twas to bless such souls as these
            The Lord of Angels came.

          We bring them, Lord, in thankful hands,
            And yield them up to thee;
          Joyful that we ourselves are thine,
            Thine let our children be.

                    Philip Doddridge (1702–51)

This is a three-verse abbreviation of a hymn in five verses, entitled 'Christ's condescending Regard to little Children: Mark 10: 14', from Doddridge's *Hymns founded on Various Texts in the Holy Scriptures* (1755). It originally finished as follows (beginning halfway through verse 3):

          Joyful that we ourselves are thine,
            Thine let our offspring be.

          Ye little flock, with pleasure hear;
            Ye children, seek his face;
          And fly with transport to receive
            The blessings of his grace.

          If orphans they are left behind,
            Thy guardian care we trust,
          That care shall heal our bleeding hearts,
            While weeping o'er their dust.

These last two verses are better omitted, for they oscillate between addressing the children, thinking about the fate of orphans, and (rather suddenly) reflecting on infant mortality. The three verses which are preserved make a neat and quietly reflective hymn, very suitable for expressing the responsible role of parents or godparents at the Sacrament of Baptism, while also emphasizing the tenderness of the occasion. The originating quotation from St Mark's Gospel contains the words 'Suffer the little children to come unto me, and forbid them not: for of such is the kingdom of God.'

Doddridge uses this verse together with the image of Christ as the good shepherd, whose 'charms' are 'all engaging': this may be an echo of a beautiful paragraph by Bishop Berkeley, in which he writes (in a *Guardian* essay of 1713) of 'Virtue', which 'has in herself the most engaging charms':

and Christianity, as it places her in the strongest light, and adorned with all her native attractions, so it kindles a new fire in the soul, by adding to them the unutterable rewards which attend her votaries in an eternal state.

Berkeley's essay, which is entitled 'Happiness obstructed by Free-Thinkers', was an attack on scepticism: his emphasis on the happiness to be found in the practice of virtue and religion is one which looks forward to Doddridge's sweet-tempered hymns.

The usual tune for these words is DUBLIN, attributed to John Andrew Stevenson (who lived there), and published in 1825. It can also be sung to BELMONT, from William Gardiner's *Sacred Melodies*, volume 1 (1812).

84
Ye servants of the Lord,
Each in his office wait,
Observant of his heavenly word,
And watchful at his gate.

Let all your lamps be bright,
And trim the golden flame;
Gird up your loins as in his sight,
For awful is his name.

Watch! 'tis your Lord's command,
And while we speak, he's near;
Mark the first signal of his hand,
And ready all appear.

O happy servant he,
In such a posture found!
He shall his Lord with rapture see,
And be with honour crowned.

Christ shall the banquet spread
With his own royal hand,
And raise that faithful servant's head
Amidst the angelic band.

Philip Doddridge (1702–51)

From *Hymns founded on Various Texts in the Holy Scriptures* (1755). It was entitled 'The active Christian, Luke 12: 35–38'. Originally the penultimate line was 'And raise that fav'rite servant's head', but the emendation is justified.

The verses from Luke 12 exhort the Christian to 'let your loins be girded about, and your lights burning'. They are like good servants, whom the Lord finds watching when he returns, 'that when he cometh and knocketh, they may open unto him immediately'. The spreading of the banquet comes from verse 37, which describes the master rewarding his faithful servants: 'he shall gird himself, and make them to sit down to meat, and will come forth and serve them.' It makes the hymn suitable for Holy Communion, as well as for Advent.

Its crisp and economical style is characteristic of Doddridge, who was an admirer of Racine and the French neoclassical style; it is also typical of his encouraging treatment of the gospel. Doddridge never threatens: he holds out the promise of reward for good service and faithful loyalty.

The tune is usually either ST MICHAEL, also called the OLD 134th, from its origin in the Genevan Psalter of 1551, or NARENZA, adapted by William Henry Havergal (1793–1870, father of Frances Ridley Havergal) from a sixteenth-century German Catholic tune, and used in *Hymns Ancient and Modern*.

85   Christians, awake, salute the happy morn
             Whereon the Saviour of the world was born;
             Rise to adore the mystery of love,
             Which hosts of angels chanted from above;
             With them the joyful tidings first begun
             Of God incarnate and the virgin's son.

             Then to the watchful shepherds it was told,
             Who heard the angelic herald's voice, 'Behold,
             I bring good tidings of a Saviour's birth
             To you and all the nations of the earth;
             This day hath God fulfilled his promised word,
             This day is born a Saviour, Christ the Lord.'

             He spake; and straightway the celestial choir
             In hymns of joy, unknown before, conspire.
             The praises of redeeming love they sang,
             And heaven's whole orb with alleluias rang;
             God's highest glory was their anthem still,
             Peace upon earth, and unto men goodwill.

             To Bethlehem straight the enlightened shepherds ran,
             To see the wonder God had wrought for man:
             Then to their flocks, still praising God, return,
             And their glad hearts with holy rapture burn;
             Amazed, the wondrous tidings they proclaim,
             The first apostles of his infant fame.

             Like Mary, let us ponder in our mind
             God's wondrous love in saving lost mankind;
             Trace we the babe, who hath retrieved our loss,
             From his poor manger to his bitter cross;
             Tread in his steps, assisted by his grace,
             Till man's first heavenly state again takes place.

Then may we hope, the angelic hosts among,
To sing, redeemed, a glad triumphal song;
He that was born upon this joyful day
Around us all his glory shall display;
Saved by his love, incessant we shall sing
Eternal praise to heaven's almighty king.

John Byrom (1692–1763)

This hymn was written in 1749 as a poem of three paragraphs (of 16, 20, and 16 lines). It was first published, in a version of 48 lines, in Byrom's *Miscellaneous Poems* (1773). This text may be found in *The New Oxford Book of Christian Verse*, edited by Donald Davie (1981). There have been many variations from the original wording in different hymn-books.

Byrom wrote the poem as a Christmas present for his daughter Dolly, and gave it to her on Christmas Day, 1749, headed 'Christmas Day. For Dolly' (the manuscript may still be seen at Chetham's Library in Byrom's native city of Manchester). Its division into six-line verses was owing to the tune, which was written for these words by John Wainwright, organist of Byrom's parish church at Stockport, and played at Byrom's house on the following Christmas morning, 1750. It was printed in the six-line form in Thomas Cotterill's *Selection of Psalms and Hymns* (8th edition, 1819). Cotterill, a Sheffield clergyman, was helped in this selection by the poet and hymn-writer James Montgomery, who may have drawn Cotterill's attention to it.

This is a magnificent hymn for Christmas morning, not used as much as it should be, perhaps because congregations are used to shorter and less demanding texts. Wesley Milgate, in *Songs of the People of God*, remarks that 'even assisted by the exhilaration of Christmas morning, the average congregation might find a hymn of this scope as much as it can comfortably render.'

It is based on the account of the angels and the shepherds, and the final touching reference to Mary, in Luke 2: 1–20. It also echoes, naturally enough, Milton's 'On the Morning of Christ's Nativity', which has the same phrase in the first line, 'happy morn', and goes on to observe that

The Babe lies yet in smiling Infancy,
That on the bitter cross
Must redeem our loss;
So both himself and us to glorifie: (151–4)

Byrom's inclusion of these phrases is evidence of his debt to Milton, but the hymn is strongly Byrom's own, given an eighteenth-century 'feel' by its use of heroic couplets and by its formal and precise diction. It is the story of the Incarnation shaped into couplets; and the line 'To Bethlehem straight the enlightened shepherds ran' is strikingly concerned (as poets such as Pope and scientists such as Newton were) with light and with 'illumination'. It is interesting as showing the word 'enlightened' before 'the Enlightenment' became a word for the philosophical character of the eighteenth century itself. Here it is only one example of a sustained dignity and controlled enthusiasm which are delightfully present in this hymn.

The tune is YORKSHIRE, by John Wainwright (1723–68), written and played as described above. It was first printed in Caleb Ashworth's *Collection of Tunes* (c.1760), with the name MORTRAM (it has since been given other names, including the more appropriate STOCKPORT). Archibald Jacob, in *Songs of Praise Discussed*, described it as 'this splendid tune . . . The prevalent movement of the melody is upward, expressing the festive spirit of the words, but there is sufficient downward motion, partially in the 4th and wholly in the 5th, to act as a counterpoise, and, by its position, to emphasize the joyous reascent of the final line.' In Wainwright's own *Collection of Psalm Tunes, Anthems, Hymns and Chants* (1766) the last line was headed 'Chorus': the last line is then repeated as a refrain (as still happens in some parts of Yorkshire and Lancashire).

86   Father of mercies, in thy word,
    What endless glory shines!
For ever be thy name adored
    For these celestial lines.

Here may the blind and hungry come,
    And light and food receive;
Here shall the meanest guest have room,
    And taste and see and live.

Here may the wretched sons of want
    Exhaustless riches find;
Riches, above what earth can grant,
    And lasting as the mind.

Here the fair tree of knowledge grows,
    And yields a free repast;
Sublimer sweets than nature knows
    Invite the longing taste.

Here the Redeemer's welcome voice
    Spreads heavenly peace around;
And life and everlasting joys
    Attend the blissful sound.

O may these heavenly pages be
    My ever dear delight,
And still new beauties may I see,
    And still increasing light.

Divine instructor, gracious Lord,
Be thou for ever near;
Teach me to love thy sacred word,
And view my Saviour there.

Anne Steele (1717–78)

This hymn on the Holy Scriptures (originally in twelve verses) was first published in Anne Steele's *Poems on Subjects Chiefly Devotional* (1760), in which her name appeared as 'Theodosia' ('gift of God'). As 'Theodosia', she became widely known in the eighteenth century as a Baptist hymn-writer, especially after 1769, when she was introduced to a wider public by Caleb Evans, Baptist minister and hymnologist. The fourth edition of J. Ash and C. Evans's *A Collection of Hymns adapted to Public Worship* (1769), contained no fewer than 62 hymns by 'T' (for 'Theodosia').

Anne Steele was not the first woman hymn-writer, but she was the first to become widely known. Her life, which was otherwise uneventful, had a deeply tragic episode when her fiancé was drowned on the morning of her wedding: her suffering is reflected in the titles of some of her hymns, such as 'Desiring a cheerful resignation to the Divine Will', and 'The Presence of God the only comfort in affliction'. She became a prototype of the hymn-writing woman, living a quiet life and enduring sorrow: her example was followed by many nineteenth-century woman hymn-writers. As the writer of a book entitled *Lady Hymn Writers*, published in 1892, put it, 'a quiet life suited her best'.

This is the only hymn by Anne Steele which has survived (in a modernized form) into the present-day *Baptist Praise and Worship* (1991). Other hymn-books have allowed it to fall out of use: this is a pity, because it is a very good hymn of gratitude for the treasures of Holy Scripture, expressed in terms of riches, food, sound, and light.

One tune associated with these words is ANGMERING, by C. H. H. Parry, which dates from 1902; an alternative is TILTEY ABBEY, by A. H. Brown (1830–1926), a reflective and beautiful tune, which climbs high in the third line, and descends gently at the end. Another is SOUTHWELL, by H. S. Irons (1834–1905).

{6}

Charles Wesley

Into the Latitudinarian calm of the Church of England in the early eighteenth century came two serious-minded young clergymen, John and Charles Wesley. Their conduct at Oxford as members of the Holy Club, and their disciplined mode of living, led to their being called 'Methodists': and from 1738 onwards, John and Charles Wesley preached through the whole of Britain, often facing dangerous mobs and rented rioters. John presided over what was, in effect, the beginning of a new church in 1784; Charles never left the Church of England. John left behind his journals and sermons, and the memory of him as the father of his people; Charles left behind an astonishing body of hymns.

John Wesley came to know the power of hymns during his voyage to Georgia in 1735, when his fellow-passengers were hymn-singing Moravians. With characteristic eagerness, Wesley learnt German from their hymns, and produced his own book, *A Collection of Psalms and Hymns*, in Charlestown in 1737. After the failure of his mission to Georgia, he returned to England, and, with his brother, produced many hymn-books between 1738 and 1780, when the 'Large Hymn Book', *A Collection of Hymns for the Use of the People called Methodists*, was published.

John Wesley made some fine translations from the German; Charles wrote almost all the English ones. His output was extraordinary: even now, no one is quite sure how many hymns he wrote. His enthusiasm permeates every verse: it is controlled by a craftsmanship which came from his classical education, and by a natural poetic skill. Again and again a line or a verse of Charles Wesley's hymns seems to be exactly right, to say what it wants to say with a richness of vocabulary and an economy of diction that are instantly recognizable as the work of a master.

His first hymn, written on his conversion on 21 May 1738 (three days before his brother John's) began 'Where shall my won'dring soul begin?' It is the same question that was asked by Samuel Crossman and John Mason— 'what may I say?' And it is almost as if the rest of Charles Wesley's hymn-writing life was spent in trying to find the words to say what he wanted to say about what his brother called 'experimental and practical divinity'—a faith that is based on experience and on practice rather than on theory. The result is a vast body of work, with some masterpieces, wide-ranging, superbly written, and filled with energy and life.

87 And can it be, that I should gain
    An interest in the Saviour's blood?
Died he for me, who caused his pain?
    For me, who him to death pursued?
Amazing love! How can it be
That thou, my God, shouldst die for me?

  'Tis mystery all: the Immortal dies!
    Who can explore his strange design?
In vain the first-born seraph tries
    To sound the depths of love divine.
'Tis mercy all! Let earth adore,
Let angel minds enquire no more.

He left his Father's throne above—
    So free, so infinite his grace—
Emptied himself of all but love,
    And bled for Adam's helpless race.
'Tis mercy all, immense and free;
For, O my God, it found out me!

Long my imprisoned spirit lay
    Fast bound in sin and nature's night;
Thine eye diffused a quickening ray—
    I woke, the dungeon flamed with light;
My chains fell off, my heart was free,
I rose, went forth, and followed thee.

No condemnation now I dread;
    Jesus, and all in him, is mine!
Alive in him, my living Head,
    And clothed in righteousness divine,
Bold I approach the eternal throne,
And claim the crown, through Christ, my own.

Charles Wesley (1707–88)

This is classic statement of joy and enthusiasm from a newly converted believer. The impassioned rhetoric of this hymn suggests an overwhelming and powerful response to some great event such as a 'new birth', and it probably belongs to the period shortly after the Wesleys' 'conversion' in May 1738. The so-called 'conversion hymn', 'Where shall my wond'ring soul begin', was written in the same metre. Both were published in *Hymns and Sacred Poems* (1739), where 'And can it be' was entitled 'Free Grace'.

The excitement is even more obvious in the original punctuation:

> And can it be, that I should gain
>   An Int'rest in the Saviour's blood!
> Dy'd He for Me?—who caus'd his Pain!
>   For Me? who Him to Death pursu'd.
> Amazing Love! how can it be
> That Thou, my God, shouldst die for Me?

There were six verses in the original text: between the present verses 4 and 5 there was a characteristic statement (for Wesley) of 'feeling' the power of saving grace:

> Still the small inward Voice I hear,
>   That whispers all my Sins forgiv'n;
> Still the atoning blood is near,
>   That quench'd the Wrath of hostile Heav'n:
> I feel the Life his Wounds impart;
> I feel my Saviour in my Heart.

The 'now' of 'No condemnation now I dread' follows naturally and fittingly after this verse.

This hymn is a powerful statement of belief in the doctrine of 'Free Grace', and the sense of freedom from sin that accompanies an assurance of salvation (signified by Charles Wesley's use of Acts 16: 23–32 in verse 4). Theologians have also pointed to Wesley's versification of the kenotic theory in verse 3 ('Emptied himself of all but love'). Poetically it is an astonishingly assured statement of a post-conversion experience: the thrice-repeated 'for me' in verse 1 is a recognition of the personal impact of it, and the echoes of ''Tis mystery all' and ''Tis mercy all' carry the appropriate response of wonder and amazement.

The hymn has become a favourite with British Methodists, as a classic statement of an ardent and enthusiastic belief in 'Free Grace'; and particularly when sung to the rousing tune SAGINA, by Thomas Campbell, published in *The Bouquet* (1825). In that book, as the name implies, each of the tunes was named after a flower (Sagina is the name of a genus of the pink (dianthus) family). The tune, with its bouncy repeats and vigorous rhythms, has often been seen as unsuitable for words of such devotional intensity, and in successive books there have been attempts to dislodge it as the dominant tune (LANSDOWN, by A. Beer; DIDSBURY, by Cyril Taylor; and ABINGDON by Erik Routley); but none has succeeded.

88
O for a thousand tongues to sing
  My great Redeemer's praise,
The glories of my God and King,
  The triumphs of his grace!

My gracious Master, and my God,
  Assist me to proclaim,
To spread through all the earth abroad
  The honours of thy name.

Jesus! the name that charms our fears,
  That bids our sorrows cease;
'Tis music in the sinner's ears,
  'Tis life, and health, and peace.

He breaks the power of cancelled sin,
  He sets the prisoner free;
His blood can make the foulest clean,
  His blood availed for me.

He speaks, and listening to his voice,
  New life the dead receive;
The mournful, broken hearts rejoice,
  The humble poor believe.

Hear him, ye deaf; his praise, ye dumb,
  Your loosened tongues employ;
Ye blind, behold your Saviour come,
  And leap, ye lame, for joy!

See all your sins on Jesus laid:
  The Lamb of God was slain;
His soul was once an offering made
  For every soul of man.

In Christ, your Head, you then shall know,
  Shall feel, your sins forgiven,
Anticipate your heaven below,
  And own that love is heaven.

Charles Wesley (1707–88)

The importance of his conversion for Charles Wesley is indicated by the fact that he kept the day in remembrance each year. This hymn, from *Hymns and Sacred Poems* (1740), was entitled 'For the Anniversary Day of one's Conversion'. It was a long hymn of eighteen verses, beginning with three which emphasize the particular occasion of its composition:

Glory to God, and praise, and love
  Be ever, ever given,
By saints below and saints above,
  The Church in earth and heaven.

On this glad day the glorious Sun
Of Righteousness arose;
On my benighted soul He shone,
And fill'd it with repose.

Sudden expired the legal strife;
'Twas then I ceas'd to grieve;
My second, real, living life
I then began to live.

This is a classic statement of the 'new birth' associated with conversion; since Charles Wesley had experienced this on 21 May 1738, it seems likely that the hymn was written a year later. The present selection extracts the hymn from its local and personal associations, and makes it eminently suitable for general use as a hymn of praise to the great Redeemer (originally written 'dear Redeemer'). It has been especially prominent in Methodist use since John Wesley chose it to open *A Collection of Hymns for the Use of the People called Methodists* in 1780. It remained the first hymn in subsequent Wesleyan Methodist books, and the tradition was followed in the *Methodist Hymn Book* of 1933. The final verse of the present text began 'With me, your Chief, you then shall know'.

Like many of Charles Wesley's hymns, it contains complex interweavings of passages from the Old and New Testaments, mainly from the Psalms and Isaiah 35 linked with Philippians 2: 5–13. It celebrates Christ's soul as the offering for the sins of the whole world, and in the process that soul 'breaks the power of cancelled sin': sin (the Fall) is cancelled by the Cross, but its power is also broken for the future.

The idea of the thousand tongues may have come from Charles Wesley's conversations in the months before his conversion with the Moravian Peter Böhler, who said 'Had I a thousand tongues I would praise Him with them all'. There is also a German hymn, by Johann Mentzner (1658–1734) beginning 'O dass ich tausend zungen hätte'. It would also be characteristic of Charles Wesley's art to have taken Isaac Watts's 'Begin, my tongue, some heavenly theme' and multiplied it a thousandfold.

British Methodists use two principal tunes. The first is RICHMOND, by Thomas Haweis (1734–1820) from his *Carmina Christo* ('Songs to Christ') of 1792, which is a fine dignified tune with a grand climax at the end of line 3. The second is LYDIA, by Thomas Phillips (1735–1807), a tune with lively rhythms, unexpected leaps, and a repetition of the last line of each verse. It was described as a tune associated with 'the Independent meeting' in George Eliot's *Scenes of Clerical Life* (1857). American and Canadian books use AZMON, a German tune adapted by the great American musician Lowell Mason; other tunes associated with the hymn include UNIVERSITY; LYNGHAM; and ARDEN, by George Thalben-Ball (1896–1987).

89

    Christ, whose glory fills the skies,
        Christ, the true, the only light,
    Sun of Righteousness, arise,
        Triumph o'er the shades of night;
    Day-spring from on high, be near;
    Day-star, in my heart appear.

    Dark and cheerless is the morn
        Unaccompanied by thee;
    Joyless is the day's return,
        Till thy mercy's beams I see,
    Till they inward light impart,
    Glad my eyes, and warm my heart.

    Visit then this soul of mine,
        Pierce the gloom of sin and grief;
    Fill me, radiancy divine,
        Scatter all my unbelief;
    More and more thyself display,
    Shining to the perfect day.

                        Charles Wesley (1707–88)

This hymn was described by James Montgomery as 'one of Charles Wesley's loveliest progeny'. It was published in *Hymns and Sacred Poems* (1740), where it was entitled 'A Morning Hymn'. It is a most assured and confident poetic statement of the idea found in the 'Benedictus' (Luke 1: 68–79). Charles Wesley would have been familiar with it in the version of the *Book of Common Prayer*, where it is sung after the Second Lesson at Morning Prayer:

Through the tender mercy of our God: whereby the day-spring from on high hath visited us; To give light to them that sit in darkness, and in the shadow of death; and to guide our feet into the way of peace.   (verses 78–9)

The hymn brilliantly combines this metaphorical reading of the light and darkness imagery with the actual morning, in which the Christian awakes to find the skies filled with light and knows it to be the light of Christ's glory. Thus every morning starts with praise. The hymn also makes use of the Old Testament image of the Messiah as the Sun of Righteousness (as in Malachi 4: 2) or of light, as in Isaiah 42: 5–7, where the Lord is 'a light of the Gentiles':

To open the blind eyes, to bring out the prisoners from the prison, and them that sit in darkness out of the prison house.

In Charles Wesley's New Testament reading the light is 'inward light', and the 'radiancy divine' pierces the gloom which is caused by sin and grief. The hymn is one of the many hymns by him which deal with the release from the prison of sin, although here the image is of darkness: its springy rhythm conveys joy and gladness, as it celebrates the mercy of Christ and looks to (and prays for) 'the perfect day', the cloudless day of His final coming.

The three verses are economical, absolutely functional in that there are no distractions from the theme, and wonderfully accommodated to the rhythm and metre. It could be said of the first line that, as Christ's glory fills the skies, so the words exactly fill the line, beginning a hymn which is rare in its taut control and imaginative power.

It has been fortunate in having some fine tunes. The one found in many books is RATISBON, a German tune found in J. G. Werner's *Choral-Buch zu den neuen protestantischen Gesangbüchern* of 1815, and arranged by William Henry Havergal for the first edition of *Hymns Ancient and Modern* (1861), where it was set to these words. An alternative is HEATHLANDS, by Henry Smart (1813–79). Both tunes are invigorating to sing, and carry the words well. The *English Hymnal* set it to the tune for Psalm 135 in the Genevan Psalter of 1562, which it called MINISTRES DE L'ÉTERNEL.

90

Hark! the herald angels sing
Glory to the new-born King,
Peace on earth, and mercy mild,
God and sinners reconciled.
Joyful, all ye nations, rise,
Join the triumph of the skies;
With the angelic host proclaim:
Christ is born in Bethlehem.
 Hark! the herald-angels sing
 Glory to the new-born King.

Christ, by highest heaven adored,
Christ, the everlasting Lord,
Late in time behold him come,
Offspring of a virgin's womb.
Veiled in flesh the Godhead see!
Hail the incarnate Deity!
Pleased as man with man to dwell,
Jesus, our Immanuel:

Hail the heaven-born Prince of Peace!
Hail, the Sun of Righteousness!
Light and life to all he brings,
Risen with healing in his wings.
Mild he lays his glory by,
Born that man no more may die,
Born to raise the sons of earth,
Born to give them second birth:

Charles Wesley (1707–88)

In *Hymns and Sacred Poems* (1739), Wesley published a series of five hymns in the same metre, 77.77, celebrating five great festivals of the church, Christmas Day, the Epiphany, Easter Day, Ascension Day, and Whit Sunday. This was the 'Hymn for Christmas Day': it is particularly notable for its first line in the original version, 'Hark how all the Welkin rings' (re-introduced, in a praiseworthy attempt to be authentic, in the 1904 edition of *Hymns Ancient and Modern*, to universal displeasure).

Wesley was a fine poet, and his original opening should be more widely appreciated, although it will never dislodge the present text. It is a strong line, and it was carefully chosen: the welkin is not only the sky but also 'the abode of the Deity . . . the celestial regions, heaven' (*Oxford English Dictionary*, sense 2b), and the word is also used 'in phrases descriptive of loud sounds, as *to make the welkin ring*' (sense 2c). *OED* quotes Somerville's *The Chase*, published four years earlier than Wesley's hymn in 1735: 'The Welkin rings, Men, Dogs, Hills, Rocks, and Woods/ In the full Consort join'. It would be like Wesley to appropriate a phrase from a recently published poem, so that the sounds that make the welkin ring are now the transforming sounds of the message of the Incarnation (linking up, in the original, with a phrase in verse 2, 'Universal Nature say'). Verses 1 and 2 in the original were as follows:

> Hark how all the Welkin rings
> "Glory to the Kings of Kings,
> "Peace on Earth, and Mercy mild,
> "God and Sinners reconcil'd!

> Joyful all ye Nations rise,
> Join the Triumph of the Skies,
> Universal Nature say
> "Christ the Lord is born to Day!"

The second line is a clear misprint: the manuscript (in the John Rylands University Library of Manchester) has 'King of Kings'. That 1739 printing has ten four-line stanzas: 1–6 contain the familiar lines, with slight variations (the end of the modern text's verse 2 is 'Pleas'd as Man with Men t'appear/ Jesus, our Immanuel here!'). Verses 7–10, however, show how crucial it was for Wesley to set the Incarnation in the context of the Fall:

> Come, Desire of Nations, come,
> Fix in Us thy humble Home,
> Rise, the Woman's Conqu'ring Seed,
> Bruise in Us the Serpent's Head.

> Now display thy saving Pow'r,
> Ruin'd Nature now restore,
> Now in Mystic Union join
> Thine to Ours, and Ours to Thine.

Adam's likeness, Lord, efface,
Stamp thy Image in its Place,
Second Adam from above,
Reinstate us in thy Love.

Let us Thee, tho' lost, regain,
Thee, the Life, the Inner Man:
O! to All Thyself impart,
Form'd in each Believing Heart.

The present lines 1 and 2, with the alteration from 'the Welkin rings' to 'the herald angels sing', were the work of George Whitefield, in his *Collection of Hymns for Social Worship* of 1753; and the present verse 1 lines 7 and 8 are from Martin Madan's *A Collection of Psalms and Hymns extracted from Various Authors* (1760).

In its abbreviated form, this has become one of the best-loved Christmas hymns, now invariably in three eight-line verses and sung to the tune MENDELSSOHN, which requires the addition of a very effective refrain. It was adapted by W. H. Cummings, then organist of Waltham Abbey, from a chorus in Mendelssohn's *Festgesang*, first performed in 1840. It was first published as a hymn tune in 1857, in Richard R. Chope's *Congregational Hymn and Tune Book*, and firmly established as the tune for this hymn by *Hymns Ancient and Modern* (1861), which first gave it the name MENDELSSOHN.

91   Hail the day that sees him rise,
                        Alleluia!
            Ravished from our wistful eyes!
            Christ, awhile to mortals given,
            Reascends his native heaven:

            There the glorious triumph waits:
            Lift your heads, eternal gates;
            Wide unfold the radiant scene;
            Take the King of Glory in!

            Him though highest heaven receives,
            Still he loves the earth he leaves;
            Though returning to his throne,
            Still he calls mankind his own:

            See! He lifts his hands above;
            See! He shows the prints of love;
            Hark! His gracious lips bestow
            Blessings on his church below:

Master, parted from our sight,
High above yon azure height,
Grant our hearts may thither rise,
Following thee beyond the skies:

There we shall with thee remain,
Partners of thy endless reign;
There thy face forever see,
Find our heaven of heavens in thee!

Charles Wesley (1707–88)

This is another of the hymns on the great festivals of the church published in *Hymns and Sacred Poems* (1739). It was entitled 'Hymn for Ascension-Day', and had ten verses. It has become a classic statement of the Ascension-tide doctrine of the triumphant return of the Son of God to His native heaven, with a wonderfully human (and very daring) touch in 'Still he loves the earth he leaves'. It follows the Collect for Ascension Day in the *Book of Common Prayer*:

Grant, we beseech thee, Almighty God, that like as we do believe thy only-begotten Son our Lord Jesus Christ to have ascended into the heavens; so we may also in heart and mind thither ascend, and with him continually dwell, who liveth and reigneth with thee and the Holy Ghost, one God, world without end. Amen.

The influence of this collect is clearly seen in the last six lines of the present text. In the original, the last three verses, 8–10, show it more clearly:

Grant, tho' parted from our Sight,
High above yon azure Height,
Grant our Hearts may thither rise,
Following Thee beyond the Skies.

Ever upward let us move
Wafted on the Wings of Love,
Looking when our Lord shall come,
Longing, gasping after Home.

There we shall with Thee remain,
Partners of thy endless Reign,
There thy face unclouded see,
Find our Heav'n of Heav'ns in Thee!

The 'longing, gasping' is very characteristic of the intensity and physicality of Charles Wesley's verse. An earlier verse, the original verse 6, shows his fine vocabulary and ingenious thought:

Still for us his Death he pleads;
Prevalent, He intercedes;
Near Himself prepares our Place,
Harbinger of human Race.

'Harbinger' is here used exactly, of one who goes before to prepare lodgings, and 'prevalent' as 'Having great power or force; effective, powerful'(*Oxford English Dictionary*, sense 1) or as 'Having the superiority or ascendancy; predominant, victorious' (sense 2). In verse 2, the first line was originally

> There the pompous Triumph waits

in which 'pompous' is used in its original sense of 'characterized by pomp or stately show; magnificent, splendid; processional' (*OED*, sense 1).

The hymn is a splendid example of Charles Wesley's most vigorous and energetic style, and it is also interesting to note the debt to the Prayer Book. It is perhaps significant that John Wesley, when choosing hymns for the 'Large Hymn Book', *A Collection of Hymns for the Use of the People called Methodists* (1780), omitted this hymn: he was preparing a book which expressed individual religious experience rather than the liturgical year. Charles Wesley always retained his allegiance to the Church of England and its practices, and this hymn is an early example.

The usual tune is ASCENSION, written by William Henry Monk (1823–89) for the first edition of *Hymns Ancient and Modern* (1861). It was one of Monk's most successful contributions to that book. Other tunes for this hymn have been LLANFAIR and CHISLEHURST.

92

Jesu, lover of my soul,
   Let me to thy bosom fly,
While the nearer waters roll,
   While the tempest still is high;
Hide me, O my Saviour hide,
   Till the storm of life is past;
Safe into the haven guide,
   O receive my soul at last!

Other refuge have I none,
   Hangs my helpless soul on thee;
Leave, ah, leave me not alone,
   Still support and comfort me.
All my trust on thee is stayed,
   All my help from thee I bring;
Cover my defenceless head
   With the shadow of thy wing.

Thou, O Christ, art all I want;
　　More than all in thee I find;
Raise the fallen, cheer the faint,
　　Heal the sick, and lead the blind.
Just and holy is thy name,
　　I am all unrighteousness;
False and full of sin I am,
　　Thou art full of truth and grace.

Plenteous grace with thee is found,
　　Grace to cover all my sin;
Let the healing streams abound,
　　Make and keep me pure within.
Thou of life the fountain art;
　　Freely let me take of thee;
Spring thou up within my heart,
　　Rise to all eternity.

　　　　　　Charles Wesley (1707–88)

From *Hymns and Sacred Poems* (1740), where it had five verses. The omitted
verse emphasized the dramatic nature of this hymn:

　　Wilt thou not regard my call?
　　　　Wilt thou not accept my prayer?
　　Lo! I sink, I faint, I fall!
　　　　Lo, on thee I cast my care!
　　Reach me out thy gracious hand!
　　　　While I of thy strength receive,
　　Hoping against hope I stand,
　　　　Dying, and behold I live!

　　From the moment of its wonderful opening, 'Jesu, lover . . .', in which the
intimacy of 'Jesu' plays such a crucial part, this hymn proclaims itself as a
work of unusual intensity. It sets the closeness and protectiveness of the
Saviour (emphasized by the tender word 'bosom') against the storms and
tempests of life; and it relates the images of safety—the haven, the refuge,
the 'shadow of thy wing'—to the helpless and defenceless self. Although that
self is 'false and full of sin', it can still find comfort in the grace of God: and
that grace, with its healing streams and its fountain, will keep the sinner in
everlasting life. Every stage of the hymn leads on to the next, and relates
back to the central truth of Jesus as the lover of the human soul, however
undeserving it may be.
　　The hymn is full of images from the psalms: the haven (Psalm 107), the
shadow of thy wing (Psalm 91), the fountain (Psalm 36); but they are set in
the context of a human drama of sin and forgiveness. Another debt, subsumed into the intensity of the poem's imagery, is to Matthew Prior's
Solomon:

> We weave the Chaplet, and We crown the Bowl;
> And smiling see the nearer Waters roll;
> 'Till the strong Gusts of raging Passion rise;
> 'Till the dire Tempest mingles Earth and Skies; . . .

Solomon is in love with the servant Abra, and is a slave to his passions. Wesley, on the other hand, has no doubt where his love is:

> Thou, O Christ, art all I want;
> More than all in thee I find . . .

The 'nearer waters' make a superb contrast to the bosom of the loving Saviour, and it is not difficult to see what they are—the waters of the storm, close by, rolling towards the defenceless soul. That soul has the comfort of knowing that, however false and full of sin it is, there is a loving God ('But thou sparest all, for they are thine, O Lord, thou lover of souls'—Wisdom 11: 26).

The 'nearer waters' have caused some trouble to the literal-minded: as Percy Dearmer remarked, referring to Julian's *Dictionary of Hymnology*, 'Dr Julian devotes nearly half a column to explaining this inspired poetic epithet by an analysis of the behaviour of waves in some local kinds of storm.' Dearmer quoted a number of clumsy attempts to rewrite the first four lines, adding sharply: 'It did not always occur to the compilers of hymnals that a little understanding of poetry is necessary for their work.'

The hymn is a powerful statement of some deep psychological truths, concerned with danger and safety, and with sin and forgiveness, with a final verse which prays for healing and life. But it would not be so compelling if it were not written with such control and such deep emotion—the control and the emotion balancing one another quite beautifully. A line such as 'Leave, ah, leave me not alone' is a cry that is articulated through the syllables, and the interruption, 'ah', makes a deeply moving plea. The interaction between the sinning self and the forgiving Christ, which is found everywhere in this hymn, is also marvellously conveyed in the second half of verse 3 through the figure of chiasmus, in which the 'I am . . . I am' is enclosed within the divine attributes, 'Just and holy . . . truth and grace':

> *Just and holy* is thy name,
>   *I am* all unrighteousness;
> False and full of sin *I am*,
>   Thou art full of *truth and grace*.

John Wesley did not include this magnificent hymn in *A Collection of Hymns for the Use of the People called Methodists* of 1780, it is said because he disliked terms of endearment addressed to God. It is hard to see this as a valid objection: the whole point of the hymn is the tender and loving presence of the Saviour in a world where the sinner feels helpless; and Charles Wesley has not been afraid to give intense expression to that love, and to the life which it brings, so movingly described in the final verse.

This is one of those hymns, like 'Abide with me' and 'Rock of Ages', about which legends accumulate. Some of those about the circumstances of composition seem unlikely; but there seems no reason to doubt the story of the soldier in the American Civil War who was about to shoot a picket from the other side when he heard him singing 'Cover my defenceless head/ With the shadow of thy wing'.

There are two great tunes to this hymn. The best-known is ABERYSTWYTH, by Joseph Parry (1841–1903), who was Professor of Music at University College, Aberystwyth, from 1873–9. It is a very grand Welsh tune, with fine harmonies, that rises and falls to great effect and leads to a splendid climax in the penultimate line. Almost as moving, and easier to sing for smaller congregations, is J. B. Dykes's HOLLINGSIDE, set to this hymn in the first edition of *Hymns Ancient and Modern* in 1861. At lines 7 and 8 it repeats the tune for lines 3 and 4 in each verse, thus drawing attention to the variation in the other lines.

93   Soldiers of Christ, arise,
        And put your armour on,
        Strong in the strength which God supplies
        Through his eternal Son;

        Strong in the Lord of Hosts,
        And in his mighty power,
        Who in the strength of Jesus trusts
        Is more than conqueror.

        Stand then in his great might,
        With all his strength endued,
        But take, to arm you for the fight,
        The panoply of God;

        That, having all things done,
        And all your conflicts passed,
        Ye may o'ercome through Christ alone,
        And stand entire at last.

        Stand then against your foes,
        In close and firm array;
        Legions of wily fiends oppose
        Throughout the evil day;

        But meet the sons of night,
        But mock their vain design,
        Armed in the arms of heavenly light,
        Of righteousness divine.

Leave no unguarded place,
No weakness of the soul;
Take every virtue, every grace,
And fortify the whole;

Indissolubly joined,
To battle all proceed;
But arm yourselves with all the mind
That was in Christ, your Head.

Charles Wesley (1707–88)

This hymn first appeared in John Wesley's tract, *The Character of a Methodist*, published in 1742, entitled 'The whole armour of God, Ephesians 6'. It subsequently appeared in *Hymns and Sacred Poems* (1749) in a section of 'Hymns for Believers'.

It was originally a very long hymn, containing no fewer than sixteen eight-line verses in Double Short Metre. It has always been shortened for congregational use, with selections made in various ways. The present text is that of the *Methodist Hymn Book* of 1933, which prints the first four verses intact. They are divided here into four line (Short Metre) verses, as they are in a number of hymn books which use the four-line tune, ST ETHELWALD.

In its original form, the hymn went on to elaborate on the military imagery of Ephesians 6:

But, above all, lay hold
On faith's victorious shield;
Armed with that adamant and gold
Be sure to win the field;

If faith surround your heart,
Satan shall be subdued,
Repelled his every fiery dart,
And quenched with Jesu's blood. . . .

To keep your armour bright
Attend with constant care;
Still walking in your Captain's sight,
And watching unto prayer;

Ready for all alarms,
Steadfastly set your face,
And always exercise your arms,
And use your every grace.

It continues by exhorting the Christian soldier 'Pray, without ceasing pray'. The reference to 'adamant and gold' in the shield is one of many echoes of Milton in this hymn. In *Paradise Lost*, Book VI, Satan is 'armed in adamant and gold' and the loyal angels proceed to battle 'indissolubly firm'. Because that book deals with the battle in heaven between the forces of good and those of evil, it would naturally have been in Charles Wesley's mind when writing the hymn; but the principal source, as its first title indicates, is Ephesians 6, where St Paul uses the extended comparison of the Christian life with that of a soldier. From this passage comes not only the idea of the shield, but also the magnificent image of 'the panoply of God', the 'whole armour' (from the Greek word *panoplia*).

The heavily accented double short metre is characteristic of what George H. Findlay called 'Charles Wesley's fighting metre'. It helps to produce a very unusual hymn-singing experience: the hymn is plain but forceful, using words such as 'might' and 'mighty', together with 'strong' and 'strength'. The repetition of these words provides emphasis, and this is contrasted with exotic and polysyllabic words such as 'panoply', 'fortify', and 'indissolubly'. This style was the subject of an apt note by Percy Dearmer in *Songs of Praise Discussed*: 'The mastered simplicity of this, its faultless technique, its sagacity in the use of imperfect rhymes, are signs of high accomplishment'.

In John Wesley's 1780 *Collection of Hymns for the Use of the People called Methodists*, this hymn was appropriately set to a tune entitled 'Handel's March' (it appears, with the name JERICHO TUNE, in the *Methodist Hymn Book*, to the words 'Forth rode the knights of old'). It became well known, however, when it was introduced into the first edition of *Hymns Ancient and Modern* (1861) with a tune specially written for these words by William Henry Monk. This excellent four-line tune, ST ETHELWALD, was the standard tune for many years, and is still found in most books. A more vigorous, syncopated eight-line tune, Elgar-like in its grandeur, was written by E. W. Naylor (1867–1934) and called FROM STRENGTH TO STRENGTH. Naylor, who was organist of Emmanuel College, Cambridge, wrote it for the College chapel: it was published in pamphlet form, and included in *The Public School Hymn Book* (1919). Its pulsing rhythms make it very suitable for young people singing about the Church Militant here on earth.

94　　　　　　　　　Gentle Jesus, meek and mild,
　　　　　　　　　　Look upon a little child,
　　　　　　　　　　Pity my simplicity,
　　　　　　　　　　Suffer me to come to thee.

　　　　　　　　　　Fain I would to thee be brought;
　　　　　　　　　　Dearest Lord, forbid it not;
　　　　　　　　　　In the kingdom of thy grace
　　　　　　　　　　Give a little child a place.

　　　　　　　　　　Fain I would be as thou art;
　　　　　　　　　　Give me thine obedient heart:
　　　　　　　　　　Thou art pitiful and kind;
　　　　　　　　　　Let me have thy loving mind.

　　　　　　　　　　Let me above all fulfil
　　　　　　　　　　God my heavenly Father's will;
　　　　　　　　　　Never his good spirit grieve,
　　　　　　　　　　Only to his glory live.

　　　　　　　　　　Lamb of God, I look to thee;
　　　　　　　　　　Thou shalt my example be:
　　　　　　　　　　Thou art gentle, meek, and mild;
　　　　　　　　　　Thou wast once a little child.

　　　　　　　　　　Thou didst live to God alone;
　　　　　　　　　　Thou didst never seek thine own;
　　　　　　　　　　Thou thyself didst never please:
　　　　　　　　　　God was all thy happiness.

　　　　　　　　　　Loving Jesu, gentle Lamb,
　　　　　　　　　　In thy gracious hands I am:
　　　　　　　　　　Make me, Saviour, what thou art;
　　　　　　　　　　Live thyself within my heart.

　　　　　　　　　　I shall then show forth thy praise,
　　　　　　　　　　Serve thee all my happy days;
　　　　　　　　　　Then the world shall always see
　　　　　　　　　　Christ, the holy child, in me.

　　　　　　　　　　　　Charles Wesley (1707–88)

This children's hymn was first published in *Hymns and Sacred Poems* (1742), and later in *Hymns for Children* (1763) in a section headed 'Hymns for the Youngest'. It had fourteen verses, divided into two parts of seven verses each. Its first line has become a classic example of a certain kind of image of Jesus for children: so much so, that it has been omitted from the most recent Methodist book, *Hymns and Psalms* (1983). That book begins with 'Loving Jesus [for 'Jesu'], gentle Lamb', and prints a different selection of verses.

　　The decision to omit the original first verse is understandable, for 'gentle', 'meek' and 'mild' are no longer adjectives which have much appeal. However, they do signify important characteristics of human behaviour, and the line deserves to be remembered; especially as it leads into the next three lines, which have a direct simplicity (using that word with great precision in line 3) which is both true to life and attractive. The verses then continue, using the seven-syllable couplets with great skill, to give the effect of short, simple insights. At the same time, the hymn is profound in its recognition of the child's relationship to Jesus, who is now the 'gentle Lamb': He is a lamb which would be attractive to a child, a woolly lamb, but also the Lamb that was slain for the redemption of the world. Blake used the same idea in 'The Lamb', from *Songs of Innocence*, in which the child tells the Lamb who made it:

> He is callèd by thy name,
> For he calls himself a Lamb;
> He is meek and he is mild,
> He became a little child:
> I a child, and thou a lamb,
> We are callèd by his name.

To read Wesley's hymn beside Blake's poem is to realize how subtle Blake was in describing both Creation and Redemption, but also to understand how good Charles Wesley was (fifty years before Blake) at representing the 'voice' of childhood innocence.

Several tunes have been used for these words, but two in particular have become closely associated with them. INNOCENTS was first published in 1851, and used by William Henry Monk for the first edition of *Hymns Ancient and Modern* (1861), though not for this hymn. In 1915 Martin Shaw (1875–1958) wrote GENTLE JESUS for Percy Dearmer's church, St Mary's, Primrose Hill, and it later appeared in *Songs of Praise*. Each of these tunes carries the sentiments with great delicacy and charm.

95   Come, O thou Traveller unknown,
          Whom still I hold, but cannot see;
      My company before is gone,
          And I am left alone with thee;
      With thee all night I mean to stay,
      And wrestle till the break of day.

      I need not tell thee who I am,
          My misery and sin declare;
      Thyself hast called me by my name;
          Look on thy hands, and read it there.
      But who, I ask thee, who art thou?
      Tell me thy name, and tell me now.

      In vain thou strugglest to get free,
          I never will unloose my hold;
      Art thou the Man that died for me?
          The secret of thy love unfold:
      Wrestling, I will not let thee go
      Till I thy name, thy nature know.

      Wilt thou not yet to me reveal
          Thy new unutterable name?
      Tell me, I still beseech thee, tell;
          To know it now resolved I am:
      Wrestling, I will not let thee go
      Till I thy name, thy nature know.

      What though my shrinking flesh complain
          And murmur to contend so long?
      I rise superior to my pain:
          When I am weak, then I am strong;
      And when my all of strength shall fail
      I shall with the God-man prevail.

      Yield to me now—for I am weak,
          But confident in self-despair!
      Speak to my heart, in blessings speak,
          Be conquered by my instant prayer:
      Speak, or thou never hence shalt move,
      And tell me if thy name is LOVE.

      'Tis Love! 'Tis Love! Thou diedst for me;
          I hear thy whisper in my heart.
      The morning breaks, the shadows flee,
          Pure Universal Love thou art:
      To me, to all, thy mercies move—
      Thy nature, and thy name, is LOVE.

My prayer hath power with God; the grace
  Unspeakable I now receive;
Through faith I see thee face to face;
  I see thee face to face, and live!
In vain I have not wept and strove—
Thy nature, and thy name, is LOVE.

I know thee, Saviour, who thou art—
  Jesus, the feeble sinner's friend;
Nor wilt thou with the night depart,
  But stay, and love me to the end;
Thy mercies never shall remove,
Thy nature, and thy name, is LOVE.

The Sun of Righteousness on me
  Hath rose with healing in his wings;
Withered my nature's strength; from thee
  My soul its life and succour brings;
My help is all laid up above:
Thy nature, and thy name, is LOVE.

Contented now upon my thigh
  I halt, till life's short journey end;
All helplessness, all weakness, I
  On thee alone for strength depend;
Nor have I power from thee to move:
Thy nature, and thy name, is LOVE.

Lame as I am, I take the prey,
  Hell, earth, and sin with ease o'ercome;
I leap for joy, pursue my way,
  And as a bounding hart fly home;
Through all eternity to prove,
Thy nature, and thy name, is LOVE.

Charles Wesley (1707–88)

This is the twelve-verse text of a hymn originally printed in fourteen verses in *Hymns and Sacred Poems* (1742). The present version is the one which was used by John Wesley for the 1780 *Collection of Hymns for the Use of the People called Methodists*, with two small exceptions: in verse 2 line 2 it read 'misery or sin'; and in verse 7 line 5 'To me, to all, thy bowels move', using 'bowels'—considered as the seat of the tender and sympathetic affections— to mean pity, compassion, feeling, 'heart' (*Oxford English Dictionary*, sense 3). This was common in the seventeenth and eighteenth centuries, but since Wesley uses 'mercies' elsewhere in the hymn, the removal of the archaic phrase is justified. The full fourteen-verse text is printed in the American *United Methodist Church Hymnal* of 1989, though as a supplement to a four-verse text set to music, as if the editors did not expect it to be sung.

As a 'Sacred Poem' (although it makes a magnificent hymn), 'Wrestling Jacob', as it was originally called, shows Charles Wesley's imaginative grasp of a situation at its finest. The episode of Jacob at the ford of Jabbok (Genesis 32: 24–32) is intensely dramatic in itself, the solitary combat of two adversaries: 'And Jacob was left alone; and there wrestled a man with him until the breaking of the day.' As Matthew Henry put it in his *Commentary*, to which Charles Wesley was indebted for his interpretation of this passage, 'they had no seconds'. Henry's comment is a reminder of the element of conflict and struggle in the poem: Wesley is putting himself in the place of Jacob, and encountering God in wrestling with Him as an adversary. Through the closeness of physical effort, the wrestler comes to know his opponent, better than he could in any other way; and here the poet resolves that he never will unloose his hold (the word 'hold' is, of course, a technical term in wrestling), and never let go until he knows the name of his opponent.

The principal difference between this and a normal wrestling match is that the human wrestler triumphs in his weakness—'When I am weak, then I am strong'. When his strength fails, he will prevail, and he is 'confident in self-despair'. These paradoxes point to a struggle that is fully realized in the verse, but which has another meaning: Wesley brilliantly converts it into an emblem of Christian experience, in which human weakness and sin are touched by the forgiving grace of God.

Jacob says 'I will not let thee go, except thou bless me' (verse 26), whereupon his opponent says 'What is thy name?' Wesley changes this, so that the poet/reader/singer asks that question. He becomes a representative figure of humanity, struggling with the God-Man in the darkness, seeking to find out the true nature of His adversary. This identity has been hinted at in verses 2 and 3: 'Look on thy hands and read it there' suggests the hands of the crucified Christ, as shown to Thomas (John 20: 27), and 'Art thou the Man that died for me?' similarly points forward to 1 John 3: 16: 'Hereby perceive we the love of God, because he laid down his life for us'.

The hymn becomes a search to know God, and to know his true essence, his nature and his name, which is LOVE (given capitals for emphasis). The excited repetition in verse 7 captures the moment of discovery, which is whispered (the heads of the wrestlers being close together): ''Tis Love! 'Tis Love!' And from that moment onward every verse ends with the same line, 'Thy nature, and thy name, is LOVE.' The evangelical interpretation of the old legend of Jacob at the ford is complete, and rich with multiple meanings, gathered from all parts of the Bible. One wonder is that the wrestler has come so close to God, and survived: 'I see thee face to face, and live!' (Genesis 32: 30). He has done so 'through faith' (verse 8), and comes to an awareness of full salvation as 'the morning breaks, the shadows flee' (verse 7). After that point, the hymn is a celebration of the great mystery of redeeming love, as he has come to know the other, 'Jesus, the feeble sinner's friend', the Sun of Righteousness who has 'risen with healing in his wings'.

One final adaptation of the story remains. As Jacob 'halted upon his thigh', so the redeemed sinner is marked by the encounter to the end of his life. And although he is lame (perhaps 'lame' in a worldly sense, in that he puts himself at a disadvantage by his Christian experience), he 'takes the prey' as he overcomes hell, earth, and sin (they become his 'prey', as if he were some masterful creature: the phrase is from Isaiah 33: 23). So at the end he 'flies home' to God, like a bounding hart: his lameness disappears (as it does in Isaiah 35: 6: 'Then shall the lame man leap as an hart') as he leaves life, and the poem, transported and lost in the radiance of eternal life.

James Montgomery greatly admired Wesley's hymn, 'in which, with consummate art, he has carried on the action of a lyrical drama'; and Isaac Watts said 'that single poem, *Wrestling Jacob*, was worth all the verses he himself had written' (recorded by John Wesley in his obituary tribute to his brother).

It is hard to find a tune which will carry such dramatic words (although the whole hymn is rarely sung, and a number of books print versions of four or six stanzas). The difficulty is indicated by the way in which a number of books print several tunes. Probably the most widely used is Samuel Sebastian Wesley's WRESTLING JACOB, written, as its name implies, for this hymn and set to it in *The European Psalmist* of 1872. Others include DAVID'S HARP, by Robert King, from Henry Playford's *Divine Companion* of 1701, which is used in the *English Hymnal*; and Carlton Young's delightful setting of a Scottish folk tune (perhaps almost too sweetly lyrical for these words) in the *United Methodist Church Hymnal*.

96   Come, thou long-expected Jesus,
                                   Born to set thy people free,
                                From our fears and sins release us,
                                   Let us find our rest in thee.

                                Israel's strength and consolation,
                                   Hope of all the earth thou art,
                                Dear desire of every nation,
                                   Joy of every longing heart.

                                Born thy people to deliver,
                                   Born a child and yet a king,
                                Born to reign in us for ever,
                                   Now thy gracious kingdom bring.

                                By thy own eternal Spirit
                                   Rule in all our hearts alone;
                                By thy all-sufficient merit
                                   Raise us to thy glorious throne.

                                         Charles Wesley (1707–88)

From *Hymns for the Nativity of our Lord* (1744), where it appeared in two eight-line verses. Although it was written and published in a book of Christmas hymns, it is now more frequently used in the season of Advent. Its uniqueness comes from its skilful conjunction of several elements into one simple-sounding discourse. Those elements include the Old Testament promise of the Messiah, 'Israel's strength and consolation' who has been long expected and who will set his people free; the New Testament story of the birth of the child who is also a king (Matthew 2: 6); and the idea of the Christ-child not only as the strength and consolation of Israel, but also the hope of all the earth, a Christ who is born for the Gentiles as well as the Jews.

   To those elements is added a metaphorical layer of meaning, in which the freedom of line 2 is the freedom from sin and death, and the joy that is felt in the heart. The 'governor, that shall rule my people Israel' (Matthew 2: 6) becomes the Christ who, through the Holy Spirit, is invited to 'rule in all our hearts alone' and in due course to bring us to heaven ('Raise us to thy glorious throne'). It is an unobtrusive but very effective transference from the narrative of the Incarnation to the application of that narrative to the spiritual state of the Christian in prayer.

   This hymn is frequently sung to a German tune, STUTTGART, probably by Christian Friedrich Witt (1660–1716), which was published in his Lutheran book, *Psalmodia Sacra*, in 1715. It appeared in the first edition of *Hymns Ancient and Modern* (1861) set to 'Earth has many a noble city', but it has now become associated primarily with the present hymn. It is also often sung to John Stainer's CROSS OF JESUS, from his oratorio *The Crucifixion* of 1887, which fits the lines sweetly but less grandly than STUTTGART.

97

> Glory be to God on high,
>   And peace on earth descend!
> God comes down, He bows the sky,
>   And shows Himself our Friend:
> God the invisible appears!
>   God, the blest, the great I AM,
> Sojourns in this vale of tears,
>   And Jesus is his Name.
>
> Him the angels all adored,
>   Their Maker and their King;
> Tidings of their humbled Lord
>   They now to mortals bring.
> Emptied of His majesty,
>   Of His dazzling glories shorn,
> Being's Source begins to be,
>   And God Himself is born!
>
> See the eternal Son of God
>   A mortal son of man;
> Dwelling in an earthly clod,
>   Whom heaven cannot contain!
> Stand amazed, ye heavens, at this!
>   See the Lord of earth and skies;
> Humbled to the dust He is,
>   And in a manger lies.
>
> We, the sons of men, rejoice,
>   The Prince of Peace proclaim;
> With heaven's host lift up our voice,
>   And shout Immanuel's name:
> Knees and hearts to Him we bow;
>   Of our flesh and of our bone,
> Jesus is our Brother now,
>   And God is all our own.

Charles Wesley (1707–88)

This spectacular hymn is from *Hymns for the Nativity of our Lord* (1744). It is based on the Christmas story as told by St Luke, beginning with a reference to Luke 2: 14; this is cleverly interwoven with St Paul's commentary on the Incarnation from Philippians 2, especially verses 8 and 10:

And being found in fashion as a man, he humbled himself, and became obedient unto death, . . . That at the name of Jesus every knee should bow, of things in heaven, and things in earth . . .

This hymn is not widely known outside British Methodist books (it is not in the American *United Methodist Hymnal*, for example) but it deserves inclusion because it is Charles Wesley's most dramatic Christmas hymn.

The play of sound and word ('Being's source begins to be') at the end of verse 2 is particularly impressive: Donald Davie, quoting this verse, said that in such lines of Charles Wesley 'we encounter audacities, imaginative abstractings, that . . . ought to leave us gasping' (*Dissentient Voice*, 1982: 21). The contrast between the complexity of this line and the simplicity of 'And God himself is born!' is wonderfully managed. And throughout, there is a powerful contrast between the 'dazzling glories' of 'the Lord of earth and skies' and the dwelling in an earthly clod (originally 'earthy clod', which is even more striking).

The amazing transformation of the Eternal Son of God into a mortal son of man means that, in the hymn's final lines, 'Jesus is our Brother now,/ And God is all our own.' The human response is to rejoice, and to 'shout Immanuel's name' in another line that vividly conveys the excitement of Wesley's perception. 'Shouting' was a part of his very physical reaction to moments of great joy: 'We sang and shouted all the way to Oxford', he noted in his journal for September 1738, in the first months of his converted enthusiasm.

The hymn is usually sung to AMSTERDAM, a tune found in John Wesley's *A Collection of Tunes Set to Music, as they are commonly sung at the Foundery* (1742). It was an adaptation of a German chorale in J. A. Freylinghausen's *Geistreiches Gesangbuch* (1704). The Foundery was an abandoned cannon foundry in Moorfields, London, used by the local Methodist society for its meetings in the early years after the Wesleys' conversion; so this must be one of the earliest of Methodist tunes.

98   Ye servants of God,
                           Your Master proclaim,
                    And publish abroad
                           His wonderful name;
                    The name all-victorious
                           Of Jesus extol;
                    His kingdom is glorious,
                           And rules over all.

                    God ruleth on high,
                           Almighty to save;
                    And still he is nigh,
                           His presence we have;
                    The great congregation
                           His triumph shall sing,
                    Ascribing salvation
                           To Jesus our King.

                    Salvation to God,
                           Who sits on the throne!
                    Let all cry aloud,
                           And honour the Son:
                    The praises of Jesus
                           The angels proclaim,
                    Fall down on their faces,
                           And worship the Lamb.

                    Then let us adore,
                           And give him his right,
                    All glory and power,
                           All wisdom and might;
                    All honour and blessing,
                           With angels above,
                    And thanks never-ceasing,
                           And infinite love.

                  Charles Wesley (1707–88)

First published in *Hymns for Times of Trouble and Persecution* (1744), where it was printed in a 10 10.11 11. metre. The 'trouble and persecution' of the title referred to the difficulties experienced by the early Methodists, but also to the problems of national life, which culminated in the rebellion of Prince Charles Edward Stuart in 1745.

The hymn was reprinted in the more familiar short-line form in *Hymns on the Great Festivals, and Other Occasions* (1746). This book contained twenty-four hymns, set to tunes by Charles Wesley's friend John Frederick Lampe (1703–51). In this edition the present hymn was entitled 'The Triumph of Faith', and the same title appears above the tune. There were six verses: the ones which are generally omitted were those which would have had a particular appropriateness in 1746, describing contemporary problems in images of storm and tempest:

> The Waves of the Sea
>   Have lift up their Voice,
> Sore troubled that We
>   In Jesus rejoice:
> The Floods they are roaring,
>   But Jesus is here:
> While we are adoring
>   He always is near.

> Men, Devils engage;
>   The Billows arise,
> And horribly rage,
>   And threaten the Skies:
> Their Fury shall never
>   Our Stedfastness shock:
> The weakest Believer
>   Is built on a Rock.

These verses are based upon Psalm 93: 'The floods have lifted up, O Lord . . . The Lord on high is mightier than the noise of many waters, yea, than the mighty waves of the sea.' However, it is a relief to turn from this assertive and defiant mode to the more general 'God ruleth on high', which allows the hymn to recover its successful poetic mode of sweeping grandeur. It is indeed one of the great inclusive hymns of praise, neatly containing the doctrine of the Incarnate Word and the Holy Spirit ('And still he is nigh, his presence we have') but based principally on the adoration of the Lamb from Revelation 7: 9–12.

At least part of the grand effect of the hymn comes from the use of the word 'all', which occurs in three of the four verses. God rules over all (verse 1), and it is the duty of all to 'cry aloud' with praises (verse 3) which are 'all glory and power, all wisdom and might' (verse 4). The repetition suggests a crescendo, which builds up to a climax, ending on a magnificent development from the repeated 'all . . . all' to the words 'infinite love'.

There are two fine tunes which are used for this hymn, both called LAUDATE DOMINUM ('Praise the Lord') because both were written for Sir H. W. Baker's hymn 'O praise ye the Lord! praise him in the height' . The better known, by Parry, was used with Baker's words in his anthem 'Hear my words, O ye people' of 1894, and found its way into *Hymns Ancient and Modern* in a supplement of 1916. The other tune, by H. J. Gauntlett, was set to Baker's hymn when it first appeared in the second edition of *Hymns Ancient and Modern* (1875). Some hymn-books print Parry's striking organ accompaniment to the unison singing of verse 4, with a double 'Amen' that responds to the magnificence of the words and the musical setting.

99   Father of everlasting grace,
            Thy goodness and thy truth we praise,
               Thy goodness and thy truth we prove;
            Thou hast, in honour of thy Son,
            The gift unspeakable sent down,
               The Spir't of life, and power, and love.

            Send us the Spirit of thy Son,
            To make the depths of Godhead known,
               To make us share the life divine;
            Send him the sprinkled blood to apply,
            Send him our souls to sanctify,
               And show and seal us ever thine.

            So shall we pray, and never cease,
            So shall we thankfully confess
               Thy wisdom, truth, and power, and love;
            With joy unspeakable adore,
            And bless and praise thee evermore,
               And serve thee as thy hosts above:

            Till, added to that heavenly choir,
            We raise our songs of triumph higher,
               And praise thee in a bolder strain,
            Outsoar the first-born seraph's flight,
            And sing, with all our friends in light,
               Thy everlasting love to man.

                        Charles Wesley (1707–88)

From *Hymns of Petition and Thanksgiving for the Promise of the Father*, sub-titled 'Hymns for Whitsunday' and published at Bristol in 1746. This was the first hymn, which started the book of 32 hymns with a strong text. The original had eight verses. The verses that are usually omitted contain a powerful vision of the promise of the Comforter (from John 14: 16–17), first seen in the context of the Old Testament, in which 'The Prophecy' and 'The Promise' are fulfilled by 'The Grace'. The prophecy is found in Genesis 3: 15, in which the serpent is told 'I will put enmity between thee and the woman, and between thy seed and her seed; it shall bruise thy head, and thou shalt bruise his heel'; the promise is sworn to Abraham, in Genesis 22: 15–18, that in his seed 'shall all the nations of the earth be blessed'. Wesley was following a traditional reading of these passages, found, for example, in Milton, *Paradise Lost* X. 182 ff., and XII. 147 ff. Verses 2 to 5 contain a tradi-tional Covenant theology, transformed by Wesley's imagination into the promise of the Holy Spirit:

Thou hast THE PROPHECY fulfill'd,
The grand Orig'nal Compact seal'd,
    For which thy Word and Oath were join'd:
THE PROMISE to our Fallen Head
To every Child of Adam made,
    Is now pour'd out on all Mankind.

The purchas'd Comforter is given,
For Jesus is return'd to Heaven,
    To claim, and then THE GRACE impart:
Our Day of Pentecost is come,
And GOD vouchsafes to fix his Home
    In every poor expecting Heart.

Father, on Thee whoever call,
Confess the Promise is for All,
    While every one that asks receives,
Receives the Gift, and Giver too,
And witnesses that Thou art true,
    And in the Spirit walks, and lives.

Not to a single Age confin'd,
For every Soul of Man design'd,
    O GOD, we now That Spirit claim:
To us the Holy Ghost impart,
Breathe Him into our panting Heart,
    Thou hear'st us ask in JESU'S Name.

This hymn has been known mainly to Methodists, by whom it is highly valued: it appeared in John Wesley's *A Collection of Hymns for the Use of the People called Methodists* (1780) in the section quaintly entitled 'Groaning for full Redemption'. However, it was included in *The Australian Hymn Book*, and there are signs that it may be making its way into wider circulation, most notably by its inclusion in *Common Praise* (2000), the new edition of *Hymns Ancient and Modern*.

As so often with Charles Wesley, it begins on earth and ends in heaven, proceeding from the gift of the Holy Spirit to the ultimate rejoicing of the heavenly choir. It links the promise of the Holy Spirit as Comforter, from John 14 and John 16, with a complex series of New Testament references, especially to 1 Peter 1: 2.

The tune to which this hymn is usually sung is STAMFORD, which carries the words with a rare vigour and fluidity, suited to the way in which the lines run on and interconnect. It was composed by Samuel Reay and first published in John Dobson's *Tunes New and Old* (1864). Reay was organist of Newark parish church, not far from Stamford, from 1864 to 1901.

100   Rejoice, the Lord is King!
            Your Lord and King adore;
            Mortals, give thanks, and sing,
            And triumph evermore:
                Lift up your heart, lift up your voice;
                Rejoice! Again I say: Rejoice!

            Jesus the Saviour reigns,
            The God of truth and love;
            When he had purged our stains,
            He took his seat above:

            His kingdom cannot fail,
            He rules o'er earth and heaven;
            The keys of death and hell
            Are to our Jesus given:

            He sits at God's right hand
            Till all his foes submit,
            And bow to his command,
            And fall beneath his feet:

            Rejoice in glorious hope;
            Jesus the Judge shall come,
            And take his servants up
            To their eternal home:
                We soon shall hear the archangel's voice;
                The trump of God shall sound: Rejoice!

                        Charles Wesley (1707–88)

From *Hymns for our Lord's Resurrection* (1746). It had six verses, with an
original verse 5 as follows:

            He all his Foes shall quell,
            Shall all our Sins destroy,
            And every Bosom swell
            With pure Seraphic Joy;
                Lift up your heart, lift up your voice;
                Rejoice! Again I say: Rejoice!

This verse, which is understandably omitted in modern printings, is characteristic of Wesley's enthusiasm, his pride in the achievements of Christ
figured in the image of the swelling bosom. What remains of the hymn is an
economical statement of the final triumph of Jesus as Saviour and Judge, as
stated in the Apostles' Creed: 'He ascended into heaven, and sitteth at the
right hand of God the Father Almighty; from whence He shall come to judge
the quick and the dead.' The rule of Christ is connected with his
Resurrection in Ephesians 1: 19–22, which speaks of God's mighty power—

Which he wrought in Christ, when he raised him from the dead, and set him at his
own right hand in the heavenly places, . . . And hath put all things under his feet . . .

The hymn is a meditation and expansion of Philippians 4: 4: 'Rejoice in the Lord alway: and again I say, Rejoice.' It begins with an allusion to the first and last verses of Psalm 97: 'The Lord reigneth, let the earth rejoice' and 'Rejoice in the Lord, ye righteous; and give thanks at the remembrance of his holiness.' As these phrases begin and end the psalm, and the verse from Philippians, so the word 'rejoice' opens and closes this hymn. The wording of the refrain, until the final verse, is from the *Sursum Corda* in the eucharistic liturgy, 'Lift up your hearts'. The final verse is a thrilling reminder of 1 Corinthians 15, which in this hymn takes up the reference to 'mortals' in verse 1:

The trumpet shall sound, and the dead shall be raised incorruptible, and we shall be changed . . . For this corruptible must put on incorruption, and this mortal must put on immortality.

The mastery of structure and the density of allusion are rare even for Charles Wesley: they make this the greatest of all triumph hymns.

In its earliest years, this hymn was probably sung to an appropriately named tune, RESURRECTION, by Wesley's friend John Frederick Lampe (1703–51), printed in *Hymns on the Great Festivals and Other Occasions* (1746). It is now invariably sung to GOPSAL, a tune which was once called ON THE RESURRECTION: it was one of three tunes by George Frideric Handel discovered in 1826 by Charles Wesley's son Samuel in the library of the Fitzwilliam Museum, Cambridge. The name GOPSAL refers to Gopsal Hall in Leicestershire, the home of Charles Jennens, who arranged the texts for Handel's *Messiah*.

101   Love Divine, all loves excelling,
           Joy of heaven, to earth come down,
       Fix in us thy humble dwelling,
           All thy faithful mercies crown.
       Jesu, thou art all compassion,
           Pure unbounded love thou art;
       Visit us with thy salvation,
           Enter every trembling heart.

       Come, almighty to deliver,
           Let us all thy life receive;
       Suddenly return, and never,
           Never more thy temples leave.
       Thee we would be always blessing,
           Serve thee as thy hosts above,
       Pray, and praise thee, without ceasing,
           Glory in thy perfect love.

       Finish then thy new creation,
           Pure and spotless let us be;
       Let us see thy great salvation,
           Perfectly restored in thee:
       Changed from glory into glory,
           Till in heaven we take our place,
       Till we cast our crowns before thee,
           Lost in wonder, love, and praise!

                    Charles Wesley (1707–88)

From *Hymns for those that seek, and those that have Redemption in the Blood of Jesus Christ* (1747). It is almost always printed in three verses (or six verses of four lines each), but originally there were four. Verse 2 was

       Breathe, O breathe thy loving Spirit
           Into every troubled breast,
       Let us all in thee inherit,
           Let us find that second rest;
       Take away our power of sinning,
           Alpha and Omega be,
       End of faith, as its beginning,
           Set our hearts at liberty.

It has been suggested that this verse was dropped by John Wesley in his 1780 *Collection of Hymns for the Use of the People called Methodists* because it was controversial (presumably because it admits the possibility of continuing to sin). It deals with the complex problem of 'the second blessing' ('that second rest' of line 4 of this verse), which is a blessing which follows and confirms the conversion experience. The contents part of the 1780 *Collection* illustrates the process as John Wesley saw it: Part III deals with conversion, with sections entitled 'Praying for Repentance', 'For Mourners convinced of Sin', and 'For Mourners brought to the Birth'; Part IV with the post-conversion experience of 'Believers', who are 'Rejoicing, Fighting, Praying, Watching, Working, Suffering' and then 'Groaning for Full Redemption', 'Brought to the Birth', 'Saved', and 'Interceding for the Word'. For a full discussion of Wesley's theology, including a reference to this verse, see the modern edition of the 1780 *Collection*, volume 7 of *The Works of John Wesley*, edited by Franz Hildebrandt and Oliver A. Beckerlegge (Oxford, 1983: 16–19).

The three verses that remain make a hymn that has become justly famous and beloved, better known than almost any other hymn of Charles Wesley. In *Hymns Ancient and Modern* it was printed in six four-line verses, and set to a tune by John Stainer: most other books use the original eight-line verse form. This gives a very satisfying three movements: the prayer for the Saviour to visit the trembling heart; the receiving of grace, so that the redeemed soul can pray and praise; and the finishing of the new creation, ending with the final transformation into the full glory of heaven. The reference is to 2 Corinthians 5: 17: 'if any man be in Christ, he is a new creature', and it is expressed by one of Charles Wesley's favourite metaphors, that of the soul which is 'lost', lost in God, lost in wonder, love, and praise. The last line is an adaptation from Addison's

> Transported with the view, I'm lost
> In wonder, love, and praise.

Charles Wesley's placing of 'lost' at the beginning of the last line is crucial to the heightened effect of this last sublime verse.

The opening is modelled on a lyric from Dryden's *King Arthur* (1691), the 'Song sung by Venus in honour of Britannia' in Act II:

> Fairest Isle, all isles excelling,
> Seat of pleasures, and of loves;
> Venus here will choose her dwelling,
> And forsake her Cyprian groves.

Wesley characteristically takes over a classical reference and makes a Christian point: instead of Venus, the goddess of love, leaving Cyprus for the British Isles, Divine Love is to leave heaven and dwell in the human heart (if we take 'to earth come down' as an adjectival phrase, the meaning is that it has already come). Another classical reference is to Ovid's *Metamorphoses* (which Wesley would have studied at school), not only because Ovid's poem deals with change and transformation, as the third verse does here, but also because there is a particular story of divinities coming to earth: in Book VIII, Jupiter and Mercury are entertained by Baucis and Philemon in their humble dwelling ('parva quidem, stipulis et canna tecta palustri'—'poor, and thatched with reeds from the marsh'). The kind old couple are rewarded by dying together; they are transformed into trees, guarding the temple ('Never more thy temples leave').

Charles Wesley wrote 'Let us all thy life receive' in the 1747 printing (verse 2, line 2). In *A Collection of Hymns for the Use of the People called Methodists* of 1780 John Wesley amended 'life' to 'grace', which is acceptable, but less apposite to the Incarnational theology of the hymn as a whole. 'Grace' remained in Methodist books until *Hymns and Psalms* (1983); other denominations have tended to print 'life'. Charles Wesley's precision of thought is well seen in 'life' (from John 10: 10, 'I am come that they may have life, and have it more abundantly'); and his ingenious use of his complex sources in this hymn is coupled with a sweeping and energetic verse style that uses such Biblical references neatly and fittingly to produce the greatest of all hymns on Christian love.

The hymn has a strong 8.7.8.7.D metre, and it has been fortunate to attract a number of fine tunes. The first was Purcell's setting of Dryden's lyric, which Wesley may have had in his mind when writing the words. It appeared in several eighteenth-century hymn-books, named WESTMINSTER, and was set to the present hymn in the Wesleys' *Select Hymns with Tunes Annext* (1761). After almost two hundred years of neglect, it has recently been revived, and is one of the three tunes in the present Methodist book, *Hymns and Psalms*. Another tune is John Stainer's charming LOVE DIVINE, set to the four-line verses in the 1889 Supplement to the 1875 edition of *Hymns Ancient and Modern*. Grander and more responsive to the sublime element of the hymn are the three splendid Welsh tunes which have been associated with it in various books: MORIAH, HYFRYDOL, and (most frequently) BLAEN-WERN, written by W. P. Rowlands (1860–1937).

102   Lo! He comes with clouds descending,
         Once for favoured sinners slain;
       Thousand thousand Saints attending
         Swell the triumph of his train:
           Alleluia!
         God appears, on earth to reign.

       Every eye shall now behold him
         Robed in dreadful majesty;
       Those who set at nought and sold him,
         Pierced and nailed him to the tree,
           Deeply wailing,
         Shall the true Messiah see.

       Those dear tokens of his passion
         Still his dazzling body bears,
       Cause of endless exultation
         To his ransomed worshippers:
           With what rapture
         Gaze we on those glorious scars!

       Yea, amen! let all adore thee,
         High on thine eternal throne;
       Saviour, take the power and glory,
         Claim the kingdom for thine own:
           O come quickly!
         Everlasting God, come down!

           Charles Wesley (1707–88), and others

This hymn was first published in approximately this form in *Hymns of Intercession for all Mankind* (1758), although verse 4 line 5 was originally 'Jah, Jehovah!', quoting Psalm 68: 4. It seems to have been a rewriting of a hymn by John Cennick (1718–55), a follower of John Wesley and George Whitefield who became a Moravian minister. Cennick's hymn appears in the fifth edition of his *Collection of Sacred Hymns* (1752). Two of the five verses will give an indication of Cennick's enthusiasm, and (by contrast) Wesley's fine control:

(1)   Lo! he cometh, countless trumpets
         Blow before his bloody sign!
       'Midst ten thousand saints and angels,
         See the Crucified shine,
           Allelujah!
         Welcome, welcome bleeding Lamb!

(4)   All who love him view His glory,
         Shining in his bruised Face:
       His dear Person on the rainbow,
         Now His people's heads shall raise:
           Happy mourners!
         Now on clouds he comes! he comes!

Martin Madan's *Collection of Psalms and Hymns* (1760) printed a further version containing some Cennick and some Wesley, together with other changes; and since then there have been many variations in the printings of this hymn. It is a magnificent hymn, with a powerful tune, but like many sublime hymns it treads a narrow line between being too wildly enthusiastic (as in Cennick's version) and being too restrained. Charles Wesley's version deals with this problem finely and with sensitivity. Some modern rewritings err on the side of control, and take the stuffing out of the hymn. *Rejoice and Sing*, for example, replaces

> Deeply wailing
> Shall the true Messiah see

with

> Lord have mercy,
> let us all thine Advent see.

In any traditional version it is a very powerful hymn, usually sung during the season of Advent with particular reference to the Second Coming. In this it follows the second part of the Collect for the First Sunday in Advent:

. . . that in the last day, when he shall come again in his glorious Majesty to judge both the quick and the dead, we may rise to the life immortal, . . .

In Charles Wesley's original printing it was in a section entitled 'Thy Kingdom Come', and it is full of references to Revelation, especially to 1: 7: 'Behold, he cometh with clouds; and every eye shall see him, and they also which pierced him: and all kindreds of the earth shall wail because of him. Even so, Amen.'

This hymn is almost always sung to the tune HELMSLEY. That tune is said to have been written by Thomas Olivers, one of John Wesley's preachers (who wrote the words of 'The God of Abraham praise'): it was printed with the name OLIVERS in the second edition of Wesley's *Select Hymns with Tunes Annext* (1765). It is close to a tune named HELMSLEY found in Martin Madan's *A Collection of Psalm and Hymn Tunes* (1769). It may have been given the name by Dr Richard Conyers, vicar of Helmsley in Yorkshire, who published *A Collection of Psalms and Hymns, from various authors: for the use of serious and devout Christians of every denomination* in 1767. The use of the word 'serious' (meaning 'serious in matters of religion') indicates his book's evangelical affiliations: it was one of the earliest Church of England hymnbooks, and helped to encourage hymn-singing in the north of England (a fifth edition was printed in York in 1788).

103   Let saints on earth in concert sing
             With those whose work is done;
        For all the servants of our King
             In heaven and earth are one.

        One family, we dwell in him,
             One Church, above, beneath;
        Though now divided by the stream,
             The narrow stream of death.

        One army of the living God,
             To his command we bow;
        Part of the host have crossed the flood,
             And part are crossing now.

        E'en now to their eternal home
             There pass some spirits blest;
        While others to the margin come,
             Waiting their call to rest.

        Jesu, be thou our constant guide;
             Then, when the word is given,
        Bid Jordan's narrow stream divide,
             And bring us safe to heaven.

                    Charles Wesley (1707–88) and others

This is a well-known text, taken from *Hymns Ancient and Modern,* of a longer and finer hymn, which is still known to Methodists. It is also, in Percy Dearmer's words, 'a curious and extreme example of the "cooking" of a hymn', the making of a new dish from raw materials. In its original form, it is from Charles Wesley's *Funeral Hymns,* second series (1759). Some of the new version is found in the sixth edition of Thomas Cotterill's *Selection of Psalms and Hymns* (1815): Cotterill was a Sheffield man, and a friend of James Montgomery, who may have been responsible for the new text: its effective plainness would be characteristic of Montgomery's work.

Although this makes a neat and precise hymn on the Communion of Saints, Charles Wesley's original version is immeasurably superior in imaginative grasp: Wesley seems to be able to picture the greeting between the living and the dead, and the last verse, with its hope of heaven, refers back to the story of Moses with a breathtaking rightness:

                    Come, let us join our friends above
                         That have obtained the prize,
                    And on the eagle wings of love
                         To joys celestial rise:
                    Let all the saints terrestrial sing
                         With those to glory gone;
                    For all the servants of our King,
                         In earth and heaven, are one.

One family, we dwell in him,
    One church, above, beneath,
Though now divided by the stream,
    The narrow stream of death:
One army of the living God,
    To his command we bow;
Part of his host have crossed the flood,
    And part are crossing now.

Ten thousand to their endless home
    This solemn moment fly;
And we are to the margin come,
    And we expect to die;
His militant, embodied host
    With wishful looks we stand,
And long to see that happy coast,
    And reach that heavenly land.

Our old companions in distress
    We haste again to see,
And eager long for our release,
    And full felicity:
Ev'n now by faith we join our hands
    With those that went before,
And greet the blood-besprinkled bands
    On the eternal shore.

Our spirits too shall quickly join,
    Like theirs with glory crowned,
And shout to see our captain's sign,
    To hear his trumpet sound.
O that we now might grasp our guide!
    O that the word were given!
Come, Lord of Hosts, the waves divide,
    And land us all in heaven.

The imagery is traditional, but seldom has it been deployed with such skill: the singer rises to become a part of the Communion of Saints on the eagle wings of love, and yet that sublime achievement is also linked with the idea of the 'one family' in heaven and on earth. Death is the traditional narrow stream, but those who cross it do so because they are 'blood-besprinkled' (from Hebrews 9 and 10, where the sprinkling of blood by Moses over the people of Israel is seen as a figure of the saving blood of Jesus Christ, and from 1 Peter 1: 2: 'through sanctification of the Spirit, unto obedience and sprinkling of the blood of Jesus Christ').

Jesus is the captain, but the typology of Moses as the liberator and leader is everywhere in this hymn. The 'one family' of verse 2 suggests the children of Israel, who came 'to the margin' of the Red Sea, expecting to die (verse 3) but who were delivered by the dividing of the waves. In this way the hymn reaches back into Old Testament legend with a New Testament application. It also draws upon Puritan tradition: the central image of the stream of death is found unforgettably in John Bunyan's *The Pilgrim's Progress*, which in turn influenced Isaac Watts's 'There is a land of pure delight' (no. 67), which is echoed at the end of verse 3 of Wesley's version.

The shorter version is usually sung to DUNDEE, from the *Scottish Psalter*, where it was originally one of the twelve 'common tunes' (not assigned to any particular psalm). It was called DUNDY TUNE in Thomas Ravenscroft's *The Whole Booke of Psalmes* of 1621. The longer version is best sung to ST MATTHEW, a fine swinging tune by William Croft (1678–1727), also associated with 'Thine arm, O Lord, in days of old'.

104
    Forth in thy name, O Lord, I go,
      My daily labour to pursue;
    Thee, only thee, resolved to know,
      In all I think, or speak, or do.

    The task thy wisdom hath assigned
      O let me cheerfully fulfil;
    In all my works thy presence find,
      And prove thine acceptable will.

    Preserve me from my calling's snare,
      And hide my simple heart above,
    Above the thorns of choking care,
      The gilded baits of worldly love.

    Thee may I set at my right hand,
      Whose eyes my inmost substance see,
    And labour on at thy command,
      And offer all my works to thee.

    Give me to bear thy easy yoke,
      And every moment watch and pray,
    And still to things eternal look,
      And hasten to thy glorious day;

    For thee delightfully employ
      Whate'er thy bounteous grace hath given,
    And run my course with even joy,
      And closely walk with thee to heaven.

                Charles Wesley (1707–88)

From *Hymns and Sacred Poems* (1749), where it was one of forty-three 'Hymns for Believers'. It was headed 'Before Work'.

In *Songs of Praise Discussed*, Percy Dearmer commented on verse 3 that it 'strikes just the notes of social duty and avoidance of anxiety that are prominent in modern religion'. That verse marvellously complicates and deepens the hymn, setting worldly ambition and careerism into the context of something more important, the idea of work done cheerfully and for God, with the gifts that He has given (oddly, the verse is missing from most Methodist books). Wesley was clearly anxious that work should be done 'cheerfully' and 'delightfully' ('with experience of delight, delightedly'—*Oxford English Dictionary*, sense 2, where this example is quoted) rather than intensely and with narrow ambitions.

He also had in mind Romans 12: 2: 'And be not conformed to this world: but be ye transformed by the renewing of your mind, that ye may prove what is that good, and acceptable, and perfect, will of God'. This is referred to in verse 2, line 4, where Wesley is seeking to 'prove' ('find out by experience', *OED* sense 3) what is God's acceptable will. The line appears awkward to sing, however, and this crucial reference has often been lost in modern printings (amended to the less precise 'And prove thy good and perfect will'). The hymn is therefore not just a prayer for cheerful working; it is rich with the tensions of religious duty and worldly ambition, and with the need to set work in the context of divine service.

The customary tune for this hymn is SONG 34 (ANGELS' SONG) by Orlando Gibbons, written for George Wither's *Hymns and Songs of the Church* (1623). It was set to the present words in John Wesley's *Select Hymns with Tunes Annext* (1761), and has been associated with them from that time onwards.

105   O thou who camest from above
            The pure celestial fire to impart,
         Kindle a flame of sacred love
            On the mean altar of my heart!

         There let it for thy glory burn
            With inextinguishable blaze,
         And trembling to its source return,
            In humble prayer and fervent praise.

         Jesus, confirm my heart's desire
            To work, and speak, and think for thee;
         Still let me guard the holy fire,
            And still stir up thy gift in me;

         Ready for all thy perfect will,
            My acts of faith and love repeat,
         Till death thy endless mercies seal,
            And make the sacrifice complete.

                        Charles Wesley (1707–88)

First published in *Short Hymns on Select Passages of the Holy Scriptures* (1762), on Leviticus 6: 13: 'The fire shall ever be burning upon the altar; it shall never go out.' It was originally in two eight-line stanzas. Wesley characteristically applies this Old Testament text as a metaphor for the human heart, giving it a vivid personal application, especially in the original, where the final line was 'And make my sacrifice complete'.

Wesley's lines contain many passing allusions to biblical texts, especially to the descent of the Holy Ghost at Pentecost (Acts 2: 3) and to the image of fire in Luke 12: 49. The hymn thus invests the original text from Leviticus with a New Testament application: in verse 4, for example, 'perfect will' is taken from Romans 12: 2 and the 'acts of faith and love' are from I Thessalonians 1: 3. The modern editors of *A Collection of Hymns for the Use of the People called Methodists* have pointed to a series of debts, not only to biblical phrases, but also to eighteenth-century poetry: Pope used the phrase 'celestial fire' (*An Essay on Criticism*: 195), and 'holy fire' was used by Edward Young in 'The Last Day' and by Richard Blackmore in 'A Hymn to the Sacred Spirit'. Wesley's debt to the *Book of Common Prayer* is found in verse 3, line 4, where the phrase 'stir up' echoes the Collect for the twenty-fifth Sunday after Trinity: 'Stir up, we beseech thee, O Lord, the wills of thy faithful people . . .'.

It is part of a hymn of great firmness and strength: the 'O thou' at the beginning is echoed by 'Jesus' at the opening of verse 3 (originally verse 2, the opening of the second verse); and the long metre lines are organized with great skill. Thus 'kindle', the main verb, comes at precisely the right moment in verse 1; there is a fine balance in verse 2, with 'humble prayer and fervent praise', and that verse accommodates the wonderful six-syllable 'inextinguishable'. Against the steady beat, and strong rhetoric, Wesley introduces the unexpected and enlivening variation of the trochaic 'Ready' at the opening of verse 4; returning to regularity as the verse proceeds, so that the final line is steadily iambic, ending very satisfyingly with 'complete'. As the last verse ends, the line, and the hymn, and the meditation, and the heart's sacrifice, are all complete.

The best-known tune for this hymn is S. S. Wesley's HEREFORD, used in *Hymns Ancient and Modern*. Some Methodist books have used WILTON, by Samuel Stanley (1767–1822), but HEREFORD seems now to be the preferred tune.

{7}

The Later Eighteenth Century

This is the period of the earliest collections of hymns for public worship, apart from John Wesley's early *Collection of Psalms and Hymns*. George Whitefield printed *A Collection of Hymns for Social Worship* in 1753; Martin Madan, chaplain to the Lock Hospital in London, produced his collection in 1760; Richard Conyers's *Collection of Psalms and Hymns* was printed in York in 1767; and Augustus Montague Toplady followed with *Psalms and Hymns for Public and Private Worship* in 1776. Meanwhile the Baptists Caleb Evans and John Ash had produced their own book in 1769; while the Congregationalists had John Rippon's *A Collection of Hymns from Various Authors, intended as a Supplement to Dr Watts* (1787). Clearly there was a great deal of encouragement to sing hymns in certain religious circles.

The hymn-writing of the second half of the eighteenth century was dominated by the Evangelical Revival, with its emphasis on personal salvation through the blood of Jesus Christ. William Cowper's 'There is a fountain fill'd with blood/ Drawn from Emmanuel's veins' is a graphic example of that impassioned belief; and John Newton's 'Amazing grace' is another example of the strong sense of sin and of the power of Jesus Christ to overcome it. Newton's own life, as a sailor and as the master of a slave ship, was a dramatic example of the power of Christ to change people's lives: he became a clergyman, at Olney, and then at St Mary Woolnoth in London, where his memorial tablet can still be seen, testifying to his change of heart. Similarly, Augustus Montague Toplady's 'Rock of Ages, cleft for me' signals a need to trust in the saving power of Jesus, not in his own righteousness, or even in his own penitence.

Two followers of John Wesley appear in this section: Thomas Olivers, who accompanied Wesley on some of his journeys, and who ran Wesley's 'Print Room' for a time; and Edward Perronet, who disliked the Church of England and preached against it so vehemently that he quarrelled with Wesley over the matter. Also associated with the early Methodists was William Williams, the 'sweet singer of Wales', two of whose magnificent hymns are printed here.

Christopher Smart, who lived during this period, was one of the great religious poets of the eighteenth century: his mystical *Jubilate Agno* is an astonishing performance, in which (as Robert Browning put it) he 'lit language straight from soul'. His hymns are not so well known, but one, 'Where is this stupendous stranger?', has recently found a place in a number of hymn-books.

In Scotland during this period, the church produced the *Translations and Paraphrases* in 1781, following an uncertain period of trial collections from 1745 onward. They contain some of the finest examples of biblical paraphrase, and three of them have been included.

106
The God of Abraham praise
Who reigns enthroned above,
Ancient of everlasting Days,
    And God of love:
Jehovah, great I AM,
By earth and heaven confest;
We bow and bless the sacred name
    For ever blest.

The God of Abraham praise,
    At whose supreme command
From earth we rise, and seek the joys
    At his right hand:
We all on earth forsake,
    Its wisdom, fame, and power;
And him our only portion make,
    Our Shield and Tower.

Though nature's strength decay,
    And earth and hell withstand,
To Canaan's bounds we urge our way
    At his command:
The watery deep we pass,
    With Jesus in our view;
And through the howling wilderness
    Our way pursue.

The goodly land we see,
    With peace and plenty blest:
A land of sacred liberty
    And endless rest;
There milk and honey flow,
    And oil and wine abound,
And trees of life for ever grow,
    With mercy crowned.

There dwells the Lord our King,
    The Lord our Righteousness,
Triumphant o'er the world of sin,
    The Prince of Peace:
On Sion's sacred height
    His Kingdom he maintains,
And glorious with his saints in light
    For ever reigns.

He keeps his own secure,
He guards them by his side,
Arrays in garment white and pure
    His spotless Bride:
With streams of sacred bliss,
Beneath serener skies,
With all the fruits of Paradise,
    He still supplies.

Before the great Three-One
They all exulting stand,
And tell the wonders he hath done
    Through all their land:
The listening spheres attend,
And swell the growing fame,
And sing in songs which never end
    The wondrous name.

The God who reigns on high
The great archangels sing,
And 'Holy, Holy, Holy,' cry,
    'Almighty King!
Who was, and is the same,
And evermore shall be:
Jehovah, Father, great I AM,
    We worship thee.'

Before the Saviour's face
The ransomed nations bow,
O'erwhelmed at his almighty grace
    For ever new;
He shows his prints of love—
They kindle to a flame,
And sound through all the worlds above
    The slaughtered Lamb.

The whole triumphant host
Give thanks to God on high;
'Hail, Father, Son, and Holy Ghost!'
    They ever cry:
Hail! Abraham's God, and mine!
(I join the heavenly lays)
All might and majesty are thine,
    And endless praise.

Thomas Olivers (1725–99)

This amazing hymn is based on the Hebrew Yigdal, the summary of the
Jewish faith chanted between cantor and congregation in Jewish worship. It
was versified into a hymn form by Max Landsberg and Newton Mann, and

later recast by W. C. Gannett, as 'Praise to the living God'. Olivers took the tune, which he had heard sung by the great cantor Meyer Leoni (or Lyon), and wrote his hymn to fit the tune, giving a specifically Christian content to the words. The hymn had twelve verses: the present text is that of *Hymns Ancient and Modern New Standard*, where it is still printed in this ten-verse form (as it is in *Common Praise*, though with different capitalization). This text changes the original 'I' form into 'We' throughout, to make the hymn more congregational.

Olivers was an early follower of John Wesley, who valued him highly. He was a cobbler by trade, who was converted by George Whitefield in Bristol, and who became a fervent preacher and a formidable controversialist in the pamphlet wars that raged around early Methodism. His daring hymn shows why the Methodists were distrusted on account of their enthusiasm: its verses proceed from earth to heaven in an ecstasy of imaginative excitement. In one of the omitted verses, it also shows the wonder of spiritual experience—'He calls a worm his friend'. The hymn was first printed in leaflet form, with the title *A Hymn to the God of Abraham, In Three Parts: Adapted to a celebrated Air, sung by the Priest, Signior Leoni, etc., at the Jews' Synagogue, in London.* John Wesley then printed some of the verses in his *Sacred Harmony* (1780), and they were included in subsequent early Methodist hymn-books.

The verses are packed with biblical references, and with the imagery associated with the visions of Revelation. The opening is from Exodus 3: 6 and 3: 14: 'I am the God of thy father, the God of Abraham', and 'I AM THAT I AM'. From there the Exodus experience serves as the metaphor for the pilgrimage of the soul until the Promised Land is reached, the glory of which occupies Olivers to the end of the hymn.

The tune is LEONI, named after Meyer Leoni (Leoni was the liturgical name for Meyer Lyon), which Olivers is said to have heard about 1770, and which inspired the unusual form and metre of the splendid verses.

107   All hail the power of Jesu's name;
                         Let angels prostrate fall;
                       Bring forth the royal diadem
                         To crown him Lord of all.

                       Crown him, ye morning stars of light,
                         Who fixed this floating ball;
                       Now hail the strength of Israel's might,
                         And crown him Lord of all.

                       Crown him, ye Martyrs of your God,
                         Who from his altar call;
                       Praise him whose way of praise ye trod,
                         And crown him Lord of all.

                       Ye seed of Israel's chosen race,
                         Ye ransomed of the fall,
                       Hail him who saves you by his grace,
                         And crown him Lord of all.

                       Hail him, ye heirs of David's line,
                         Whom David Lord did call;
                       The God Incarnate, Man Divine,
                         And crown him Lord of all.

                       Sinners, whose love can ne'er forget
                         The wormwood and the gall,
                       Go spread your trophies at his feet,
                         And crown him Lord of all.

                       Let every tribe and every tongue
                         To him their hearts enthral,
                       Lift high the universal song,
                         And crown him Lord of all.

                       Edward Perronet (c.1726–92), and others

This hymn dates from 1779 and 1780, and is clearly an expression of the Evangelical Revival of the eighteenth century. The first verse was printed in the *Gospel Magazine* for November 1779, and an eight-verse text appeared in the same magazine in 1780, with the title 'On the Resurrection. The Lord is King'.

The hymn has been the subject of many alterations over the years, beginning with John Rippon's *Selection of Hymns* of 1787, where a version was printed with the title 'The Spiritual Coronation, Canticles 3: 11'. The reference is to the Song of Songs: 'Go forth, O ye daughters of Zion, and behold king Solomon with the crown wherewith his mother crowned him in the day of his espousals, and in the day of the gladness of his heart.' By applying Solomon's crowning to this hymn, the Old Testament reference is seen as Solomon prefiguring Christ.

The original text is full of awkward phrases and coded references. Verse 3, line 3, for example, was 'Extol the Stem-of-Jesse's Rod' (from Isaiah 11: 1), and Perronet's final verse was

> Let every tribe and every tongue
> That bound creation's call,
> Now shout in universal song
> The crowned Lord of all.

Rippon's version was:

> O that with yonder sacred throng
> We at his feet may fall,
> We'll join the everlasting song,
> And crown him Lord of all.

The text used here is from the *English Hymnal*. In spite of all the alterations (there is a particularly radical rewriting of the text in *Songs of Praise*) the hymn has survived very well: its most distinctive feature is the continuous rhyme with 'all', which allows the variations on a sound—'gall', 'fall', 'ball'—to have a chiming effect while expressing different aspects of the Evangelical experience.

The hymn's continued popularity, however, must have something to do with its spectacular tunes. In the 1779 printing, the first verse appeared with a tune entitled SHRUBSOLE, now known as MILES LANE, which remains the tune in many books. It is a fine rousing tune, with an appropriate rising repetition of 'crown him' making a natural crescendo. It was written by William Shrubsole (1760–1806) and named after a chapel in Miles Lane, London, with which he may have been associated.

DIADEM, a nineteenth-century tune, is even more extraordinary. It was written by James Ellor (1819–99), and is frequently found in Methodist books and in the Salvation Army repertoire (it is most effective when played by a band). The repetitions in this tune require the second line of each verse to be sung twice, and then 'crown him' is sung no less than eight times, six repetitions with an opening and a concluding phrase.

Another fine tune is LADYWELL, composed for these words in *The Public School Hymn Book* (1919) by W. H. Ferguson (1874–1950).

108   Rock of Ages, cleft for me,
                      Let me hide myself in thee;
                      Let the Water and the Blood,
                      From thy riven side which flowed,
                      Be of sin the double cure,
                      Cleanse me from its guilt and power.

                      Not the labours of my hands
                      Can fulfil thy law's demands;
                      Could my zeal no respite know,
                      Could my tears for ever flow,
                      All for sin could not atone;
                      Thou must save, and thou alone.

                      Nothing in my hand I bring,
                      Simply to thy cross I cling;
                      Naked, come to thee for dress;
                      Helpless, look to thee for grace;
                      Foul, I to the fountain fly;
                      Wash me, Saviour, or I die.

                      Whilst I draw this fleeting breath,
                      When mine eyes are closed in death,
                      When I soar through tracts unknown,
                      See thee on thy judgment throne;
                      Rock of ages, cleft for me,
                      Let me hide myself in thee.

                      Augustus Montague Toplady (1740–78)

The first appearance of the famous first line of this hymn was in October
1775, in the *Gospel Magazine*:

Yet, if you fall, be humbled, but do not despair. Pray afresh to God, who is able to
raise you up, and set you on your feet again. Look to the blood of the covenant; and
say to the Lord, from the depths of your heart—

                      Rock of Ages, cleft for me,
                      Let me hide myself in Thee!
                      Foul I to the fountain fly:
                      Wash me, Saviour, or I die.

   In the *Gospel Magazine* for the following March 1776, Toplady (who had
by then become editor) published a bizarre article, entitled 'A remarkable
Calculation: Introduced here, for the sake of the spiritual Improvement sub-
joined. Questions and Answers, relative to the National Debt'. Noting that
the National Debt was so large that it would never be paid off, Toplady
argued that human beings would incur the same kind of unpayable debt
because they would never achieve 'legal sanctity' and because they break
God's laws 'every second of [their] sublunary duration'. The result was what
he called 'Our dreadful account', second by second:

At *ten* years old each of us is chargeable with 315 millions and 36 thousand sins. At *twenty*, with 630 millions, and 720 thousand. At *thirty*, with 946 millions and 80 thousand . . . .

At the end of this calculation, Toplady argued that although the debt grew every day, 'Christ hath redeemed us from the curse of the Law; being made a curse for us (Gal. iii. 13)'. 'This, This will not only *counter*-balance, but infinitely *over*-balance, ALL the sins of the WHOLE believing world'. Beneath this followed 'Rock of ages, cleft for me', under the title 'A living and dying PRAYER for the HOLIEST BELIEVER in the world'.

The only alteration to this first printing is in verse 4, line 2, which was originally 'When my eye-strings break in death'. The eye-strings, or tendons, were supposed to break or crack at the moment of death.

Toplady was a Calvinist of an extreme persuasion, author of *The Historical Proof of the Doctrinal Calvinism of the Church of England* (1774). He engaged in a fierce pamphlet war with the Arminian John Wesley and his followers. His hymn has become his claim to fame: Julian's *Dictionary of Hymnology* argues that 'no other English hymn can be named which has laid so broad and firm a grasp upon the English-speaking world.' Julian, who traces many subsequent versions of the hymn, also notes that there have been several translations of it into Latin, including W. E. Gladstone's 'Jesus, pro me perforatus'.

There are many references to rock in the Old Testament, including Exodus 33: 22: 'I will put thee [Moses] in a cleft of the rock, and will cover thee with my hand'; but the hymn probably owes more to St Paul's famous typology in 1 Corinthians 10: 4: 'for they drank of that spiritual Rock that followed them: and that Rock was Christ.' Toplady may also have known Charles Wesley's *Hymns on the Lord's Supper* (1745), which reprints as a Preface John Wesley's abridgement of Dr Daniel Brevint's *The Christian Sacrament and Sacrifice*. Brevint's book contains the following:

O Rock of Israel, Rock of Salvation, Rock struck and cleft for me, let those two streams of blood and water which once gushed out of Thy side bring down pardon and holiness into my soul; and let me thirst after them now, as if I stood upon the mountain whence sprung this water, and near the cleft of that rock, the wounds of my Lord, whence gushed this sacred blood.

Charles Wesley used the rock image in hymn 27 of *Hymns on the Lord's Supper*, which has a first line that anticipates Toplady's in its grandeur, but which then becomes quite different:

> Rock of Israel, cleft for me,
> For us, for all Mankind,
> See, thy feeblest Followers see
> Who call thy Death to mind: . . .

Another hymn inspired by the passage from Brevint is 31, which is closer to Toplady:

> O Rock of our Salvation, see
> The Souls that seek their Rest in Thee,
> Beneath thy cooling Shadow hide,
> And keep us, Saviour, in thy Side,
> By Water and by Blood redeem,
> And wash us in the mingled Stream.

Fine though these hymns are, neither has quite the magical quality of Toplady's lines. James Montgomery noted 'a peculiarly ethereal spirit' in Toplady's hymns, 'in which, whether mourning or rejoicing, praying or praising, the writer seems absorbed in the full triumph of faith, and "whether in the body or out of the body, caught up into the third heaven", and beholding unutterable things.'

The usual, very dignified, tune is REDHEAD No. 76, also known as PETRA ('Rock'), by Richard Redhead (1820–1901), published in his *Church Hymn Tunes, Ancient and Modern* of 1853. It was set to this hymn in *Hymns Ancient and Modern* (1861), where it was given the name PETRA. It is a fitting accompaniment to the words, with its long pauses and plangent melody. American books tend to use another tune entitled TOPLADY; it was written (in 1830) for this hymn by Thomas Hastings (1784–1872).

109   Amazing grace! (how sweet the sound)
         That sav'd a wretch like me!
       I once was lost, but now am found,
         Was blind, but now I see.

       'Twas grace that taught my heart to fear,
         And grace my fears reliev'd;
       How precious did that grace appear,
         The hour I first believ'd!

       Thro' many dangers, toils and snares,
         I have already come;
       'Tis grace has brought me safe thus far,
         And grace will lead me home.

       The Lord has promis'd good to me,
         His word my hope secures;
       He will my shield and portion be,
         As long as life endures.

Yes, when this flesh and heart shall fail,
  And mortal life shall cease;
I shall possess, within the vail,
  A life of joy and peace.

The earth shall soon dissolve like snow,
  The sun forbear to shine;
But God, who call'd me here below,
  Will be for ever mine.

John Newton (1725–1807)

This is from *Olney Hymns* (1779), the book which Newton edited, containing hymns by himself and William Cowper, who was a member of his congregation: Cowper had gone to live at Olney to 'sit under' Newton, a noted Evangelical clergyman.

This hymn has been so altered by hymn-book editors that it seems sensible to print the original text. It comes from Book I of *Olney Hymns*, *On Select Passages of Scripture*, under the heading ' I. Chronicles. Faith's review and expectation. Chap. xvii. 16, 17'. Those verses read:

And David the king came and sat before the Lord, and said, Who am I, O Lord God, and what is mine house, that thou hast brought me hitherto? And yet this was a small thing in thine eyes, O God; for thou hast also spoken of thy servant's house for a great while to come, and hast regarded me according to the estate of a man of high degree, O Lord God.

The theme of undeserved favour is taken over by Newton and used as a metaphor for the operation of divine grace. Its contrast between the original state of the 'wretch' and 'a life of joy and peace' is simple but forceful: the opening phrase, 'Amazing grace', is quite common in eighteenth-century hymnody, but placed at the beginning it acquires a boldness which is both crude and effective. Similarly, the images of being lost, and being blind, and of coming home, are simple but powerful. The ballad-like stanzas suggest a forceful, if simple, statement of faith: indeed, the words and the tune together take the hymn form close to that of a folk song or ballad.

The hymn also gains force from Newton's own history, especially as he contemplates the many dangers, toils, and snares through which he has come, and his being brought 'home'. His extraordinary life included a time as a sailor, first as a wild and godless youth and later as the master of a slave ship: he experienced storms and other adventures, notably a storm in a leaking vessel in 1748, but also through the whole of his reckless youth. He settled in Liverpool after giving up the slave trade, and fell under the influence of Wesley and Whitefield; from there he took Holy Orders, becoming curate of Olney in Buckinghamshire in 1764. There he built up a strong and fervently Evangelical congregation, including the poet William Cowper and Cowper's friend Mary Unwin. He and Cowper combined to produce *Olney Hymns* in 1779. Perhaps as a result of his early experiences, however, Newton's hymns often describe dangers and storms, as in 'Begone unbelief' ('With Christ in the vessel/ I smile at the storm'). They become metaphors for the spiritual life, but have an authenticity that comes from Newton's own experience.

This hymn has had an unusual history. It has always been popular in the USA and Canada, where it is often printed (as in *The United Methodist Hymnal* and in *Voices United*) with a different final verse:

> When we've been there ten thousand years,
>   Bright shining as the sun,
> We've no less days to sing God's praise
>   Than when we'd first begun.

This is from *A Collection of Sacred Ballads* (1790); the author is unknown.

In Great Britain this hymn disappeared from use for nearly two hundred years (Julian's *Dictionary of Hymnology* described it as 'unknown to modern collections'). It was revived by a pipe band (the tune suits the bagpipes) and then by popular singers in the 1970s, and its appeal was seized upon by a delighted Church, which promptly began to reprint this neglected piece of eighteenth-century Evangelicalism.

The tune is an American folk melody, found in *Virginia Harmony* (1831), edited by James P. Carrell and David S. Clayton, and harmonized for this hymn by the American composer Edwin O. Excell (1851–1921) for his *Coronation Hymns* of 1910. It has, however, been reharmonized many times since then.

110
> Glorious things of thee are spoken,
>   Zion, City of our God!
> He, whose word cannot be broken,
>   Form'd thee for his own abode:
> On the rock of ages founded,
>   What can shake thy sure repose?
> With salvation's walls surrounded
>   Thou may'st smile at all thy foes.
>
> See! the streams of living waters,
>   Springing from eternal love,
> Well supply thy sons and daughters,
>   And all fear of want remove:
> Who can faint while such a river
>   Ever flows their thirst t'assuage?
> Grace, which like the Lord, the Giver,
>   Never fails from age to age.

Round each habitation hov'ring,
 See the cloud and fire appear!
For a glory and a cov'ring,
 Shewing that the Lord is near:
Thus deriving from their banner
 Light by night, and shade by day;
Safe they feed upon the Manna
 Which he gives them when they pray.

Blest inhabitants of Zion,
 Wash'd in the Redeemer's blood!
Jesus, whom their souls rely on,
 Makes them kings and priests to God:
'Tis his love his people raises
 Over self to reign as kings
And as priests, his solemn praises
 Each for a thank-off'ring brings.

Saviour, if of Zion's city
 I, through grace, a member am,
Let the world deride or pity,
 I will glory in thy name:
Fading is the worldling's pleasure,
 All his boasted pomp and show;
Solid joys and lasting treasure
 None but Zion's children know.

John Newton (1725–1807)

From *Olney Hymns* (1779), where it is hymn 60 of Book I, *On Select Passages of Scripture*. It is entitled 'Zion, or the city of God', and comes in a section on Isaiah, with a reference to Isaiah 33: 27–8. This is clearly a mistake, for there are only 24 verses in that chapter. It probably refers to verses 20 and 21:

Look upon Zion, the city of our solemnities: thine eyes shall see Jerusalem a quiet habitation, a tabernacle that shall not be taken down; not one of the stakes thereof shall ever be removed, neither shall any of the cords thereof be broken. But there the glorious Lord will be unto us a place of broad rivers and streams; wherein shall go no galley with oars, neither shall gallant ship pass thereby.

The reference to galleys and ships would have caught Newton's eye since, before becoming a clergyman in 1764 he had been a seaman (see the notes to 'Amazing grace', no. 109). In this hymn, his early experience gives particular force to his inspired choice of adjective at the end of verse 5: 'solid joys' contrasts wonderfully with all that is changeable and ephemeral ('Fading', which is the worldling's pleasure), but 'solid' also suggests land rather than sea.

The hymn is often printed in a three-verse form, using verses 1, 2, and 5. One or other of verses 3 and 4 are also sometimes included, and there are versions which use conflations of the two to make an eight-line stanza. In any version, this is a grand hymn, an exercise in the sublime: Newton's enthusiasm is here energetically employed to display the glories of Zion. The hymn uses scriptural references abundantly, holding them within a tight and assured verse form. For example, the first two lines (as *Olney Hymns* points out) are a quotation from Psalm 87: 3: 'Glorious things are spoken of thee [Zion], O city of God.'

The particular skill of this verse form is the use of double rhymes at the end of the odd-numbered lines, which (by contrast) gives additional force to the rhymes on the even numbers. It makes for a verse form which is strong and supple, rich with allusion and also wide-ranging, from Isaiah to the Psalms, and from Exodus in verse 3 to Revelation in verse 4 ('kings and priests to God' is from Revelation 1: 6). At the same time, Newton's Calvinism, which is found in verse 5—'Saviour, if of Zion's city'—referring to the possibility of being one of the elect, now reads like an appropriate humility. An amendment such as 'Saviour, since of Zion's city', which is found in some hymn-books, seems to be too full of assurance.

The traditional tune for this hymn is AUSTRIA, by Franz Joseph Haydn, who was almost Newton's contemporary (1732–1809). AUSTRIA, or AUSTRIAN HYMN as it is sometimes called, is a product of the Austro-Hungarian Empire, and its grandeur reflects its origin: it was written for the birthday of the Austrian Emperor in 1797, to the words 'Gott erhalte Franz den Kaiser'. Haydn later used it as the theme with variations for the slow movement of his String Quartet in C, 'The Emperor'. It was published as a tune for hymn-singing in Edward Miller's *Sacred Music* (1802): it became associated with this hymn in the 1889 Supplement to the second edition of *Hymns Ancient and Modern* (1875), and for many years was inseparable from it.

As so often happens, however, a hymn with one good tune seems to attract another. In this case, the new tune is ABBOT'S LEIGH, by Cyril Taylor (1907–91), a lovely flowing tune composed in 1941. Abbot's Leigh, near Bristol, was the wartime headquarters of the Religious Affairs Department of the BBC, and Taylor composed the tune one Sunday morning during his time there. It was used in *Hymns Ancient and Modern Revised* (1950) and in Taylor's own *BBC Hymn Book* (1951). It has since been used for other hymns in this metre, but remains particularly associated with this one. It is even preferred to AUSTRIA in some books (*Rejoice and Sing* prints it alone, and *Common Praise* prints it as the first tune) for these words. It is certainly one of the best tunes written in the twentieth century: its only disadvantage is the steep drop to D (when in the key of D major) in the penultimate bar, which is all too easily ignored by congregations. 'Please', said Cyril Taylor, rehearsing on one occasion, 'please try to get the last line right!'

111

How sweet the name of Jesus sounds
 In a believer's ear!
It soothes his sorrows, heals his wounds,
 And drives away his fear.

It makes the wounded spirit whole,
 And calms the troubled breast;
'Tis manna to the hungry soul,
 And to the weary rest.

Dear name! the rock on which I build,
 My shield and hiding place,
My never-failing treasury, filled
 With boundless stores of grace!

Jesus! my Shepherd, Brother, Friend,
 My Prophet, Priest, and King.
My Lord, my Life, my Way, my End,
 Accept the praise I bring.

Weak is the effort of my heart,
 And cold my warmest thought;
But when I see thee as thou art,
 I'll praise thee as I ought.

Till then I would thy love proclaim
 With every fleeting breath;
And may the music of thy name
 Refresh my soul in death.

John Newton (1725–1807)

Newton's habitual force and energy is here transmuted into sweetness, and 'sweet' is the key word in line 1. The hymn comes from *Olney Hymns* (1779), where it is hymn 57 of Book I, *On Select Passages of Scripture*. It is entitled 'The name of Jesus', and comes under 'Solomon's Song', with a reference to The Song of Solomon 1: 3:

Because of the savour of thy good ointments thy name is as ointment poured forth, therefore do the virgins love thee.

 Newton's fertile imagination seized upon the idea of a name as the savour of good ointment and turned it into 'How sweet . . .', thereafter developing the theme abundantly in his own energetic way. His original verse 4 is usually omitted:

By thee my pray'rs acceptance gain,
 Altho' with sin defil'd;
Satan accuses me in vain,
 And I am own'd a child.

In the present verse 4 Newton originally wrote 'Jesus! my Shepherd, Husband, Friend' ('husband' in the sense of 'ship's husband', perhaps—*Oxford English Dictionary*, sense 4b—one who attends to a ship's stores and provisions). That verse, with its catalogue of names, recalls Isaac Watts's 'Join all the glorious names', but also has a strong poetic resonance, with savour after savour of the sweet-sounding name being brought out for inspection. It has already been likened to a rock and a treasury in verse 3: it is now replete with images from the Old and the New Testaments.

The directness and vigour of this hymn make it one of the best for general use. Newton stresses the power of the name of Jesus to soothe and heal, and give courage, to heal wounds and to calm, to feed and to give rest. The name of Jesus, in other words, has something to apply to every situation; and the human response should be praise throughout the whole of life ('With every fleeting breath'). The last two lines crown the hymn: after all the other experiences comes music, 'the music of thy name', which refreshes the soul in death, at the last moment of life and after it.

The tune which is almost always used for this hymn is ST PETER, by Alexander Robert Reinagle (1799–1877). He was organist of St Peter-in-the-East Church in Oxford (now a College Library), after which the tune takes its name. It was first published in Reinagle's *Psalm Tunes for the Voice and Pianoforte* (c.1830), and subsequently in his *Collection of Psalm and Hymn Tunes, Chants and Other Music as sung in the Parish Church of St Peter-in-the-East, Oxford* (1840). From there it found its way to these words in the first edition of *Hymns Ancient and Modern* (1861).

112
    God moves in a mysterious way
      His wonders to perform;
    He plants his footsteps in the sea,
      And rides upon the storm.

    Deep in unfathomable mines
      Of never-failing skill,
    He treasures up his bright designs,
      And works his sovereign will.

    Ye fearful saints, fresh courage take;
      The clouds ye so much dread
    Are big with mercy, and shall break
      In blessings on your head.

    Judge not the Lord by feeble sense,
      But trust him for his grace;
    Behind a frowning providence
      He hides a smiling face.

His purposes will ripen fast,
  Unfolding every hour;
The bud may have a bitter taste,
  But sweet will be the flower.

Blind unbelief is sure to err,
  And scan his work in vain;
God is his own interpreter,
  And he will make it plain.

William Cowper (1731–1800)

This delightful hymn on the wonders of God was first published anonymously in John Newton's *Twenty-six Letters on religious Subjects; to which are added Hymns, etc. by Omicron* (1774). It later appeared in other places such as the *Gospel Magazine*, and finally in *Olney Hymns* (1779), where it was identified as one of Cowper's by the letter C. It was entitled 'Light shining out of darkness'.

The fact that this hymn was composed in 1773, shortly before Cowper suffered a severe breakdown, has led some critics to suggest that this hymn is an expression of despair. Nothing could be further from the truth. Cowper certainly recognizes that there are things to be feared ('The clouds ye so much dread'), but they are clouds which are full of mercy and blessing. Similarly, the 'frowning providence' hides a smiling face, and the 'bitter taste' of the bud gives way to the beauty of the flower. It is the Christian's duty and joy to interpret the signs of God's providence: and the concluding verse sums up beautifully the hymn's subject. Belief is needed, and then God, who is the great Interpreter (Genesis 40: 8) will make everything clear. Without that interpretation, His ways are mysterious and His 'bright designs' are hidden. The hymn is therefore one of trust and hope, and the perception of the goodness of God (even if it seems to be hidden) is the 'Light shining out of darkness' of the hymn's title.

Cowper went to live at Olney in 1767, to become a member of Newton's congregation. Newton encouraged him to write hymns, of which this is one; many of them were later published in *Olney Hymns*, although Newton contributed the greater number. Cowper's hymns have a fine sensitivity to nature, and a moving awareness of the fluctuations of the human soul.

The tune most frequently used for this hymn is LONDON NEW, from Edward Miller's *The Psalmes of David* (1635). It was published in John Playford's *Psalms & Hymns in Solemn Musick* (1671), and in Playford's *The Whole Book of Psalms* (1677) it was called LONDON NEW in order to distinguish it from LONDON. It was used for this hymn in *Hymns Ancient and Modern* (1861), and, as so often, the association of words and music has remained. It is sometimes sung to IRISH, an eighteenth-century tune (used for 'Thy kingdom come! on bended knee').

113

Sometimes a light surprizes
    The christian while he sings;
It is the Lord who rises
    With healing in his wings:
When comforts are declining,
    He grants the soul again
A season of clear shining
    To cheer it after rain.

In holy contemplation,
    We sweetly then pursue
The theme of God's salvation,
    And find it ever new:
Set free from present sorrow,
    We cheerfully can say,
E'en let th' unknown to-morrow,
    Bring with it what it may:

It can bring with it nothing
    But he will bear us thro';
Who gives the lilies clothing
    Will clothe his people too:
Beneath the spreading heavens,
    No creature but is fed;
And he who feeds the ravens,
    Will give his children bread.

Tho' vine, nor fig-tree neither,
    Their wonted fruit should bear,
Tho' all the fields should wither,
    Nor flocks, nor herds, be there:
Yet God the same abiding,
    His praise shall tune my voice;
For while in him confiding,
    I cannot but rejoice.

        William Cowper (1731–1800)

From *Olney Hymns* (1779), where it is hymn 48 of Book III, *On the Rise, Progress, Changes, and Comforts of the Spiritual Life*. Its title is 'Joy and peace in believing'. The text above is taken from the first edition, with some alterations to misprints in the final verse, which has 'The vine' in line 1 and 'whither' in line 3. The colon at the end of verse 2 replaces the original full stop, to indicate the (very unusual) link between the conditional clause in verse 2 and the main clause in verse 3.

    Newton's plan of Book III of *Olney Hymns* was based on the processes of 'experimental religion' so dear to the Evangelicals of the eighteenth century. Newton's pattern is as follows: I. Solemn Addresses to Sinners; II. Seeking, Pleading, Hoping; III. Conflict; IV. Comfort; V. Dedication and Surrender;

VI. Cautions; VII. Praise; VIII. Short Hymns. This hymn comes in the 'Comfort' section. In it Cowper sweetly sings the joy of Christian belief, although Donald Davie has pointed out the importance of the opening 'Sometimes': 'it is only *sometimes*, on one or two Sundays out of many, that "a light surprizes" and the words take on a heartfelt meaning, "while he sings"' (Preface to *The New Oxford Book of Christian Verse*, 1981). Cowper's image for this is that of sunshine after rain: he was a walker in the countryside around Olney in all seasons and all weathers, and the image is a lovely application of the uncertainty of the English climate to the spiritual life. At the same time, the hymn dwells movingly on the promises of Jesus Christ in the Sermon on the Mount. Cowper's note to verse 2 refers the reader to Matthew 6: 34: 'Take therefore no thought for the morrow'; although what follows draws on earlier verses from that chapter (26, 28–9):

Behold the fowls of the air: for they sow not, neither do they reap, nor gather into barns; yet your heavenly Father feedeth them . . . Consider the lilies of the field, how they grow; they toil not, neither do they spin: And yet I say unto you, That even Solomon in all his glory was not arrayed like one of these.

The last verse contains a rare reference to Habakkuk (3: 17–18):

Although the fig tree shall not blossom, neither shall fruit be in the vines; the labour of the olive shall fail, and the fields shall yield no meat; the flock shall be cut off from the fold, and there shall be no herd in the stalls: Yet I will rejoice in the Lord, I will joy in the God of my salvation.

Cowper's charming and harmonious verses indicate a mind that can truly cherish these moments of peace and happiness, perhaps all the more powerfully because of the fragility of his belief and his often depressed mental state. It is as if the sunshine of this hymn shines out more clearly because of the showers with which the poet was so familiar.

There are a number of tunes to this hymn. *Songs of Praise* used LLANGLOFFAN, a Welsh tune; Methodists have traditionally used PETITION, from *Wesley's Hymns* (1877), although *Hymns and Psalms* prints as a first tune JUBILATE by C. H. H. Parry. *Rejoice and Sing* prints an Irish traditional melody, CLONMEL, and a tune by Erik Routley called CRAIGMILLAR.

114   Hark, my soul! it is the Lord;
                       'Tis thy Saviour, hear his word;
                       Jesus speaks, and speaks to thee:
                       'Say, poor sinner, lov'st thou me?

                       I deliver'd thee when bound,
                       And, when wounded, heal'd thy wound;
                       Sought thee wand'ring, set thee right,
                       Turn'd thy darkness into light.

                       Can a woman's tender care
                       Cease, towards the child she bare?
                       Yes, she may forgetful be,
                       Yet will I remember thee.

                       Mine is an unchanging love,
                       Higher than the heights above;
                       Deeper than the depths beneath,
                       Free and faithful, strong as death.

                       Thou shalt see my glory soon,
                       When the work of grace is done;
                       Partner of my throne shalt be,
                       Say, poor sinner, lov'st thou me?'

                       Lord, it is my chief complaint,
                       That my love is weak and faint;
                       Yet I love thee and adore,
                       O for grace to love thee more!

                            William Cowper (1731–1800)

After a nervous collapse in 1763, Cowper had a period of treatment at St
Albans, and then moved to Huntingdon in 1765 to live with the Revd Morley
Unwin and his wife Mary as 'a sort of adopted son'. As a consequence of
Unwin's death in an accident, he and Mary moved to Olney in 1767 (see
notes to 'God moves in a mysterious way', no. 112). This hymn was written
at Huntingdon, and published in a 'New Appendix' of 1768 to Thomas
Maxfield's *Collection of Psalms and Hymns*. It was included in other
Evangelical collections, and later in *Olney Hymns* (1779), from which the
text above is taken (modern editions prefer 'bleeding' for 'wounded' in verse
2, following a text of 1797).
     In *Olney Hymns* it is found in Book I, *On Select Passages of Scripture*, with
a reference to John 21: 16, and the title 'Lovest thou me?' The passage was a
favourite with Evangelicals in Cowper's time, because it is concerned with
Jesus's forgiveness for Peter and his indication of Peter's mission for the
future. Cowper makes of it a moving drama, in which the quiet voice of
the Saviour (perhaps the 'still, small voice' of I Kings 19) speaks insistently,
gently but also compellingly, to the 'poor sinner'. The hymn speaks over-
whelmingly of love: the questioning is accompanied by reminders of what

the Saviour has done, delicately expressed in lines of great tenderness: 'sought thee wand'ring, set thee right'. The image of maternal love in verse 3 is part of this, even though it is claimed that a mother can forget her child: Cowper is trying to indicate a love that is beyond all earthly love, which can be inconstant, even maternal love. The strength of the Saviour's love is wonderfully expressed in the echoes and balances of verse 4—higher than the heights, deeper than the depths—and in the wide-ranging connotations of the rhyme words: love/above, beneath/death. Love is everywhere: higher, deeper, unchanging in life and in death. The 'death' of that verse leads into the promise of verse 5, in which the means of grace leads into the hope of glory: as Isaac Watts put it, 'And glory ends what grace begun'.

The sinner's response in the final verse is beautifully judged. His love is 'weak and faint', which contrasts touchingly with the grandeur of the Saviour's love as it has been revealed in the main speech of the hymn. It is his 'chief complaint', using 'complaint' in the sense of illness or disease; and the hymn ends with a prayer for grace to love the Saviour more.

The best-known tune to these words, ST BEES, by John Bacchus Dykes (1823–76), was first published in Richard R. Chope's *The Congregational Hymn and Tune Book* (1862). It was set to the present words in the second edition of *Hymns Ancient and Modern* (1875), and has been associated with them ever since that time. Its unspectacular and meditative quality comes from the use of a very narrow range of notes in the first and fourth lines; the last line in particular is very well suited to the question 'lov'st thou me?' and the tune as a whole encourages reflection and dedication. Its quiet Victorian sweetness, however, was not to the taste of Vaughan Williams, who relegated it to the 'chamber of horrors' (the Appendix) in the *English Hymnal*. He set the hymn to a unison tune by Ivor Atkins, WHITE LADIES ASTON, or to SAVANNAH (usually associated with 'Love's redeeming work is done', to which its briskness is much better suited). *Songs of Praise* set it to a German tune, FREUEN WIR UNS, and *Hymns and Psalms* also has a tune by William H. Harris (1883–1973) called PETERSFIELD.

115   Where is this stupendous stranger?
       Prophets, shepherds, kings, advise:
       Lead me to my Master's manger,
       Show me where my Saviour lies.

       O most mighty, O most holy,
       Far beyond the seraph's thought,
       Art thou then so mean and lowly
       As unheeded prophets taught?

       O the magnitude of meekness!
       Worth from worth immortal sprung;
       O the strength of infant weakness,
       If eternal is so young!

       God all-bounteous, all-creative,
       Whom no ills from good dissuade,
       Is incarnate, and a native
       Of the very world he made.

                    Christopher Smart (1722–71)

This hymn, entitled 'The Nativity of our Lord and Saviour Jesus Christ' is
from Smart's *Hymns and Spiritual Songs for the Fasts and Festivals of the
Church of England*, published with his *Translation of the Psalms* in 1765. The
four verses are a selection from Smart's nine verses, and a rewriting of one of
their obscurities—'Swains of Solyma, advise'—in verse 1. The 'swains of
Solyma' [Judaea] are the shepherds, and in Smart's original text presumably
the verse is spoken by the Wise Men or Three Kings, which is no longer
possible in the altered version.

      Smart's *Jubilate Agno* is one of the most astonishing religious poems ever
written, and traces of his extraordinary imagination can be seen in the way
in which his poetry captures the wonder of the Incarnation in these verses.
In some of the omitted ones (two of these were used in *Songs of Praise* 1925),
we see his idea that the whole creation looks fresher, is milder, and sings for
joy at the birth of the Saviour. This is the text in the Oxford edition of
Smart's *Poetical Works*:

                Nature's decorations glisten
                  Far above their usual trim;
                Birds on box and laurel listen
                  As so near the cherubs hymn.

                Boreas no longer winters
                  On the desolated coast;
                Oaks no more are riv'n in splinters
                  By the whirlwind and his host.

> Spinks and ousels sing sublimely,
> 'We too have a Saviour born';
> Whiter blossoms burst untimely
> On the blest Mosaic thorn.

Spinks (chaffinches) and ousels (blackbirds) sing for joy because the day-spring from on high has visited us, so that the north wind (Boreas) no longer dominates: the thorn is the Glastonbury thorn, which traditionally blossomed at Christmas and was said to be from the staff brought to England by Joseph of Arimathea, connected with the blossoming staff of Aaron (Numbers 17). These are all images from Smart's strange and attractive mind, which gives this hymn its unusual and touching atmosphere, ending with a superb rendering of the great paradox of the Incarnation.

Smart was neglected for many years, except by a few perceptive individuals such as Robert Browning, but he enjoyed a revival in the twentieth century. Percy Dearmer printed five of his poems in *Songs of Praise*, including a selection of verses from this one. This is the only one which has remained in use. It was printed in *More Hymns for Today* (1980), and from there in *Hymns Ancient and Modern New Standard* (1983). It is also found in *Rejoice and Sing* (1991) and in *Common Praise* (2000).

No single tune has become established for it, which is a pity. Perhaps the most familiar of the set tunes is HALTON HOLGATE, by William Boyce (1710–79), set as a second tune in *More Hymns for Today*, where the first tune is SHEET, by Cyril Taylor (1907–91). *Common Praise* drops SHEET, keeping HALTON HOLGATE as a first tune, with a second tune by Bryan Kelly (1934–), CASTIGLIONE. *Songs of Praise* used an eighteenth-century Swiss tune, ENGADINE, and *Rejoice and Sing* uses OTTERY ST MARY, by Henry G. Ley (1887–1962).

116

Guide me, O thou great Jehovah,
Pilgrim through this barren land;
I am weak, but thou art mighty,
Hold me with thy powerful hand:
Bread of heaven,
Feed me till I want no more.

Open thou the crystal fountain,
Whence the healing stream doth flow;
Let the fire and cloudy pillar
Lead me all my journey through:
Strong Deliverer,
Be thou still my strength and shield.

When I tread the verge of Jordan,
Bid my anxious fears subside;
Death of death, and hell's destruction,
Land me safe on Canaan's side:
Songs of praises
I will ever give to thee.

William Williams (1717–91),
tr. Peter Williams (1722–96) and others

This famous hymn was first published in Welsh, entitled 'Nerth i fyned trwy'r Anialwch' ('A Prayer for strength to go through the Wilderness of the World'). It appeared in William Williams's *Y Mor o Wydr* ('the sea of glass'), Carmarthen, 1762, with five verses. Peter Williams of Carmarthen made an English translation of verses 1, 3, and 5, which was published in 1771; William Williams then made his own translation of verses 3 and 4, following it with another verse, so that a text of four verses (Peter's translation of verse 1, William's of verses 3 and 4 plus the extra verse) appeared in leaflet form, *c.*1772. It was promptly included in the fifth edition of *A Collection of Hymns* printed for the Countess of Huntingdon's Connexion. A three-verse hymn had already appeared, probably in 1771, in the undated edition of *A Collection of Hymns sung in the Countess of Huntingdon's Chapels in Sussex.* There have been many variations of the text since that time. For example, *Hymns Ancient and Modern* and the *English Hymnal* have always printed 'Guide me, O thou great Redeemer' as a first line.

William Williams 'Pantycelyn' (he lived at a farm of that name near Llandovery) here produces the supreme example of biblical typology, in which Old Testament episodes prefigure the life and work of Jesus Christ. In this case, the operative text is Exodus 16, in which the children of Israel, travelling through the wilderness (the 'barren land' of verse 1, line 2) received manna ('bread of heaven'). This episode is quoted by Jesus, who describes Himself as 'the bread of life', in John 6: 31 ff. The fire and the cloudy pillar are from Exodus 13: 21–2, in which 'the Lord went before them by day in a pillar of cloud, to lead them the way; and by night in a pillar of fire, to give them light'. At the end of the journey, the children of Israel came to the river Jordan, and crossed over into the promised land of Canaan (Joshua 3), which has traditionally been a symbol for the end of the journey of life and the arrival in heaven. The third verse therefore concludes the hymn with a moving prayer in the face of impending death. The prayer for guidance and sustenance, for help on the journey of life, concludes very beautifully with the recognition of heaven as the final destination. Indeed, the hymn is sometimes printed with the text: 'This God is our God for ever and ever; He will be our guide even unto death', from Psalm 48: 14.

Nineteenth-century hymn-books used various tunes, most commonly PILGRIMAGE, by Sir George Elvey. The *English Hymnal* and *Songs of Praise* used a Welsh hymn tune called CAERSALEM. But in 1905 a tune called RHONDDA was composed by John Hughes (1873–1932) for a Baptist Singing Festival at Pontypridd: it was first used in an English book in the *Methodist Hymn Book* (1933), and has since become justly famous, sung throughout the world. CWM RHONDDA, as it is now called, is a truly 'popular' tune, sung at rugby matches when Wales are playing, as well as on great religious occasions. But it is also capable of a quiet and reflective rendering, suitable for the prayerful mood of the hymn. Welsh hymn books do not use this tune, however, preferring CAPEL Y DDOL or LLAN BAGLAN. (See the article by Alan Luff in the *Bulletin* of the Hymn Society, 215, April 1998, to which I am much indebted, and his *Welsh Hymns and their Tunes*, 1990.)

117
    Ride on, Jesu, all-victorious,
      Bear thy sword upon thy side;
    None on earth can e'er withstand thee,
      Nor yet hell, for all its pride:
    At thy mighty name tremendous
      Every foe is forced to yield;
    Hushed in awe, creation trembles:
      Come then, Jesu, take the field.

    Rescue now our souls from bondage,
      In thy morn of victory,
    Batter down the doors of Babel,
      Break the bars and set us free:
    Let thy rescued hosts, exulting,
      Troop to freedom, wave on wave,
    Like the surge of mighty waters:
      O come quickly, come and save!

Hark! I hear already, faintly,
Songs of victory from afar,
Where the heirs of thy redemption
Hail thy triumph in the war.
Clad in robes of shining glory,
Palms of conquest in each hand,
Joyful hosts, to freedom marching,
Enter now the promised land.

William Williams (1717–91),
tr. Gwilym Owen Williams (1913–90)

This hymn is by William Williams ('Pantycelyn'), 'the sweet singer of Wales' and the author of 'Guide me, O thou great Jehovah'. It was published in his collection entitled *Gloria in Excelsis* (1772), with five verses. The present text is a translation of verses 2, 3, and 4 by Gwilym Williams, made for his enthronement as Bishop of Bangor in 1957. It is a hymn which wonderfully uses the imagery of conflict between good and evil: in that battle, the victorious Jesus comes not only to defeat the forces of evil but also to free his people from the bondage of sin. They 'troop to freedom', like an army of released captives, and (in the final verse) join the hosts of the redeemed in the triumphant march to the promised land. The hymn sustains the mood of exultation without ever becoming strident or boastful: it is an exercise in the exalted strain of hymnody, which, through words and music, transcends our ordinary responses to the world and fixes our minds on something higher.

In Robert Graves's delightful poem, 'Welsh Incident', 'The sun was shining', and

The Harlech Silver Band played *Marchog Jesu*
On thirty-seven shimmering instruments,
Collecting for Carnarvon's (Fever) Hospital Fund

but the tune they were using is not specified. It is usually HYFRYDOL, by R. H. Prichard (1811–87), published in 1844. It has been associated with many hymns, but is particularly appropriate for this one: it is recorded that the original Welsh text was sung to it at a meeting in London addressed by David Lloyd George in 1914 to encourage the formation of a regiment of the London Welsh.

118

Behold the amazing gift of love
   The Father hath bestowed
On us, the sinful sons of men
   To call us sons of God.

Concealed as yet this honour lies,
   By this dark world unknown,
A world that knew not when he came,
   E'en God's eternal Son.

High is the rank we now possess,
   But higher we shall rise;
Though what we shall hereafter be
   Is hid from mortal eyes.

Our souls, we know, when he appears,
   Shall bear his image bright;
For all his glory, full disclosed,
   Shall open to our sight.

A hope so great and so divine
   May trials well endure,
And purge the soul from sense and sin,
   As Christ himself is pure.

Scottish Translations and Paraphrases, 1781

This paraphrase was one of those which were designed to broaden the range of material for singing in Scottish services. Until the eighteenth century, the Church of Scotland had used metrical psalms only: drafts and experiments were made, beginning in 1745 (not an auspicious year, with a full-scale rebellion in progress), to extend this to cover other passages from the Bible. This draft aroused opposition in the General Assembly, and it was brought to fruition only in 1781. This paraphrase, probably by William Cameron, is a good example of the genre. It is based upon 1 John 3: 1–3, and two of its verses follow a paraphrase by Isaac Watts, entitled 'Adoption' in *Hymns and Spiritual Songs* (1707), beginning

Behold what wondrous grace
The Father hath bestowed
On sinners of a mortal race
To call them sons of God.

The paraphrase is notable for its assured rhythms, and for its strong sense of human possibility, and its expression of the hope of glory.

   The usual tune in Scotland is NEWINGTON, sometimes called ST STEPHEN, by William Jones of Nayland in Suffolk. It was published in England in 1789, set to Psalm 23 of the 'Old Version'; in Scotland it was printed in R. A. Smith's *Sacred Music . . . sung in St George's Church, Edinburgh* (1828). Its fine vigour has much to do with the popularity of this paraphrase in

Scotland. An alternative tune is ABRIDGE, another tune which was given the name ST STEPHEN in A. M. Thomson's *Sacred Harmony, for the Use of St George's Church, Edinburgh*, published in 1820.

119

Behold! the mountain of the Lord
  In latter days shall rise
On mountain tops above the hills,
  And draw the wondering eyes.

To this the joyful nations round,
  All tribes and tongues shall flow;
Up to the hill of God, they'll say,
  And to his house we'll go.

The beam that shines from Sion hill
  Shall lighten every land;
The King who reigns in Salem's towers
  Shall all the world command.

Among the nations he shall judge;
  His judgments truth shall guide;
His sceptre shall protect the just,
  And quell the sinner's pride.

No strife shall rage, nor hostile feuds
  Disturb those peaceful years;
To ploughshares men shall beat their swords,
  To pruning-hooks their spears.

No longer hosts encountering hosts
  Shall crowds of slain deplore:
They hang the trumpet in the hall
  And study war no more.

Come then, O house of Jacob, come
  To worship at his shrine;
And, walking in the light of God,
  With holy beauties shine.

Scottish Translations and Paraphrases, 1781,
probably by Michael Bruce (1746–67)

This energetic and striking Scottish paraphrase of Isaiah 2: 2–5 is a revision of an earlier version which began 'In latter days, the mount of God,/ His sacred house, shall rise'. This is of unknown authorship, but was included in the trial version of *Translations and Paraphrases* prepared by the Church of Scotland in 1745. The present version was claimed as his own by John

Logan, minister of South Leith; but Logan had borrowed (and then allowed to be destroyed) Bruce's manuscript poems after his death, and there is some suggestion that this was one of Bruce's paraphrases, written for a singing class at Kinnesswood, Kinross-shire, where he lived and worked during his vacations from Edinburgh University until his death at a very early age.

The paraphrase is well known in Scotland: its image of the mountain and the hills is well suited to the Scottish landscape, and the coming of universal peace is signified by a flowing of all the nations to the house of God on Sion's hill. The biblical phrases are incorporated into the verses with a dignified rhetoric that is in the best tradition of metrical psalmody.

In *The Scottish Psalter* (1929) the recommended tune for this paraphrase is GLASGOW, a fine eighteenth-century tune from T. Moore's *The Psalm Singer's Pocket Companion* (Glasgow, 1756). It has done much to ensure the popularity of this version.

120
How bright these glorious spirits shine!
    Whence all their white array?
How came they to the blissful seats
    Of everlasting day?

Lo! these are they from sufferings great,
    Who came to realms of light,
And in the blood of Christ have washed
    Those robes which shine so bright.

Now with triumphal palms, they stand
    Before the throne on high,
And serve the God they love, amidst
    The glories of the sky.

His presence fills each heart with joy,
    Tunes every mouth to sing:
By day, by night, the sacred courts
    With glad hosannas ring.

Hunger and thirst are felt no more,
    Nor suns with scorching ray;
God is their sun, whose cheering beams
    Diffuse eternal day.

The Lamb which dwells amidst the throne
    Shall o'er them still preside;
Feed them with nourishment divine
    And all their footsteps guide.

'Mong pastures green he'll lead his flock,
Where living streams appear;
And God the Lord from every eye
Shall wipe off every tear.

Scottish Translations and Paraphrases, 1781,
based on Isaac Watts (1674–1748)

This paraphrase of Revelation 7: 13–17 comes originally from Isaac Watts's *Hymns and Spiritual Songs* (1707), where it was entitled 'The Martyrs glorified: Rev 7, 13 ff. &c'. Watts's first line was 'These glorious minds, how bright they shine'.

It was rewritten for a draft of the Scottish Church's *Translations and Paraphrases* of 1745–51, which was never published (see 'Behold the amazing gift of love', no. 118). It was then altered again for the official *Translations and Paraphrases* of 1781. The alterations were claimed as the work of William Cameron (1751–1811) by his daughter, and there seems no reason to dispute this: Cameron, who was minister of Kirknewton, Midlothian, certainly had a considerable hand in the revision of the earlier attempt. It is interesting to see the little glimpse of Psalm 23 in the final verse (paraphrasing 'living fountains of waters', but adding the green pastures).

This is such a fine paraphrase of the magnificent verses of Revelation, and is so useful as a hymn for All Saints' Day, that in the nineteenth century it became popular outside the Scottish Church. It crossed the Border in the first edition of *Hymns Ancient and Modern* (1861), and it is still in use in the latest edition, *Common Praise* (2000). In *Songs of Praise* Percy Dearmer, reacting against the 'Blood' imagery of verse 2, altered it to the more fastidious

And by the grace of Christ have won
Those robes that shine so bright.

As a paraphrase in common metre, it has been set to many tunes. Those recommended in *The Scottish Psalter* are ST ASAPH, an entirely unsuitable opera-style tune by Giovanni Marie Giornovichi, and GLOUCESTER, a much finer setting from Thomas Ravenscroft's *Psalter* of 1621. *Hymns Ancient and Modern* used a German tune, NORMANTON, and more recently STRACATHRO, and SENNEN COVE, by W. H. Harris (1883–1973). *Songs of Praise* and the *English Hymnal* used a Scottish tune, BALLERMA, first printed in Glasgow in 1833. The best tune for these words, however, is John Bacchus Dykes's BEATITUDO, which seems Victorian and sentimental when set to some words, but not to these.

{8}

The Romantic Movement and the Early Nineteenth Century

The Romantic period interest in the sublime is found in the hymn by John Bowring, where he describes the Cross 'Towering o'er the wrecks of time':

> All the light of sacred story
> Gathers round its head sublime.

The Cross is no longer so insistently connected with the blood of the Lamb; and the eighteenth-century concern with individual salvation gives way at this point to a hymnody of adoration, sometimes celebrating the God of the natural world:

> Thy bountiful care what tongue can recite?
> It breathes in the air, it shines in the light,
> It streams from the hills, it descends to the plain,
> And sweetly distils in the dew and the rain.

The grace of God is here pictured as a series of mountain streams; similarly, James Montgomery portrays the coming of Christ as a new spring: 'He shall come down like showers/ Upon the fruitful earth'.

Montgomery is the greatest nonconformist hymn-writer after Watts: his hymns are full of the most accurate insight into what is involved in human life, including a deeply felt sense of the need of prayer. He was a well known poet in his day; so was Reginald Heber, author of 'From Greenland's icy mountains'. Both were more famous than the obscure William Blake, from whose poetry comes the greatest of all hymns of national reform, 'And did those feet in ancient time'. Its use of 'England' prevents its use elsewhere, but it is an inspirational text of the period.

Heber was not allowed to publish his hymns, but they appeared after his death in the same year as John Keble's *The Christian Year*. The popularity of Keble's poems, which were closely connected to the *Book of Common Prayer*, coincided with a time when the Church was beginning to see the possibility of hymns. Heber had advocated the singing of hymns, pointing out their power among the nonconformists and evangelicals; and in the first half of the century they began to be seen as more respectable, and less of a 'party badge' (as John Ellerton later put it). The hymns of Henry Francis Lyte were a very good example of the growing interest in hymn-singing: and such books as Edward Bickersteth's *Christian Psalmody* (1833) and William Mercer's *Church Psalter and Hymn Book* (1854) began to be used. Meanwhile, children's hymns were being written, and Cecil Frances Alexander's *Hymns for Little Children* (1848) became very successful. The stage was set for the great hymns of the Victorian age which were to follow.

121

And did those feet in ancient time
    Walk upon England's mountains green?
And was the holy Lamb of God
    On England's pleasant pastures seen?
And did the Countenance Divine
    Shine forth upon our clouded hills?
And was Jerusalem builded here
    Among these dark Satanic mills?

Bring me my bow of burning gold;
    Bring me my arrows of desire;
Bring me my spear—O clouds, unfold!
    Bring me my chariot of fire!
I will not cease from mental fight,
    Nor shall my sword sleep in my hand
Till we have built Jerusalem
    In England's green and pleasant land.

William Blake (1757–1827)

This is from Blake's *Milton*, written sometime around 1800–4, and engraved
c.1809, but never published, in the normal sense of that word (Blake made
individual copies of his work for sale, and only four copies of *Milton* are
known). It was one of Blake's 'Prophetic Books', and in the original the
poem is followed by 'Would to God that all the Lord's people were
prophets! *Numbers* xi 29'.

The references to England have made this of limited use as a hymn inter-
nationally, but its effect is so powerful that it takes its place in England as
one of the great expressions of social protest and of hope. It works through
a system of complex symbols, which are more powerful than straight preaching in verse might be. Blake imagines a time before the Fall (which was,
of course, the subject of Milton's great poem, *Paradise Lost*) when—as he
suggests—Christ walked the earth, including England, and Jerusalem was
here (Blake was probably thinking of London, but it could be any city).
Now, in the early nineteenth century, the evidence of a fallen world is all
around him. The 'dark Satanic mills' are perhaps the factories of the industrial revolution; but Blake uses 'mills' elsewhere as symbols of anything
which would grind down the soul, reduce its individuality, and extinguish its
prophetic fire. So the 'Satanic mills' could be the whole edifice of modern
civilization, the work of the devil, a corrupt society which is dark under the
clouded skies. The second verse uses more traditional prophetic imagery,
especially that of the chariot, to call for a power that will fight against
corruption, wickedness, and all the ills of modern life, until the new
Jerusalem is built again in England.

Blake's work slowly became known during the nineteenth century, and in
the last years of it this poem was taken up by reforming groups such as the

Christian Socialist Society, which used the last four lines as a motto on the title page of its magazine. It was used in its entirety at a thanksgiving service in the Albert Hall by the supporters of Women's Suffrage in 1916. At that service it was sung to Parry's great tune for the first time: it entered mainstream English hymnody with *Songs of Praise* in 1925.

JERUSALEM, by Sir Hubert Parry (1848–1918) was written for Blake's words at the suggestion of Robert Bridges. Parry's colleague and friend, Sir Walford Davies, remembered 'one memorable morning in 1916':

> We looked at it long together in his room at the Royal College of Music, and I recall vividly his unwonted happiness over it. One momentary act of his should perhaps be told here. He ceased to speak, and put his finger on the note D in the second stanza where the words 'O clouds unfold' break his rhythm. I do not think any word passed about it, yet he made it perfectly clear that this was the one note and one moment of the song which he treasured.

Percy Dearmer noted that the verses had already become well enough known to be in the minds of the compilers of the *English Hymnal* in 1906, but that there was no suitable tune for it. It was Parry's tune which made the poem into a singable hymn: Parry 'made a tune so exalted, and fitting so marvellously with the words, that Blake's *Jerusalem* had become possible for an ordinary congregation.'

The verses were not called 'Jerusalem', which is the title of one of Blake's other Prophetic Books; but there can be little doubt that Dearmer was right in other respects, and that Parry's tune and Blake's words together have become a marvellous expression of the idea of a good society. They have been sung countless times by organizations and societies dedicated to the idea of a better country, and have become an anthem of hope and idealism: perhaps most notably in 1945, after the Second World War, when the hope for a better world was articulated by those who sang it following the victory of the Labour Party at the General Election.

122

Brightest and best of the sons of the morning,
    Dawn on our darkness, and lend us thine aid;
Star of the East, the horizon adorning,
    Guide where our infant Redeemer is laid.

Cold on his cradle the dew-drops are shining,
    Low lies his head with the beasts of the stall:
Angels adore him in slumber reclining,
    Maker and Monarch and Saviour of all.

Say, shall we yield him, in costly devotion,
    Odours of Edom and offerings divine?
Gems of the mountain and pearls of the ocean,
    Myrrh from the forest or gold from the mine?

Vainly we offer each ample oblation,
    Vainly with gifts would his favour secure;
Richer by far is the heart's adoration,
    Dearer to God are the prayers of the poor.

Brightest and best of the sons of the morning,
    Dawn on our darkness, and lend us thine aid;
Star of the East, the horizon adorning,
    Guide where our infant Redeemer is laid.

          Reginald Heber (1783–1826)

This is one of the best known hymns for the Epiphany. It was one of Heber's earliest hymns, published in the *Christian Observer* in November 1811. It was later published in Heber's *Hymns written and adapted to the Weekly Church Service of the Year* (1827). As early as 1820, mindful of the success of hymns in Methodist and other nonconformist chapels, he had asked permission from the Archbishop of Canterbury, Charles Manners-Sutton, and the Bishop of London, William Howley, to publish such a book: they refused to permit its appearance, and it was not until after his sudden death that his widow was able to bring it out. It contained hymns by others, including H. H. Milman's 'Ride on, ride on in majesty'; but the majority were by Heber himself.

    The decision to publish may have been connected with Heber's untimely death. He became Bishop of Calcutta in 1823, and discharged his duties with energy and distinction for three years. At Trichinopoly, he preached to a large congregation and confirmed those who were prepared; after which he went to what was described as 'a large cold bath', probably a plunge pool, and died, perhaps from shock at the cold water on a hot day. His death caused a sensation: he became the glorious exemplar of dedicated missionary-bishop, giving his life for the furtherance of the gospel. A contemporary engraving shows his body being carried from the bath by his servant and his chaplain, the latter immaculately attired in a frock coat and top hat.

This hymn begins with a most delicate portrayal of the Christ-child in the manger, to whom the singers (like the wise men) are led by the star. When the singers arrive, they see the dewdrops on his Cradle, and the sleeping baby, adored by watching angels. Heber then gives a rather obvious sermon: rich presents are not wanted, but the heart's adoration and the prayers of the poor will be welcomed. The repetition of the first verse at the end is like the revisiting of a picture in an art gallery, so that we are left with the lovely vision of the infant Jesus.

Julian's *Dictionary of Hymnology* tells us that 'few hymns of merit have troubled compilers more than this.' The problem seems to have been that 'its use involved the worshipping of a star', and that its metre was 'too suggestive of a solemn dance'. It was perhaps for these reasons that it was not included in *Hymns Ancient and Modern* until 1916; but such absurd scruples have disappeared long ago, banished by the sheer charm of Heber's vision. The prayer that the star may 'dawn on our darkness', is reminiscent of the Advent Collect—'that we may cast away the works of darkness' and of the Third Collect at Evening Prayer—'Lighten our darkness, we beseech thee, O Lord'.

For a hymn with such long lines, in the 11.10.11.10 metre, this has been blessed by a remarkable number of successful tunes. Probably the best-known are EPIPHANY, by J. F. Thrupp (1827–67) and LIEBSTER IMMANUEL, a German tune printed in Jena in 1679, together with SPEAN, by John Frederick Bridge (1844–1924). Another more recent tune is JESMIAN, composed at the request of Sir Walford Davies by George Thalben-Ball (1896–1987) for the *BBC Hymn Book* (1951).

123

By cool Siloam's shady rill
How sweet the lily grows!
How sweet the breath, beneath the hill,
Of Sharon's dewy rose!

Lo! such the child whose early feet
The paths of peace have trod,
Whose secret heart with influence sweet
Is upward drawn to God.

By cool Siloam's shady rill
The lily must decay;
The rose, that blooms beneath the hill,
Must shortly fade away:

And soon, too soon, the wintry hour
Of man's maturer age
Will shake the soul with sorrow's power,
And stormy passion's rage.

O thou, whose infant feet were found
Within thy Father's shrine,
Whose years, with changeless virtue crowned,
Were all alike divine:

Dependent on thy bounteous breath,
We seek thy grace alone,
In childhood, manhood, age, and death,
To keep us still thine own.

Reginald Heber (1783–1826)

This hymn, entitled 'Christ a Pattern for Children. Luke ii. 40', was first published in the *Christian Observer*, April 1812, in a different form beginning 'By cool Siloam's shady fountain'. It was later rewritten in common metre, and appeared in Heber's *Hymns written and adapted to the Weekly Church Service of the Year* (1827), published by his widow after his death. It was placed there at the First Sunday after Epiphany. It begins with a verse of seductive beauty, but then develops into a stern reminder of the shortness of life and the passing of time.

Perhaps for this reason, the middle two verses were often omitted. Thus softened, it became a touching hymn of childlike trust, with a reminder of the pattern of Christ's own childhood, from Luke 2: 40: 'And the child grew, and waxed strong in spirit, filled with wisdom: and the grace of God was upon him.'

The beautiful use of Siloam in line 1 refers to the waters of Shiloah 'that go softly' in Isaiah 8: 6: the stream ran near Mount Zion and beside Calvary, and Heber would have known Milton's reference to it as

Siloa's brook that flowed
Fast by the oracle of God

in the opening lines of *Paradise Lost*. It may also be a reference to the pool of Siloam in John 9: 7, as a place of healing. 'Sharon's dewy rose' is a reference to The Song of Solomon 2: 1: 'I am the rose of Sharon, and the lily of the valleys.' Together these references suggest a mysterious and beautiful abundance, and lead into the description of the child as a natural and lovely flower. This makes the subsequent reminder of ageing and mortality all the more poignant.

This hymn was at one time very popular, sung to its tune BELMONT, probably by William Gardiner (1769–1853), published in his *Sacred Melodies*, volume 1 (1812). It was made famous when sung to these words by the Glasgow Orpheus Choir under Sir Hugh Roberton, in the early years of the wireless. It seems to have dropped out of hymn-books in recent years, even in Scotland, where it was greatly loved.

124   From Greenland's icy mountains,
                    From India's coral strand,
              Where Afric's sunny fountains
                    Roll down their golden sand,
              From many an ancient river,
                    From many a palmy plain,
              They call us to deliver
                    Their land from error's chain.

              What though the spicy breezes
                    Blow soft o'er Java's isle:
              Though every prospect pleases,
                    And only man is vile;
              In vain with lavish kindness
                    The gifts of God are strown;
              The heathen in his blindness
                    Bows down to wood and stone.

              Can we, whose souls are lighted
                    With wisdom from on high,
              Can we to men benighted
                    The lamp of life deny?
              Salvation! O salvation!
                    The joyful sound proclaim,
              Till each remotest nation
                    Has learned Messiah's name.

> Waft, waft, ye winds, his story,
> And you, ye waters, roll,
> Till like a sea of glory,
> It spreads from pole to pole:
> Till o'er our ransomed nature
> The Lamb for sinners slain,
> Redeemer, King, Creator,
> In bliss returns to reign.

Reginald Heber (1783–1826)

This was written at Wrexham in 1819, on the eve of Whit Sunday, when there was to be a collection throughout the country for the Society for the Propagation of the Gospel. It was published in the *Evangelical Magazine*, July 1821, and again in the *Christian Observer* in February 1823, not long before Heber's departure for India as Bishop of Calcutta. It was later published in his *Hymns written and adapted to the Weekly Church Service of the Year*, published in 1827, a year after his death.

The hymn is a conspicuous example of that fervent belief in the need to convert the world to Christianity which led Heber and others to lay down their lives in the mission field. Heber, a distinguished scholar and poet, became an example to many, and his life of courageous dedication was followed by missionaries throught the century. Often they would leave Britain in the knowledge that their life expectancy in places such as West Africa could be reckoned in months rather than years.

It is in the light of such heroism that this hymn is best understood. The whole hymn assumes the need for Christianity, and the second verse would now be thought quite unacceptable. It is printed here not in an attempt to revive it but to give the full flavour of a particular kind of nineteenth-century missionary hymn. In this case the hymn's geography—the icy mountains of Greenland, the coral strand of India—is enchanting: the mind registers the golden sands and the palmy plain as illustrative pictures in an early map or travel book. Into this comes the awareness that 'every prospect pleases, and only man is vile', and the heartfelt need for missionaries to go out and enlighten 'the heathen in his blindness'. To-day, with our respect for Islam, Hinduism, Buddhism, and other religions, such beliefs are untenable: but at the time they were the motive for countless noble and altruistic acts of heroism.

The hymn must have been well known, because it was parodied by Kipling, using the voice of the English soldier:

> The 'eathen in 'is blindness bows down to wood an' stone;
> 'E don't obey no orders unless they is 'is own;
> 'E keeps 'is side-arms awful: 'e leaves 'em all about,
> An' then comes up the Regiment an' pokes the 'eathen out.

In spite of such treatment, Heber's hymn remains as an astonishing piece of missionary rhetoric, ending with a vision of the winds and waters joining in the great process of bringing about the coming of the kingdom of God upon earth.

The tune, MISSIONARY, sometimes called MISSIONARY HYMN, was written by Lowell Mason (1792–1872), one of the great American sacred musicians of the nineteenth century. He was working as a bank clerk in Savannah, Georgia, in 1823, when a lady in that town, receiving a copy of Heber's words from Britain, asked him to set them to music. It has also been sung to AURELIA (used for 'The church's one foundation').

125   Holy, Holy, Holy! Lord God Almighty!
               Early in the morning our song shall rise to thee;
           Holy, Holy, Holy! merciful and mighty!
               God in three Persons, blessed Trinity!

           Holy, Holy, Holy! all the Saints adore thee,
               Casting down their golden crowns around the glassy sea;
           Cherubim and Seraphim falling down before thee,
               Which wert, and art, and evermore shalt be.

           Holy, Holy, Holy! though the darkness hide thee,
               Though the eye of sinful man thy glory may not see,
           Only thou art holy, there is none beside thee
               Perfect in power, in love, and purity.

           Holy, Holy, Holy! Lord God Almighty!
               All thy works shall praise thy name, in earth and sky and sea;
           Holy, Holy, Holy! merciful and mighty!
               God in three Persons, blessed Trinity!

                                        Reginald Heber (1783–1826)

This hymn, which is the most widely known of all hymns for Trinity Sunday, was first published in the third edition (1826) of *A Selection of Psalms and Hymns for the Parish Church of Banbury*, and subsequently in Heber's *Hymns written and adapted to the Weekly Church Service of the Year* (1827, published after Heber's death in India). It is based on the traditional *Ter Sanctus* of the Mass.

Its imagery comes principally from chapters 4 and 5 of Revelation, with 'a sea of glass like unto crystal' from 4: 6 (William Law used the same phrase, 'glassy sea' in *The Spirit of Love*, 1752–4). To this are added references from the Old Testament: 'Early in the morning' is from Isaiah 26: 9, or Psalm 63: 1: 'early will I seek thee'. The darkness of verse 3, line 1 is reminiscent of

Exodus 20: 21: '... and Moses drew near unto the thick darkness where God was'.

This rich combination of Old Testament and New Testament imagery is entirely suitable for Trinity Sunday: Heber's art is to blend the repetitions of 'Holy! Holy! Holy!' with suitable variations in each verse. The result is a powerful combination of images which explore the sublime mystery of the Holy Trinity, combining it with the aspirations of human worship. Thus although sin prevents us from seeing the glory of God, and his perfection, the congregation on earth ('early in the morning', verse 1) can unite with the saints and with the cherubim and seraphim (verse 2).

The three-in-one of the Holy Trinity is emphasized by Heber's use of triple combinations in the verse, which echo the rhythm of the *Ter Sanctus*: 'saints ... cherubim ... seraphim'; 'wert ... art ... shalt be'; 'power ... love ... purity'; and finally, 'earth and sky and sea', which brings the hymn back from heaven to earth, and also from the richness of the Psalm and Exodus imagery to its starting point in Revelation, this time from 5: 13: 'And every creature which is in heaven, and on the earth, and under the earth, and such as are in the sea, and all that are in them, heard I saying, Blessing, and honour, and glory, and power, be unto him that sitteth upon the throne, and unto the Lamb for ever and ever.'

The magnificence of the lines has been fittingly given the tune NICAEA, by John Bacchus Dykes (1823–76): its majestic grandeur carries the long lines effortlessly, and the words have become inseparable from it. It is sometimes thought of as Dykes's finest tune.

126   Ride on! ride on in majesty!
      Hark, all the tribes hosanna cry;
      Thine humble beast pursues his road
      With palms and scattered garments strowed.

      Ride on! ride on in majesty!
      In lowly pomp ride on to die;
      O Christ, thy triumphs now begin
      O'er captive death and conquered sin.

      Ride on! ride on in majesty!
      The wingèd squadrons of the sky
      Look down with sad and wondering eyes
      To see the approaching sacrifice.

      Ride on! ride on in majesty!
      Thy last and fiercest strife is nigh;
      The Father, on his sapphire throne,
      Expects his own anointed Son.

Ride on! ride on in majesty!
In lowly pomp ride on to die;
Bow thy meek head to mortal pain,
Then take, O God, thy power, and reign.

Henry Hart Milman (1791–1868)

First published in Reginald Heber's *Hymns written and adapted to the Weekly Church Service of the Year* (1827), as the hymn for Palm Sunday. Although the book was published after Heber's untimely death in 1826, he had been collecting material from his friends for some time; and it included twelve hymns by Milman, of which this is the best known. Heber also tried to get some contemporary poets to help, but he wrote to Milman after receiving some of his hymns (including this one): 'a few more such hymns and I shall neither need nor wait for the aid of Scott and Southey.'

It is a hymn which captures the powerful drama of Palm Sunday. The 'majesty' of Christ's entry into Jerusalem is contrasted with the humility of his entry on an ass, the 'humble beast' of verse 1; and the whole occasion is filled with dramatic irony, because as the hymn is sung, the conclusion of the story is clearly in the singer's mind. The events of Palm Sunday are seen against 'the approaching sacrifice': so the first line of every verse (the repetition is itself a powerful piece of rhetoric) is followed by its commentary, full of foreboding in the first part, but signalling the triumph of the Resurrection and Ascension in the last two verses. The sense that Jesus is riding into Jerusalem to face His last and most terrible ordeal is very strong: and our foreknowledge of what is going to happen gives a powerful and complex significance to the event itself. Milman exploits this brilliantly, especially in the third verse, where the angels, unable to alter the course of events, look on in wonder and sorrow.

There are several tunes for this hymn. The best-known is WINCHESTER NEW, which goes back to a German book of 1690. It seems to have been brought to England by John Wesley, in his *Collection of Tunes Set to Music, as they are commonly sung at the Foundery* (1742), where it was called SWIFT GERMAN TUNE. After a number of changes in both metre and harmony, it was given its present form by William Henry Havergal (1793–1870, father of Frances Ridley Havergal), who published it in his *Old Church Psalmody* of 1847. Slightly altered, it appeared in the first edition of *Hymns Ancient and Modern* (1861), set to this hymn and others, including 'On Jordan's bank the Baptist's cry'. Another tune is ST DROSTANE, by John Bacchus Dykes (1823–76), with a surprising drop at the end of the second line, but a good build-up in the third line and a moving last musical phrase. St Drostane (*c.*600) was a disciple (and in some accounts a nephew) of St Columba. Dykes named a number of his tunes after northern or Scottish saints.

127

Angels from the realms of glory,
 Wing your flight o'er all the earth;
Ye, who sang creation's story,
 Now proclaim Messiah's birth;
  Come and worship,
 Worship Christ, the new-born King.

Shepherds in the field abiding,
 Watching o'er their flocks by night,
God with man is now residing,
 Yonder shines the infant light;
  Come and worship,
 Worship Christ, the new-born King.

Sages, leave your contemplations;
 Brighter visions gleam afar;
Seek the great desire of nations,
 Ye have seen his natal star;
  Come and worship,
 Worship Christ, the new-born King.

Saints before the altar bending,
 Watching long with hope and fear,
Suddenly the Lord descending,
 In his temple shall appear;
  Come and worship,
 Worship Christ, the new-born King.

Sinners, wrung with true repentance,
 Doomed for guilt to endless pains,
Justice now revokes your sentence,
 Mercy calls you; break your chains:
  Come and worship,
 Worship Christ, the new-born King.

James Montgomery (1771–1854)

This vigorous Nativity hymn first appeared in the newspaper, the *Sheffield Iris*, of which Montgomery was the editor, on Christmas Eve 1816. It was later published, with slight alterations, in Montgomery's *The Christian Psalmist* (1825), under the title 'Good tidings of great joy to all people'. Many hymn-books substitute a verse from another hymn for the final stanza:

Though an infant now we view him,
 He shall fill his Father's throne;
Gather all the nations to him,
 Every knee shall then bow down:
  Come and worship,
 Worship Christ, the new-born King.

This makes a good ending, but it loses Montgomery's careful structure: following the first verse, there are the shepherds and then the wise men; then there is another contrast, between saints and sinners. The final verse, appealing to the sinners, is highly appropriate because it echoes the Psalm for Christmas morning, Psalm 85, especially verse 10: 'Mercy and truth are met together: righteousness and peace have kissed each other.'

James Montgomery was a well known poet, highly thought of by his contemporaries such as Shelley and Byron. He was also a newspaper editor, fearless in his denunciation of evils such as the slave trade. He was twice imprisoned, first for printing a poem which celebrated the fall of the Bastille, and on the second occasion for criticizing the behaviour of the Sheffield police during a riot. His hymns are vigorous and strong, and his prefatory essay to *The Christian Psalmist* has some claim to be the best essay on hymnody ever written.

In nineteenth-century books such as *Hymns Ancient and Modern* this hymn was sung to a tune by H. S. Irons (1834–1905) called ST OSMUND, but in *The Oxford Book of Carols* (1928) it was set by Martin Shaw to a French carol tune: that tune was taken up by Percy Dearmer in the enlarged edition of *Songs of Praise* (1931), where it was named IRIS, in a happy recollection of Montgomery's newspaper. This is now the customary (and best known) tune for the hymn; but alternatives are FENITON COURT, by E. J. Hopkins (1818–1901), LLANDINAM, by Thomas Williams (1807–94), and LEWES, by John Randall (1715–99).

128   Hail to the Lord's Anointed,
    Great David's greater Son!
Hail, in the time appointed,
    His reign on earth begun!
He comes to break oppression,
    To set the captive free,
To take away transgression,
    And rule in equity.

He comes, with succour speedy,
    To those who suffer wrong;
To help the poor and needy,
    And bid the weak be strong;
To give them songs for sighing,
    Their darkness turn to light,
Whose souls, condemned and dying,
    Were precious in his sight.

He shall come down like showers
    Upon the fruitful earth,
And love, joy, hope, like flowers,
    Spring in his path to birth;
Before him, on the mountains,
    Shall peace, the herald, go;
And righteousness, like fountains,
    From hill to valley flow.

Arabia's desert-ranger
    To him shall bow the knee;
The Ethiopian stranger
    His glory come to see;
With offerings of devotion
    Ships from the isles shall meet,
To pour the wealth of ocean
    In tribute at his feet.

Kings shall fall down before him,
    And gold and incense bring;
All nations shall adore him,
    His praise all people sing;
To him shall prayer unceasing
    And daily vows ascend,
His kingdom still increasing,
    A kingdom without end.

O'er every foe victorious,
    He on his throne shall rest;
From age to age more glorious,
    All-blessing and all-blest.
The tide of time shall never
    His covenant remove;
His name shall stand for ever,
    That name to us is Love.

       James Montgomery (1771–1854)

This is a free paraphrase of Psalm 72, written in 1821 for a 'Moravian Ode', a leaflet for use at Christmas, possibly by the Moravian church at Fulneck, near Leeds. Montgomery recited it at a Missionary meeting in Liverpool in April 1822, and the Methodist scholar Adam Clarke, who was present, took it to print beside Psalm 72 in his *Commentary on the Bible* (1822). It also appeared in the *Evangelical Magazine* in May 1822. The complete text is a hymn of eight verses, usually shortened to four or five. The last line, which was originally 'His name—what is it? Love', was altered by Montgomery himself; later hymn-books often printed their own version of this line—'His changeless name of Love', as in *Hymns Ancient and Modern*.

The hymn is a magnificent commentary on the coming of the Kingdom of

Christ, which is linked with the ending of oppression and the coming of spring. Montgomery, who was a considerable poet, was a friend of Shelley, and his hymn has many affinities with Shelley's great drama, *Prometheus Unbound*, published in 1820. In the drama, the end of Jupiter's tyranny is accompanied by the revival of life on earth, in the spring, as Prometheus is freed. Montgomery here writes a Shelleyan drama in miniature, linking it with the coming of the kingdom of God upon earth.

The tune is usually CRÜGER (HERRNHUT), from a melody by Johann Crüger in his *Neues vollkömliches Gesangbuch* (1640). It was set to these words by William Henry Monk in the first edition of *Hymns Ancient and Modern* (1861), and it has been closely associated with them since that time. It is one more example of Monk's genius in finding the appropriate tune for the words. The word Herrnhut refers to the Moravian settlement in Germany, from which others such as Fulneck came. Another tune for these words is ELLACOMBE, usually used for 'The day of resurrection'.

129   Prayer is the soul's sincere desire,
               Uttered or unexpressed;
           The motion of a hidden fire,
               That trembles in the breast.

           Prayer is the burden of a sigh,
               The falling of a tear,
           The upward glancing of an eye,
               When none but God is near.

           Prayer is the simplest form of speech
               That infant lips can try,
           Prayer the sublimest strains that reach
               The majesty on high.

           Prayer is the contrite sinner's voice,
               Returning from his ways;
           While angels in their songs rejoice,
               And cry, 'Behold, he prays!'

           Prayer is the Christian's vital breath,
               The Christian's native air,
           His watchword at the gates of death:
               He enters heaven with prayer.

           In prayer on earth the saints are one,
               In word, and deed, and mind,
           When with the Father and his Son
               Sweet fellowship they find.

Nor prayer is made on earth alone;
    The Holy Spirit pleads,
And Jesus, on the eternal throne,
    For sinners intercedes.

O Thou, by whom we come to God,
    The Life, the Truth, the Way,
The path of prayer Thyself hast trod:
    Lord, teach us how to pray!

James Montgomery (1771–1854)

This was written in 1818, and included in Montgomery's *The Christian Psalmist* (1825) under the heading 'What is prayer?' It was written at the request of Edward Bickersteth for his *Treatise on Prayer*, and was published in broadsheet form with three other hymns (including 'Lord, teach us how to pray aright') for the use of Sunday schools in Sheffield. Montgomery said that he had received more praise for this hymn than for any other that he had written.

It is the greatest of all hymns on the difficult subject of prayer. Montgomery understood that prayer could be spoken or unspoken, and that it came from the heart, often in a sigh or a tear: he also knew that it could be both simple and sublime. It is the breath of life, and the 'watchword' at the gate of death. Montgomery, as so often, is wonderfully economical and inclusive: verse after verse adds to our understanding, until the final verse brings us to the way, and the truth, and the life (from John 14: 6), and to the Jesus who was asked by one of His disciples 'Lord, teach us to pray' (from Luke 11: 1, beautifully fitted in here as a conclusion).

Several tunes have been used for this hymn, including WIGTOWN, from the *Scottish Psalter* (1635); NOX PRAECESSIT, by John Baptiste Calkin (1827–1905); MENDIP, used in the *English Hymnal* (1906) for 'There is a land of pure delight'; and others, such as AYRSHIRE, NUN DANKET ALL, and ROCHESTER.

130
   For ever with the Lord!
    Amen; so let it be:
  Life from the dead is in that word,
    'Tis immortality.
   Here in the body pent,
    Absent from him I roam,
  Yet nightly pitch my moving tent
    A day's march nearer home.

   My father's house on high,
    Home of my soul, how near
  At times, to faith's foreseeing eye,
    Thy golden gates appear!
   Ah! then my spirit faints
    To reach the land I love,
  The bright inheritance of saints,
    Jerusalem above.

   For ever with the Lord!
    Father, if 'tis thy will,
  The promise of that faithful word
    Even here to me fulfil.
   Be thou at my right hand,
    Then can I never fail;
  Uphold thou me, and I shall stand;
    Fight, and I must prevail.

   So when my latest breath
    Shall rend the veil in twain,
  By death I shall escape from death
    And life eternal gain.
   Knowing as I am known,
    How shall I love that word,
  And oft repeat before the throne:
    For ever with the Lord!

   James Montgomery (1771–1854)

First published in an annual, *The Amethyst*, in 1835, and then in Montgomery's *Poet's Portfolio* in the same year. It was headed 'At Home in Heaven. 1 Thess. iv. 17', and was in two parts. The present text, which is found in many hymn-books, is a selection from Montgomery's four-line verses.

The verse from 1 Thessalonians occurs in an account of the Second Coming: 'Then we which are alive and remain shall be caught up together with them in the clouds, to meet the Lord in the air: and so shall we ever be with the Lord.' Montgomery's variation on the last phrase allows the mind to dwell on the various joys of heaven while still on the earth, pitching its moving tent nearer and nearer the final home. The image of the tent is a deeply moving variant of the usual image of the journey or pilgrimage of life: now each night's sleep is a pitching of the tent (easy to imagine in days when the bed-curtains were drawn round to keep out the draughts), and each day's work is a day's march along the road. In some texts, such as that in *Church Hymns with Tunes* (1874) the second half of verse 1 is given as the second half of each verse, allowing the mind to come back again and again to the idea of coming 'nearer home'; while some versions of the tune have a refrain, which takes up the words 'Nearer home': 'nearer home, nearer home, a day's march nearer home'. Sung at a funeral, these lines can be deeply affecting: Montgomery said that he had received more indications of approval for this hymn than for any other, except for his lines on prayer.

The tune is usually called NEARER HOME, after the hymn, or WOODBURY after its American composer, Isaac Baker Woodbury (1819–58). It was first published in *The Choral Advocate* in 1852, and was arranged by Arthur Sullivan for *Church Hymns with Tunes* (1874), of which he was the music editor. It appeared a year later in the second edition of *Hymns Ancient and Modern* (1875), using Sullivan's arrangement. *The Primitive Methodist Hymnal* of 1889 included the refrain, for some unknown reason calling the tune BREMEN. Another tune, by Martin Shaw (1875–1958), was written for these words and called, appropriately, MOVING TENT.

131   New every morning is the love
Our wakening and uprising prove;
Through sleep and darkness safely brought,
Restored to life, and power, and thought.

New mercies, each returning day,
Hover around us while we pray;
New perils past, new sins forgiven,
New thoughts of God, new hopes of heaven.

If on our daily course our mind
Be set to hallow all we find,
New treasures still, of countless price,
God will provide for sacrifice.

Old friends, old scenes, will lovelier be,
As more of heaven in each we see:
Some softening gleam of love and prayer
Shall dawn on every cross and care.

We need not bid, for cloistered cell,
Our neighbour and our work farewell,
Nor strive to wind ourselves too high
For sinful man beneath the sky:

The trivial round, the common task,
Would furnish all we ought to ask,—
Room to deny ourselves, a road
To bring us daily nearer God.

Only, O Lord, in thy dear love
Fit us for perfect rest above;
And help us this and every day
To live more nearly as we pray.

John Keble (1792–1866)

This is a selection of verses from the opening poem of Keble's *The Christian Year* (1827), entitled 'Morning'. The complete poem begins with an address to the 'Hues of the rich unfolding morn', and goes on to contrast those who 'day by day to sin awake' with those who are 'timely happy, timely wise':

Oh! timely happy, timely wise,
Hearts that with rising morn arise!
Eyes that the beam celestial view,
Which evermore makes all things new!

This verse (which has been used to open the hymn in some books) emphasizes Keble's belief that those who are 'timely wise' will find joy in doing God's will day-by-day, not necessarily by a life of prayer and meditation ('cloistered cell') or by mysticism and vision (winding ourselves too high), but in the ordinary ways of life. The quotation on the title-page of *The Christian Year* is 'In quietness and in confidence shall be your strength' (from Isaiah 30: 15), and Keble loves to celebrate the simple goodness of the Christian life.

The Christian Year was perhaps the most popular book of religious poems ever published. It provided nineteenth-century readers with a poem for every Sunday of the year, and was a poetic commentary which enriched and illuminated the *Book of Common Prayer*. In the Preface Keble said that 'the object of the present publication will be attained, if any person find assistance from it in bringing his own thoughts and feelings into more entire unison with those recommended and exemplified in the Prayer Book.' It went through edition after edition, inspiring generations of Anglicans (and others) to aim for a quiet acceptance of their lot, and for simplicity and gentleness.

'Morning' is headed with a quotation from Lamentations 3: 22, 23: 'His compassions fail not. They are new every morning.' Keble's celebration of God's mercies leads him into a meditation on trust and inner content, and on the unspectacular action of the daily round and the common task. It states the themes of trust and peace which will recur in *The Christian Year*: throughout the book Keble implies a contrast between the sacred year and the ordinary year of the early nineteenth century with its anxieties and problems. He saw his own time, as Matthew Arnold was later to do, as one 'when excitement of every kind is sought after with a morbid eagerness', and he endeavoured to bring the reader's thoughts and feelings into a better state, which for him was exemplified in the Church of England and its Prayer Book. He spoke of 'that *soothing* tendency in the Prayer Book, which it is the chief purpose of these pages to exhibit'. This opening poem, therefore, celebrates a calm and unstressful goodness, mindful of the mercies of God every morning and trying to live the Christian life without fuss and in simple service. The gentle strength of the last verse, so plain in its message and so powerful in its verse form, expresses this admirably.

The tune invariably used is MELCOMBE, by Samuel Webbe (1740–1816), called 'the elder' to distinguish him from his equally musical son. He is named as the composer in Ralph Harrison's *Sacred Harmony* of 1791, where the tune was given its name: that name probably refers to Melcombe Regis, a part of Weymouth made famous in the late eighteenth century by the sea-bathing visits of George III. The tune was used for this hymn in the first edition of *Hymns Ancient and Modern* (1861), and has always been associated with it since that time. Archibald Jacob (in *Songs of Praise Discussed*) described its qualities as follows: 'The build of the tune is interesting; the structure of the first two lines is similar, and is again paralleled in the last line, the analogy here being strengthened by the occurrence of two downward impulses, while, as a counterpoise, the third line presents the movement upward, that is to say inverted. The result is an extremely well-balanced tune, of great dignity.'

132
    Blest are the pure in heart,
    For they shall see our God;
    The secret of the Lord is theirs,
    Their soul is Christ's abode.

    The Lord, who left the heavens
    Our life and peace to bring,
    To dwell in lowliness with men,
    Their pattern and their King;

    Still to the lowly soul
    He doth himself impart,
    And for his dwelling and his throne
    Chooseth the pure in heart.

    Lord, we thy presence seek;
    May ours this blessing be;
    Give us a pure and lowly heart,
    A temple meet for thee.

    John Keble (1792–1866) and others

This hymn has two sources. The first and third verses are by John Keble, from the poem entitled 'The Purification' [of the Blessed Virgin Mary] in *The Christian Year* (1827). They were the first and last verses of a poem of seventeen stanzas. To these are added verses 2 and 4, as they were in W. J. Hall and E. Osler's *Psalms and Hymns adapted to the Services of the Church of England* of 1836, usually called 'the *Mitre Hymn Book*' because of the bishop's mitre on the front cover.

This composite text was probably the work of one or both of the compilers of the *Mitre Hymn Book*, and was frequently reprinted in this form, sometimes with a doxology in the same short metre:

> All glory, Lord, to thee
> Whom heaven and earth adore;
> To Father, Son, and Holy Ghost,
> One God for evermore.

According to Percy Dearmer, Keble approved of the text as it stands. He was generous with his poetry, and seems not to have minded the interpolations of others. Dearmer added an odd note to this hymn: 'He [Keble] was too good a writer of English to confuse purity with the specific virtue of chastity, as is so often done in the use of this hymn' (*Songs of Praise Discussed*). In fact, the poem's inspiration seems to have been the obvious one of the Beatitudes: 'Blessed are the pure in heart: for they shall see God' (Matthew 5: 8). Keble slips this beautifully into the short metre stanza with the minimum of alteration, as if the hymn were self-effacing, allowing the Bible (in the Authorized Version of 1611, of course) to speak for itself. But then comes the striking word: 'The *secret* of the Lord is theirs'. In that word 'secret' is contained a whole doctrine, that of the Oxford Movement with its emphasis on Reserve, in which the high and holy mysteries should not be spoken of too openly and obviously. Keble's 'secret' is the intimate knowledge of God given to the pure in heart, and that intimacy is to be preserved by the same quiet confidence that is found in the hymn, in which the Short Metre is used to express simple thoughts quickly and without a flourish.

The tune usually associated with this hymn is FRANCONIA, by William Henry Havergal (1793–1870), derived from an eighteenth-century German tune found in Johann Balthasar König's *Harmonischer Liederschatz* published in Frankfurt (in Franconia) in 1738. It was set to this hymn in *Hymns Ancient and Modern* (1861), and was one of the associations of words and tune for which that book became famous.

133   Sun of my soul, thou Saviour dear,
               It is not night if thou be near:
                 O may no earth-born cloud arise
                 To hide thee from thy servant's eyes!

               When the soft dews of kindly sleep
               My wearied eyelids gently steep,
                 Be my last thought, how sweet to rest
                 For ever on my Saviour's breast.

               Abide with me from morn till eve,
               For without thee I cannot live:
                 Abide with me when night is nigh,
                 For without thee I dare not die.

               If some poor wandering child of thine
               Have spurned, today, the voice divine,
                 Now, Lord, the gracious work begin;
                 Let him no more lie down in sin.

               Watch by the sick: enrich the poor
               With blessings from thy boundless store:
                 Be every mourner's sleep tonight
                 Like infants' slumbers, pure and light.

               Come near and bless us when we wake,
               Ere through the world our way we take,
                 Till in the ocean of thy love
                 We lose ourselves in heaven above.

                              John Keble (1792–1866)

This delicate and touching evening hymn is the second poem in *The Christian Year* (1827), entitled 'Evening', with the reference: 'Abide with us: for it is toward evening, and the day is far spent. *St. Luke* xxiv. 29.' This text, which also forms the starting point for Henry Francis Lyte's 'Abide with me' (no. 142), is gracefully integrated into verse 3, which carries the neat antithesis of 'without thee I cannot live . . . . without thee I dare not die'.

In *The Christian Year* the poem begins with the setting sun—"'Tis gone, that bright and orbèd blaze'—and with the traveller who has to 'press' on his way 'in darkness and in weariness'. Verse 3 (the present verse 1) turns the idea inward, so that the Saviour is now 'Sun of my soul' (paralleling Milton's meditation on his blindness at the beginning of Book III of *Paradise Lost*, which asks for 'celestial light' to 'shine inward'). The hymn becomes a prayer for the presence of God, for his forgiveness for sinners, and his help to those in need—the sick, and those who mourn.

These verses were included in the first edition of *Hymns Ancient and Modern* (1861), which selected six from the original fourteen, including verses for 'the Rulers of this Christian land' and another for 'thy Priests', both showing Keble's attachment to the *Book of Common Prayer*.

The gentleness and tenderness of this hymn are well served by its two principal tunes, ABENDS by Herbert Oakeley (1830–1903) and HURSLEY from a Catholic Songbook of the eighteenth century, c.1775. In the first edition of *Hymns Ancient and Modern* HURSLEY was used. Its simplicity is attractive, especially when taken slowly: if it is played too quickly it becomes too light-hearted for these words. Indeed, Oakeley composed ABENDS for this hymn because he claimed that HURSLEY resembled a drinking song in Mozart's *The Marriage of Figaro*, 'Se vuol ballare'. 'To hear "Sun of my soul, thou Saviour dear" sung to a lively tune, unsuitable to sacred words', he wrote, 'often has the effect of driving me out of church.' His tune first appeared in the Irish *Church Hymnal* of 1874, and had become the 'first tune' in the second edition of *Hymns Ancient and Modern* by 1875. ABENDS is still the first tune in the latest edition, *Common Praise* (2000), which prints a second tune, BIRLING, from a nineteenth-century Nottingham collection.

It would be interesting to know which tune D. H. Lawrence, who came from a mining village in Nottinghamshire, had in his mind when he thought of this hymn, many years after having sung it as a child: 'This was the last hymn at the board school. It did not mean to me any Christian dogma or salvation. Just the words, "Sun of my soul, thou Saviour dear", penetrated me with wonder and the mystery of twilight' ('Hymns in a Man's Life', 1928). The *Congregational Church Hymnal* of 1887, which Lawrence would have used in the chapel at Eastwood, included both HURSLEY and ABENDS, together with a third, WHITBURN, by H. Baker (also known as ELIM or HESPERUS).

134   The head that once was crowned with thorns
                 Is crowned with glory now;
            A royal diadem adorns
                 The mighty Victor's brow.

            The highest place that heaven affords
                 Is his, is his by right,
            The King of kings and Lord of lords,
                 And heaven's eternal light,

            The joy of all who dwell above,
                 The joy of all below
            To whom he manifests his love
                 And grants his name to know.

            To them the cross, with all its shame,
                 With all its grace, is given,
            Their name an everlasting name,
                 Their joy the joy of heaven.

> They suffer with their Lord below,
> They reign with him above,
> Their profit and their joy to know
> The mystery of his love.
>
> The cross he bore is life and health,
> Though shame and death to him;
> His people's hope, his people's wealth,
> Their everlasting theme.
>
> Thomas Kelly (1769–1855)

This hymn was first published in Kelly's *Hymns on Various Passages of Scripture*, published in Dublin in 1820. It is based on Hebrews 2: 10: 'For it became him . . . in bringing many sons unto glory, to make the captain of their salvation perfect through sufferings'. Verse 5 uses part of a verse from 2 Timothy 2: 12: 'If we suffer, we shall also reign with him.'

It is likely that Kelly, who was a priest of the Church of Ireland (and who was forbidden to preach by his archbishop, probably because of the vehement evangelicalism of his sermons), knew the work of John Bunyan, which he echoes, either consciously or unconsciously. Bunyan's most recent editor, Graham Midgley, points out the debt to Bunyan's 'One Thing is Needful':

> The head that once was crowned with thorns
> Shall now with glory shine;
> The heart that broken was with scorns
> Shall flow with life divine.

Both Bunyan and Kelly work by strong contrasts. Thorns lead to glory; suffering below leads to reigning above. These reach a climax in the final verse, in which the pattern is reversed, 'life and health' preceding 'shame and death'; as though the final ending is now dominant, and the suffering leading up to it is in the past. The hymn thus becomes a vivid recognition of the Passion of Christ (signalled instantly by the 'thorns' of the first line), seen through the knowledge of His final triumph. The firm handling of the stanzas, with their rhetoric of repetition, contains this vast message with a controlled energy that is very powerful.

The tune is ST MAGNUS, probably by Jeremiah Clarke (*c*.1673–1707), organist of St Paul's Cathedral, and music-master to Queen Anne. It was set to these words in the *Appendix* (1868) to the first edition of *Hymns Ancient and Modern*. It is a magnificent tune, rising to a wonderful climax at the beginning of the last line. It was named ST MAGNUS in William Riley's *Parochial Harmony* (1762), probably after the beautiful church of St Magnus Martyr on the riverside below St Paul's.

135   Lead us, heavenly Father, lead us
              O'er the world's tempestuous sea;
           Guard us, guide us, keep us, feed us,
              For we have no help but thee,
           Yet possessing every blessing
              If our God our Father be.

           Saviour, breathe forgiveness o'er us;
              All our weakness thou dost know;
           Thou didst tread this earth before us,
              Thou didst feel its keenest woe;
           Lone and dreary, faint and weary,
              Through the desert thou didst go.

           Spirit of our God descending,
              Fill our hearts with heavenly joy,
           Love with every passion blending,
              Pleasure that can never cloy;
           Thus provided, pardoned, guided,
              Nothing can our peace destroy.

                     James Edmeston (1791–1867)

This hymn was first published in Edmeston's *Sacred Lyrics, set two* (1821). It was entitled 'Hymn, Written for the Children of the London Orphan Asylum'. Edmeston, who was an architect and surveyor, was greatly interested in the welfare of children in the London Orphanage.

The hymn has become a very general one, and was at one time popular at weddings. However, the original title suggests a reading of the text which is strikingly, and even disturbingly, applicable to homeless children. 'Guard us, guide us, keep us, feed us' might be addressed to a Board of Governors, and the idea that 'For we have no help but thee' is certainly applicable to those children who have no parents. The London Orphan Asylum may have been a good institution of its kind, watched over by such benevolent people as Edmeston: but the hymn's date is a reminder that only fifteen years or so later Dickens was writing *Oliver Twist* (1837–8), and that the lot of orphans in the early nineteenth century was often very sad. However, the hymn has shaken itself free from these associations to become a classic three-part hymn, addressed to Father, Son, and Holy Spirit, praying for guidance in the voyage of life.

It became well known after it was set by Arthur Sullivan to MANNHEIM in *Church Hymns with Tunes* (1874): the 1875 edition of *Hymns Ancient and Modern* followed suit. The tune was an arrangement of a German Chorale published by Friedrich Filitz (1804–76).

136   In the cross of Christ I glory,
          Towering o'er the wrecks of time;
      All the light of sacred story
          Gathers round its head sublime.

When the woes of life o'ertake me,
   Hopes deceive and fears annoy,
Never shall the cross forsake me:
   Lo! it glows with peace and joy.

When the sun of bliss is beaming
   Light and love upon my way,
From the cross the radiance streaming
   Adds more lustre to the day.

Bane and blessing, pain and pleasure,
   By the cross are sanctified;
Peace is there that knows no measure,
   Joys that through all time abide.

In the cross of Christ I glory,
   Towering o'er the wrecks of time;
All the light of sacred story
   Gathers round its head sublime.

             John Bowring (1792–1872)

This hymn was published in Bowring's *Hymns* (1825), one of his many publications. He was a voluminous writer and an indefatigable traveller: he was also a remarkable linguist, proficient in many different languages. He was knighted for his public services as a diplomat and Member of Parliament in 1854. The idea of the Cross 'towering o'er the wrecks of time' may well have been inspired by seeing a ruined church in a post-Napoleonic-war journey; although the story that it was a church in Macao cannot be true if the poem was published in 1825, before Bowring went to the Far East (where he became Governor of Hong Kong). The image is a fine one, however: it allows the reader to glimpse the Cross standing over a ruined universe: into that Cross are drawn all the emotions, the woes of life, the good moments of light and love, so that both are 'sanctified': the whole mixed state of our earthly life is summed up in these lines, and brought to the Cross which brings peace and joy. The crucial adjective, however, is 'sublime', the culminating word of the first and last verses, which sums up the majesty and wonder which Bowring is trying to capture. 'Sublime' was an important word in the Romantic period, and this hymn is a splendid example of hymn-writing in the age of Blake and Wordsworth. It is a fine variation on Galatians 6: 14, the text which also inspired Isaac Watts's 'When I survey the wondrous cross': 'But God forbid that I should glory, save in the cross of our Lord Jesus Christ . . .'.

It has been sung to many tunes, most frequently to STUTTGART (used for
'Come, thou long-expected Jesus') or LOVE DIVINE (used for 'Love divine, all
loves excelling'). An American tune, RATHBUN, is by Ithamar Conkey
(1815–67).

137

O worship the King,
  All glorious above;
O gratefully sing
  His power and his love:
Our Shield and Defender,
  The Ancient of Days,
Pavilioned in splendour,
  And girded with praise.

O tell of his might,
  O sing of his grace,
Whose robe is the light,
  Whose canopy space.
His chariots of wrath
  The deep thunder-clouds form,
And dark is his path
  On the wings of the storm.

The earth, with its store
  Of wonders untold,
Almighty, thy power
  Hath founded of old;
Hath stablished it fast
  By a changeless decree,
And round it hath cast,
  Like a mantle, the sea.

Thy bountiful care
  What tongue can recite?
It breathes in the air,
  It shines in the light;
It streams from the hills,
  It descends to the plain,
And sweetly distils
  In the dew and the rain.

> Frail children of dust,
>   And feeble as frail,
> In thee do we trust,
>   Nor find thee to fail;
> Thy mercies how tender!
> How firm to the end!
> Our Maker, Defender,
>   Redeemer, and Friend.
>
> O measureless Might,
>   Ineffable Love,
> While Angels delight
>   To hymn thee above,
> Thy humbler creation,
>   Though feeble their lays,
> With true adoration
>   Shall sing to thy praise.

Sir Robert Grant (1779–1838)

This is one of the great hymns on the magnificence of God revealed in His creation. Apart from minor differences in punctuation, this text (from the *English Hymnal*) follows the original printing except for the last four lines, which were:

> The humbler creation
>   Tho' feeble their lays,
> With true adoration
>   Shall lisp to thy praise!

This hymn appeared in *Sacred Poems*, 'by the late Right Hon. Sir Robert Grant', published in London in 1839 and edited by his brother Charles, Lord Glenelg. Grant was a lawyer, Member of Parliament, and Privy Counsellor: he was appointed Governor of Bombay in 1834 and died in India in 1838.

The posthumous publication of 1839 acknowledged that some of Grant's poems had already appeared in print, but that the copies 'vary so much from the originals as well as from each other, that it becomes necessary to present to the public a more correct and authentic version'. Among the other poems in this slim volume was a fine hymn based on the Litany, 'Saviour, when in dust to thee/ Low we bow th'adoring knee' (*English Hymnal*, 1933: 87). The present poem, entitled simply 'Psalm CIV' is a springy imitation of verses 1–10 and 24–33; it is written, perhaps by design, in the same metre as William Kethe's Psalm 104 in *The Whole Booke of Psalmes* of 1562, the 'Old Version':

My soul praise the Lord,
Speak good of his Name:
O Lord our great God,
how dost thou appear!
So passing in glory,
that great is thy fame,
Honour and Majesty
in thee shine most clear.

Grant's hymn nicely varies the five–syllable lines with two lines of six syllables (sometimes lines 5 and 7, sometimes lines 6 and 8). The nature imagery of Psalm 104 is beautifully captured in the last four lines of verse 2 and in the gentler imagery of verse 4, and superbly integrated into a wider vision of divine mercy and human adoration. The greatness of God, 'Who layeth the beams of his chambers in the waters: who maketh the clouds his chariot: who walketh upon the wings of the wind', is unobtrusively linked with the God of mercy, who is not only 'Pavilioned in splendour' but also 'Redeemer and Friend'.

The hymn is always sung to HANOVER, thought to be by William Croft (1678–1727), a magnificent and strong tune which carries the words with great conviction and sureness. It was first published in 1708, in *A Supplement to the New Version of the Psalms by Dr Brady and Mr Tate*, where it was set to Psalm 67.

138   Eternal Light! Eternal Light!
          How pure the soul must be,
       When, placed within thy searching sight,
       It shrinks not, but with calm delight,
          Can live, and look on thee!

       The spirits that surround thy throne
          May bear the burning bliss;
       But that is surely theirs alone,
       Since they have never, never known
          A fallen world like this.

       O how shall I, whose native sphere
          Is dark, whose mind is dim,
       Before the Ineffable appear,
       And on my naked spirit bear
          The uncreated beam?

       There is a way for man to rise
          To that sublime abode:
       An offering and a sacrifice,
       A Holy Spirit's energies,
          An advocate with God:

       These, these prepare us for the sight
          Of holiness above:
       The sons of ignorance and night
       May dwell in the eternal light,
          Through the eternal love!

                    Thomas Binney (1798–1874)

This hymn was written when Binney (later an eminent Congregationalist) was a young man, probably in 1826: in 1856 he wrote it out from memory for a friend, with the note 'Composed thirty years ago, while looking up at the sky, one brilliant starlight night.' It was published in the Baptist *Psalms and Hymns* (1858) and in the *New Congregational Hymn Book* (1859). It has been reprinted many times in nonconformist books, and it is good to see it coming into the Anglican tradition in *Common Praise* (2000).

It is based upon 1 John 1: 5: 'God is light, and in him is no darkness at all', although it owes much to Milton's *Paradise Lost* with its description of light at the opening of Book III:

          Hail, holy Light, offspring of heaven first-born,
          Or of the eternal co-eternal beam
          May I express thee unblamed? Since God is light,
          And never but in unapproached light
          Dwelt from eternity, dwelt then in thee,
          Bright effluence of bright essence increate.

The echoes of this can be seen in Binney's opening line, which (like Milton) repeats the word 'eternal'; and in the last line of his verse 3, where 'the uncreated beam' is derived from Milton's 'essence increate'. More importantly, the structure of Binney's hymn follows Milton. Rather unexpectedly (for a hymn) it begins in light, and then proceeds to recollect the darkness of the fallen world: the usual process of a hymn is to conduct the mind from the world towards the eternal light of heaven. Having begun with light, and described the fallen world as dark and dim, Binney then shows how the light may be recovered, through the 'energies' of the Holy Spirit, and the workings of eternal love. It renders Milton into singable verse, while retaining that sense of wonder at the brilliance of the light of God: indeed Erik Routley, in *Hymns and Human Life*, described it as 'one of the noblest and most sympathetic expressions of the "numinous" in our language'. It has immense confidence and vigour, too: a word such as 'energies' in verse 4 is quite unexpected yet wonderfully rich in meaning; while the last two lines are remarkable in their use of 'the'. The allusive element of the writing climaxes in 'the eternal love': this is *the* eternal love, the one unique and salvific love that allows for the restoration of human beings from their fallen state.

A popular tune for this hymn was for many years NEWCASTLE, by H. L. Morley (1830–1916), named after Binney's native city. More recently a tune by Erik Routley (1917–82), CHALFONT PARK, has been an alternative. Routley's attractive tune reflects his admiration for Binney's hymn. Another is TEILO SANT, a free-running tune by Jack Dobbs (1922–), set alongside CHALFONT PARK in *Rejoice and Sing* (1991).

139   Lead, kindly Light, amid the encircling gloom,
               Lead thou me on;
           The night is dark, and I am far from home,
               Lead thou me on.
           Keep thou my feet; I do not ask to see
           The distant scene; one step enough for me.

           I was not ever thus, nor prayed that thou
               Should'st lead me on;
           I loved to choose and see my path; but now
               Lead thou me on.
           I loved the garish day, and, spite of fears,
           Pride ruled my will: remember not past years.

           So long thy power hath blest me, sure it still
               Will lead me on,
           O'er moor and fen, o'er crag and torrent, till
               The night is gone,
           And with the morn those angel faces smile,
           Which I have loved long since, and lost awhile.

                    John Henry Newman (1801–90)

Newman was one of the great figures of the Victorian era, first associated with the Oxford Movement of the 1830s and 1840s and later a convert to Roman Catholicism. His conversion in 1845 was the example which many followed. This poem was written in June 1833, long before that conversion. The story of its composition is told in his *Apologia Pro Vita Sua* (1864): he had been on holiday in Italy (beginning in December 1832) with his friend Hurrell Froude and Froude's father. After leaving them in Rome, he had gone to Sicily, where he became very ill; when he recovered, he went to Palermo to catch a boat for England. After three weeks he found an orange boat bound for Marseilles, which then became becalmed in the Straits of Bonifacio. It was at that point that the poem was written, although Newman's account makes it clear that he had been disturbed about many things: the Revolution of 1830 in France; the success of the Reform Bill, and the popular hatred levelled at the bishops who had opposed it; the power of the Liberals; and the increasing influence of Parliament in the affairs of the Church. He said that he had 'fierce thoughts against the Liberals', although he and his two friends 'kept clear of Catholics throughout our tour'.

    The background to the poem was thus a disturbed one, and Newman's uneasy mind is seen thoughout, especially in the second verse. It is precisely this unease, however, which makes the poem so touching: the prayer to be guided onward is all the more moving for its hesitations and almost childlike trust. John Julian, in his *Dictionary of Hymnology*, calls it 'one of the finest lyrics of the nineteenth century', and writes of it in strikingly moving terms:

Angry at the state of disunion and supineness in the Church he still loved and in which he still believed; confident that he had 'a mission', 'a work to do in England'; passionately longing for home and the converse of friends; sick in body to prostration, and, as some around him feared, even unto death; feeling that he should not die but live, and that he must work, but knowing not what that work was to be, how it was to be done, or to what it might tend, he breathed forth the impassioned and pathetic prayer, one of the birth-pangs, it might be called, of the Oxford movement of 1833.

It was first published in the *British Magazine* (March 1834), and subsequently in *Lyra Apostolica* (1836), a collection of poems by Newman and his Anglo-Catholic friends such as John Keble and Isaac Williams. In *Lyra Apostolica* Newman added an epigraph before the poem: 'Unto the godly there ariseth up light in the darkness'. When he published it in his *Occasional Verses* in 1868, he gave it the pilgrimage epigraph, 'The Pillar of the Cloud'.

The hymn combines the idea of life as a journey (Newman said in the *Apologia* that he was convinced that 'in some sense or other he was on a journey') with the prayer to be led from darkness to light. He senses his own pride and unworthiness (in verse 2), and knows that he is 'far from home', in more than one sense: the title in some versions, 'At Sea', might be interpreted as his being 'all at sea'. In this situation, he prays to be led towards the morning light through all the intervening difficulties (the inhospitable landscape of moor and fen, crag and torrent). Then he will see the angel faces 'Which I have loved long since, and lost awhile'.

A great deal of ink has been spilt over the end of the poem. Newman himself refused to commit himself to any interpretation. In a letter of 18 January 1879 he answered in the words of John Keble, that 'poets were not bound to be critics, or to give a sense to what they had written'. He went on:

There must be a statute of limitation for writers of verse, or it would be quite tyranny if in an art which is the expression, not of truth, but of imagination and sentiment, one were obliged to be ready for examination on the transient states of mind which came upon one when home-sick, or sea-sick, or in any other way sensitive or excited.

Perhaps the most sensible explanation of the angel faces is that of Newman's friend Charles Marriott, who thought that 'the couplet touched on the idea that infants have a more intimate communion with the unseen world'. If this is so, then Newman was (perhaps unconsciously) thinking of a time ('long since') of innocence and childhood. It blends with another possible meaning, which is that of being reunited with loved ones: the hymn has spoken comfort to many because of its suggestion of seeing again the angel faces (perhaps the faces of children who have died in infancy). The word 'smile' is extraordinarily touching in this context.

This hymn received some insensitive treatment in the nineteenth century, usually from those who wanted something more specific than Newman's magic and mystery. Horatius Bonar, not content with the opening, had to establish what the 'kindly light' was, and began his version with 'Lead, Saviour, lead . . .'. Edward Bickersteth, Bishop of Exeter, added a verse in his *Hymnal Companion* of 1870, with a note to the 1876 edition saying that 'it was added by the Editor from a sense of need, and from a deep conviction that the heart of the belated pilgrim can only find rest in the Light of Light.' The verse was as follows:

> Meantime along the narrow rugged path,
>> Thyself hast trod,
> Lead, Saviour, lead me home in Child-like faith
>> Home to my God,
> To rest for ever after earthly strife
> In the calm light of everlasting life.

The bishop's intervention was unnecessary and tactless: Newman's hymn contains all that is necessary to express this idea. Bickersteth turned poetry into dogma, and the mysterious into the conventional ('rugged path', 'earthly strife').

There are a number of tunes to this hymn, in spite of its unusual metre. The best known is probably by John Bacchus Dykes (1823–76), given the name LUX BENIGNA ('kindly light') by the compilers of *Hymns Ancient and Modern* when they printed it in the *Appendix* of 1868. Newman modestly thought that the popularity of the hymn was owing to this tune. He told the Revd George Huntington, the Rector of Tenby: 'But you see it is not the Hymn, but the *Tune*, that has gained the popularity! The Tune is Dykes's, and Dr Dykes was a great Master' (J. T. Fowler, *Life and Letters of John Bacchus Dykes*,1897: 104). Almost as good are SANDON, by C. H. Purday (1799–1885), and PATMOS, by Samuel Sebastian Wesley (1810–76).

As a reaction to the grand Victorian qualities of these tunes, some twentieth-century books have preferred a tune entitled ALBERTA, by William Henry Harris (1883–1973), organist for many years of St George's Chapel, Windsor. Harris wrote the tune while travelling on a train between Calgary and Edmonton in the province of Alberta. It was first used in a hymn-book in the enlarged edition of *Songs of Praise* (1931). Another fine twentieth-century tune is BONIFACIO, by David Evans (1874–1948), music editor of the *Church Hymnary* (1927).

140   Just as I am, without one plea
             But that thy blood was shed for me,
             And that thou bidst me come to thee,
                  O Lamb of God, I come!

             Just as I am, and waiting not
             To rid my soul of one dark blot,
             To thee whose blood can cleanse each spot,
                  O Lamb of God, I come!

             Just as I am, though tossed about
             With many a conflict, many a doubt,
             Fightings and fears within, without,
                  O Lamb of God, I come!

             Just as I am, poor, wretched, blind;
             Sight, riches, healing of the mind,
             Yea, all I need, in thee to find,
                  O Lamb of God, I come!

             Just as I am, thou wilt receive,
             Wilt welcome, pardon, cleanse, relieve;
             Because thy promise I believe,
                  O Lamb of God, I come!

             Just as I am—thy love unknown
             Has broken every barrier down—
             Now to be thine, yea, thine alone,
                  O Lamb of God, I come!

             Just as I am, of that free love
             The breadth, length, depth, and height to prove,
             Here for a season, then above,
                  O Lamb of God, I come!

                  Charlotte Elliott (1789–1871)

This hymn was written in 1834. Charlotte Elliott, who was an invalid, lived with her brother, Henry Venn Elliott, an Evangelical vicar in Brighton. She had had a sleepless night, 'tossed about/ With many a conflict', and was too ill to help him at a church bazaar to raise money for the building of a school for the daughters of poor clergy. As Percy Dearmer put it succinctly: 'While every one at Westfield Lodge was out and busy over the bazaar, she lay in greater misery than ever, and determined to fight it out then and there; so she took a pen and wrote this hymn.'

Its success was phenomenal, as her brother noted: 'In the course of a long ministry, I hope I have been permitted to see some fruit of my labours; but I feel far more has been done by a single hymn of my sister's.' It was first published in leaflet form in 1835, and then (in a text of six verses) in the second edition of *The Invalid's Hymn Book* of 1836. The full text appeared in Elliott's *Hours of Sorrow Cheered and Comforted* in the same year. In *The*

Invalid's Hymn Book, it was given the quotation from John 6: 37: 'Him that cometh unto me I will in no wise cast out.' It is notable not only for its powerful rhythms and intense desire for acceptance, but also for its references to cleansing and healing: it is one of the few hymns to mention 'healing of the mind' as associated with a sense of salvation.

This is one of those hymns which has a different tune in different parts of the world. In Great Britain, there are two principal tunes, both of which effectively carry the words, with strong stresses on the fourth syllable of each line. The oldest is MISERICORDIA, by Henry Smart (1813–79), which rises to an E flat to carry the final 'O *Lamb* of God, I come!' Another is SAFFRON WALDEN, by Arthur Henry Brown (1830–1926), in which the high point is reached in the third line, and the last line becomes a quiet prayer.

The tune used in American, Australian, and Canadian books is WOOD-WORTH, by William Batchelder Bradbury (1816–68). It was used for this hymn in Ira D. Sankey's *Sacred Songs and Solos*, and has been a favourite for evangelical campaigns, such as those of Dr Billy Graham, since then. It is a highly emotional tune, requiring a sighing repeat of 'I come!' on a falling third at the end.

141   Praise, my soul, the King of heaven;
      To his feet thy tribute bring.
    Ransomed, healed, restored, forgiven,
      Who like me his praise should sing?
      Praise him! Praise him!
      Praise the everlasting King!

    Praise him for his grace and favour
      To our fathers in distress;
    Praise him, still the same for ever,
      Slow to chide and swift to bless.
      Praise him! Praise him!
      Glorious in his faithfulness.

    Father-like, he tends and spares us;
      Well our feeble frame he knows;
    In his hands he gently bears us,
      Rescues us from all our foes.
      Praise him! Praise him!
      Widely as his mercy flows.

> Angels, help us to adore him;
> Ye behold him face to face;
> Sun and moon, bow down before him,
> Dwellers all in time and space.
> Praise him! Praise him!
> Praise with us the God of grace!
>
> Henry Francis Lyte (1793–1847)

This robust and sparkling hymn of praise was first published in Lyte's collection of his own paraphrases, *The Spirit of the Psalms* (1834). It is based on Psalm 103, in the version that Lyte would have known from the *Book of Common Prayer*:

Praise the Lord, O my soul: and all that is within me praise his holy Name. Praise the Lord, O my soul: and forget not all his benefits; who forgiveth all thy sin: and healeth all thine infirmities; Who saveth thy life from destruction: and crowneth thee with mercy and loving-kindness . . .

The hymn had another verse (sometimes printed after verse 3 in the text above) which was printed in brackets:

> Frail as summer's flower we perish:
> Blows the wind and it is gone.
> But, while mortals rise and perish,
> God endures unchanging on.
> Praise him! Praise him!
> Praise the high eternal One!

This corresponds nicely to verses 15–17 of the psalm ('The days of man are but as grass: for he flourisheth as a flower of the field. For as soon as the wind goeth over it, it is gone . . .'); but lines 3 and 4 are weaker than the rest of the hymn, and the verse is better omitted (as the original printing suggested it might be). The almost overwhelming sense of jubilation is nicely communicated in some texts, principally that of *Hymns Ancient and Modern*, which change 'Praise him! Praise him!' to 'Alleluia! Alleluia!'

The hymn shows Lyte as joyfully praising the providence of God, but the hymn has much in common with his other masterpiece, 'Abide with me'. In particular, Lyte consistently emphasizes the reliability of God, His saving care for humanity, and His capacity to 'tend and spare' us ('He will not alway be chiding: neither keepeth he his anger for ever.') In addition, the hymn shows a remarkable and unobtrusive rhetoric, in which some lines have their word order inverted. This gives a strange strength to the hymn, often pairing the simple lines with the complicated ones.

The popularity of this hymn has undoubtedly been aided by its celebrated tune, PRAISE MY SOUL, by John Goss (1800–80), organist of St Paul's Cathedral. As the name implies, it was written for this hymn, and first published in 1869: it requires the first four syllables of each verse to be sung to the same note, before (in this case) leaping a fourth. An alternative tune, REGENT SQUARE, is by Henry Smart (1813–79). It is another tune of immense energy and vigour.

142   Abide with me; fast falls the eventide;
       The darkness deepens; Lord, with me abide!
       When other helpers fail, and comforts flee,
       Help of the helpless, O abide with me.

       Swift to its close ebbs out life's little day;
       Earth's joys grow dim, its glories pass away;
       Change and decay in all around I see;
       O thou who changest not, abide with me.

       I need thy presence every passing hour;
       What but thy grace can foil the tempter's power?
       Who like thyself my guide and stay can be?
       Through cloud and sunshine, Lord, abide with me.

       I fear no foe, with thee at hand to bless;
       Ills have no weight, and tears no bitterness.
       Where is death's sting? where, grave, thy victory?
       I triumph still, if thou abide with me.

       Hold thou thy cross before my closing eyes;
       Shine through the gloom, and point me to the skies;
       Heaven's morning breaks, and earth's vain shadows flee:
       In life, in death, O Lord, abide with me!

           Henry Francis Lyte (1793–1847)

This moving and stately hymn may date from 1847, though one theory is that it was written twenty years before, when Lyte was nursing a dying friend. There seems no reason to doubt the story that a version in manuscript was given to a relative on Sunday 5 September 1847, on the last occasion that Lyte preached in Brixham church, where he was perpetual curate. He left for the Continent soon afterwards, in an attempt to recover his health, and died in the south of France, at Nice, on 20 November. In the different versions of the text there are slight variations: for example, one text has 'The darkness thickens' in verse 1, later changed to 'The darkness deepens'.

  The five-verse text is that of the first edition of *Hymns Ancient and Modern* (1861), which has been adopted as the customary version for singing. The original hymn had three more verses, between the present verses 2 and 3:

Not a brief glance, I beg, a passing word;
But as Thou dwell'st with Thy disciples, Lord,
Familiar, condescending, patient, free,
Come not to sojourn, but abide with me.

Come not in terrors, as the King of kings,
But kind and good, with healing in Thy wings,
Tears for all woes, a heart for every plea,—
Come, Friend of sinners, and thus bide with me.

Thou on my head in early youth didst smile;
And, though rebellious and perverse meanwhile,
Thou hast not left me, oft as I left Thee,
On to the close, O Lord, abide with me.

These three verses would not only make the hymn too long, but words such
as 'condescending' and 'familiar' now have the wrong connotations for a
hymn that depends on the fine sustaining of a serious tone throughout. In
addition, these verses detract from the remarkable unity of the five verse-
text, which proceeds from the initial statement of evening to the acknowledgment of death, praying at each step for comfort and help. The hymn
moves from an earthly darkness towards a heavenly light, meditating on the
transience of life and on the changes and chances of this fleeting world. At
the centre of Lyte's thought is God, 'O thou who changest not': the idea
came from Henry Vaughan, whose poems Lyte edited, and who wrote (in
'My soul, there is a country', no. 51) of 'One who never changes/ Thy God,
thy life, thy cure.' Contrasted with that unchanging God is the uncertainty
and instability of earthly life, as changeable and fickle as the weather:
'Through cloud and sunshine, Lord, abide with me.'

The long and beautiful lines allow the reader or singer to feel the movement of the hymn slowly and carefully, and to understand the unobtrusive
connection between 'the eventide' (which is the evening time and—to those
who live by the sea, as Lyte did—the evening tide). The evening tide signifies
the end of the day, and the metaphor is made clear in the first line of verse 2:
'Swift to its close ebbs out life's little day'. Life, in the sight of God, is as
short as a day; and death is the ebbing of our life, the going out of the tide.
It is in this context that we have to see the need for a God in whom to trust.
Lyte's hymn expresses that trust, but is also touchingly aware of human
vulnerability and frailty: the combination is very powerful in speaking to the
human condition.

In the manuscript version, the hymn is preceded by the quotation from
Luke 24: 29, telling the story of the journey to Emmaus: 'Abide with us; for
it is toward evening, and the day is far spent.' This hospitality is based on the
literal fact of the closing day: Lyte's genius takes the quotation and turns it
into a metaphor for human life in all its brevity. At the same time, by changing 'Abide with us' into 'Abide with me', he deepens the feeling by making

it speak to the individual, in prayer or meditation: John Ellerton thought the hymn 'almost too intense and personal for congregational use'.

Perhaps because it speaks so clearly about human hopes and fears, the hymn is very popular, and rightly so: it is sung on public occasions such as the Cup Final, and is often used at funerals. It has the ability to communicate to those who can feel through its poetry what they cannot always believe through doctrine.

Even so, the hymn might not have been so popular if it had not had the advantage of a wonderfully appropriate tune, William Henry Monk's EVEN-TIDE. Monk, who was the musical editor of *Hymns Ancient and Modern*, wrote it (according to his wife) 'at a time of great sorrow' when he had been watching 'the glory of the setting sun'. Lyte himself wrote a tune for the words, and it has also been sung to a four-line form of the OLD 124th and to a tune by S. S. Wesley entitled ORISONS. None of these has seriously challenged Monk's tune as the ideal setting for these words: together, words and music make one of the most moving examples of the art of the hymn.

143

I heard the voice of Jesus say,
  'Come unto me and rest;
Lay down, thou weary one, lay down
  Thy head upon my breast':
I came to Jesus as I was,
  Weary, and worn, and sad;
I found in him a resting-place,
  And he has made me glad.

I heard the voice of Jesus say,
  'Behold, I freely give
The living water; thirsty one,
  Stoop down, and drink, and live';
I came to Jesus, and I drank
  Of that life-giving stream;
My thirst was quenched, my soul revived,
  And now I live in him.

I heard the voice of Jesus say,
  'I am this dark world's light;
Look unto me, thy morn shall rise,
  And all thy day be bright':
I looked to Jesus, and I found
  In him my star, my sun;
And in that light of life I'll walk
  Till travelling days are done.

Horatius Bonar (1808–89)

This hymn was written at Kelso, Roxburghshire, when Bonar was a minister there, before he left the Church of Scotland at the Great Disruption of 1843 (he became an eminent figure in the Free Church of Scotland). It was first published in his *Hymns, Original and Selected* (1846), and subsequently in his *Hymns of Faith and Hope*, first series (1857), with the title 'The Voice from Galilee'. It is a hymn in which each verse uses a biblical text: verse 1 is based on Matthew 11: 28; verse 2 on John 4: 10–14; and verse 3 on John 8: 12.

There are two principal tunes for this hymn, and they represent interesting divergences of musical taste. VOX DILECTI, by John Bacchus Dykes (1823–76), was written for these words, and printed in the *Appendix* (1868) to the first edition of *Hymns Ancient and Modern*. It is a tune which typifies a Victorian sensibility: Dykes increases the plaintiveness of the first half of each verse, and stresses its contrast to the comfort of the second half, by changing key from G minor into G major.

In the *English Hymnal* (1906), Ralph Vaughan Williams (1872–1958) rejected this tune, and supplied in its place an English folk tune, KINGSFOLD. This vigorous tune carried the words well, and was used in many books, taking precedence over VOX DILECTI for much of the twentieth century. Only in the last two decades did the shadow of the *English Hymnal*'s rejection of Victorianism begin to lift.

KINGSFOLD is still the preferred tune in some books, such as *The Australian Hymn Book* of 1977 and the Canadian *Voices United* of 1996. But Dykes's skill can be seen, if by implication only, in Wesley Milgate's comment on KINGSFOLD in *Songs of the People of God*, the 'Companion' to *The Australian Hymn Book*: 'the organist might consider changing the accompaniment at this point [half way through the verse] to a clearer and slightly more brilliant texture.' What has to be effected by the organist here was achieved by Dykes in VOX DILECTI with his spectacular key change. Tallis's THE THIRD TUNE has also been used for this hymn.

144

Jesus lives! thy terrors now
     Can, O death, no more appal us;
Jesus lives! by this we know
     Thou, O grave, canst not enthral us.
          Alleluia!

Jesus lives! henceforth is death
     But the gate of life immortal;
This shall calm our trembling breath,
     When we pass its gloomy portal.
          Alleluia!

Jesus lives! for us he died;
     Then, alone to Jesus living,
Pure in heart may we abide,
     Glory to our Saviour giving.
          Alleluia!

Jesus lives! our hearts know well
     Nought from us his love shall sever;
Life, nor death, nor powers of hell
     Tear us from his keeping ever.
          Alleluia!

Jesus lives! to him the throne
     Over all the world is given;
May we go where he is gone,
     Rest and reign with him in heaven.
          Alleluia!

Christian Fürchtegott Gellert (1715–69),
tr. Frances Elizabeth Cox (1812–97)

This is a translation of an eighteenth-century German hymn. Gellert's 'Jesus lebt! mit ihm auch ich', was first published in his *Geistliche Oden und Lieder* in 1757. Cox's translation appeared in her *Sacred Hymns from the German* of 1841. It followed Gellert by being in six-line verses, each (except the last) ending 'This shall be my confidence' (from 'Diess ist meine Zuversicht'). Thus a six-line verse would run as follows:

Jesus lives! to Him the throne
     High o'er heaven and earth is given;
I may go where he is gone,
     Live and reign with him in heaven:
God through Christ forgives offence;
This shall be my confidence.

Cox altered the verse form herself, and it was printed with 'Alleluia!' in her *Hymns from the German* of 1864. The four-line version had existed well before that date, first in Gilbert Rorison's *Hymns and Anthems adjusted to the Church Services throughout the Christian Year* (1851) and then in F. H.

Murray's *Hymnal for Use in the English Church* (1852). It was printed in *Hymns Ancient and Modern* in 1861. The alteration from a six-line stanza form to a four-line one sounds radical but is easily achieved, because the final couplet is added to the quatrain rather than being an integral and necessary part of the verse. This text went through many different changes, in word order and phrasing, and also in the ordering of the verses; so much so that even Julian's *Dictionary of Hymnology* gives up: 'To follow out the variation of text and order in later books would be bewildering.'

An example from the opening will demonstrate this. The first edition of *Hymns Ancient and Modern* printed the four-line version in a five-verse text that began 'Jesus lives! no longer now/ Can thy terrors, Death, appal us'. The problem with this was the pause at the end of the first line, when a tune was sung with a long note at that point: as Julian put it, singers were faced with 'an apparent denial of the resurrection of Jesus which some musical settings of the opening line might produce'. Cox therefore altered it to 'Jesus lives! thy terrors now/ Can no longer, Death, appal us'. It was further altered by Godfrey Thring in *A Church of England Hymn-book* of 1880 to 'Jesus lives! Thy terrors now/ Can, O Death, no more appal us'.

The dominance of the four-line form is almost certainly owing to the tune, ST ALBINUS, by H. J. Gauntlett (1805–76), written for another Easter hymn by W. J. Blew, 'Angels to our Jubilee', in *The Church Hymn and Tune Book* of 1852. It was set to Cox's words in the first edition of *Hymns Ancient and Modern* in 1861, and the words and tune have been inseparable since that time. Erik Routley thought that it 'may be the finest of all nineteenth-century English tunes' (*An English-speaking Hymnal Guide*: 44). It is named after the eighth-century English saint, Alcuin (Latin Albinus).

An alternative tune is CHRIST IST ERSTANDEN, found in *Songs of Praise*. It is an old tune, associated with a medieval Easter hymn, 'Christ ist erstanden'. Archibald Jacob noted with pleasure that 'this melody occupies the same place in German music as "Sumer is icumen in" does in English' (*Songs of Praise Discussed*: 101).

145   *Adeste, Fideles*

O come, all ye faithful,
Joyful and triumphant,
O come ye, O come ye to Bethlehem;
Come and behold him
Born the King of Angels:
 O come, let us adore him,
 O come let us adore him,
O come, let us adore him, Christ the Lord!

God of God,
Light of Light,
Lo! he abhors not the Virgin's womb;
Very God,
Begotten, not created:

See how the shepherds,
Summoned to his cradle,
Leaving their flocks, draw nigh with lowly fear;
We too will thither
Bend our joyful footsteps:

Lo! star-led chieftains,
Magi, Christ adoring,
Offer him incense, gold, and myrrh;
 We to the Christ child
Bring our hearts' oblations:

Child, for us sinners
Poor and in the manger,
Fain we embrace thee, with awe and love;
Who would not love thee,
Loving us so dearly?

Sing, choirs of angels,
Sing in exultation,
Sing, all ye citizens of heaven above:
Glory to God
In the highest:

Yea, Lord, we greet thee,
Born this happy morning,
Jesu, to thee be glory given;
Word of the Father,
Now in flesh appearing:
 O come, let us adore him,
 O come, let us adore him,
O come, let us adore him, Christ the Lord!

Latin, perhaps eighteenth century,
tr. Frederick Oakeley (1802–80) and others.

This is another nineteenth-century version of an eighteenth-century hymn. The Latin text is of Roman Catholic origin. It is found in an eighteenth-century manuscript from the College at Douai. One possibility is that the author was John Francis Wade, an English musician at the college. Verses were later added to the original by Monsignor de Borderies, a Roman Catholic catechist who was exiled to England (together with the Douai college) at the French Revolution.

The original four verses (the present verses 1, 2, 6, 7) were translated in 1841 by Frederick Oakeley for his congregation at Margaret Street Chapel, London (now All Saints, Margaret Street). They later appeared in F. H. Murray's *Hymnal for Use in the English Church* (1852) and in other books. The hymn was included in this four-verse text in *Hymns Ancient and Modern* (1861), perhaps because Murray was one of the instigators of that book. The enlarged text, printed above, includes verses translated from de Borderies' additions by W. T. Brooke, printed in *The Altar Hymnal* of 1884. Many other versions and variations have been found in nineteenth-century books. Examples include the alterations in verse 2 to 'True God of true God' and to 'Light of light eternal'.

The Latin text, and the tune that went with it, became very popular. It was sung as early as 1797 in the Chapel of the Portuguese Embassy in London, from which it acquired the name at one time of 'Portuguese Hymn'. Oakeley's translation has eclipsed all others (including those by such fine poets as Edward Caswall and J. M. Neale), and in Great Britain it has become an essential feature of many Christmas services, especially at midnight on Christmas Eve or at morning services on Christmas Day. It is a sturdy set of verses, somewhat irregular and (most unusually for a hymn) unrhyming: it is carried along by its tune, and by the succession of strong imperatives—'O come . . .'; 'Sing, choirs of angels'—ending with the joyful assent on Christmas morning: 'Yea, Lord, we greet thee'. It is a hymn that allows the congregation to respond with full hearts in the final verse.

The tune, ADESTE FIDELES, which carries the words so vigorously, may also have been by John Francis Wade. It appeared, harmonized by William Henry Monk, in *Hymns Ancient and Modern* (1861). Many different versions have been made in various keys: perhaps the best known is that by Vaughan Williams for the *English Hymnal* in the key of G, which accommodates a superb discord in the first line.

146

> Nearer, my God, to thee,
>   Nearer to thee!
> E'en though it be a cross
>   That raiseth me,
> Still all my song shall be,
> Nearer, my God, to thee,
>   Nearer to thee!
>
> Though, like the wanderer,
>   The sun gone down,
> Darkness be over me,
>   My rest a stone,
> Yet in my dreams I'd be
> Nearer, my God, to thee,
>   Nearer to thee!
>
> There let the way appear
>   Steps unto heaven;
> All that thou sendest me
>   In mercy given;
> Angels to beckon me
> Nearer, my God, to thee,
>   Nearer to thee!
>
> Then, with my waking thoughts
>   Bright with thy praise,
> Out of my stony griefs
>   Bethel I'll raise;
> So by my woes to be
> Nearer, my God, to thee,
>   Nearer to thee!
>
> Or if on joyful wing
>   Cleaving the sky,
> Sun, moon, and stars forgot,
>   Upwards I fly,
> Still all my song shall be,
> Nearer, my God, to thee,
>   Nearer to thee!
>
> Sarah Flower Adams (1805–48)

This famous hymn was written in 1840. Together with twelve other hymns by Sarah Flower Adams, it was published by W. J. Fox, a celebrated Unitarian minister, in *Hymns and Anthems* (1841), a book compiled for his congregation in South Place Chapel, Finsbury, London (Sarah Flower Adams was a member of this congregation). It was common for Unitarian chapels to have their own individual hymn-book at this time, before the widespread adoption of James Martineau's *Hymns for The Christian Church and Home* (1840); but no other book can boast of having included an original hymn that was to become so celebrated. It was included in the first edition of *Hymns Ancient and Modern* (1861), and has accumulated a whole literature of stories around it, including the legend that it was played by the band of the *Titanic* as the liner was sinking (this is now thought not to be true).

It is a skilful rewriting of the story of Jacob's dream (Genesis 28: 10–22). Its Unitarian origins are seen in the third line, where the Cross is not the sign of the Atonement but the Cross of earthly trouble and suffering. Jacob's situation is used to portray the speaker/singer of the lines as a wanderer, in the darkness, with the sun gone down and with only a stone for a pillow. In this comfortless place, the wanderer dreams of heaven, and rejoices in mercy. As Jacob said 'this is none other but the house of God, and this is the gate of heaven' (verse 17), and in the hymn it is clear that the sufferer feels near to God. The stone of the pillow becomes the 'stony griefs' out of which 'Bethel I'll raise', even as Jacob took the stone on which he had slept and set it up for a pillar (verse 18). By this time the hymn is expressing more than suffering: the waking thoughts are 'Bright with thy praise', and the last verse describes a mystical flight, the soul transformed into rapture in its journey upwards to God.

It presents a very powerful mixture of human suffering illuminated by the practice of the presence of God. It is a pity that this hymn has found no place in some modern books, such as *Rejoice and Sing* and *Hymns Ancient and Modern New Standard* (it has been restored to the 'A&M' repertoire in *Common Praise*). Its Unitarianism may be responsible: in the nineteenth century, for example, William Walsham How took it upon himself to write a version beginning 'Nearer to Thee, my God', which he described as 'a paraphrase of Mrs Adams's hymn, expressing more definitely Christian faith, and better adapted for congregational worship'. It was described by John Julian, in his *Dictionary of Hymnology*, as 'the least musical of Bp. How's hymns' (which might have been guessed from the first line).

The best-known tune is J. B. Dykes's HORBURY, written for this hymn at Horbury in Yorkshire, and used for it in the first edition of *Hymns Ancient and Modern* (1861). Another fine Victorian tune is Arthur Sullivan's PROPIOR DEO ('Nearer to God'), which is found in *The Hymnary* (1872), and then in *Church Hymns with Tunes* (1874) of which Sullivan was the musical editor. There is a modem tune by Erik Routley, WILMINGTON, named after the Kent village where Routley was a Congregational minister from 1945 to 1948.

147

All things bright and beautiful,
  All creatures great and small,
All things wise and wonderful,
  The Lord God made them all.

Each little flower that opens,
  Each little bird that sings,
He made their glowing colours,
  He made their tiny wings.
All things . . .

The rich man in his castle,
  The poor man at his gate,
God made them high or lowly,
  And ordered their estate.
All things . . .

The purple headed mountain,
  The river running by,
The sunset and the morning,
  That brightens up the sky;
All things . . .

The cold wind in the winter,
  The pleasant summer sun,
The ripe fruits in the garden,
  He made them every one;
All things . . .

The tall trees in the greenwood,
  The meadows where we play,
The rushes by the water
  We gather every day;
All things . . .

He gave us eyes to see them,
  And lips that we might tell
How great is God Almighty,
  Who has made all things well.
All things . . .

Cecil Frances Alexander (1818–95)

This hymn on God as Creator is from Mrs Alexander's *Hymns for Little Children* (1848), under the heading from the Apostles' Creed—'Maker of Heaven and Earth'. Its strength comes from its unquestioning simplicity of language and idea, as the child celebrates the small things of nature (flowers, the colours of birds) and the magnificent ones (sunsets, mountains).

Modern hymn-books tend to omit verse 6, as being too exclusively rural, and as having no relevance to the lives of modern city children; and very few books have ever printed verse 3 (*Hymns Ancient and Modern*, up to 1916, was an exception). Percy Dearmer called verse 3 'the appalling verse' in *Songs of Praise Discussed*: the problem has always been that, whatever her intention, Mrs Alexander seems here to be suggesting that God is responsible for a social and economic system that is full of inequality. It seems probable that she was trying to include all people, rich and poor, within the compass of God's creative power; as Maurice Frost rather tartly put it, in the *Historical Companion to Hymns Ancient and Modern*, 'Most modern hymnbook compilers omit the stanza, though why rich and poor do not qualify as part of God's creation is never explained.' Frost was probably correct in identifying Alexander's original intention; but her words appear, at first sight, to encourage the idea that God 'ordered' human beings into classes, the rich and the poor, the fortunate and the unfortunate.

Apart from this, the hymn has an instant appeal: it states its position neatly and simply, with a catchy rhythm and a lively series of images (even though it does overdo the adjective 'tiny'). Its two splendid tunes have done much to ensure its popularity: it is a hymn which seems instantly to bring to mind a primary school class singing from *Songs of Praise* on a sunny summer morning.

One tune, by William Henry Monk, was called ALL THINGS BRIGHT AND BEAUTIFUL, and sometimes KEATS (presumably in recognition of the poet's love for the natural world). It dates from the *Home Hymn Book* of 1887, and was included in the 1889 *Supplement* to the second edition of *Hymns Ancient and Modern*. The other tune, ROYAL OAK, has its origins in a Royalist melody of the seventeenth century, 'The twenty-ninth of May', celebrating the Restoration of Charles II in 1660 (the title refers to the oak tree in which he is supposed to have hidden after the Battle of Worcester in 1651). The tune was arranged by Martin Shaw, and became widely known and loved through its inclusion in *Songs of Praise* (1925).

148   Once in royal David's city
              Stood a lowly cattle-shed,
           Where a mother laid her baby
              In a manger for his bed:
           Mary was that mother mild,
           Jesus Christ her little child.

           He came down to earth from heaven
              Who is God and Lord of all
           And his shelter was a stable,
              And his cradle was a stall;
           With the poor and mean and lowly
           Lived on earth our Saviour holy.

           And through all his wondrous childhood
              He would honour and obey,
           Love, and watch the lowly maiden
              In whose gentle arms he lay.
           Christian children all must be
           Mild, obedient, good as he.

           For he is our childhood's pattern
              Day by day like us he grew,
           He was little, weak, and helpless,
              Tears and smiles like us he knew;
           And he feeleth for our sadness,
           And he shareth in our gladness.

           And our eyes at last shall see him,
              Through his own redeeming love,
           For that child so dear and gentle
              Is our Lord in heaven above;
           And he leads his children on
           To the place where he is gone.

           Not in that poor lowly stable,
              With the oxen standing by,
           We shall see him; but in heaven,
              Set at God's right hand on high;
           When like stars his children crowned
           All in white shall wait around.

                 Cecil Frances Alexander (1818–95)

From Mrs Alexander's *Hymns for Little Children* (1848), for the article of the
Apostles' Creed, 'who was conceived by the Holy Ghost, born of the Virgin
Mary'. It has become universally loved as a Christmas hymn, often used as
an opening processional hymn for a carol service, following the example of
King's College, Cambridge. The singing of the first verse as a solo on such
an occasion can provide a moment of beauty that is unsurpassed in hymn-
singing.

The words show Mrs Alexander at her best, even though there has been a good deal of earnest modern raging at the idea of the meek and obedient child of verse 3 (and some poor rewriting in modern books). The hymn is really the rendering of the gospel as a children's story, beginning 'Once' (for 'Once upon a time'), and naming the main characters as if for the first time. The attention which this demands (and gets) from children (and adults) suggests that for a moment the normal adult censorships are suspended: in this world of magic, a child is born in a stable, and the children who listen, breathlessly, to the narrative, will one day find themselves changed into stars, in attendance around the throne of God.

In other words, the hymn is part of the magic of Christmas, and depends on that magic: those who grumble about it forget that, in Dickens's words, 'it is good to be children sometimes, and never better than at Christmas, when its mighty Founder was a child himself.' To say that Mrs Alexander's children are unreal in this post-Freudian age is to rationalize the Christmas spirit out of existence.

The words are full of Christmas magic, but the popularity of the hymn owes much to the tune by Henry John Gauntlett (1805–76), entitled IRBY. It was first published in 1849 as a tune for these words, and appeared in the *Appendix* (1868) to the first edition of *Hymns Ancient and Modern*. It can be a slow processional, or used more quickly: it repeats its phrases with great effect, and manages to combine stateliness with a lovely running melody. The harmonization by Gauntlett is sometimes varied by using a skilful arrangement by Arthur Henry Mann (1850–1929), who was organist at King's College, Cambridge, where he started the tradition of a Christmas Eve service of nine lessons and carols.

149

There is a green hill far away,
  Without a city wall,
Where the dear Lord was crucified
  Who died to save us all.

We may not know, we cannot tell,
  What pains he had to bear;
But we believe it was for us
  He hung and suffered there.

He died that we might be forgiven,
  He died to make us good,
That we might go at last to heaven
  Saved by his precious blood.

> There was no other good enough
>   To pay the price of sin;
> He only could unlock the gate
>   Of heaven, and let us in.
>
> O dearly, dearly has he loved,
>   And we must love him too,
> And trust in his redeeming blood,
>   And try his works to do.

Cecil Frances Alexander (1818–95)

From Mrs Alexander's *Hymns for Little Children* (1848), under the heading from the Apostles' Creed, 'Suffered under Pontius Pilate, was crucified, dead, and buried'. It was written in easy language for children, with the doctrine of the Atonement explained in the simplest terms; but its straightforward dignity means that it is one of those rare children's hymns that can be sung without embarrassment by people of all ages. Only in the final line does the language of the hymn shift to a child's register.

It is an unusual hymn, from the first line onwards: the 'green hill' which is 'far away' seems to belong to a far-off, imagined landscape. It is a hill 'without a city wall', which further increases the sense of mystery: most hills do not have city walls, so why is this one so described? One answer is that 'without' means 'outwith' (or outside), and many modern books have amended the line to read 'outside a city wall'. This is certainly clear, though the mystery is lost.

After the first lines, the hymn becomes a touching and very simple exposition of the doctrine that Christ died for our sins, and that His blood is a 'redeeming blood' which is used 'to save us all'. The simple progress of the hymn makes the repetition of 'dearly, dearly' in the last verse even more effective than it might have been: the words convey a deepening of emotion, and also a double meaning—that Christ loved mankind dearly, and in a way that cost Him dearly.

The tune to these words is HORSLEY, by William Horsley (1774–1858), organist of the Charterhouse and friend of Mendelssohn. It was first published in 1844, and was set to these words in the *Appendix* (1868) to the first edition of *Hymns Ancient and Modern*; it has been associated with them invariably since that time.

{9}

The High Victorian Period

The growing appreciation of the importance of hymns during the first half of the nineteenth century led to their gradual incorporation into services of the Church of England. A number of hymn-books appeared during the 1840s and 1850s to assist those who wished to include hymns in services: and in 1861 *Hymns Ancient and Modern* was published, 'for use in the Services of the Church', to great effect. When the editors produced a *Supplement* in 1868, they spoke of 'their deep gratitude to Almighty God for the marvellous success with which He has been pleased to bless their former work'.

Many streams of hymnody contributed to *Hymns Ancient and Modern*. Indeed, one of the reasons why it was so successful was the fact that the editors followed Keble's advice to 'make it comprehensive'. Among those streams were the fine metrical translations of John Mason Neale, which brought to Victorian England the great treasures of ancient hymnody; the German hymns of the Reformation, translated by Catherine Winkworth and others; and the hymns of Charles Wesley and Isaac Watts, which were beginning to shake off the notoriety which attached to them from their associations with Methodists and Congregationalists. The book also included two hymns from America.

Once the Church of England had come to accept hymns as a part of worship, the way was open for their own writers to produce them. The second half of the nineteenth century was the time of major hymn-writers such as John Ellerton, William Chatterton Dix, William Walsham How, and others. It also saw a great increase in the hymn-writing of women. At the same time, the performance of church music improved in the hands of such figures as Samuel Sebastian Wesley, Sir George Elvey, Sir John Stainer, and other cathedral organists: this was the age of the Victorian hymn tune, by fine composers such as John Bacchus Dykes, Arthur Sullivan, Joseph Barnby, Henry John Gauntlett, John Goss, and E. J. Hopkins. A master at setting words to music was William Henry Monk, whose name has appeared frequently in these pages.

150

Be thou my guardian and my guide,
And hear me when I call;
Let not my slippery footsteps slide,
And hold me lest I fall.

The world, the flesh, and Satan dwell
Around the path I tread;
O save me from the snares of hell,
Thou quickener of the dead.

And if I tempted am to sin,
And outward things are strong,
Do thou, O Lord, keep watch within,
And save my soul from wrong.

Still let me ever watch and pray,
And feel that I am frail;
That if the tempter cross my way,
Yet he may not prevail.

Isaac Williams (1802–65)

This hymn dates from early in the reign of Queen Victoria, when the Church of England was shaken by the controversies surrounding the Oxford Movement. The group of Oxford men who gathered round Newman and Keble were concerned about a Church which they saw as too liberal in its beliefs, and about government interference in religious appointments. They were known also as 'Tractarians', because their ideas were expounded in a series of pamphlets entitled 'Tract . . .'.

This restrained but effective hymn is from Williams's *Hymns on the Catechism* (1842), based on the prayer from The Lord's Prayer 'And lead us not into temptation'. Some hymn-books print Williams's original 'Be thou our guardian', with the plural throughout, which makes it closer to the originating text.

Williams's hymn, simple though it seems, is reticent for a purpose. As a prominent member of the Oxford Movement, and an associate of Newman and Keble, Williams held Tractarian views on matters poetical and religious. He was the author of Tracts 80 and 87, both entitled 'On Reserve in Communicating Religious Knowledge'; and this hymn is characteristic of the doctrine of Reserve, of not talking too openly and easily about the high and sacred truths of religion. Its simple prayer to be guarded from sin and guided from temptation is therefore not only an effective hymn (for all ages) but also an example of the restraint with which (in the Tractarian view) religious matters should be addressed. *Hymns Ancient and Modern* added a doxology, 'To Father, Son and Holy Ghost', but most hymn-books print the text above. The text is sometimes headed with Psalm 17: 5: 'O, hold Thou up my goings in Thy paths; that my footsteps slip not.'

It is invariably sung to the tune ABRIDGE, by Isaac Smith (1734–1805), to which it was set in the *Appendix* (1868) to the first edition of *Hymns Ancient and Modern*.

151

Firmly I believe and truly
　God is three, and God is one;
And I next acknowledge duly
　Manhood taken by the Son.

And I trust and hope most fully
　In that manhood crucified;
And each thought and deed unruly
　Do to death, as he has died.

Simply to his grace and wholly
　Light and life and strength belong,
And I love supremely, solely,
　Him the holy, him the strong.

And I hold in veneration,
　For the love of him alone,
Holy Church as his creation,
　And her teachings as his own.

Adoration ay be given,
　With and through the angelic host,
To the God of earth and heaven,
　Father, Son, and Holy Ghost.

John Henry Newman (1801–90)

The next two hymns are out of sequence chronologically, but Newman was so central to the Oxford Movement and to the development of Roman Catholicism in Britain, that they are placed here. This hymn is from Part I of 'The Dream of Gerontius', published in the Roman Catholic periodical *The Month* in May and June 1865, and later made famous by Elgar's setting of 1900. It was first used as a hymn in the *English Hymnal* (1906).

In Newman's poem it is sung by the dying Gerontius (the word means 'little old man') as a final statement of his belief. It is a hymn which economically and gracefully states some principal doctrines of the Holy Catholic Church: the Holy Trinity, the Incarnation, the Crucifixion, and the uniqueness of Holy Church as created by God and as having authority. It is not often found in nonconformist books, but has been a favourite credal hymn in the *English Hymnal* and *Hymns Ancient and Modern* for much of the twentieth century.

A tune often used is SHIPSTON, one of the tunes brilliantly imported into the *English Hymnal* by Ralph Vaughan Williams from English folk-music, and described in that book as 'English Traditional Melody'. It had been published in *English County Songs* (1893), edited by Lucy Broadwood and J. A. Fuller-Maitland: Lucy Broadwood had found it at Halford, near Shipston-on-Stour, Warwickshire. As a setting for Newman's solemn words, the ballad tune works surprisingly well. *Hymns Ancient and Modern* uses HALTON HOLGATE, from a melody by William Boyce (*c.*1710–79).

152   Praise to the Holiest in the height,
            And in the depth be praise,
         In all his words most wonderful,
            Most sure in all his ways.

         O loving wisdom of our God!
            When all was sin and shame,
         A second Adam to the fight
            And to the rescue came.

         O wisest love! that flesh and blood
            Which did in Adam fail,
         Should strive afresh against the foe,
            Should strive and should prevail;

         And that a higher gift than grace
            Should flesh and blood refine,
         God's presence and his very self,
            And essence all-divine.

         O generous love! that he who smote
            In man for man the foe,
         The double agony in man
            For man should undergo;

         And in the garden secretly,
            And on the cross on high,
         Should teach his brethren, and inspire
            To suffer and to die.

         Praise to the Holiest in the height,
            And in the depth be praise,
         In all his words most wonderful,
            Most sure in all his ways.

            John Henry Newman (1801–90)

From Part II of Newman's 'The Dream of Gerontius'. It was first used in a hymn-book in the *Appendix* of 1868 to the first edition of *Hymns Ancient and*

Modern. The narrative at this point of Newman's poem shows Gerontius dying and entering purgatory, in which, the angel promises:

> Swiftly shall pass thy night of trial here,
> And I will come and wake thee on the morrow.

It would be difficult to find a hymn that so subtly and completely describes the providence of God and the ministry of Christ. The *felix culpa* or 'fortunate Fall' which was the subject of twelve books of Milton's *Paradise Lost* is here expounded in six verses. In this reading of the problem of evil, it was the loving wisdom of God which ordained that Adam should fall, and that Christ, the second Adam, should restore mankind. The principal statement of this is the summary by St Paul as part of his extended and magnificent discussion of the question in 1 Corinthians 15:

For since by man came death, by man came also the resurrection of the dead. For as in Adam all die, even so in Christ shall all be made alive.

Both St Paul and Newman emphasize that it is important and appropriate that as flesh and blood failed in Adam, so flesh and blood (in the Incarnate Word, Jesus Christ) should finally succeed in overcoming evil. This leads Newman into stating his belief (verse 4) that the Incarnation was 'a higher gift than grace', involving the very presence of God Himself on earth. That verse has been the subject of some prejudice and controversy. Wesley Milgate, writing in *Songs of the People of God* (the 'Companion' to *The Australian Hymn Book*) describes it thus:

Suspicious Protestants have been known to circle warily around v.4 . . . on the ground that it implied the doctrine of Transubstantiation; but this is surely a radical misreading of the text . . . 'Refine' has something of the old alchemists' idea that purifying a substance 'dignified' or 'ennobled' it; human flesh and blood was thus ennobled in Christ by being inhabited by God himself (cf. Heb. 2: 10–11, 14).

The achievement of Christ through His Passion and death is set out in verses 5 and 6. In His 'generous love' He underwent 'the double agony in man', a compressed phrase which is explained in verse 6: it is the agony in the garden, and the pain and suffering on the Cross. He does this 'in man for man', Newman's neat and pithy summation of the Incarnate Word, Christ becoming man in order to save mankind.

These verses carry so much doctrine in such a little space, that it is almost essential to begin and end the hymn with a psalm-like verse, enclosing the profound meditation in a general expression of praise. This allows the mind to have time to tease out the meanings so deftly woven into the middle verses. The result is a hymn that is both profound in its doctrine, and satisfying in its response to that doctrine.

The tune which is probably most often associated with these words is

GERONTIUS, written by John Bacchus Dykes (1823–76) for the 1868 *Appendix to Hymns Ancient and Modern* in which the hymn first appeared. It is one of Dykes's finest tunes, a reworking of his tune ALMSGIVING ('O Lord of heaven and earth and sea'); it carries the words 'height' and 'depth' an octave apart on a high and low D (in the key of G major), and ends with a suitably simple fourth line. There are other fine tunes used for this hymn, notably RICHMOND (in the *English Hymnal*, part of that book's reaction against Victorian tunes), and BILLING by the Roman Catholic musician Sir Richard Runciman Terry (1865–1938), Director of Music at Westminster Cathedral, and music editor of the *Westminster Hymnal* (1912). One would expect Terry to have had a particular affinity with these words by Cardinal Newman, and his tune certainly seems to have been inspired by something out of the ordinary, as effective in its way as Dykes's original setting. In the USA it is sometimes called NEWMAN. A further tune is CHORUS ANGELORUM, by Arthur Somervell (1863–1937), used in *Rejoice and Sing* (1991) and other books.

153
　　　　See amid the winter's snow,
　　　　Born for us on earth below,
　　　　See, the tender Lamb appears,
　　　　Promised from eternal years.

　　　　Hail, thou ever blessed morn!
　　　　Hail, redemption's happy dawn!
　　　　Sing through all Jerusalem:
　　　　Christ is born in Bethlehem!

　　　　Lo, within a manger lies
　　　　He who built the starry skies,
　　　　He who, throned in height sublime,
　　　　Sits amid the cherubim.

　　　　'Say, ye holy shepherds, say,
　　　　What your joyful news to-day:
　　　　Wherefore have ye left your sheep
　　　　On the lonely mountain steep?'

　　　　'As we watched at dead of night,
　　　　Lo, we saw a wondrous light:
　　　　Angels, singing peace on earth,
　　　　Told us of a Saviour's birth.'

　　　　Sacred infant, all divine,
　　　　What a tender love was thine
　　　　Thus to come from highest bliss
　　　　Down to such a world as this!

Teach, O teach us, holy Child,
By thy face so meek and mild,
Teach us to resemble thee,
In thy sweet humility.

Virgin Mother, Mary blest,
By the joys that fill thy breast,
Pray for us that we may prove
Worthy of the Saviour's love.

Edward Caswall (1814–78)

Edward Caswall has already appeared in the first section of this book as a fine translator of early hymns. He was an Anglican vicar who converted to Roman Catholicism, following the example of Newman. His *Lyra Catholica* (1849) did much to encourage an interest in early Latin hymnody.

This hymn was published in *The Masque of Mary, and Other Poems* (1858), entitled 'Christmas', because it is a Christmas tradition to pray for the intercession of the Christ child and the Blessed Virgin Mary (Protestant churches which use this hymn have tended to omit the final verse). The hymn takes the story of the birth of Christ from Luke 2: 1–20, and (especially in verse 2) delights to explore the paradox that within a manger lies the God 'who built the starry skies'. The love of God in descending to earth is recorded in verse 5, which refers to 2 Corinthians 8: 9: 'though he was rich, yet for our sakes he became poor'.

The theology of the Incarnation is skilfully blended with other elements in this hymn, notably a simple drama in which some anonymous passer-by asks the shepherds a simple question about what they are doing (someone who had noticed them as St Luke describes them in verse 20, on the way back to their sheep: 'and the shepherds returned, glorifying and praising God'). This is followed by the prayers of intercession through the Christ child and the Blessed Virgin.

There is also a pictorial element, signified by 'See' in the first verse, which sets the birth in a time of snow. This is part of a tradition, from Milton to Christina Rossetti ('Snow had fallen, snow on snow'). In Milton's Ode 'On the Morning of Christ's Nativity', the snow falls as pure whiteness to cover the corruptions of a fallen world. Nature 'woos the gentle air'—

To hide her guilty front with innocent Snow,
And on her naked shame,
Pollute with sinful blame,
The Saintly Vail of Maiden white to throw,
Confounded, that her Makers eyes
Should look so neer upon her foul deformities.

By the nineteenth century this flamboyant idea had become a generalized shorthand for the birth of Christ in the middle of winter, which has a strong imaginative appeal for anyone north of the Alps (a rather absurd literal-mindedness about snow in the Holy Land seems to have been responsible for some books amending to 'See! in yonder manger low').

These elements of picture, theology, drama, and prayer are held together by the splendid refrain, which uses the repetition of 'Hail' like a chiming bell. It makes a fine contrast to the swiftly changing verses, and gives the hymn continuity and stability. It records the prophecy in Isaiah 40 ('Speak ye comfortably to Jerusalem') and has a prophetic grandeur which contrasts beautifully with the narrative and dramatic modes.

The customary tune, called OXFORD or HUMILITY was composed by John Goss (1800–80), organist of St Paul's Cathedral from 1838 to 1872. It was first published in Bramley and Stainer's *Christmas Carols: New and Old* (1871).

154

Souls of men! why will ye scatter
   Like a crowd of frightened sheep?
Foolish hearts! why will ye wander
   From a love so true and deep?

Was there ever kindest shepherd
   Half so gentle, half so sweet,
As the Saviour who would have us
   Come and gather round his feet?

There's a wideness in God's mercy
   Like the wideness of the sea;
There's a kindness in his justice
   Which is more than liberty.

There is welcome for the sinner,
   And more graces for the good;
There is mercy with the Saviour,
   There is healing in his blood.

There is grace enough for thousands
   Of new worlds as great as this;
There is room for fresh creations
   In that upper home of bliss.

For the love of God is broader
   Than the measures of man's mind,
And the heart of the Eternal
   Is most wonderfully kind.

But we make his love too narrow
   By false limits of our own;
And we magnify his strictness
   With a zeal he will not own.

There is plentiful redemption
　In the blood that has been shed;
There is joy for all the members
　In the sorrows of the Head.

If our love were but more simple,
　We should take him at his word,
And our lives would be all sunshine
　In the sweetness of our Lord.

Frederick William Faber (1814–63)

Faber was one of the most prominent and energetic of the Roman Catholic converts. He founded a branch of the 'Priests of the Congregation of St Philip Neri' at the Brompton Oratory in London, and this hymn was first published in *Oratory Hymns* (1854). It was entitled 'Come to Jesus', and had eight verses. It was later enlarged to thirteen verses, and published in Faber's *Hymns* of 1862.

The first two verses have often been omitted in modern hymn-books, to allow the hymn to begin with the striking 'There's a wideness in God's mercy', and also to avoid the gender-based language of 'Souls of men'. The original version, however, begins with two dramatic questions and the fine image of the sea: it is taken from Job 11, which asks the question (verse 7) 'Canst thou by searching find out God?', and responds (verse 9) 'The measure thereof is longer than the earth, and broader than the sea.' Faber carefully shapes this towards the mercy of God, and produces a most un-usual hymn about it: he makes a direct approach to the anxious believer, who believes that his or her shortcomings will result in divine disfavour. God's love is more wonderful than our limited vision can understand. As one of the omitted verses puts it, 'His fondness/ Goes far out beyond our dreams'. The antepenultimate verse of the present text, verse 9 of the original, states this beautifully, though it has not always found favour: the *Companion* to the American *Hymnal 1982* even says 'hardly anyone has dared include st. 9'. It is not clear why this should be seen as more daring than other parts of this extraordinary hymn: Faber as a hymn-writer was nothing if not extravagant, here and elsewhere.

In this context, Faber's favourite adjective 'sweet' has some justification. We live, as the final verse says, in the 'sweetness' of God's love, which means that we do not have to run from Him like frightened sheep; rather, God in Christ would wish us to be like the little children who gathered round His feet. It is this concept which gives 'wonderfully' a new and fresh meaning: 'wonderfully kind' is no longer just a superlative, but the adverb has a fullness of meaning which is usually forgotten. Faber's enthusiasm for the idea even leads him into the 'sunshine' image, which has often been seen as unbecoming: both *Hymns and Psalms* and *Rejoice and Sing* amend to the safe and conventional 'And our lives would be illumined'. This takes away something of the unique atmosphere of Faber's hymn, but is probably more acceptable to most readers.

One tune used in Britain is CROSS OF JESUS, by John Stainer (1840–1901), from his oratorio *The Crucifixion* (1887); hymn-books in other countries have printed a variety of tunes, including the twentieth-century ST HELENA by Calvin Hampton, and nineteenth-century tunes such as WELLESLEY, by Lizzie S. Tourjee, or BEECHER, by John Zundel, named after Henry Ward Beecher, minister of Plymouth Congregational Church, Brooklyn, and brother of Harriet Beecher Stowe, the author of *Uncle Tom's Cabin* (visiting London, Mrs Stowe thought little of English preachers: 'Oh for half-an-hour of my brother Henry!', she wrote). Other tunes used have been OMNI DIE, SUSSEX, and ST MABYN.

155 Hark! hark, my soul! Angelic songs are swelling
         O'er earth's green fields, and ocean's wave-beat shore;
     How sweet the truth those blessèd strains are telling
         Of that new life when sin shall be no more!
             Angels of Jesus, Angels of light,
             Singing to welcome the pilgrims of the night!

     Onward we go, for still we hear them singing,
         Come, weary souls, for Jesus bids you come:
     And, through the dark, its echoes sweetly ringing,
         The music of the gospel leads us home.
             Angels of Jesus . . .

     Far, far away, like bells at evening pealing,
         The voice of Jesus sounds o'er land and sea,
     And laden souls, by thousands meekly stealing,
         Kind Shepherd, turn their weary steps to thee.
             Angels of Jesus . . .

     Rest comes at length; though life be long and dreary,
         The day must dawn, and darksome night be past;
     All journeys end in welcomes to the weary,
         And heaven, the heart's true home, will come at last.
             Angels of Jesus . . .

     Angels! sing on, your faithful watches keeping,
         Sing us sweet fragments of the songs above;
     While we toil on, and soothe ourselves with weeping,
         Till life's long night shall break in endless love.
             Angels of Jesus, Angels of light,
             Singing to welcome the pilgrims of the night!

                     Frederick William Faber (1814–63)

First published in Faber's *Oratory Hymns* (1854), with the title 'The Pilgrims of the Night'. The five-verse text is the usual one for hymn-books, omitting two from the original seven (verses 2 and 6):

> Darker than night life's shadows fall around us,
>   And, like benighted men, we miss our mark;
> God hides himself, and grace hath scarcely found us,
>   Ere death finds out his victims in the dark.
>   *Angels of Jesus* . . .
>
> Cheer up, my soul! faith's moonbeams softly glisten
>   Upon the breast of life's most troubled sea;
> And it will cheer thy drooping heart to listen
>   To those brave songs which angels mean for thee.
>   *Angels of Jesus* . . .

These omitted verses show very clearly the character of this remarkable hymn. The first suggests darkness and night, both in life and in death, with the sinister image of death finding out his victims in the dark; the second shows the moonbeams of faith, and hears the songs of the angels, floating over the dark landscape of our human life. That landscape is an integral part of the hymn: the angelic songs are heard (but only if we listen) over green fields and across the sea, in a world through which we travel in darkness and with difficulty. Eventually rest will come, and the fragments of the songs which we have heard will become part of a world of song and light and everlasting life.

Faber's emotionalism, and his uninhibited use of such imagery, demonstrate his love of a sentiment that comes close to sentimentality. But his sentiment, however excessive it may seem, touches a tender spot: Faber is cheering on the soul, recognizing the troubles of life, and holding out the promise of the final homecoming. If we listen to the angels, we can hear something that will encourage us: and here the refrain is all important. As we sing the hymn, the refrain comes again and again, set against the four-line verses, with their admonitions and their descriptions of the world in which we live. The refrain, in other words, is a perpetual reminder of the song of the angels, as a counterpoint to the long lines of each verse: it is as though the hymn enacts the process which it describes with such a strong sense of atmosphere. Perhaps this is why, when sung at a funeral, the effect of this hymn can be overwhelming.

The hymn was made widely known when it was printed in the *Appendix* (1868) to the first edition of *Hymns Ancient and Modern*. It was set there to two tunes: the better of them, by Henry Smart (1813–79), is known as PILGRIMS, and was composed for these words. In the *English Hymnal* (1906), the hymn was set to a tune entitled PILGRIMS OF THE NIGHT, adapted from a Swiss song, 'La Suissesse au Bord du Lac', by Jacques Nicolas Goulé, sometimes therefore called LA SUISSESSE.

156   My God, how wonderful thou art,
          Thy majesty how bright,
        How beautiful thy mercy-seat,
          In depths of burning light!

        How dread are thine eternal years,
          O everlasting Lord,
        By prostrate spirits day and night
          Incessantly adored!

        How beautiful, how beautiful,
          The sight of thee must be,
        Thine endless wisdom, boundless power,
          And awful purity!

        O, how I fear thee, living God,
          With deepest, tenderest fears,
        And worship thee with trembling hope,
          And penitential tears!

        Yet I may love thee too, O Lord,
          Almighty as thou art,
        For thou hast stooped to ask of me
          The love of my poor heart.

        No earthly father loves like thee,
          No mother, half so mild,
        Bears and forbears as thou hast done
          With me thy sinful child.

        Father of Jesus, love's reward,
          What rapture will it be
        Prostrate before thy throne to lie,
          And gaze and gaze on thee.

              Frederick William Faber (1814–63)

This hymn was first published in *Jesus and Mary: or, Catholic Hymns for Singing and Reading* (1849), with the title 'The Eternal Father'. It had nine verses, but most hymn-books print seven of them.

It is characteristic of Faber's enthusiasm in its highly dramatic portrayal of the soul in heaven. The word 'rapture' in the last verse draws in to itself much of what has gone before, to characterize a certain devotional bliss. The word 'bliss' occurs in one of the omitted verses, and indicates the emotional approach to the Eternal Father:

          Only to sit and think of God,
            O what a joy it is!
          To think the thought, to breathe the name,
            Earth has no higher bliss!

Adjectives such as 'bright, 'burning', 'endless', 'boundless', and 'awful' join with the thrice-repeated 'beautiful'; and the depths of heaven are not dark, but are depths of light. The vision of 'awful purity' inspires fear, as it should, but the fear is a 'deepest, tenderest' emotion; similarly, worship is made up of tears, and trembling hope, giving way to love. Love is the subject of the second part of the hymn, in which God is father, mother, and 'love's reward'. God 'bears and forbears', in a neat echo, and to love God is to know or be like Jesus, who is thus the 'reward' of love. The greatest joy of the singer will be to become one of the prostrate spirits around the throne of God.

The imagery is intense and strong, and not for the fastidious or the faint-hearted. It is a perfect example of its kind, a baroque extravagance in words: its only equivalent is in some spectacular, or even garish, church architecture. Its consciousness of sin, and of spiritual poverty, gives way to rapture: and both states are portrayed with an intensity that is strangely effective.

The customary tune is WESTMINSTER, by James Turle (1802–82), organist of Westminster Abbey from 1831 to 1875. It was set to these words in the first edition of *Hymns Ancient and Modern* (1861), and is yet another example of William Henry Monk's genius for finding the right tune to fit the words.

157   Lord, thy word abideth,
             And our footsteps guideth;
             Who its truth believeth
             Light and joy receiveth.

             When our foes are near us,
             Then thy word doth cheer us,
             Word of consolation,
             Message of salvation.

             When the storms are o'er us,
             And dark clouds before us,
             Then its light directeth,
             And our way protecteth.

             Who can tell the pleasure,
             Who recount the treasure,
             By thy word imparted
             To the simple hearted?

             Word of mercy, giving
             Succour to the living;
             Word of life, supplying
             Comfort to the dying.

O that we discerning
Its most holy learning,
Lord, may love and fear thee,
Evermore be near thee.

Sir Henry Williams Baker (1821–77)

This hymn was written for the first edition of *Hymns Ancient and Modern* (1861). Baker was the principal editor, and the driving force behind the book, and he was largely responsible for its success. He was vicar of Monkland, Herefordshire, in 1851, and on the death of his father in 1859 he inherited a baronetcy.

The hymn is based on Psalm 119: 105: 'Thy word is a lamp unto my feet, and a light unto my path.' Its short lines, of six syllables, make the rhymes more important, especially because Baker uses 'feminine rhyme' (rhyming on two syllables, with the second unstressed). Thus, after only four syllables, the rhyme arrives; and it is skilfully used to embody the central messages of the hymn: the word abideth and guideth; whoever believeth, receiveth; and so on. It is a rhyming gospel, with neat and subtle variations; and it is written throughout in a lucid and unaffected style. As Julian's *Dictionary of Hymnology* said of Baker's technique:

Poetical figures, far-fetched illustrations, and difficult compound words, he entirely eschewed. In his simplicity of language, smoothness of rhythm, and earnestness of utterance, he reminds one forcibly of the saintly Lyte.

The tune, RAVENSHAW, was one of many written or adapted by William Henry Monk for *Hymns Ancient and Modern* (1861). It was taken from a medieval German tune found in Michael Weisse's *Ein neu Gesangbuchlein* of 1531, and has become closely associated with these words.

158
Eternal Father, strong to save,
Whose arm doth bind the restless wave,
Who bidd'st the mighty ocean deep
Its own appointed limits keep:
    O hear us when we cry to thee
    For those in peril on the sea.

O Saviour, whose almighty word
The winds and waves submissive heard,
Who walkedst on the foaming deep,
And calm amid its rage didst sleep:
    O hear us when we cry to thee
    For those in peril on the sea.

O sacred Spirit, who didst brood
Upon the chaos dark and rude,
Who bad'st its angry tumult cease,
And gavest light and life and peace:
    O hear us when we cry to thee
    For those in peril on the sea.

O Trinity of love and power,
Our brethren shield in danger's hour;
From rock and tempest, fire and foe,
Protect them wheresoe'er they go:
    And ever let there rise to thee
    Glad hymns of praise from land and sea.

William Whiting (1825–78)

This hymn was written in 1860, and almost immediately found its way into the first edition of *Hymns Ancient and Modern* (1861), though in an altered form. Whiting, who was a schoolmaster, must have known his Milton, because there are echoes of *Paradise Lost* in verses 1 and 3. The first is to Book VII. 166–7, in which God is speaking to the Son:

ride forth, and bid the deep
Within appointed bounds be heaven and earth, . . .

and verse 3 is indebted to Book I. 19–21, in which the poet prays for inspiration to the Holy Spirit:

thou from the first
Wast present, and with mighty wings outspread
Dove-like sat'st brooding on the vast abyss . . . .

The first of these borrowings is even more evident in Whiting's first version, which began 'O Thou Who bidd'st the ocean deep'. This was altered by the editors of *Hymns Ancient and Modern*; the hymn was later rewritten by Whiting in its present form, which dates from 1869.

The hymn also echoes Psalm 107: 23–30, with its description of 'they that go down to the sea in ships, that do business in great waters', with its sublime description of the storm, and the final coming into harbour.

It is a stately Trinitarian hymn, praying in turn to Father, Son, and Holy Ghost, and ending with the resounding 'O Trinity of love and power'. But to those who have served in the Royal Navy it is known as 'The Sailor's Hymn', sung on Sundays whenever 'the exigencies of the service' allowed. Thus it was sung during the meeting between Churchill and Roosevelt in the North Atlantic on the ill-fated *Prince of Wales* during the Second World War. It has also been used on such great and solemn occasions as the funeral of President John F. Kennedy. It was sung many times during the Falklands War of 1982, and became at that time a deeply felt national prayer for those who were setting out for the South Atlantic. It is also used to great effect in Benjamin Britten's *Noye's Fludde*.

The noble prayer of this hymn is well suited to the powerful tune written for it in *Hymns Ancient and Modern* by John Bacchus Dykes (1823–76), with its remarkable climbing tenor and bass in line 1. It was appropriately named MELITA (Malta), after the island on which St Paul was shipwrecked.

159   As with gladness men of old
Did the guiding star behold,
As with joy they hailed its light,
Leading onward, beaming bright;
So, most gracious Lord, may we
Evermore be led to thee.

As with joyful steps they sped,
Saviour, to thy lowly bed,
There to bend the knee before
Thee whom heaven and earth adore;
So may we with willing feet
Ever seek thy mercy-seat.

As they offered gifts most rare
At thy cradle rude and bare;
So may we with holy joy,
Pure and free from sin's alloy,
All our costliest treasures bring,
Christ, to thee our heavenly king.

Holy Jesus, every day
Keep us in the narrow way;
And, when earthly things are past,
Bring our ransomed souls at last
Where they need no star to guide,
Where no clouds thy glory hide.

In the heavenly country bright
Need they no created light;
Thou its light, its joy, its crown,
Thou its sun which goes not down;
There for ever may we sing
Alleluias to our king.

William Chatterton Dix (1837–98)

This is one of the best-known hymns of the Epiphany. It was written, according to a note on the manuscript, 'about 1860 during an illness', and was first published in Dix's *Hymns of Love and Joy* (1861), a small collection of hymns for private circulation. In the same year it appeared in a Bristol hymn-book, the *St Raphael's Hymnal*, prepared for the church of that name (see the note on Dix at no. 163); and in the first edition of *Hymns Ancient and Modern*. The text was later slightly revised, with Dix's approval.

Its simplicity of stanza form and its predictable rhymes and rhythms conceal an art which is unobtrusive and economical: the first three verses all begin with an extended simile, 'As', then inviting the singer to transfer the episode of the wise men into his or her own life, using the word 'So'. There is then a graceful transition from earthly things to heavenly ones, following the pattern of a Collect in the *Book of Common Prayer*.

The tune has always been known as DIX from its close association with this hymn. This has its own irony, because Dix is known to have disliked it. It comes from a chorale melody by a German composer, Conrad Kocher (1786–1872), published in 1838, which was adapted and harmonized by William Henry Monk (1823–89), the musical editor of *Hymns Ancient and Modern*. It is a pity that Charles Villiers Stanford's ORIENT, written for a collection of carols published in 1894 and reprinted in the *Methodist Hymn Book*, has not been more widely adopted.

160

Forty days and forty nights
  Thou wast fasting in the wild;
Forty days and forty nights
  Tempted, and yet undefiled;

Sunbeams scorching all the day;
  Chilly dew-drops nightly shed;
Prowling beasts about thy way;
  Stones thy pillow, earth thy bed.

Shall not we thy sorrow share,
  And from earthly joys abstain,
Fasting with unceasing prayer,
  Glad with thee to suffer pain?

And if Satan, vexing sore,
  Flesh or spirit should assail,
Thou, his vanquisher before,
  Grant we may not faint or fail.

So shall we have peace divine;
  Holier gladness ours shall be;
Round us, too, shall angels shine,
  Such as ministered to thee.

Keep, O keep us, Saviour dear,
  Ever constant by thy side;
That with thee we may appear
  At the eternal Eastertide.

George Hunt Smyttan (1822–70)
and Francis Pott (1832–1909)

This is the best known of all hymns for Lent. A version by Smyttan was published in 1856, and used by Pott for his *Hymns Fitted to the Order of Common Prayer* (1861). It also appeared in the same year in the first edition of *Hymns Ancient and Modern*. Pott reduced Smyttan's nine-verse text to six verses, and radically altered them; since then his own version has often been tampered with. The text printed above is that of *Hymns Ancient and Modern* (1861).

The hymn is closely connected with the Gospel for the First Sunday in Lent (Matthew 4: 1–11) and with the Collect for that Sunday:

O Lord, who for our sake didst fast forty days and forty nights; give us grace to use such abstinence, that, our flesh being subdued to the Spirit, we may ever obey thy godly motions in righteousness, and true holiness, to thy honour and glory . . .

Pott succeeds in producing a very real sense of relief and comfort after the pain of the earlier verses, and the hymn is a good indicator of the reward of Easter after the privations of Lent.

The tune, HEINLEIN, is wonderfully suited to the words, its minor chords suggesting the struggle with temptation and the privations of Christ in the wilderness. It is by Martin Herbst (*c*.1654–81); although at one time it was thought to be by Paul Heinlein, from whom it takes its name.

161

Come, ye thankful people, come,
Raise the song of harvest home:
All is safely gathered in,
Ere the winter storms begin;
God our maker doth provide
For our wants to be supplied:
Come to God's own temple, come,
Raise the song of harvest home!

All the world is God's own field
Fruit unto his praise to yield;
Wheat and tares together sown,
Unto joy or sorrow grown;
First the blade, and then the ear,
Then the full corn shall appear:
Grant, O harvest Lord, that we
Wholesome grain and pure may be.

For the Lord our God shall come,
And shall take his harvest home;
From his field shall in that day
All offences purge away;
Give his angels charge at last
In the fire the tares to cast:
But the fruitful ears to store
In his garner evermore.

Even so, Lord, quickly come,
Bring thy final harvest home:
Gather thou thy people in,
Free from sorrow, free from sin;
There, for ever purified,
In thy garner to abide:
Come, with all thine angels, come,
Raise the glorious harvest home!

Henry Alford (1810–71),

From Alford's *Psalms and Hymns* (1844), from which it was taken into *Hymns Ancient and Modern* (1861), though with a greatly altered text, which the author did not like: it included a final verse (still found in *Hymns Ancient and Modern New Standard*) with the saints in heaven

> All upon the golden floor
> Praising thee for evermore:

Alford altered his own poem for his *Poetical Works*, fourth edition (1865) to a form that is close to the present well-known version. This is the text which appears in many hymn-books, although the *English Hymnal* begins the final verse with 'Then, thou Church Triumphant come', and this has been followed by *Common Praise* (2000).

Most hymn-books print four verses, but *Rejoice and Sing* abbreviates further; to avoid the severe warning of verse 3: the omission is entirely in keeping with modern worship, which (in Pope's words) 'never mentions hell to ears polite'.

Alford, who was a Greek scholar and a poet (a friend of Tennyson and Hallam at Cambridge) became Dean of Canterbury in 1857. Before that he had worked for eighteen years in the parish of Wymeswold, in rural Leicestershire, which would have given him an insight into the importance of harvest time in a country community. Indeed, one of the hymn's most attractive features is its use of the traditional phrase 'Harvest Home!' in three of the four verses printed above. 'Raise the song of harvest home!' at the end of verse 1 neatly appropriates the traditional festivities and brings them inside the parish church, asking for God's blessing upon the fruits of the earth.

At the same time, Alford the parish priest allows his country congregation to think of the Bible: of the parable of the wheat and the tares (Matthew 13: 24–30), and of the sower in Mark 4, where (verse 28, echoed in verse 2 of the hymn) 'the earth bringeth forth fruit of herself; first the blade, then the ear, after that the full corn in the ear.' Throughout, Alford skilfully uses the idea of harvest as a metaphor for the Christian life, and as a parable.

The use of this hymn as a pre-eminent hymn at harvest time is in part owing to its wonderfully vigorous tune, ST GEORGE'S, WINDSOR, by Sir George Job Elvey (1816–93). The tune was named after the Royal Chapel: Elvey was organist of St George's Chapel, Windsor, from 1835 to 1882. The tune first appeared in E. H. Thorne's *Selection of Psalm and Hymn-Tunes* (London, 1858), set to James Montgomery's 'Hark! the song of jubilee'. Its association with the present words began with the first edition of *Hymns Ancient and Modern* (1861), and tune and words together have been a stirring and enjoyable feature of harvest festivals ever since.

162   *Wir pflügen und wir streuen*

We plough the fields, and scatter
 The good seed on the land,
But it is fed and watered
 By God's almighty hand:
He sends the snow in winter,
 The warmth to swell the grain,
The breezes, and the sunshine,
 And soft, refreshing rain.
  All good gifts around us
   Are sent from heaven above;
  Then thank the Lord, O thank the Lord,
   For all his love.

He only is the maker
 Of all things near and far;
He paints the wayside flower,
 He lights the evening star;
The winds and waves obey him,
 By him the birds are fed;
Much more to us, his children,
 He gives our daily bread.
  All good gifts around us
   Are sent from heaven above;
  Then thank the Lord, O thank the Lord,
   For all his love.

We thank thee then, O Father,
 For all things bright and good,
The seed-time and the harvest,
 Our life, our health, our food:
Accept the gifts we offer
 For all thy love imparts,
And, what thou most desirest,
 Our humble, thankful hearts.
  All good gifts around us
   Are sent from heaven above;
  Then thank the Lord, O thank the Lord,
   For all his love.

    Matthias Claudius (1740–1815),
   tr. Jane Montgomery Campbell (1817–78)

This German harvest hymn was first published in a portrait of country life entitled 'Paul Erdmann's Fest'. It appeared in the fourth part (1782) of a series, in a newspaper published at Wandsbeck, near Hanover, entitled *Der Wandsbecker Bote*. Claudius, who wrote under the pseudonym 'Asmus', was the chief contributor to the newspaper: he has been described as 'the father of German popular journalism' and 'a poet with a delight in the minor happenings of life'. His essays and articles were collected as *Asmus omnia sua secum portans, oder sämmtliche Werke des Wandsbecker Bothen, 1775–1812* ('containing all of Asmus within it; or the collected works of the Wandsbeck messenger').

In 'Paul Erdmann's Fest', neighbours come at harvest time to sing a 'Peasant's Song', in four-line verses, at Paul's party. The third verse began 'Wir pflügen . . .': Jane Montgomery Campbell's translation uses verses 3, 5, 7, 9, 10, 13 to make three verses of eight lines, with a refrain to fit the tune.

The translation of this (by now) very popular German song was included in a collection by Charles S. Bere, *A Garland of Song; an English Liederkranz* ('song-wreath') published in 1861. It first appeared, slightly altered, as a hymn in the *Appendix* (1868) to the first edition of *Hymns Ancient and Modern*, from which it made its way into many hymn-books. It is a robust and cheerful harvest hymn, retaining many of the features which made it an effective folk song—a strong rhythm, a boldness of speech, and a simplicity of idea. Its deep popular appeal in Germany is shown by a beautiful scene in a short story by the novelist Elizabeth Gaskell, 'Six Weeks at Heppenheim' (1862), in which the English visitor observes the villagers gathering round the local pastor, bare-headed, to sing it at the grape harvest. It is a moment in which the hard manual labour of the harvest is transformed and given religious significance.

The hymn is sometimes printed with a text from Psalm 145: 15: 'The eyes of all wait upon Thee, and Thou givest them their meat in due season.' The refrain is sometimes linked with James 1: 17: 'Every good gift and every perfect gift is from above . . .'.

The tune is usually called WIR PFLÜGEN, but occasionally DRESDEN or CLAUDIUS. It was written by Johann Abraham Peter Schulz, and first published in a school song-book, *Lieder im Volkston* (Berlin, 1782–90). Words and music were reprinted in a Hamburg collection of folk songs, Wichern's *Unsere Lieder* of 1844. Campbell's words are well fitted to the tune, which Julian's *Dictionary of Hymnology* rather fastidiously described as 'popular and somewhat boisterous'.

163   Alleluia, sing to Jesus,
               His the sceptre, his the throne;
             Alleluia, his the triumph,
               His the victory alone;
             Hark, the songs of peaceful Sion
               Thunder like a mighty flood;
             Jesus, out of every nation
               Hath redeemed us by his blood.

             Alleluia, not as orphans
               Are we left in sorrow now;
             Alleluia, he is near us,
               Faith believes, nor questions how;
             Though the cloud from sight received him,
               When the forty days were o'er,
             Shall our hearts forget his promise,
               'I am with you evermore'?

             Allleluia, bread of angels,
               Thou on earth our food, our stay;
             Alleluia, here the sinful
               Flee to thee from day to day;
             Intercessor, friend of sinners,
               Earth's redeemer, plead for me,
             Where the songs of all the sinless
               Sweep across the crystal sea.

             Alleluia, King eternal,
               Thee the Lord of lords we own;
             Alleluia, born of Mary,
               Earth thy footstool, heaven thy throne:
             Thou within the veil hast entered,
               Robed in flesh, our great High Priest;
             Thou on earth both priest and victim
               In the Eucharistic Feast.

             Alleluia, sing to Jesus,
               His the sceptre, his the throne;
             Alleluia, his the triumph,
               His the victory alone;
             Hark, the songs of peaceful Sion
               Thunder like a mighty flood;
             Jesus, out of every nation
               Hath redeemed us by his blood.

                     William Chatterton Dix (1837–98)

This hymn was written in 1866, 'the author's design being to assist in sup-
plying a then acknowledged lack of Eucharistic hymns in Church of England
hymnals' (Julian's *Dictionary of Hymnology*). It was first published in Dix's

Altar Songs (1867), with the title, 'Redemption by the Precious Blood'. A year later it was included in the *Appendix* (1868) to the first edition of *Hymns Ancient and Modern*.

The Eucharistic theme is evident in verse 3, with its reference to Christ as the food and stay, to whom the sinful turn. At every point it is a spectacular and dramatic hymn, with its very allusive style, picking up biblical references in the manner of Charles Wesley. The most notable one is the idea of Jesus as High Priest (from Hebrews, chapters 3 to 9), and the vision of Revelation 5: 9: 'Thou hast redeemed us to God by thy blood out of every kindred, and tongue, and people, and nation.' It is also closely linked with the feast of the Ascension in verse 2. Verse 3 of the hymn contains the great appeal to Jesus the intercessor and redeemer, which returns to the Eucharistic theme, though now linked with the ascended one in heaven; while in verse 4 the Incarnate Word, who was 'born of Mary' is now both priest and victim in the Eucharistic feast.

Dix was a Bristolian. His father, a medical man, must have hoped that his son would be a poet, because he called him William (perhaps after Shakespeare) and Chatterton (after Thomas Chatterton, 1752–70, the Bristol poet who died young and tragically). His son lived up to his father's expectations, publishing several collections of religious poetry, with a predilection for 'High Church' ritual. This hymn is an imitation of the 'Alleluia' hymns in ancient liturgies, revived in the nineteenth century by such translators as John Mason Neale.

In *Hymns Ancient and Modern* this hymn was set to a tune by Samuel Sebastian Wesley called ALLELUIA. But in the *English Hymnal* (1906) Ralph Vaughan Williams set it to the magnificent Welsh tune HYFRYDOL, by R. H. Prichard (1811–87), and that tune carries the words so well that it has become the usual setting for them.

164   O praise ye the Lord!
                                     Praise him in the height;
                                 Rejoice in his word,
                                     Ye angels of light;
                                 Ye heavens adore him
                                     By whom ye were made,
                                 And worship before him,
                                     In brightness arrayed.

                                 O praise ye the Lord!
                                     Praise him upon earth,
                                 In tuneful accord,
                                     Ye sons of new birth;
                                 Praise him who hath brought you
                                     His grace from above,
                                 Praise him who hath taught you
                                     To sing of his love.

                                 O praise ye the Lord,
                                     All things that give sound;
                                 Each jubilant chord,
                                     Re-echo around;
                                 Loud organs, his glory
                                     Forth tell in deep tone,
                                 And sweet harp, the story
                                     Of what he hath done.

                                 O praise ye the Lord!
                                     Thanksgiving and song
                                 To him be outpoured
                                     All ages along:
                                 For love in creation,
                                     For heaven restored,
                                 For grace of salvation
                                     O praise ye the Lord!

                            Sir Henry Williams Baker (1821–77)

This splendid hymn of praise was written for the 1875 edition of *Hymns Ancient and Modern,* of which Baker was the chief editor. The success of the 1861 edition had led to an *Appendix* of 1868, and then to this second edition. The hymn is a straightforward hymn of praise, inspired mainly by Psalm 148 and Psalm 150; there are also echoes of the General Thanksgiving in verse 4: 'We bless thee for our creation, preservation, and all the blessings of this life; but above all, for thine inestimable love in the redemption of the world by our Lord Jesus Christ; for the means of grace, and for the hope of glory.'

    In the original printing, this hymn was accompanied by a tune written for it by H. J. Gauntlett (1805–76), entitled LAUDATE DOMINUM (a Latin version of the first line). It is now more frequently sung to another tune of the same name by C. H. H. Parry (1848–1918). Parry wrote it when he used Baker's words for the concluding part of an anthem, 'Hear my words, ye people', in 1894. It makes a magnificent hymn of praise, especially with the spectacular running organ accompaniment to verse 4, followed by the double 'Amen'.

165

The King of love my Shepherd is,
   Whose goodness faileth never;
I nothing lack if I am his
   And he is mine for ever.

Where streams of living water flow
   My ransomed soul he leadeth,
And, where the verdant pastures grow,
   With food celestial feedeth.

Perverse and foolish oft I strayed,
   But yet in love he sought me,
And on his shoulder gently laid,
   And home, rejoicing, brought me.

In death's dark vale I fear no ill
   With thee, dear Lord, beside me;
Thy rod and staff my comfort still,
   Thy cross before to guide me.

Thou spread'st a table in my sight;
   Thy unction grace bestoweth;
And oh, what transport of delight
   From thy pure chalice floweth!

And so through all the length of days
   Thy goodness faileth never:
Good Shepherd, may I sing thy praise
   Within thy house for ever.

Sir Henry Williams Baker (1821–77)

This very Victorian paraphrase of the twenty-third Psalm was first printed in the *Appendix* (1868) to the first edition of *Hymns Ancient and Modern*, of which Baker was the principal editor. It is a skilful adaptation of that psalm for the Anglican church of the nineteenth century. The image of the good shepherd with the lamb upon his shoulder appears in many stained-glass windows of the period; and the spreading of the table becomes a recognition of the power of the Sacraments. The 'unction', or anointing with oil, bestows grace, and the chalice at Holy Communion gives a 'pure transport' of delight: so that the singing of praise 'within thy house for ever' suggests not only the life everlasting, but also a lifetime spent in the service of the church, as Baker's was. He said the words of the third verse on his deathbed.

The metre is strongly iambic, 8.7.8.7., but with a lovely feminine rhyme (rhyming on two syllables, with the second unstressed) in the second and fourth lines. It was given the flowing tune DOMINUS REGIT ME, which emphasizes the unusual metre, by John Bacchus Dykes (1823–76). The name comes from the first line of Psalm 23 in the Vulgate, or Latin Bible. The *English Hymnal* was refused permission to use this tune, and chose the Irish traditional melody ST COLUMBA instead: Vaughan Williams, who usually disliked Victorian tunes, regretted that the committee were not allowed to use 'such a beautiful tune'. ST COLUMBA has remained an alternative tune in many books; there is also a delicate and charming modern tune by Brian Hoare (1935–) called CLIFF LANE, used as an alternative in *Hymns and Psalms*.

166

Crown him with many crowns,
The Lamb upon his throne;
Hark, how the heavenly anthem drowns
All music but its own:
Awake, my soul, and sing
Of him who died for thee,
And hail him as thy matchless King
Through all eternity.

Crown him the Virgin's Son,
The God incarnate born,
Whose arm those crimson trophies won
Which now his brow adorn:
Fruit of the mystic Rose,
As of that Rose the stem,
The root whence mercy ever flows,
The babe of Bethlehem.

Crown him the Lord of love;
Behold his hands and side,
Rich wounds yet visible above
In beauty glorified:
No angel in the sky
Can fully bear that sight,
But downward bends his burning eye
At mysteries so bright.

Crown him the Lord of peace,
Whose power a sceptre sways
From pole to pole, that wars may cease,
And all be prayer and praise:
His reign shall know no end,
And round his piercèd feet
Fair flowers of paradise extend
Their fragrance ever sweet.

Crown him the Lord of years,
The Potentate of time,
Creator of the rolling spheres,
Ineffably sublime.
All hail, Redeemer, hail!
For thou hast died for me;
Thy praise shall never, never fail
Throughout eternity.

Matthew Bridges (1800–94)

This hymn, from Bridges's *Hymns of the Heart* (1851) was made popular by its inclusion in the *Appendix* (1868) to the first edition of *Hymns Ancient and Modern*. It is a stirring hymn of triumph, made the more powerful by its strong tunes: recalling the medieval tradition, Christ is the Virgin's son but also (as God) the creator of the Virgin, so that He is both 'fruit of the mystic Rose (the Blessed Virgin Mary) and the 'stem' of that Rose, while being also the 'root' of mercy. He then becomes the 'Lord of love' by His suffering on the Cross, and the 'Lord of peace' in the coming of His kingdom. Finally He is 'Lord of time', both Creator and Redeemer.

During the 1870s, objections were made to Bridges's words, perhaps because of the complex references to the Blessed Virgin Mary; and Godfrey Thring (1823–1903) produced an alternative version, printed in his *Hymns and Sacred Lyrics* (1874). Some hymn-books use verses from Bridges and Thring to make a composite hymn: *Hymns Ancient and Modern* has always stood by Bridges, with some slight alterations, and the 1868 text is the one printed here. It may have offended some Victorians, but it is immensely superior to Thring's version in its imaginative realization of the power and love of Christ.

The usual tune, DIADEMATA ('crowns') was written for these words in *Hymns Ancient and Modern* by Sir George Job Elvey (1816–93), organist of St George's Chapel, Windsor, for forty-seven years: it makes a magnificent setting for the text, march-like and joyful without ever becoming mechanical or strident. Other tunes include CORONA, by Richard Runciman Terry (1865–1938) and another tune also called CORONA, by Charles Hylton Stewart (1884–1932).

167   Now the day is over,
                 Night is drawing nigh,
             Shadows of the evening
                 Steal across the sky.

             Now the darkness gathers,
                 Stars begin to peep,
             Birds, and beasts, and flowers
                 Soon will be asleep.

             Jesu, give the weary
                 Calm and sweet repose;
             With thy tenderest blessing
                 May mine eyelids close.

             Grant to little children
                 Visions bright of thee;
             Guard the sailors tossing
                 On the deep blue sea.

             Comfort every sufferer
                 Watching late in pain;
             Those who plan some evil
                 From their sin restrain.

             Through the long night watches
                 May thine angels spread
             Their white wings above me,
                 Watching round my bed.

             When the morning wakens,
                 Then may I arise
             Pure, and fresh, and sinless
                 In thy holy eyes.

             Glory to the Father,
                 Glory to the Son,
             And to thee, blest Spirit,
                 Whilst all ages run.

             Sabine Baring-Gould (1834–1924)

This simple but lovely evening hymn was first published in the *Church Times* in 1867, and included in the *Appendix* (1868) to the first edition of *Hymns Ancient and Modern*. It became very popular, and was included in most hymn-books until recent times: its quiet understatement has not commended itself to most modern editors.

It uses the short lines very well, often in two-line units: the 6 5. 6 5. metre seems to produce attractive children's hymns, as with 'Daisies are our silver'; and although this is not specifically a children's hymn (it prays for them in verse 4), it has many features which are associated with a child's sensibility, such as the angels watching round the bed in verse 6. The singer of this hymn, child or adult, prays in short and straightforward phrases for the weary, the children, for sailors, for those in pain, and for those tempted to sin; and the final prayer is for the singer, that he or she may arise refreshed and innocent.

Baring-Gould was an unusual man, the eldest son of a Devonshire squire in the village of Lew Trenchard on the edge of Dartmoor. While a curate at Horbury Bridge, Yorkshire, where he wrote 'Onward, Christian soldiers', he courted and married a mill girl, whom he sent to be educated and made into a lady. He became a country vicar in Yorkshire and Essex, and finally of Lew Trenchard (in 1881). He wrote a fifteen-volume *Lives of the Saints* between 1872 and 1877, and other voluminous works which are now forgotten, such as *Curious Myths of the Middle Ages* (1866–8) and *The Origins and Development of Religious Belief* (1869–70); but what will not be forgotten are the Devonshire songs which he collected, including 'Widecombe Fair'.

He was also an amateur musician: the simplicity of his verses is matched by his own tune, EUDOXIA. Its uncomplicated musical phrases make an apt setting for such words.

168   Onward, Christian soldiers,
                 Marching as to war,
             With the Cross of Jesus
                 Going on before.
             Christ the Royal Master
                 Leads against the foe;
             Forward into battle,
                 See his banners go!
                     Onward, Christian soldiers,
                         Marching as to war,
                     With the Cross of Jesus
                         Going on before.

             At the sign of triumph
                 Satan's host doth flee:
             On then, Christian soldiers,
                 On to victory.
             Hell's foundations quiver
                 At the shout of praise;
             Brothers, lift your voices,
                 Loud your anthems raise.
                     Onward, Christian soldiers, . . .

Like a mighty army,
    Moves the church of God;
Brothers, we are treading
    Where the saints have trod;
We are not divided,
    All one body we,
One in hope and doctrine,
    One in charity.
        Onward, Christian soldiers, . . .

Crowns and thrones may perish,
    Kingdoms rise and wane,
But the church of Jesus
    Constant will remain;
Gates of hell can never
    'Gainst that church prevail;
We have Christ's own promise,
    And that cannot fail.
        Onward, Christian soldiers, . . .

Onward, then, ye people,
    Join our happy throng,
Blend with ours your voices
    In the triumph song;
Glory, laud, and honour
    Unto Christ the king,
This through countless ages
    Men and angels sing.

        Onward, Christian soldiers,
        Marching as to war,
        With the Cross of Jesus
        Going on before.

Sabine Baring-Gould (1834–1924)

This astonishing hymn could hardly be more different from the tranquil
'Now the day is over' by the same author: but what the two hymns have in
common is an appeal to children. This hymn was written, when Baring-
Gould was a curate in Yorkshire, for the children of Horbury Bridge, near
Wakefield: it was published in the *Church Times*, 15 October 1864, with the
title 'Hymn for Procession with Cross and Banners'. It was designed to be
sung as the children processed on Whit Monday. It came into general use
after it was published in the *Appendix* (1868) to the first edition of *Hymns
Ancient and Modern*.

The hymn is a fascinating example of the way in which the hymnody of
the Church Militant can be used for children. All children like dressing up
and 'playing soldiers', and here they have an opportunity to do so with
gusto. It seems that they need only to shout, and Satan's host will flee: here

and at other points the hymn seems singularly optimistic. For example, the idea that the Church is 'not divided' seems untrue; but the ringing declaration that the gates of hell will never prevail against it has the sanction of the words of Jesus in Matthew 16: 18.

The hymn, like many strong texts, lends itself to parody. Percy Dearmer tells the story (in *Songs of Praise Discussed*) of the low-church bishop who did not like processions with crosses, whereupon the choir processed out of the vestry singing 'With the Cross of Jesus/ Left behind the door'.

Baring-Gould wrote the hymn to a tune from Haydn, which was called ST ALBAN, and it was published with that tune in its early years. The great march tune by which it is now universally known, with its thumping bass notes in the chorus, was written by Arthur Sullivan, and published in *The Musical Times* in 1871. Sullivan naturally used it in *Church Hymns with Tunes* (1874), of which he was the musical editor, and it has become universally associated with these words. Its name, ST GERTRUDE, was a deft compliment to Mrs Gertrude Clay-Ker-Seymour, in whose house Sullivan was staying when he wrote the tune.

169 *Igjennem Nat og Traengsel*

Through the night of doubt and sorrow
  Onward goes the pilgrim band,
Singing songs of expectation,
  Marching to the Promised Land.

Clear before us through the darkness
  Gleams and burns the guiding light;
Brother clasps the hand of brother,
  Stepping fearless through the night.

One the light of God's own presence
  O'er his ransomed people shed,
Chasing far the gloom and terror,
  Brightening all the path we tread;

One the object of our journey,
  One the faith which never tires,
One the earnest looking forward,
  One the hope our God inspires.

One the strain that lips of thousands
  Lift as from the heart of one;
One the conflict, one the peril,
  One the march in God begun;

One the gladness of rejoicing
On the far eternal shore,
Where the One Almighty Father
Reigns in love for evermore.

Onward, therefore, pilgrim brothers,
Onward with the Cross our aid;
Bear its shame, and fight its battle,
Till we rest beneath its shade.

Soon shall come the great awaking,
Soon the rending of the tomb;
Then the scattering of all shadows,
And the end of toil and gloom.

Bernhardt Severin Ingemann (1789–1862),
tr. Sabine Baring-Gould (1834–1924)

This is the only Danish hymn to have become widely known in English-speaking countries, which is odd when one remembers that one of the great European hymn-writers, N. F. S. Grundtvig, wrote prolifically and splendidly for the Danish church hymn-book.

This hymn, 'Igjennem Nat og Traengsel', was published in *Nyt Tillaeg til Evangelisk-christelig Psalmebog* (1859). Dr R. F. Littledale (1833–90), hymn-writer and editor of *The People's Hymnal* (1867), asked Baring-Gould to look through the Danish hymn-book and produce translations of any text that he thought interesting. Baring-Gould translated several hymns, of which this is the survivor. Verse 2, line 3 is amended in modern books to 'Pilgrim clasps the hand of pilgrim'.

Part of the reason for this hymn's survival when Baring-Gould's other translations have disappeared must be that it has always attracted good tunes. *Hymns Ancient and Modern* used ST OSWALD, by J. B. Dykes (1823–76), one of Dykes's most vigorous and energetic tunes; but the most common tune in twentieth-century books is Martin Shaw's splendid MARCHING, which dates from 1915 and was used in *Songs of Praise*, where it was very successful and from which it became widely known.

170

  O Jesus, I have promised
   To serve thee to the end;
  Be thou for ever near me,
   My master and my friend;
  I shall not fear the battle
   If thou art by my side,
  Nor wander from the pathway
   If thou wilt be my guide.

  O let me feel thee near me:
   The world is ever near;
  I see the sights that dazzle,
   The tempting sounds I hear;
  My foes are ever near me,
   Around me and within;
  But Jesus, draw thou nearer,
   And shield my soul from sin.

  O let me hear thee speaking
   In accents clear and still,
  Above the storms of passion,
   The murmurs of self-will;
  O speak to reassure me,
   To hasten or control;
  O speak, and make me listen,
   Thou guardian of my soul.

  O Jesus, thou hast promised
   To all who follow thee,
  That where thou art in glory
   There shall thy servant be;
  And, Jesus, I have promised
   To serve thee to the end;
  O give me grace to follow,
   My master and my friend.

  O let me see thy footmarks,
   And in them plant mine own;
  My hope to follow duly
   Is in thy strength alone;
  O guide me, call me, draw me,
   Uphold me to the end,
  And then in heaven receive me,
   My Saviour and my friend.

   John Ernest Bode (1816–74)

This hymn was written for the confirmation of the author's daughter and
two sons in 1866, so that it originally began 'O Jesus, we have promised'. It
became a classic hymn for confirmation, so much so that Percy Dearmer (in

Songs of Praise Discussed) reported that bishops were complaining to their clergy about its overuse. It was published in leaflet form by the SPCK in 1868, and rapidly made its way into nineteenth-century hymn-books, such as the second edition of *Hymns Ancient and Modern* (1875). It is based on John 12: 26: 'If any man serve me, let him follow me; and where I am, there shall also my servant be . . .'. Originally it had six verses, but most hymn-books print four verses, or five, as above. It has a fine and energetic progression through the verses: it even succeeds in incorporating, without too much trouble, an echo of 'Good King Wenceslas' at the beginning of the last verse.

Its continued success has something to do with the two tunes with which it has been associated. The first is DAY OF REST, by James William Elliott (1833–1915), so called because it was first used for 'O day of rest and gladness'. This tune was used for Bode's hymn in *Hymns Ancient and Modern* (1875), and the words and music became closely associated. Recent hymn-books have tended to prefer the unison splendour of W. H. Ferguson's WOLVERCOTE, written sometime before 1913, and printed in *The Public School Hymn Book* (1919). At that time Ferguson (1874–1950) was chaplain and musical director of Lancing College, and the tune is very appropriate for a Public School chapel. Other tunes have been the American MISSIONARY HYMN, used in the *English Hymnal*, and the Welsh MEIRIONYDD, found in *Songs of Praise*.

171   Fight the good fight with all thy might,
Christ is thy strength, and Christ thy right;
Lay hold on life, and it shall be
Thy joy and crown eternally.

Run the straight race through God's good grace,
Lift up thine eyes, and seek his face;
Life with its way before us lies,
Christ is the path, and Christ the prize.

Cast care aside, lean on thy guide;
His boundless mercy will provide;
Trust, and thy trusting soul shall prove
Christ is its life, and Christ its love.

Faint not nor fear, his arms are near,
He changeth not, and thou art dear;
Only believe, and thou shalt see
That Christ is all in all to thee.

John Samuel Bewley Monsell (1811–75)

This comes from Monsell's *Hymns of Love and Praise for the Church's Year* (1863), one of many hymn-books of the Victorian period which sought to provide hymns in close association with the Prayer Book. This one was placed at the Nineteenth Sunday after Trinity, although it seems to have no connection with the Collect, Epistle, or Gospel for that day except in its general sense of the Christian life. It is based on two texts: 'Fight the good fight of faith, lay hold on eternal life' (1 Timothy 6: 12), and 'let us run with patience the race that is set before us' (Hebrews 12: 1).

The hymn attained wide popularity through *Church Hymns with Tunes* (1874) and the second edition of *Hymns Ancient and Modern* (1875), from which this text is taken. It is full of images which Susan Tamke, in *Make a Joyful Noise unto the Lord* (1978), noted as 'the language of the public-school boy: competition, fighting, racing, winning prizes.' It is also, of course, the language of St Paul and of the author of the Epistle to the Hebrews.

Monsell was a noted hymn-writer, popular in his own day, and a parish priest, vicar of Egham, Surrey, 1853–70, and of St Nicholas', Guildford, 1870–5: he was tragically killed during building works for the restoration of the church, when a stone fell from the roof.

The words are most frequently set to DUKE STREET, attributed to John Hatton (died 1793), who lived in Duke Street, Windle, St Helens. *Church Hymns with Tunes* used PENTECOST, by William Boyd, written for 'Come, Holy Ghost, our souls inspire', but used for these words (to the composer's initial consternation) by Arthur Sullivan, the music editor. The example was followed by *Hymns Ancient and Modern*, but DUKE STREET (used in *Church Hymns*, 1903) seems now to be preferred.

172

O worship the Lord in the beauty of holiness,
   Bow down before him, his glory proclaim;
With gold of obedience and incense of lowliness,
   Kneel and adore him: the Lord is his name.

Low at his feet lay thy burden of carefulness,
   High on his heart he will bear it for thee,
Comfort thy sorrows, and answer thy prayerfulness,
   Guiding thy steps as may best for thee be.

Fear not to enter his courts in the slenderness
   Of the poor wealth thou wouldst reckon as thine;
Truth in its beauty, and love in its tenderness,
   These are the offerings to lay on his shrine.

These, though we bring them in trembling and fearfulness,
   He will accept for the name that is dear;
Mornings of joy give for evenings of tearfulness,
   Trust for our trembling, and hope for our fear.

O worship the Lord in the beauty of holiness,
   Bow down before him, his glory proclaim;
With gold of obedience and incense of lowliness,
   Kneel and adore him: the Lord is his name!

John Samuel Bewley Monsell (1811–75)

This is taken from *Hymns of Love and Praise for the Church's Year* (1863), later modified for Monsell's *The Parish Hymnal* (1873), where it is placed at the Fourth Sunday after Easter. As with 'Fight the good fight', this placing is not easy to understand, because this is in part an Epiphany hymn, as the references to gold and incense in the first verse suggest: it is also possible that Monsell had in mind Bishop Heber's 'Brightest and best of the sons of the morning', which is close not only in sentiment but in rhythm.

The arresting and beautiful first line comes from the Old Testament, where it appears three times (1 Chronicles 16: 29; Psalm 29: 2; and Psalm 96: 9). It gives a strong and unusual rhythm to the hymn: the metre of 12.10.12.10., with 13–syllable lines in the first and last verses, creates a remarkable running effect.

The first tune used for this hymn was SANCTISSIMUS, by W. H. Cooke, from the *Bristol Tune Book* of 1881. It is now more usually sung to a German tune, WAS LEBET, from a manuscript book of 1754, *Choral-Buch vor Johann Heinrich Rheinhardt*.

173

Beneath the Cross of Jesus
    I fain would take my stand—
The shadow of a mighty rock
    Within a weary land;
A home within a wilderness,
    A rest upon the way,
From the burning of the noontide heat
    And the burden of the day.

O safe and happy shelter,
    O refuge tried and sweet,
O trysting-place where heaven's love
    And heaven's justice meet!
As to the holy patriarch
    That wondrous dream was given,
So seems my Saviour's Cross to me
    A ladder up to heaven.

There lies beneath its shadow,
    But on the further side,
The darkness of an open grave
    That gapes both deep and wide;
And there between us stands the Cross,
    Two arms outstretched to save,
Like a watchman set to guard the way
    From that eternal grave.

Upon that Cross of Jesus
    Mine eye at times can see
The very dying form of One
    Who suffered there for me.
And from my stricken heart, with tears,
    Two wonders I confess,—
The wonders of redeeming love,
    And my own worthlessness.

I take, O Cross, thy shadow,
    For my abiding-place;
I ask no other sunshine than
    The sunshine of his face:
Content to let the world go by,
    To know no gain nor loss,—
My sinful self my only shame,
    My glory all—the Cross.

        Elizabeth Cecilia Clephane (1830–69)

This dramatic hymn was first published as part of a longer poem in the
Family Treasury, a Scottish Presbyterian magazine, in 1872. After Clephane's
death, a number of her poems appeared in this magazine between 1872 and

1874, under the heading of 'Breathings on the Border' (she lived at Melrose, in Roxburghshire, where she was greatly loved for her deeds of charity and her kindness to the poor).

This hymn is centred on the Cross, which is incorporated into a series of different images which describe the progress of the soul: so that the Cross seems to be itself, yet also to be found in every part of human life, in an anticipation of a 'Cross-centred' theology. It is the shadow of a great rock in a weary land (from Isaiah 32: 2), a home, a rest from the heat of the day, a shelter; it then becomes a trysting-place, where mercy and justice meet (from Psalm 85), and a ladder up to heaven like that of Jacob (the 'holy patriarch', from Genesis 28); it then becomes a watchman or guard, with its arms stretched out to prevent the sinner from falling into the open grave. Finally, it becomes a source of wonder, and a cause of glory to the repentant sinner. It is thus an expression of an evangelical theology that is profoundly moving in its imaginative vision of the pervasive presence of the Cross.

Probably the best-known tune for these words is BENEATH THE CROSS OF JESUS, by Ira D. Sankey (1840–1908), the singer in the Moody and Sankey evangelical partnership, and the editor of *Sacred Songs and Solos*. It has the marks of Sankey's style in that book, with its strong rhythms and repeated notes, together with an affecting fall of a fifth in the last line. Other tunes include GLORIA, by R. L. De Pearsall (1795–1856) used by the *English Hymnal* (with Sankey's tune relegated to the Appendix, Vaughan Williams's 'chamber of horrors'), and HELDER, by Bartholomaeus Helder (1585–1635) used for this hymn in the *BBC Hymn Book* (1951). Another tune is ST CHRISTOPHER, composed for these words by Frederick C. Maker (1844–1927), published in *The Bristol Tune Book* (1881).

174   Lord, speak to me, that I may speak
          In living echoes of thy tone;
       As thou hast sought, so let me seek
          Thy erring children lost and lone.

       O lead me, Lord, that I may lead
          The wandering and the wavering feet;
       O feed me, Lord, that I may feed
          Thy hungering ones with manna sweet.

       O strengthen me, that, while I stand
          Firm on the rock, and strong in thee,
       I may stretch out a loving hand
          To wrestlers with the troubled sea.

       O teach me, Lord, that I may teach
          The precious things thou dost impart;
       And wing my words, that they may reach
          The hidden depths of many a heart.

       O give thine own sweet rest to me,
          That I may speak with soothing power
       A word in season, as from thee,
          To weary ones in needful hour.

       O fill me with thy fullness, Lord,
          Until my very heart o'erflow
       In kindling thought and glowing word,
          Thy love to tell, thy praise to show.

       O use me, Lord, use even me,
          Just as thou wilt, and when, and where,
       Until thy blessed face I see,
          Thy rest, thy joy, thy glory share.

          Frances Ridley Havergal (1836–79)

This hymn was written in 1872, and published in leaflet form in the same year. It was included in Havergal's *Under the Surface* (1874), with the title 'A Worker's Prayer' and the text 'None of us liveth unto himself' (Romans 14: 7). It was included in the second edition of *Hymns Ancient and Modern* in 1875.

Frances Ridley Havergal was a remarkable woman: a fine musician, a poet, a good walker, a swimmer, and a mountain climber. Her sister Maria's memoir describes her as excelling in these things, and as being deeply conscious of the blessings of this life (her early death was owing to peritonitis, and not to the invalidism which afflicted so many Victorian women hymnwriters). This hymn is a sustained prayer to take the fullness of life and pass it on to others, especially to those less fortunate than herself. As in her 'Consecration Hymn', 'Take my life, and let it be', she longs to make use of her many talents in the service of the Lord. It is as one sought by Christ that she wishes to seek for the lost; it is as one sure of her way, and well nourished in the spirit, that she longs to lead others and feed them; it is as a natural swimmer that she longs to help those struggling in the water. The hymn is filled with this imagery of receiving and giving, as Frances Ridley Havergal gives full expression to her ardent and passionate self. The result is a hymn which is a prayer in two directions: for a full and energetic life, and for the surrender of that life in worship and service.

In *Hymns Ancient and Modern* this hymn was originally set to MELCOMBE, by Samuel Webbe (*c.*1740–1816). Methodist books use GALILEE, by Philip Armes (1836–1908) and *Rejoice and Sing* uses FULDA, dating from 1815.

175

Take my life, and let it be
Consecrated, Lord, to thee;
Take my moments and my days,
Let them flow in ceaseless praise.

Take my hands, and let them move
At the impulse of thy love;
Take my feet, and let them be
Swift and beautiful for thee.

Take my voice, and let me sing
Always, only, for my King;
Take my lips, and let them be
Filled with messages from thee.

Take my silver and my gold,
Not a mite would I withhold;
Take my intellect, and use
Every power as thou shalt choose.

Take my will, and make it thine;
It shall be no longer mine;
Take my heart: it is thine own;
It shall be thy royal throne.

Take my love; my Lord, I pour
At thy feet its treasure-store;
Take myself, and I will be
Ever, only, all for thee.

Frances Ridley Havergal (1836–79)

Written 4 February 1874, and first published in Havergal's *Loyal Responses* of 1878. The 'loyal responses' were those of a subject to her King, and the book is full of Havergal's intense enthusiasm. This was given first place in the collection: it was originally written in two-line verses, under a quotation from the Holy Communion service in the *Book of Common Prayer*: 'Here we offer and present unto Thee, O Lord, ourselves, our souls and bodies, to be a reasonable, holy, and lively sacrifice unto Thee.'

Havergal entitled it 'Consecration Hymn', and it is a superb expression of dedication, by a young woman who had tremendous energy and many talents: she was a good musician, a poet, and a fine athlete. References to the hands, the voice, the feet, and the lips, suggest that she was conscious of all that she had to offer: while the inclusion of the intellect (alongside the will and the heart) is nicely sensitive to the importance of thinking about God, and saves the hymn from being predominantly emotional and physical.

The story of the composition of the hymn, told in Havergal's own words, demonstrates the evangelical ardour of her nature. She had gone on a visit to Areley House, in Worcestershire:

There were ten persons in the house, some unconverted and long prayed for, some converted, but not rejoicing Christians. He gave me the prayer 'Lord, give me *all* in this house!' And He just *did*! Before I left the house every one had got a blessing. The last night of my visit, after I had retired, the governess asked me to go to the two daughters. They were crying, &c.; then and there both of them trusted and rejoiced; it was nearly midnight. I was too happy to sleep, and passed most of the night in praise and renewal of my own consecration; and these little couplets formed themselves, and chimed in my heart one after another till they finished with '*Ever*, Only, ALL for Thee!'

In a later letter she wrote of her intention to 'let my life from this day answer really to that couplet' (as she did: writing religious poetry, editing her father's sacred music, giving away money).

In some hymn-books, the hymn is given a quotation from Romans 12: 1: 'present your bodies a living sacrifice, holy, acceptable unto God, which is your reasonable service.' This idea is given additional sharpness by Havergal's sense of herself as a woman, for the image which she uses in the final verse is that of Mary Magdalen pouring out her treasure-store, the alabaster box of ointment, at the feet of Jesus (Luke 7: 36–50). It makes a most beautiful and fitting climax to the hymn.

The traditional tune for this hymn is CONSECRATION, formerly known as PATMOS (the name was probably changed because of its strong association with this particular hymn). It was written by Frances Ridley Havergal's father, William Henry Havergal (1793–1870), and printed in his *Psalmody* (1871), edited by Frances and published after his death. This is the tune which she used herself, and which she recommended. It is a neat and simple tune, given character by the sudden drop in line 3, but the last line is weak. An alternative setting, more lingering, sweet, and emotional, is NOTTINGHAM, from the Kyrie of the 'Twelfth Mass', a work once thought to be by Mozart, but no longer attributed to him. In *Hymns Ancient and Modern* an alternative tune is given as INNOCENTS (as used for 'Gentle Jesus, meek and mild'); also effective is J. B. Dykes's ST BEES (usually used for 'Hark! my soul, it is the Lord'), and a modern tune, EMMA, by Paul Leddington Wright (1951–).

176
    And art thou come with us to dwell,
      Our prince, our guide, our love, our Lord,
    And is thy name Immanuel,
      God present with his world restored?

    The heart is glad for thee: it knows
      None now shall bid it err or mourn,
    And o'er its desert breaks the rose
      In triumph o'er the grieving thorn.

    Thou bringest all again; with thee
      Is light, is space, is breadth, and room
    For each thing fair, beloved, and free,
      To have its hour of life and bloom.

    Each heart's deep instinct unconfessed;
      Each lowly wish, each daring claim;
    All, all that life hath long repressed
      Unfolds, undreading blight or blame.

    Thy reign eternal will not cease;
      Thy years are sure, and glad, and slow;
    Within thy mighty world of peace
      The humblest flower hath leave to blow.

    The world is glad for thee! The heart
      Is glad for thee! And all is well,
    And fixed, and sure, because thou art,
      Whose name is called Immanuel.

              Dora Greenwell (1821–82)

This hymn is made up of verses from the final section of an extended poem by Dora Greenwell entitled 'Veni, Veni, Emmanuel', published in her *Carmina Crucis* ('Songs of the Cross') in 1869. It is an unusual variant on the 'O come, O come, Immanuel' theme because it uses the imagery of spring and rebirth to signify the coming of Christ. It is also a most interesting example of the work of a woman hymn-writer.

The poem is the climax of a book which has throughout wrestled with problems of belief: in the words of Greenwell's biographer, Constance Maynard, who wrote an introduction to the poem in 1906, 'the note of modern scepticism is clear in it, and yet it is dominated by the note of faith.'

In this final poem, Maynard suggested, 'every shadow flees away before this triumphant sunrise.'

The hymn is in some respects a Christmas hymn, but 'Immanuel' here is not the child in the manger: instead there is a vision of Christ as prince, guide, and lord, coming to liberate the earth from its spiritual winter. In this respect it is a revealing poem about Dora Greenwell herself. She lived a sad and unfulfilled life, living for eighteen years in Durham with her widowed mother, who discouraged her friendships and who had no sympathy with her longing for a freer and fuller life. The inner conflict and unhappiness can be discerned in the hymn: while it celebrates the coming of spring ('Thou bringest all again') it also recognizes that what unfolds, like a flower, is 'All, all that life hath long repressed'. Long before modern psychology, Dora Greenwell had an awareness of repression and its cruel dangers. Its opposite is conveyed in the flower image, which is found again in 'its hour of life and bloom', and is made explicit in 'The humblest flower hath leave to blow'. The coming of Christ will allow the undernourished soul to flourish, and the world will be glad; and the hymn ends with a brave echo of another woman writer on spiritual matters, Julian of Norwich ('And all shall be well, and all manner of thing shall be well'). Dora Greenwell looks through her pain to a world in which God is ever present, God with us, Immanuel.

The tune set to this hymn in *Rejoice and Sing* is GONFALON ROYAL, which is really too hearty; more suitable is ST SEPULCHRE, by George Cooper (1820–76), organist of the Church of the Holy Sepulchre in Newgate Street (where his father was organist before him, and his son after him). This has been the tune in the *Methodist Hymn Book* (1933) and its successor, *Hymns and Psalms* (1983).

177

In heavenly love abiding,
    No change my heart shall fear;
And safe is such confiding,
    For nothing changes here:
The storm may roar without me,
    My heart may low be laid;
But God is round about me,
    And can I be afraid?

Wherever he may guide me,
    No want shall turn me back;
My Shepherd is beside me
    And nothing can I lack:
His wisdom ever waketh,
    His sight is never dim;
He knows the way he taketh,
    And I will walk with him.

Green pastures are before me,
    Which yet I have not seen;
Bright skies will soon be o'er me,
    Where the dark clouds have been:
My hope I cannot measure,
    My path to life is free;
My Saviour has my treasure,
    And he will walk with me.

Anna Laetitia Waring (1820–1910)

This beautiful meditation on trustfulness was first published in Waring's *Hymns and Meditations* (1850), with the title 'Safety in God'. It reflects Waring's sense of the instability of earthly happiness, and her reliance on the God who stilled the storm (in verse 1, where 'without', as in Alexander's 'There is a green hill', means 'outwith', or outside). The second verse carries on the theme with an extended reference to Psalm 23; and the third verse is a reminder of instability, figured in the weather for the journey of life—dark clouds, followed by bright skies.

The word 'abiding' perhaps comes from John 15: 10: 'If ye keep my commandments, ye shall abide in my love.' There are also echoes of Psalm 34: 1–8 throughout the hymn. Its rhythms and rhymes are very skilfully managed; although with the tune PENLAN, with its strong beats, verse 3, line 4 is sometimes amended to 'Where darkest clouds have been'.

The tune PENLAN is by David Jenkins (1848–1915), Professor of Music at University College, Aberystwyth. It was composed at Aberystwyth for the wedding of the local Member of Parliament, T. E. Ellis, in 1898. Ellis died in the following year, and the tune was first published in the Welsh magazine *Cymru* in May 1899, set to a poem in his memory.

178   In the bleak mid-winter
Frosty wind made moan,
Earth stood hard as iron,
Water like a stone;
Snow had fallen, snow on snow,
Snow on snow,
In the bleak mid-winter,
Long ago.

Our God, heaven cannot hold him
Nor earth sustain;
Heaven and earth shall flee away
When he comes to reign:
In the bleak mid-winter
A stable place sufficed
The Lord God Almighty,
Jesus Christ.

Enough for him, whom cherubim
Worship night and day,
A breastful of milk.
And a mangerful of hay;
Enough for him, whom angels
Fall down before,
The ox and ass and camel
Which adore.

Angels and archangels
May have gathered there,
Cherubim and seraphim
Thronged the air:
But only his mother
In her maiden bliss
Worshipped the Belovèd
With a kiss.

What can I give him,
Poor as I am?
If I were a shepherd
I would bring a lamb;
If I were a wise man
I would do my part;
Yet what I can I give him—
Give my heart.

          Christina Rossetti (1830–94)

This was published in Christina Rossetti's *Poems* (1892), with a note saying 'before 1872'. It is a most beautiful rendering of the Christmas scene, with the apparent simplicity and artlessness of a medieval carol: in fact, such verses are only possible with the highest art. They record the Incarnation as happening in the cold of winter, as Milton does in his Ode 'On the Morning of Christ's Nativity':

> It was the winter wild
> While the heaven-born child
> All meanly wrapped in the rude manger lies; . . .

Milton goes on to use the idea that it snowed at the birth of Christ, in order to cover the fallen world with a blanket of pure snow. Rossetti takes up Milton's ideas, and adds her own magic: the repetition of 'snow on snow' beautifully suggests the snow falling and falling, and the images for frosted earth and water are those of iron and stone.

The imagery of winter suddenly gives way at the start of the second verse to the vision of a God whom heaven cannot hold, nor earth sustain (suffice): the majesty of that opening gives way to the utter simplicity of the child in the manger, Jesus Christ. The use of the name at the end of verse 2 is a kind of statement in itself: our God, whom heaven cannot hold, is now the baby Jesus Christ. The next two verses fill in the details of the picture: because of the short lines, each touch seems separate, clearly defined, as sharp as a medieval illumination.

The final verse is strangely interesting. At first sight, it seems like an expected response, a dedication to the Christ child, and it can, of course, be sung by anyone. But Elizabeth Cosnett (author of 'Can we by searching find out God', no. 242) has acutely observed that 'when a woman wrote these words women were largely excluded from the professions and from higher education'. She has no job, like the shepherd; no degree, like the wise men. As Cosnett points out (*Bulletin of the Hymn Society* 205, 1995) this does not invalidate the more general reading of the verse; but it gives a special sharpness and poignancy to the last verse for those who wish to find it.

The tune, CRANHAM, was written by Gustav Holst (1874–1934) for the *English Hymnal* (1906). Its apparent simplicity conceals a wonderful art, which is able to accommodate the irregularity of the lines with great skill. As Percy Dearmer wrote: 'the verses surge and tumble, carried along for singing by the swing of the tune' (*Songs of Praise Discussed*). A very fine anthem setting by Harold Darke (1888–1976) has also become much admired and used.

179

Love came down at Christmas,
Love all lovely, Love divine;
Love was born at Christmas,
Star and angels gave the sign.

Worship we the Godhead,
Love incarnate, Love divine;
Worship we our Jesus:
But wherewith for sacred sign?

Love shall be our token,
Love be yours and love be mine,
Love to God and all men,
Love for plea and gift and sign.

Christina Rossetti (1830–94)

These verses first appeared in Rossetti's *Time Flies: A Reading Diary* (1885), entitled 'Christmastide'. It was first used as a hymn in the *Oxford Hymn Book* (1908), and then by Percy Dearmer (an enthusiast for using English poets as potential sources of hymns) in *Songs of Praise* (1925). It is based on 1 John 4: 7–11.

The sublime simplicity of this hymn is the mark of a very great writer. Rossetti makes the account of the Incarnation as plain as possible ('Star and angels gave the sign'): then in verse 2 the singer becomes a worshipper, like one of the shepherds or the wise men, and the sign of that worship is love. Love is the 'Love incarnate' which is also 'Love divine' in verse 2: it is also 'our token', seen in our love to others and to the world. It thus becomes, in the last line (altered by Rossetti herself from its original 'Love the universal sign') a plea (to God), a gift (to the world), and a sign (evidence in our lives that Christ has come to the world).

A frequently used tune is HERMITAGE, by Reginald Owen Morris (1886–1948), a teacher at the Royal College of Music. It is an unassuming and beautiful tune which it is impossible to sing boldly, or even loudly, and its haunting melody suits the words well. Other tunes include GARTAN, a traditional Irish air, and LOVE INCARNATE, by Edgar Pettman (1866–1943).

180

For the beauty of the earth,
  For the beauty of the skies,
For the love which from our birth
  Over and around us lies:
  Christ our God, to thee we raise
  This our sacrifice of praise.

For the beauty of each hour
  Of the day and of the night,
Hill and vale, and tree and flower,
  Sun and moon and stars of light:

For the joy of ear and eye,
  For the heart and brain's delight,
For the mystic harmony
  Linking sense to sound and sight:

For the joy of human love,
  Brother, sister, parent, child,
Friends on earth, and friends above,
  For all gentle thoughts and mild:

For each perfect gift of thine
  To our race so freely given,
Graces human and divine,
  Flowers of earth and buds of heaven:
  Christ our God, to thee we raise
  This our sacrifice of praise.

Folliott Sandford Pierpoint (1835–1917)

This hymn was first published in *Lyra Eucharistica: Hymns & Verses on the Holy Communion Ancient and Modern, with other Poems* (one of many nineteenth-century texts with 'Lyra' in the title), second edition, 1864, edited by Orby Shipley. It is a hymn of thanksgiving, appropriately echoing the post-Communion prayer at the Eucharist: 'we thy humble servants entirely desire thy fatherly goodness mercifully to accept this our sacrifice of praise and thanksgiving . . .'. There have been a number of alterations to this hymn: the text above is taken from the *English Hymnal*, which prints all of Pierpoint's eight verses. The five verses above were followed by three more:

For thy Bride that evermore
  Lifteth holy hands above,
Offering up on every shore
  This pure sacrifice of love:

For thy Martyrs' crown of light,
  For thy Prophets' eagle eye,
For thy bold Confessors' might,
  For the lips of infancy:

For thy Virgins' robes of snow,
For thy Maiden-mother mild,
For thyself, with hearts aglow,
Jesu, Victim undefiled:
Offer we at Thine own Shrine
Thyself, sweet Sacrament Divine.

This hymn is said to have been partly inspired by a view from a hill near Pierpoint's native city of Bath; and its nature imagery has tended to obscure its original purpose. It is often sung as a hymn of praise and thanks for the created world and for human love; and while it is placed in the 'Holy Communion' section of the *English Hymnal,* other books have seen it as expressing 'Delight in Creation' (*Hymns and Psalms*), or joy in 'All God's Created Works' (*Rejoice and Sing*). In view of the insistence on beauty (verses 1 and 2), and the lovely invocation of the world of nature, this would seem to be justified: although Pierpoint beautifully links earth and heaven, the physical and the spiritual, throughout. The climax of this is the reference to 'Graces human and divine', which are the God-given graces of human life (as well as Divine Grace) that make human life worth living: the beauty of earth, the joy of music and art, the love of friends. These are the flowers of earth, and the buds which are ready to blossom in heaven.

The refrain has often been altered, to 'Gracious God, to Thee we raise', or to 'Father, unto Thee we raise' (*Songs of Praise*). The best comment on this is by Wesley Milgate, in *Songs of the People of God,* p. 55:

Practically every recent hymnal has a different version of the refrain, apparently fearful of treading on the corns of 'liberal' theologians and those who shilly-shally with an essential part of Christian doctrine. Even in Pierpoint's day he was criticized for calling Christ 'our God', and he replied that Pliny, in his famous letter to Trajan (Ep. x. 96) wrote that Christians, when meeting for worship, sang a hymn to Christ as God; . . . .

The hymn has been fortunate in attracting two fine modern tunes, Geoffrey Shaw's ENGLAND'S LANE, an adaptation of a traditional English tune which first appeared as a hymn tune in *The Public School Hymn Book* (1919), and became firmly associated with these words in *Songs of Praise* (1925); and David Evans's LUCERNA LAUDONIAE, written for these words in the Scottish *Church Hymnary* (1927). The name means 'Lantern of the Lothians', referring to the church at Haddington, East Lothian (either to the Franciscan monastery, destroyed in 1355, or to the church which succeeded it; the minister of Haddington, G. Wauchope Stewart, was involved in the making of the 1927 book). The hymn can also be sung attractively to NORICUM, as in the *Methodist Hymn Book* of 1933.

181

The Church's one foundation
   Is Jesus Christ, her Lord;
She is his new creation
   By water and the word:
From heaven he came and sought her
   To be his holy bride,
With his own blood he bought her,
   And for her life he died.

Elect from every nation,
   Yet one o'er all the earth,
Her charter of salvation
   One Lord, one faith, one birth;
One holy name she blesses,
   Partakes one holy food,
And to one hope she presses
   With every grace endued.

Though with a scornful wonder
   Men see her sore opprest,
By schisms rent asunder,
   By heresies distrest,
Yet saints their watch are keeping,
   Their cry goes up, 'How long?'
And soon the night of weeping
   Shall be the morn of song.

'Mid toil and tribulation,
   And tumult of her war,
She waits the consummation
   Of peace for evermore;
Till with the vision glorious
   Her longing eyes are blest,
And the great Church victorious
   Shall be the Church at rest.

Yet she on earth hath union
   With God the Three in One,
And mystic sweet communion
   With those whose rest is won:
O happy ones and holy!
   Lord, give us grace that we,
Like them, the meek and lowly,
   On high may dwell with thee.

          Samuel John Stone (1839–1900)

This hymn was written by Stone in 1866, when he was a young curate at
Windsor, at a time when the Church had been rocked by a controversy
caused by John William Colenso (1814–83), Bishop of Natal. Colenso, an

energetic and thoughtful man, had published *The Pentateuch and the Book of Joshua Critically Examined* in 1862: this called into question the historical accuracy of the first five books of the Bible, and argued that Numbers and Leviticus were written much later than was thought. He was attacked on all sides, notably by Bishop Robert Gray of Cape Town, who claimed jurisdiction over the see of Natal, and who attempted unsuccessfully to have Colenso deposed from his see and excommunicated. The *Dictionary of National Biography* noted that the upper and lower houses of convocation supported Gray, but that the debates 'do not give a very high idea of the intellectual power of the bishops'.

Stone's hymn is a major legacy of this unedifying controversy, and it transcends it, partly because Stone was also writing about the Creed. He wrote a series of hymns, published as *Lyra Fidelium: Twelve Hymns on the Twelve Articles of the Apostles' Creed* (1866): the present one was on 'The Holy Catholic Church: the Communion of Saints. "He is the Head of the Body, the Church"'. The principal reference is to 1 Corinthians 3: 11: 'For other foundation can no man lay than that is laid, which is Jesus Christ.'

In the version printed above (there was a larger text written later as a processional hymn) the reference to the Colenso–Gray argument is confined to verse 3. In the original there was a verse 3 which is even stronger:

> The Church shall never perish!
>   Her dear Lord, to defend,
> To guide, sustain, and cherish,
>   Is with her to the end;
> Though there be those who hate her,
>   And false souls in her pale,
> Against or foe or traitor
>   She ever shall prevail.

What remains is in fact very splendid, partly because of the association of these words with the grandiloquent tune AURELIA, by Samuel Sebastian Wesley (1810–76). Those who criticize the tune (and there are many) clearly have not considered the extraordinary and wonderful marriage of words and music in this hymn. The tune, which dates from 1864, was first written for J. M. Neale's 'Jerusalem the Golden' ('Urbs Sion Aurea', from which it gets its name AURELIA): its setting to these words was the work of William Henry Monk, the music editor, when they appeared in the *Appendix* (1868) to the first edition of *Hymns Ancient and Modern*. The result is magnificent: it is recorded that the result of singing this hymn at St Paul's Cathedral during the Lambeth Conference of 1888 was so powerful that the singers were overwhelmed: 'it made them feel weak at the knees, their legs trembled, and they really felt as though they were going to collapse' (quoted in Wesley Milgate, *Songs of the People of God*: 154).

When he wrote 'O God of earth and altar' for the Christian Social Union in 1905, G. K. Chesterton is said to have written it with the tune AURELIA in mind because he thought that it was 'the typical tune for hymns'.

182

Saviour, again to thy dear name we raise
With one accord our parting hymn of praise;
We stand to bless thee ere our worship cease;
Then, lowly kneeling, wait thy word of peace.

Grant us thy peace upon our homeward way;
With thee began, with thee shall end the day;
Guard thou the lips from sin, the hearts from shame,
That in this house have called upon thy name.

Grant us thy peace, Lord, through the coming night;
Turn thou for us its darkness into light;
From harm and danger keep thy children free,
For dark and light are both alike to thee.

Grant us thy peace throughout our earthly life,
Our balm in sorrow, and our stay in strife;
Then, when thy voice shall bid our conflict cease,
Call us, O Lord, to thine eternal peace.

John Ellerton (1826–93)

This hymn was written in 1866, when Ellerton was vicar of Crewe Green, for the Festival of the Malpas, Middlewich, and Nantwich Choral Association. It had six stanzas, some of which are still used, for example in the *English Hymnal* and *Rejoice and Sing* versions:

Grant us thy peace, throughout our earthly life;
Peace to thy church from error and from strife;
Peace to our land, the fruit of truth and love;
Peace in each heart, thy Spirit from above:

Thy peace in life, the balm of every pain;
Thy peace in death, the hope to rise again;
In that dread hour speak thou the soul's release,
And call it, Lord, to thine eternal peace.

It is interesting, however, that both of these books go back to the text above for the last two lines, because they are so moving. That text is the one which was revised by Ellerton for the *Appendix* (1868) to the first edition of *Hymns Ancient and Modern* (1861). It was headed 'At End of Service', and prefaced by a quotation from Psalm 29: 11: 'The Lord shall give his people the blessing of peace.'

Ellerton is known as the author of two touching evening hymns, this and 'The day thou gavest, Lord, is ended'. This one concentrates on peace, remembering it as the final word of the service (in Holy Comunion): 'The peace of God, which passeth all understanding . . .'. Evening Prayer, in the *Book of Common Prayer*, ends with the grace, but that involves the same concept of peaceful dismissal. That peace depends on an inner peace, which looks forward to the eternal peace of heaven. The hymn thus begins with a congregation at worship, standing to sing and kneeling to be blessed, but moves from that to a wider concept of peace in the Church and in the world, and in the human heart. From the *Book of Common Prayer* Ellerton also takes (in verse 3) the Third Collect, 'for aid against all perils': 'Lighten our darkness we beseech thee, O Lord; and by thy great mercy defend us from all perils and dangers of this night; . . . .' Peace requires us to be preserved from danger, but also to be in light rather than in darkness.

These truths are expressed in graceful ten-syllable couplets (the metre of 'Abide with me'), which allow the mind to break each line at the halfway point, yet to feel its way gently and purposefully to the end of the line and to the final word of the last verse. When that final 'peace' is sung, it is linked with the word 'eternal', presenting us with a glimpse of an ideal world. All the hopes and fears which have been suggested in the earlier verses give way to a final suggestion of a world without harm and danger, without sin and shame, in which the worship of Evening Prayer becomes a pattern for eternal life and peace.

The tune most frequently used for this hymn is ELLERS, by E. J. Hopkins (1818–1901), organist of the Temple Church, London. Its gentle climbing melody in the first two lines gives way to a reflective third line followed by a descent to a series of E flats (with one F) at the end. The result is a tune which is beautifully suited to the mood and meaning of Ellerton's hymn. Those who do not like its Victorian mode may use Vaughan Williams's MAGDA, written for *Songs of Praise*.

183
The day thou gavest, Lord, is ended,
　The darkness falls at thy behest;
To thee our morning hymns ascended,
　Thy praise shall sanctify our rest.

We thank thee that thy Church unsleeping,
　While earth rolls onward into light,
Through all the world her watch is keeping,
　And rests not now by day or night.

As o'er each continent and island
　The dawn leads on another day,
The voice of prayer is never silent,
　Nor dies the strain of praise away.

The sun that bids us rest is waking
　Our brethren 'neath the western sky,
And hour by hour fresh lips are making
　Thy wondrous doings heard on high.

So be it, Lord; thy throne shall never,
　Like earth's proud empires, pass away;
Thy kingdom stands, and grows for ever,
　Till all thy creatures own thy sway.

John Ellerton (1826–93)

The first line of this hymn appeared as the opening of an undistinguished two-verse poem in *Church Poetry* (1855). The author is unknown. Using that line as a starting point, Ellerton wrote this evening hymn: it has since become one of the best known and most loved of all English hymns.

Ellerton's first version appeared in *A Liturgy for Missionary Meetings* (Frome, 1870), and this gives some indication of the character and purpose of the hymn. It is an evening hymn, but one which primarily celebrates the development of Christianity through the work in 'the mission field'. It was then printed in a revised version in the SPCK *Church Hymns* (1871), a hymn-book which was for some years the only serious rival to *Hymns Ancient and Modern* (Ellerton was one of its editors). In that book, it appeared under a quotation from 1 Chronicles 23: 30: '[Their office was] to stand every morning to thank and praise the Lord, and likewise at even.' When it was published in *Hymns Ancient and Modern*, in the 1889 *Supplement* to the second edition of 1875, it was associated with Psalm 113: 3: 'From the rising of the sun unto the going down of the same the Lord's name is to be praised.'

Ellerton's complex and moving hymn is oversimplified by being linked to these quotations. It begins with Genesis and ends with Revelation. It starts with God, the giver of light and of darkness (Genesis 1: 3–4); and it ends with 'all creatures' owning His sway ('And every creature which is in heaven, and on the earth, and under the earth, and such as are in the sea, and all that are in them, heard I saying, Blessing, and honour, and glory, and power, be unto him that sitteth upon the throne, and unto the Lamb for ever and ever' Revelation 5: 13.). It is a hymn which seems to draw into itself the beginning and the end of things, the patterns of morning and evening (both literally, and seen as a metaphor for life, which is why it is frequently used at funerals). In addition to this, we may note the skilful way in which it begins and ends with the worshipper in church, but (in the three middle verses) allows the imagination to see the world as spinning through space ('While earth rolls onward into light'). The first and last verses acknowledge the world of worship and prayer: the three middle verses fly over the world, watching the peoples of the world waking in their different time-zones to worship God, hour by hour. The hymn thus satisfies the demands of reality of being faithful to ourselves and our experience; and it also encompasses the visions of something greater, of a worldwide Church united in praise and prayer. Its structure is beautifully symmetrical, the three verses in the middle (in which the imagination leaps) balanced by the two on either side (which remind us of our normal Sunday lives).

In addition to the finding of the first line in *Church Poetry*, it is possible that Ellerton also knew a hymn by James Montgomery, 'The Lord's Day', which has a verse:

> Soon as the light of morning broke
> O'er island, continent, or deep,
> Thy far-spread family awoke,
> Sabbath all round the world to keep.

Both Ellerton and Montgomery explore the same idea. It must have appealed to Queen Victoria, because it was chosen as a hymn for the Diamond Jubilee celebrations of 1897: it is important to note, however, that the 'empire' which Ellerton writes of is the everlasting empire of the spirit, not an earthly one. He is quite explicit that 'earth's proud empires' will pass away; and Queen Victoria would surely have understood this. The hymn would have been wonderfully appropriate for the occasion precisely because it celebrated the Queen and Empress but also drew attention to human mortality and the transience of earthly power.

The tune which is generally associated with these words is ST CLEMENT, so named by Arthur Sullivan (perhaps with a twinkle in his eye) after the composer, Clement Cotterill Scholefield (1839–1904). The tune carries the long lines with a sweep and assurance that are admirable. The fact that it is in three-beat time has led to its disparagement by the serious-minded as a waltz tune, but it only appears waltz-like if the first beat of every bar is stressed. The *English Hymnal* relegated it: 'Another tune for this hymn', it says sniffily, referring to ST CLEMENT, 'will be found in the Appendix.' Its preferred tune was the dignified LES COMMANDEMENS DE DIEU, a Reformation tune from the Genevan Psalter by Louis Bourgeois (*c*.1510–*c*.1561); this and

JOLDWYNDS, by Charles Villiers Stanford (1852–1924), RADFORD, by Samuel Sebastian Wesley (1810–76), and ARDGOWAN, by Kenneth Finlay (1882–1974), have been placed before congregations in numerous books, but ST CLEMENT has continued to be the preferred tune on most occasions: it allows full expression to Ellerton's much-loved words.

184

For all the saints who from their labours rest,
Who thee by faith before the world confessed,
Thy name, O Jesu, be for ever blest:
    Alleluia!

Thou wast their rock, their fortress, and their might;
Thou, Lord, their captain in the well-fought fight;
Thou in the darkness drear their one true light:
    Alleluia!

O may thy soldiers, faithful, true, and bold,
Fight as the saints who nobly fought of old,
And win, with them, the victor's crown of gold:
    Alleluia!

O blest communion, fellowship divine!
We feebly struggle, they in glory shine;
Yet all are one in thee, for all are thine:
    Alleluia!

And when the strife is fierce, the warfare long,
Steals on the ear the distant triumph song,
And hearts are brave again, and arms are strong:
    Alleluia!

The golden evening brightens in the west;
Soon, soon to faithful warriors cometh rest;
Sweet is the calm of paradise the blest:
    Alleluia!

But lo, there breaks a yet more glorious day:
The saints triumphant rise in bright array;
The King of Glory passes on his way:
    Alleluia!

From earth's wide bounds, from ocean's farthest coast,
Through gates of pearl streams in the countless host,
Singing to Father, Son, and Holy Ghost:
    Alleluia!

William Walsham How (1823–97)

This magnificent hymn for All Saints' Day (and other occasions) was first published in *Hymns for Saints' Days and Other Hymns by a Layman* (1864) in which the layman was Earl Nelson (1823–1913). It was headed 'Saints'-Day Hymn. "A Cloud of Witnesses"—Heb. 12: 1'. It later appeared in *Church Hymns* (1871), of which How was one of the editors, and from there it became widely known.

The original hymn had three more verses (3–5), dealing with (3) 'the glorious company' of the Apostles, (4) the Evangelists, and (5) the Martyrs:

> For the Apostles' glorious company,
> Who, bearing forth the cross o'er land and sea,
> Shook all the mighty world, we sing to thee,
> *Alleluia!*
>
> For the Evangelists, by whose blest word,
> Like fourfold streams, the garden of the Lord
> Is fair and fruitful, be thy name adored,
> *Alleluia!*
>
> For Martyrs, who, with rapture-kindled eye,
> Saw the bright crown descending from the sky,
> And died to grasp it, thee we glorify,
> *Alleuia!*

These appear in the *Te Deum* (where How's 'Evangelists' are 'the goodly fellowship of the Prophets'), and the whole hymn is indebted to the sustained praise of that sublime poem. But its imagery suggests the final battle against evil: the unfolding of events suggests a long-drawn out and exhausting battle, in which the forces of good will at last be triumphant. The inspiration is Revelation 19 and 20. The hymn's length is there for a purpose: it allows the mind to dwell on the arduous struggle and its final end in glory. It is How's greatest hymn: he became Bishop of Wakefield in 1888, where he was much admired.

In *Church Hymns with Tunes* (1874), the music edition of the 1871 book, Arthur Sullivan set these words to an Anglican chant, as if they were a psalm. Later, Charles Villiers Stanford wrote a fine tune for *Hymns Ancient and Modern* (1904 edition), called ENGELBERG; this was superseded almost immediately by Vaughan Williams's SINE NOMINE, which is now the recognized tune. It was written for the *English Hymnal* (1906), and allows the splendour of the hymn to emerge with energy and joy. To hear this hymn sung by a large congregation, in a cathedral for example, is indeed a memorable experience. It has been suggested that the name, SINE NOMINE ('without a name'), refers to those saints who are not remembered individually but who are 'known unto God'.

185   Lord, enthroned in heavenly splendour,
First-begotten from the dead,
Thou alone, our strong defender,
Liftest up thy people's head.
Alleluia!
Jesu, true and living bread.

Here our humblest homage pay we,
Here in loving reverence bow;
Here for faith's discernment pray we,
Lest we fail to know thee now.
Alleluia!
Thou art here, we ask not how.

Though the lowliest form doth veil thee
As of old in Bethlehem,
Here as there thine angels hail thee,
Branch and flower of Jesse's Stem.
Alleluia!
We in worship join with them.

Paschal Lamb, thine offering, finished
Once for all when thou wast slain,
In its fullness undiminished
Shall for evermore remain,
Alleluia!
Cleansing souls from every stain.

Life-imparting, heavenly Manna,
Stricken Rock with streaming side,
Heaven and earth with loud hosanna
Worship thee, the Lamb who died,
Alleluia!
Risen, ascended, glorified!

George Hugh Bourne (1840–1925)

This hymn was first printed for the use of St Edmund's College, Salisbury, a Church of England college of which Bourne was the warden, in a pamphlet entitled *Seven Post-Communion Hymns* (1874). The *Supplement* (1889) to the second edition of *Hymns Ancient and Modern* (1875) printed five of the original ten verses, and thus made them widely known.

As a hymn to be sung after Holy Communion, it makes a rousing and spectacular final moment, and is eminently suitable for great occasions. It is a most unusual hymn for the nineteenth century: the abundance and complexity of its intertwining references are more like Charles Wesley than William Walsham How. It begins with 'First-begotten from the dead', from Revelation 1: 5, which is then linked with Old Testament references to lifting up the head (Genesis 40: 13; Judges 8: 28; Psalm 110: 7), and it then returns (appropriately for a Eucharistic hymn) to Jesus as the living bread (John 6: 51). In verse 3, Christ is the Stem of Jesse (Isaiah 11: 1), and in verse 4 the Lamb, the Paschal or Easter Lamb and the Lamb that was slain (1 Corinthians 5: 7; Revelation 5: 7–12). In the sacrifice of Himself He was the 'offering, finished/ Once for all', which paraphrases the Prayer of Consecration in the *Book of Common Prayer*:

who made there (by his one oblation of himself once offered) a full, perfect, and sufficient sacrifice, oblation, and satisfaction, for the sins of the whole world; . . .

The last verse reaches a climax with the use of biblical typology, in which Christ is the heavenly manna and the stricken rock. Revelation 2: 17 speaks of 'the hidden manna'; and Bourne then borrows from St Paul's sublime reinterpretation (in 1 Corinthians 10: 4) of Exodus 17: 6, in which Moses strikes the rock of Horeb: 'for they drank of that spiritual Rock that followed them: and that Rock was Christ.' In this reading, the streaming side of the wounded Christ becomes the blood and water which will save His followers. The hymn concludes with the glorious vision of the worship of the Lamb, from Revelation 5: 12.

Such spectacular words deserve a spectacular tune: one is ST HELEN, by Sir George Clement Martin (1844–1916), organist of St Paul's Cathedral, from his contribution to the *London Church Choir Association Festival Book* of 1881 (where it was used for 'Praise, my soul, the king of heaven'). It was used for the present verses in *Hymns Ancient and Modern*, and has become closely associated with them. Its high beginning (originally it was in the key of C) makes an arresting start with a thrice repeated C, and its rhythmical energy carries it on from there in an unbroken sublimity. Another tune is BRYN CALFARIA, used in the *English Hymnal* (1906) and in *Songs of Praise* (1925).

186   And now, O Father, mindful of the love
                 That bought us, once for all, on Calvary's Tree,
             And having with us Him that pleads above,
                 We here present, we here spread forth to Thee,
             That only offering perfect in Thine eyes,
             The one true, pure, immortal Sacrifice.

             Look, Father, look on His Anointed Face,
                 And only look on us as found in Him;
             Look not on our misusings of Thy grace,
                 Our prayer so languid and our faith so dim:
             For lo! between our sins and their reward
             We set the Passion of Thy Son our Lord.

             And then for those, our dearest and our best,
                 By this prevailing Presence we appeal;
             O fold them closer to Thy mercy's breast,
                 O do Thine utmost for their souls' true weal;
             From tainting mischief keep them white and clear,
             And crown Thy gifts with strength to persevere.

             And so we come; O draw us to Thy Feet,
                 Most patient Saviour, Who canst love us still;
             And by this Food, so awful and so sweet,
                 Deliver us from every touch of ill:
             In Thine own service make us glad and free,
             And grant us never more to part with Thee.

                         William Bright (1824–1901)

This hymn was first published in a Christian magazine, *The Monthly Packet of Evening Readings for Members of the English Church* (October 1873), with the title 'The Eucharistic Presentation'. It later appeared in Bright's *Hymns and Other Poems*, second edition, 1874. The text printed above, with its original capitals, is taken from the second edition of *Hymns Ancient and Modern* (1875), which printed the last four verses of a six-verse poem. The first two stanzas were as follows, with some necessarily different wording of the third verse (the present first verse):

             'Tis said, 'tis done: and like as we believe
                 That he, true God, became for us true Man;
             As, clinging to the cross, our souls receive
                 The mysteries of his redemptive plan;
             As we confess, 'He rose, and burst the tomb,—
             Went up on high,—will come to speak the doom';

So may we see the bright harmonious line
Of all those marvels stretching on to this,
A kindred master-work of power divine,
That yields a foretaste of our country's bliss,
When pilgrim hearts discern from earthly food
The quickening essence of his Flesh and Blood.

Wherefore we sinners, mindful of the love . . .
Do here present, do here spread forth . . .

The hymn takes its origin from a prayer in the Canon of the Mass beginning 'Unde et memores, Domine, nos servitui', spoken as the priest shows the chalice to the people. The translation makes the connection clear, and shows how Bright borrowed actual phrases from the prayer:

And now, Lord, we thy servants, and with us all thy holy people, calling to mind the blessed Passion of this same Christ, thy Son, our Lord, likewise his resurrection from the grave, and glorious ascension into heaven, offer to thy sovereign majesty, out of the gifts thou hast bestowed upon us, a sacrifice that is pure, holy, and unblemished, the sacred Bread of everlasting life, and the Cup of eternal salvation.

Bright became Regius Professor of Ecclesiastical History at Oxford, having previously worked in Scotland. As theological tutor at Trinity College, Glenalmond, and as Bell Lecturer in Ecclesiastical History, his views on the Reformation caused offence to the Bishop of Glasgow, who ejected him from both offices, whereupon he returned to Oxford. His hymn very beautifully records the Eucharistic celebration of the great Sacrifice, and its relationship to the individual penitent; and the third verse prays very properly for loved ones, in the manner of the prayer for the whole state of Christ's Church Militant here on earth.

The most frequently used tune for this hymn is UNDE ET MEMORES, from the Latin text, written for the second edition of *Hymns Ancient and Modern* by William Henry Monk. It marks the rhythms very beautifully with a crotchet on the third and seventh syllables of lines 1 and 3, varied to the fifth syllable in lines 2 and 4, and changed yet again in the final line of each verse. In *Common Praise* (2000) the hymn has been set to Orlando Gibbons's SONG 1 (used for 'Eternal ruler of the ceaseless round'). A modern tune for these words is John Wilson's RAVENDALE, written for these words in *The Clarendon Hymn Book* (1936).

187   Thy hand, O God, has guided
    Thy flock, from age to age;
The wondrous tale is written,
    Full clear, on every page;
Our fathers owned thy goodness,
    And we their deeds record;
And both of this bear witness,
    One Church, one Faith, one Lord.

Thy heralds brought glad tidings
    To greatest, as to least;
They bade men rise, and hasten
    To share the great King's feast;
And this was all their teaching,
    In every deed and word,
To all alike proclaiming
    One Church, one Faith, one Lord.

When shadows thick were falling,
    And all seemed sunk in night,
Thou, Lord, didst send thy servants,
    Thy chosen sons of light.
On them and on thy people
    Thy plenteous grace was poured,
And this was still their message:
    One Church, one Faith, one Lord.

Through many a day of darkness,
    Through many a scene of strife,
The faithful few fought bravely
    To guard the nation's life.
Their gospel of redemption,
    Sin pardoned, man restored,
Was all in this enfolded,
    One Church, one Faith, one Lord.

And we, shall we be faithless?
    Shall hearts fail, hands hang down?
Shall we evade the conflict,
    And cast away our crown?
Not so: in God's deep counsels
    Some better thing is stored;
We will maintain, unflinching,
    One Church, one Faith, one Lord.

> Thy mercy will not fail us,
>   Nor leave thy work undone;
> With thy right hand to help us,
>   The victory shall be won;
> And then, by men and angels,
>   Thy name shall be adored,
> And this shall be their anthem,
>   One Church, one Faith, one Lord.

Edward Hayes Plumptre (1821–91)

This hymn was first published in the *Supplement* (1889) to the 1875 edition of *Hymns Ancient and Modern*. It is one of those very grand hymns that reflects the fact that, by the 1880s, the Church of England was confidently using the hymn form in worship. In this case, it suggests a robust defence of the Church against anything that might undermine it: indeed, in its first printing, it appeared in a section entitled 'For Church Defence'. It was the work of an eminent churchman: Plumptre became Dean of Wells in 1881. Its initial inspiration comes from Ephesians 4: 4–5: 'There is one body and one Spirit . . . one Lord, one faith, one baptism', but this is developed in a particularly Victorian way: the hymn looks back to the past, and to those who guarded 'the nation's life' (presumably its spiritual life), and promises to follow their example in the present age. The later nineteenth century, by implication, is an age in which it would be all too easy to be discouraged, as verse 5 suggests: Plumptre was clearly aware of the pressures on the Church, from without and from within. His hymn asserts a vigorous defiance of the cross-currents of the age. They are unspecified, but he must have been thinking of Darwinism, or the Textual Criticism of the Bible, or of more general tendencies towards rationalism and scepticism.

In its first printing, this hymn was set to a German tune by Johann Crüger; but in 1898 a new tune, THORNBURY, was written by Basil Harwood (1859–1949) for the twenty-fifth annual festival of the London Church Choir Association. It was printed in the festival booklet, and gradually made its way into major hymn-books. It is now the usual tune; it is also sometimes used for 'O Jesus, I have promised'. Its wonderful vigour suits Plumptre's words, and helps to ameliorate their strident tone.

188
O love that wilt not let me go,
   I rest my weary soul in thee;
I give thee back the life I owe,
That in thine ocean depths its flow
   May richer, fuller be.

O light that followest all my way,
   I yield my flickering torch to thee;
My heart restores its borrowed ray,
That in thy sunshine's blaze its day
   May brighter, fairer be.

O joy that seekest me through pain,
   I cannot close my heart to thee;
I trace the rainbow through the rain,
And feel the promise is not vain,
   That morn shall tearless be.

O cross that liftest up my head,
   I dare not ask to fly from thee;
I lay in dust life's glory dead,
And from the ground there blossoms red
   Life that shall endless be.

George Matheson (1842–1906)

This hymn was published in the Church of Scotland magazine, *Life and Work*, in January 1882, and then in *The Scottish Hymnal* (1885). It was probably written in 1881. Matheson, the minister at Innellan, on the Firth of Clyde, said that he wrote it after a period of mental suffering. He also said later that 'I had the impression rather of having it dictated to me by some inward voice than of working it out myself. I am quite sure that the whole work was completed in five minutes.'

The result is an extraordinary hymn, with its imagery of ocean depths, blazing sun, rainbow and rain, dust and blossom: self-sacrifice has often been described in hymns, but never with such an intensity. In every verse, there is a giving up, which ends (verse 4) in the laying down of life: and in each case, the loss is followed by gain. The pattern of self-surrender followed by reward ends at the foot of the Cross, where the glory of earthly life is laid down; the result is the flowering of eternal life. It is a hymn which goes beyond enthusiasm into an almost ecstatic self-surrender.

The metre, 88.88.6., is unique, and the first tune, ST MARGARET, was written for these words. By a coincidence, it was also written in the Firth of Clyde, at Brodick Manse on the Isle of Arran, where A. L. Peace (1844–1912), then organist of Glasgow Cathedral, was staying. Peace wrote the tune in 1884 for the committee compiling *The Scottish Hymnal*: by yet another coincidence, it seems to have been composed with the same kind of instantaneous inspiration that gave the words to Matheson. Peace wrote:

'After reading the hymn over carefully, I wrote the music straight off, and may say that the ink of the first note was hardly dry when I had finished the tune.' Other tunes include HAMPSTEAD, by Walford Davies (1869–1941), and INNELLAN, by David Evans (1874–1948), contributed to the Scottish *Revised Church Hymnary* (1927), of which he was chief music editor.

189

God is working his purpose out, as year succeeds to year;
God is working his purpose out, and the time is drawing near;
Nearer and nearer draws the time, the time that shall surely be,
When the earth shall be filled with the glory of God as the waters cover the sea.

From utmost east to utmost west, where'er man's foot hath trod,
By the mouth of many messengers goes forth the voice of God,
'Give ear to me, ye continents, ye isles, give ear to me,
That the earth may be filled with the glory of God as the waters cover the sea.'

What can we do to work God's work, to prosper and increase
The brotherhood of all mankind, the reign of the Prince of Peace?
What can we do to hasten the time, the time that shall surely be,
When the earth shall be filled with the glory of God as the waters cover the sea?

March we forth in the strength of God with the banner of Christ unfurled,
That the light of the glorious gospel of truth may shine throughout the world;
Fight we the fight with sorrow and sin, to set their captives free;
That the earth may be filled with the glory of God as the waters cover the sea.

All we can do is nothing worth unless God blesses the deed;
Vainly we hope for the harvest-tide till God gives life to the seed;
Yet nearer and nearer draws the time, the time that shall surely be,
When the earth shall be filled with the glory of God as the waters cover the sea.

Arthur Campbell Ainger (1841–1919)

This wonderfully energetic and optimistic hymn is a product of its time and its circumstances. Ainger was a master at Eton, and the hymn was written there in 1894. It was published in leaflet form in that year, and later in the Church Missionary Society's *Hymn Book* (1899). It became widely known when it was printed in both *Hymns Ancient and Modern* (1904) and the *English Hymnal* (1906).

It was dedicated to Archbishop E. W. Benson (1829–96), whose son, A. C. Benson, was a colleague of Ainger's at Eton. It sings wonderfully well in a school chapel, and it lasted well during the twentieth century, with its wars and other horrors. It is based on Habakkuk 2: 14 or Isaiah 11: 9, both of which use the metaphor of water and sea to suggest the coming of the kingdom of God upon earth.

The tune BENSON, composed for this hymn by Millicent D. Kingham (1866–1927), was printed with the words in 1894. Another, rising to F at 'God' on the last line of each verse, is PURPOSE, by Martin Shaw. Many other tunes have been tried, but BENSON, by the almost unknown Ms Kingham, has retained its primary position.

190

Lift high the Cross, the love of Christ proclaim
Till all the world adore his sacred name.

Come, brethren, follow, where our Captain trod,
Our King victorious, Christ the Son of God:

Led on their way by this triumphant sign,
The hosts of God in conquering ranks combine:

Each new-born soldier of the Crucified
Bears on his brow the seal of him who died:

This is the sign which Satan's legions fear
And angels veil their faces to revere:

Saved by this Cross whereon their Lord was slain,
The sons of Adam their lost home regain:

From north and south, from east and west they raise
In growing unison their song of praise:

O Lord, once lifted on the glorious Tree,
As thou hast promised, draw men unto thee:

Let every race and every language tell
Of him who saves our souls from death and hell:

From farthest regions let them homage bring,
And on his Cross adore their Saviour King:

Set up thy throne, that earth's despair may cease
Beneath the shadow of its healing peace:

For thy blest Cross which doth for all atone
Creation's praises rise before thy throne:

Lift high the Cross, the love of Christ proclaim
Till all the world adore his sacred name.

George William Kitchin (1827–1912)
and Michael Robert Newbolt (1874–1956)

The original version of this hymn was written for a special festival service of the Society for the Propagation of the Gospel in Winchester Cathedral in 1887, during Kitchin's time as Dean (1883–94). It was altered by Newbolt, an Anglican priest who later became a Canon of Chester Cathedral, for the *Second Supplement* to *Hymns Ancient and Modern* (1916). It is very suitable for a processional hymn, in which the cross is literally lifted high: it expounds the meaning of the Cross as the sign of victory, and also as the means of salvation which will 'draw men' to Christ. The first image is based on the story of the Emperor Constantine's vision, when he saw the Cross and the words 'In hoc signo vinces' ('in this sign shalt thou conquer'). The second uses John 12: 32: 'And I, if I be lifted up from the earth, will draw all men unto me'. As the crucifer, or cross-bearer, carries the cross down the nave, the hymn celebrates the wonder of salvation through a 'lifting up'.

The tune, CRUCIFER, is by Sir Sydney Nicholson (1875–1947), written for these words in the 1916 *Supplement*. Nicholson was Chief Music Adviser to *Hymns Ancient and Modern*, and here he showed a fine sense of the potential of the words, the relatively subdued melody of the verses contrasting with the spectacular refrain.

191

Breathe on me, Breath of God,
Fill me with life anew,
That I may love what thou dost love,
And do what thou wouldst do.

Breathe on me, Breath of God,
Until my heart is pure;
Until with thee I will one will,
To do and to endure.

Breathe on me, Breath of God,
Till I am wholly thine;
Until this earthly part of me
Glows with thy fire divine.

Breathe on me, Breath of God:
So shall I never die,
But live with thee the perfect life
Of thine eternity.

Edwin Hatch (1835–89)

This simple yet profound hymn was first published in Hatch's privately printed volume, *Between Doubt and Prayer* (1878), and later in *Towards Fields of Light: Sacred Poems* (1890), a memorial volume published by his widow. It was given the title 'Spiritus Dei', thus linking the image of 'breath' with that of the Holy Spirit (as in the Greek, where the same word is used for 'spirit' and 'breath'; Hatch was at one time a Professor of Classics at Toronto). It was first used as a congregational hymn in Henry Allon's *Congregational Psalmist Hymnal* (1886).

The hymn takes the idea of the creating breath of God, from Genesis 2: 7, and links it with the idea of the Holy Spirit and new birth in John 3: 3–8. It brings new life and love, purity and obedience, surrender and inspiration, and finally eternal life, as the hymn moves through various stages of Christian experience and discipline towards a unity with God.

The hymn is in short metre, which makes it suitable for many tunes. The most commonly used one is probably CARLISLE, by the blind musician Charles Lockhart (1745–1815), named after the former Carlisle Chapel in London. But almost every hymn-book has a different tune to this hymn.

192

Hear us, O Lord, from heaven thy dwelling-place;
Like them of old, in vain we toil all night,
Unless with us thou go, who art the light;
Come then, O Lord, that we may see thy face.

Thou, Lord, dost rule the raging of the sea,
When loud the storm and furious is the gale;
Strong is thine arm; our little barks are frail:
Send us thy help; remember Galilee.

Our wives and children we commend to thee:
For them we plough the land and plough the deep,
For them by day the golden corn we reap,
By night the silver harvest of the sea.

We thank thee, Lord, for sunshine, dew, and rain,
Broadcast from heaven by thine almighty hand,
Source of all life, unnumbered as the sand,
Bird, beast, and fish, herb, fruit, and golden grain.

O Bread of Life, thou in thy word hast said:
'Who feeds in faith on me shall never die'.
In mercy hear thy hungry children's cry:
'Father, give us this day our daily bread!'

Sow in our hearts the seeds of thy dear love,
That we may reap contentment, joy, and peace;
And when at last our earthly labours cease,
Grant us to join thy harvest home above.

William Henry Gill (1839–1923)

This is known as 'The Manx Fishermen's Evening Hymn'. Its author, W. H. Gill, came from a Manx family, and wrote the words to a very beautiful ballad tune from the Isle of Man, which he published (with these words) in

Manx National Songs (1896). Gill lived in London for most of his life, but his roots in the Isle of Man were deep, and in writing this hymn he was mindful of the island's dependency on agriculture and fishing. There was a tradition that the Manx fishermen used to ask for God's blessing before casting their nets, and in his book Gill prefaced his hymn with these words from a prayer in the *Manx Book of Common Prayer*:

. . . that it may please thee to give and preserve to our use the kindly fruits of the earth, and to restore and continue to us the blessings of the sea, so as in due time we may enjoy them.

The long lines of this hymn give it a certain dignity: as in 'We plough the fields and scatter', the speaking voice is that of a man who works to provide food; he connects his fishing with the description of the fishermen in the New Testament. He and his fellow workers are following those who toiled all night (John 21: 3), and they have to experience storms, so that they think of him who stilled the storm (Mark 4: 37–9). They pray for daily bread, but they also link bread to the fundamentals of faith, remembering Jesus saying 'I am the bread of life' (John 6: 48, 50), a quotation which is neatly included in verse 5.

The result is a hymn which touchingly combines the fundamentals of faith with the simplest and most important kinds of work, farming and fishing. The fishermen demonstrate their faith by asking God to hear them and be with them: they ask for His help, commend their wives and children to Him, give thanks, pray for their daily bread, and finally hope for eternal life ('thy harvest home above').

This hymn is very moving in its re-creation of a state of mind in which the fishermen and farmers put their trust in God; it is strangely underused, however, not finding a place in any major hymn-books except those of the Methodists, among which it has been a favourite since 1904, when it appeared in the Wesleyan *Methodist Hymn Book*. It did however inspire the writer Malcolm Lowry (1909–57), whose collection of short stories, *Hear us O lord from heaven thy dwelling place* (1961), was published after his death. Lowry was born near Liverpool, and as a child went on holiday to the Isle of Man: echoes of the hymn occur in the stories.

The tune was published with the words in 1896, under the title 'Eaisht oo as Clash-tyn' ('Listen and hear'), and words and music are inseparable. The tune is a traditional Manx ballad tune, transformed by these words. It was given the title PEEL CASTLE in the *Methodist Hymn Book* (1904), after the castle on St Patrick's Island opposite Peel Harbour on the Isle of Man.

{10}

Nineteenth- and Early Twentieth-Century American Hymns

The nineteenth century was the first full century of American independence. It was marked by a strong hymnody almost from the beginning, and two fine American hymns crossed the Atlantic to be printed in the first edition of *Hymns Ancient and Modern*. American hymn writing was marked by a high sense of honour and moral purpose, so that poems such as Lowell's 'Once to every man and nation' and hymns such as Edmund Sears's 'It came upon the midnight clear' were calls to decision and social action.

Pride in the new and beautiful country was spoiled by the consciousness of the evils of slavery, and the Civil War was fought to remedy that evil. Julia Ward Howe's 'Battle Hymn of the Republic', written at the height of the war itself, was a stirring cry to fight for freedom. Other writers include the East Coast intellectuals, such as Oliver Wendell Holmes ('Lord of all being, throned afar'), and the Unitarian Samuel Johnson; while the Quaker poet and journalist, John Greenleaf Whittier, wrote beautifully of the love of God and the importance of quiet reflection and worship.

In a very different mode, in Chicago, the missions of Dwight L. Moody were reinforced by the potent singing of Ira D. Sankey, whose *Sacred Songs and Solos* became a best-seller, and went through many editions. Two of the writers most closely associated with the Evangelicalism of that movement were Philipp Bliss and Fanny Crosby (Frances Jane van Alstyne), both of whom are represented here. And at the end we return to the high morality of purposeful hymnody in Frederick Hosmer's 'Thy kingdom come', and Frank Mason North's New York hymn, 'Where cross the crowded ways of life'.

193
    Thou art the Way: to thee alone
      From sin and death we flee;
    And he who would the Father seek
      Must seek him, Lord, by thee.

    Thou art the Truth: thy word alone
      True wisdom can impart;
    Thou only canst inform the mind,
      And purify the heart.

    Thou art the Life: the rending tomb
      Proclaims thy conquering arm;
    And those who put their trust in thee
      Nor death nor hell shall harm.

    Thou art the Way, the Truth, the Life:
      Grant us that Way to know,
    That Truth to keep, that Life to win,
      Whose joys eternal flow.

        George Washington Doane (1799–1859)

This hymn was first published in Doane's *Songs by the Way* (1824). Doane, who subsequently became Bishop of New Jersey, his native state, wrote this as a young man: it shows astonishing confidence and maturity. It has been described as 'one of the most highly regarded American hymn texts of the nineteenth century' (*The Hymnal 1982 Companion*). It was first published in Britain by Edward Bickersteth in his *Christian Psalmody* (1833), and it was one of only two American hymns to be included in the first edition of *Hymns Ancient and Modern* (1861).

It is a simple but strong exposition of John 14: 6 ('Jesus saith unto him, I am the way, the truth, and the life: no man cometh unto the Father, but by me'). Each attribute is treated in a single verse, and the conclusion binds them into a threefold understanding. In the University of Glasgow, whose motto is 'Via, Veritas, Vita', this hymn is very properly sung on Commemoration Day.

The tune is usually ST JAMES, attributed to Raphael Courteville (*c*.1676–1772), who was organist of St James's, Piccadilly, London (some say for 81 years). It was first published anonymously in 1697 in a book of psalms and hymns for the use of 'the Parish Church and Tabernacle of St James's Westminster' (as St James's, Piccadilly, was then called). It was also published in 1708 as a metrical psalm tune, and as a tune for 'While shepherds watched their flocks by night'. The present association of words and music dates, as so many fine associations do, from the first edition of *Hymns Ancient and Modern*. An alternative is REDHEAD No. 66, by Richard Redhead (1820–1901).

194   Take up thy cross, the Saviour said,
            If thou wouldst my disciple be;
        Deny thyself, the world forsake,
            And humbly follow after me.

        Take up thy cross: let not its weight
            Fill thy weak spirit with alarm;
        His strength shall bear thy spirit up,
            And brace thy heart, and nerve thine arm.

        Take up thy cross, nor heed the shame,
            Nor let thy foolish pride rebel;
        The Lord for thee the cross endured,
            To save thy soul from death and hell.

        Take up thy cross then in his strength,
            And calmly every danger brave;
        'Twill guide thee to a better home,
            And lead to victory o'er the grave.

        Take up thy cross, and follow Christ,
            Nor think till death to lay it down;
        For only he who bears the cross
            May hope to wear the glorious crown.

        To thee, great Lord, the One in Three,
            All praise for evermore ascend;
        O grant us in our home to see
            The heavenly life that knows no end.

                    Charles William Everest (1814–77)

First published in Everest's *Vision of Death, and Other Poems* (1833). It was brought to Britain in an altered form in the *Salisbury Hymn Book* of 1857, and was one of only two American hymns to be printed in the first edition of *Hymns Ancient and Modern* (1861). This, like 'Thou art the way'(no. 193), was a young man's hymn, published when Everest was 19. This may account for a certain vagueness of imagery in the original: verse 4, line 2, for example, was 'And calmly sin's wild deluge brave'.

It is a meditation on the saying of Jesus in Mark 8: 34: 'Whosoever will come after me, let him deny himself, and take up his cross, and follow me.' It is a severe and demanding hymn, though not without the promise of strength (verses 2 and 4) and the hope of immortality (verses 5 and 6).

It is usually sung to the dignified BRESLAU, a German folk-melody from the fifteenth century. As a hymn tune, it appeared in Christian Gall's *As Hymnodus Sacer* (1625), and it was subsequently used by Bach and Mendelssohn. A frequent arrangement is from Mendelssohn's oratorio *St Paul* (1836), but it has sometimes been simplified and reharmonized, as in *Rejoice and Sing*. With the name BRESLAU, it was used no less than three times in *Hymns Ancient and Modern*, and it has remained closely associated with the present words.

195

My faith looks up to thee,
Thou Lamb of Calvary,
   Saviour divine!
Now hear me while I pray,
Take all my guilt away,
O let me from this day
   Be wholly thine.

May thy rich grace impart
Strength to my fainting heart,
   My zeal inspire;
As thou hast died for me,
O may my love to thee
Pure, warm, and changeless be,
   A living fire.

While life's dark maze I tread,
And griefs around me spread,
   Be thou my guide;
Bid darkness turn to day,
Wipe sorrow's tears away,
Nor let me ever stray
   From thee aside.

When ends life's transient dream,
When death's cold sullen stream
   Shall o'er me roll,
Blest Saviour, then in love
Fear and distrust remove;
O bear me safe above,
   A ransomed soul.

Ray Palmer (1808–87)

This hymn was written when Palmer was aged 21, shortly after his leaving Yale University. He was teaching in a girls' school in New York at the time, before going on to train for the Congregational ministry. He said that he wrote it as a private poem: 'I gave form to what I felt by writing, with little effort, the stanzas. I recollect I wrote them with very tender emotion, and ended the last lines with tears.'

The poem became a hymn a year or so later, when Palmer met Lowell Mason, the great American musician, in Boston. Mason was looking for hymn texts, and Palmer gave him this one. It was printed in *Spiritual Songs for Social Worship* (1831–2), edited by Mason and Thomas Hastings, from which it found its way into other hymn-books. It is a fine example of early nineteenth-century American hymnody, written in the same metre as 'God save our gracious king' (Samuel F. Smith's 'My country, 'tis of thee', in the same metre, was written in 1831). Julian's *Dictionary of Hymnology* described the best of Palmer's hymns as 'by their combination of thought, poetry, and devotion, . . . superior to almost all others of American origin'.

The hymn is said to have found its way to England through an older Congregationalist, Andrew Reed (1787–1862), who visited America in 1834 to receive an Honorary Degree from Yale. It was printed in *Hymns for Divine Worship* (1867), a Methodist New Connexion book, and later in Godfrey Thring's *Church of England Hymn Book* (1880), from which it found its way into the *English Hymnal* (1906) and *Songs of Praise* (1925).

The usual tune, OLIVET, was written by Lowell Mason for his 1831–2 book, and has been associated with the hymn ever since; *Songs of Praise* changed the tune in its enlarged edition to a Welsh hymn melody, DENBIGH, but OLIVET has remained a firm favourite.

196

Once to every man and nation
    Comes the moment to decide,
In the strife of truth with falsehood,
    For the good or evil side;
Some great cause, God's new Messiah,
    Offering each the bloom or blight—
And the choice goes by for ever
    'Twixt that darkness and that light.

Then to side with truth is noble,
    When we share her wretched crust,
Ere her cause bring fame and profit,
    And 'tis prosperous to be just;
Then it is the brave man chooses,
    While the coward stands aside,
Till the multitude make virtue
    Of the faith they had denied.

By the light of burning martyrs,
    Christ, thy bleeding feet we track,
Toiling up new Calvaries ever
    With the cross that turns not back.
New occasions teach new duties;
    Time makes ancient good uncouth;
They must upward still and onward
    Who would keep abreast of truth.

Though the cause of evil prosper,
Yet 'tis truth alone is strong;
Though her portion be the scaffold,
And upon the throne be wrong—
Yet that scaffold sways the future,
And, behind the dim unknown,
Standeth God within the shadow,
Keeping watch above his own.

James Russell Lowell (1819–91)

This hymn began as a poem by Lowell, in a different metre, written in 1845. It was called 'The Present Crisis', and was provoked by the war with Mexico, which Lowell and others, including Abraham Lincoln, thought would increase the power of the Southern states and therefore would enlarge the area in which slavery was accepted as normal. The poem began:

When a deed is done for Freedom, through the broad world's aching breast
Runs a thrill of joy prophetic . . .

It was published in Lowell's *Poems* (1849). Later in the century, W. Garrett Horder, a great advocate of American hymns, took Lowell's lines and made a hymn of them by shortening the lines and selecting heavily from them. He published them in his *Hymns Supplemental to Existing Collections* (1896), and then in *Worship Song* (1905), from whence it found its way into the *English Hymnal* and *Songs of Praise*. It has become a well-known hymn about ethical judgement and political action, showing the high moral tone which might be expected from an American Unitarian who was both a professor and a diplomat.

No less than three great Welsh tunes have helped to make this hymn a stirring one. The first is EBENEZER, also known as TON-Y-BOTEL, because of the story that it was found in a bottle washed up on the Welsh coast. It was composed by T. J. Williams (1869–1944), and first published as a hymn tune in 1896. The second is HYFRYDOL, by R. H. Prichard (1811–87). The third, used by the *English Hymnal* in 1933, is YN Y GLYN, by David Evans (1874–1948).

197
It came upon the midnight clear,
  That glorious song of old,
From angels bending near the earth
  To touch their harps of gold:
'Peace on the earth, good will to men,
  From heaven's all-gracious King!'
The world in solemn stillness lay
  To hear the angels sing.

Still through the cloven skies they come,
  With peaceful wings unfurled;
And still their heavenly music floats
  O'er all the weary world;
Above its sad and lowly plains
  They bend on hovering wing;
And ever o'er its Babel sounds
  The blessèd angels sing.

Yet with the woes of sin and strife
  The world has suffered long;
Beneath the angel-strain have rolled
  Two thousand years of wrong;
And man, at war with man, hears not
  The love-song which they bring:
O hush the noise, ye men of strife,
  And hear the angels sing!

And ye, beneath life's crushing load,
  Whose forms are bending low,
Who toil along the climbing way
  With painful steps and slow,
Look now! for glad and golden hours
  Come swiftly on the wing;
O rest beside the weary road,
  And hear the angels sing!

For lo! the days are hastening on,
  By prophet-bards foretold,
When, with the ever-circling years,
  Comes round the age of gold;
When peace shall over all the earth
  Its ancient splendours fling,
And the whole world give back the song
  Which now the angels sing.

Edmund Hamilton Sears (1810–76)

This Christmas hymn was first published in the *Christian Register* (Boston, Mass.) in December 1849. It is unusual in its focus on the message of the angels—'on earth peace, goodwill toward men'—to the exclusion of almost everything else in the narrative of the birth of Jesus. Sears, who was a Unitarian minister, would certainly have wanted to read the account of the Incarnation in terms of its implications for humanity: here he sees the Christmas message as coming to a weary and war-torn world, and looks for the coming of a golden age.

Sears' message has survived, in spite of the numerous wars which have taken place since he wrote the hymn: it is a part of the complex pattern of Christmas to believe that somehow we can hope for an age in which the world will, one day, be able to send back to heaven the song of the angels at Bethlehem.

The usual British tune, NOEL, is by Arthur Sullivan (1842–1900). It was written for *Church Hymns with Tunes* (1874), of which Sullivan was the music editor, and has been used ever since that time. Although 1874 was not the first appearance of the hymn in Britain (it was included in *The Hymnal Companion to the Book of Common Prayer* in 1870), the tune did much to make the words singable and popular. It is taken from a Herefordshire folk tune, used also for the carol 'Dives and Lazarus' (in Bramley and Stainer's *Christmas Carols New and Old*). In America the tune is sometimes CAROL, by R. S. Willis (1819–1900), probably first set to these words in the *Hymnal of the Methodist Epsicopal Church* (1896).

198   Mine eyes have seen the glory of the coming of the Lord;
He is trampling out the vintage where his grapes of wrath are stored;
He hath loosed the fateful lightning of his terrible swift sword:
    His truth is marching on.

I have seen him in the watch-fires of a hundred circling camps;
They have builded him an altar in the evening dews and damps;
I have read his righteous sentence by the dim and flaring lamps:
    His day is marching on.

I have read a fiery gospel, writ in burnished rows of steel:
'As ye deal with my contemners, so with you my grace shall deal;
Let the hero born of woman crush the serpent with his heel,
    Since God is marching on.'

He has sounded forth the trumpet that shall never call retreat;
He is sifting out the hearts of men before his judgement-seat;
O, be swift, my soul, to answer him; be jubilant, my feet!
    Our God is marching on.

In the beauty of the lilies Christ was born across the sea,
With a glory in his bosom that transfigures you and me;
As he died to make men holy, let us die to make men free,
    While God is marching on.

He is coming like the glory of the morning on the wave;
He is wisdom to the mighty, he is succour to the brave;
So the world shall be his footstool, and the soul of time his slave;
Our God is marching on.

Julia Ward Howe (1819–1910)

This hymn was written and published during the American Civil War, fought over the issues of independence for the Southern states and of slavery. It first appeared in the *New York Daily Tribune*, 14 January 1862, and then in the *Atlantic Monthly* for February 1862, with the title by which it is always known, 'The Battle Hymn of the Republic'.

It is a magnificent example of the 'battle hymn': of the idea that in fighting for a cause which is just and right, an army is doing the will of God. In this case, the army of the Union was fighting against the slave system, which was widely seen among Christian people in the Northern states (especially after the publication of Harriet Beecher Stowe's *Uncle Tom's Cabin* in 1852) as a fundamental evil of American society. The 'terrible swift sword' is therefore the Northern army, and the soldiers are those who were going to 'die to make men free', even as Christ died for our sins. The hymn brilliantly combines the imagery of the Church Militant with the portrayal of the war front, with its 'hundred circling camps' and its 'burnished rows of steel' (presumably the bayonets of the soldiers on parade).

It was written after seeing a review of the Union troops outside Washington on 20 November 1861. Julia Ward Howe went to the review with her husband and her pastor, James Freeman Clarke; after it was over, their carriage was stuck in the traffic, and while they were waiting they sang the tune to the words 'John Brown's body lies a-mouldering in the grave'. Clarke suggested to Mrs Howe that she should write some new words to the tune, and she did so that night in Willard's Hotel in Washington. The immediacy of her response, and the excitement of the occasion, give a wonderful urgency and power to the rhythmical lines.

The tune seems to have originated in Charleston, South Carolina, in the 1850s, as a song for a company of firemen, beginning 'Say, bummers, will you meet us'. This was changed by an Evangelical, William Steffe, to 'Say, brothers, will you meet us,/On Canaan's happy shore'. After the hanging of John Brown on 2 December 1859 for his direct action to free slaves at Harper's Ferry, the song was taken up by the 2nd Battalion of Massachusetts Infantry (which had a sergeant by the name of John Brown) and the words of 'John Brown's body' were written. Sometimes at the beginning of the Civil War other words were used, such as 'We will hang Jeff Davis on a sour apple tree' (referring to the leader of the Southern states, Jefferson Davis). The simplicity of these words is an indication of the way in which Julia Ward Howe's text transformed the crude and vengeful original into something much finer, thus capturing the idealism of a crusade.

The tune was printed with the words in April 1862, under the title 'Glory, Hallelujah' (the chorus of 'John Brown's body', sometimes found in hymn-books), and has since become closely associated with them, sometimes under the title of JOHN BROWN. It has seemed too secular a tune for some editors: in *Songs of Praise* it was headed 'For Secular use', and a tune by Martin Shaw, BATTLE SONG, was included 'For use in Church'. Another tune for the hymn is VISION, by Walford Davies (1869–1941).

199 Lord of all being, throned afar,
Thy glory flames from sun and star;
Centre and soul of every sphere,
Yet to each loving heart how near!

Sun of our life, thy quickening ray
Sheds on our path the glow of day;
Star of our hope, thy softened light
Cheers the long watches of the night.

Our midnight is thy smile withdrawn,
Our noontide is thy gracious dawn,
Our rainbow arch, thy mercy's sign,
All, save the clouds of sin, are thine.

Lord of all life, below, above,
Whose light is truth, whose warmth is love,
Before thy ever-blazing throne
We ask no lustre of our own.

Grant us thy truth to make us free,
And kindling hearts that burn for thee,
Till all thy living altars claim
One holy light, one heavenly flame.

    Oliver Wendell Holmes (1809–94)

Oliver Wendell Holmes was one of the great nineteenth-century American men of letters, a Professor of Anatomy at Harvard University, and author of many articles in the *Atlantic Monthly* which were collected together and published under various 'at the Breakfast Table' headings. This hymn was first published in December 1859, at the conclusion of the series entitled *The Professor at the Breakfast Table*, under the title of 'A Sun-day Hymn'. It was prefaced by these words:

Peace to all such as may have been vexed in spirit by any utterance these pages may have repeated! They will doubtless forget for the moment the difference in the hues of truth we look at through our human prisms, and join in singing (inwardly) this hymn to the source of the light we all need to lead us, and the warmth which alone can make us brothers.

The eirenic spirit of these words is matched by the simple strength of the hymn itself, which is entirely free from doctrinal differences, and which is universal in its emphasis on the glory of God, seen in its light, its goodness and mercy, its truth and its love. It is a fine example of the dignity and high moral tone of the nineteenth-century American hymn. It found its way into hymn-books very quickly, being reprinted in *A Collection of Hymns for the Sanctuary* (1860), and in a Methodist book of the same year.

Tunes for this hymn have also been dignified: they include UFFINGHAM, by Jeremiah Clarke (*c.*1670–1707), and MARYTON, by Henry Smith (1825–98), an Anglican clergyman who became Charles Kingsley's curate at Eversley and later the incumbent at Gibraltar. This is his only known hymn tune.

200
        City of God, how broad and far
           Outspread thy walls sublime!
        The true thy chartered freemen are
           Of every age and clime:

        One holy church, one army strong,
           One steadfast, high intent;
        One working band, one harvest-song,
           One King omnipotent.

        How purely hath thy speech come down
           From man's primeval youth!
        How grandly hath thine empire grown,
           Of freedom, love, and truth!

        How gleam thy watch-fires through the night
           With never-fainting ray!
        How rise thy towers, serene and bright,
           To meet the dawning day!

        In vain the surge's angry shock,
           In vain the drifting sands:
        Unharmed upon the eternal rock
           The eternal city stands.

                Samuel Johnson (1822–82)

From Samuel Johnson and Samuel Longfellow's *Hymns of the Spirit* (1864). It is a strong hymn, with a powerful rhythm, reflecting the grandeur of its subject. Its rhetoric is obvious: the heavy repetition in verse 2, for example, with its repeated 'one . . . one . . .', climaxes in the magnificent word 'omnipotent' at the end of the verse. This is just one of many adjectives and adverbs ('sublime', 'steadfast', 'primeval') which give strength to this hymn. In the next verse 'How purely' is echoed by 'How grandly', and the 'How' figure is carried on in the verse which follows. Eventually, after the repetition of 'In vain', the eternal city 'stands': the straightforward verb finally gives the idea of the immovable city on the eternal rock. It is all immensely impressive as a restatement of the ancient concept of the City of God, familiar from the works of St Augustine onwards. Augustine took the title of his great work *De Civitate Dei*, from Psalm 87: 3: 'Glorious things are spoken of thee, O city of God'. The city of God is symbolized by Jerusalem (considered mystically), the holy city, as opposed to Babylon, the earthly city of the flesh (and of the devil).

Johnson, who was a Unitarian minister, was a free-thinker even by the broad and tolerant Unitarian standards, and set up his own Free Church at Lynn, Massachusetts. His hymn contains no reference to Jesus or the New Testament gospel, but it has nevertheless become widely valued as a hymn about the strength of religion. Its closeness to Johnson's Unitarian origins is suggested by the reference to 'freedom, love, and truth' in verse 3.

The tune is usually RICHMOND, from Thomas Haweis's *Carmina Christo, or Hymns to the Saviour* (1792), and shortened by Samuel Webbe in his *Collection of Psalm-Tunes for Four Voices* (1808). Webbe named the tune RICHMOND: it is a robust and effective tune, rising to a splendid climax at the end of line 3.

201 Eternal ruler of the ceaseless round
  Of circling planets singing on their way;
Guide of the nations from the night profound
  Into the glory of the perfect day;
Rule in our hearts, that we may ever be
Guided and strengthened and upheld by thee.

We are of thee, the children of thy love,
  The brothers of thy well-belovèd Son;
Descend, O Holy Spirit, like a dove
  Into our hearts, that we may be as one:
As one with thee, to whom we ever tend;
As one with him, our Brother and our Friend.

We would be one in hatred of all wrong,
  One in our love of all things sweet and fair,
One with the joy that breaketh into song,
  One with the grief that trembleth into prayer,
One in the power that makes the children free
To follow truth, and thus to follow thee.

O clothe us with thy heavenly armour, Lord,
  Thy trusty shield, thy sword of love divine;
Our inspiration be thy constant word;
  We ask no victories that are not thine:
Give or withhold, let pain or pleasure be;
Enough to know that we are serving thee.

                John W. Chadwick (1840–1904)

This hymn was written by Chadwick at his graduation from the Harvard Divinity School on 19 June 1864. It is a splendidly assured hymn of dedication and commitment, grandly noble in its vision of God, and responding to that vision with a firm resolution to uphold all that is best in human life. It is thus a poem of high ideals, written by a young man of purpose and conviction. It was written during the American Civil War, and the hymn may also be seen as a response to the conflict and its aims: the third verse, in particular, may be seen as aspiring towards a society in which freedom, love, and truth can prevail.

It was published in Alfred P. Putnam's *Singers and Songs of the Liberal Faith* (Boston, Mass., 1875), a fine collection of American Unitarian hymns. It was one of the many American hymns brought to Britain by W. Garrett Horder in his *Congregational Hymns* (1884), and it has since become widely accepted.

The customary tune is SONG 1, by Orlando Gibbons (1583–1625), one of the tunes which Gibbons wrote for George Wither's *Hymns and Songs of the Church* (1623). It is noble and stately, and seems to fit the mood of Chadwick's lines perfectly.

202

O little town of Bethlehem,
  How still we see thee lie!
Above thy deep and dreamless sleep
  The silent stars go by;
Yet in thy dark streets shineth
  The everlasting light,
The hopes and fears of all the years
  Are met in thee tonight.

O morning stars, together
  Proclaim the holy birth,
And praises sing to God the King,
  And peace to men on earth;
For Christ is born of Mary;
  And, gathered all above,
While mortals sleep, the angels keep
  Their watch of wondering love.

How silently, how silently,
  The wondrous gift is given!
So God imparts to human hearts
  The blessings of his heaven.
No ear may hear his coming;
  But in this world of sin,
Where meek souls will receive him, still
  The dear Christ enters in.

Where children pure and happy
  Pray to the blessèd child,
Where misery cries out to thee,
  Son of the mother mild;
Where charity stands watching
  And faith holds wide the door,
The dark night wakes, the glory breaks,
  And Christmas comes once more.

O holy child of Bethlehem,
  Descend to us, we pray;
Cast out our sin, and enter in,
  Be born in us today.
We hear the Christmas angels
  The great glad tidings tell:
O come to us, abide with us,
  Our Lord Emmanuel.

Phillips Brooks (1835–93)

Brooks, who was an outstanding American churchman of the nineteenth century (ending up as Bishop of Massachusetts), wrote this hymn for the children of his Sunday school at Holy Trinity Church, Philadelphia. He had visited Bethlehem in 1865, and the hymn, written afterwards, beautifully captures the atmosphere of a dark night in the little town. It was printed in leaflet form some time before December 1868, when it was sung at the church in Philadelphia; from there it found its way into an American hymn-book, *The Church Porch*, published in 1874. It has become an essential and much-loved part of American Christmas services, sung to its original tune by Lewis H. Redner. It was brought to Britain by W. Garrett Horder, in his *Treasury of Hymns* of 1896, and it has become very popular, sung to Vaughan Williams's inspired setting from an English folk song.

It is written in an unusual metre, an irregular double common metre: the syllables of the fifth line of each verse have to be stretched out to meet the tune. There is also a very attractive use of internal rhyme in lines 3 and 7 of each verse: that rhyme reminds us of the hymn's origins as a Sunday school carol, because those lines have a delightful chiming quality (not unlike a nursery rhyme) which sweetens the seriousness.

Not only does the hymn beautifully describe the little town asleep in the December night; it also gracefully modulates from a description of Christmas into an examination of the meaning of Christmas: first in its encouragement of charity and faith, and then into the coming of Christ into the human heart. After the magical repetition—'How silently, how silently'—the hymn proceeds to a touching and realistic acknowledgment of the importance of Christmas in a troubled world.

The tune in the United States is traditionally Lewis H. Redner's ST LOUIS, written for this hymn in 1868, and inescapably associated with it. In Great Britain, the most popular tune is Vaughan Williams's FOREST GREEN, put to these words in a brilliant piece of intuition for the *English Hymnal* (1906). The tune was that of an English folk song, 'The Ploughboy's Dream', sung to Vaughan Williams in 1903 by a Mr Garman, of Forest Green, near Ockley in Surrey. Another charming tune is CHRISTMAS CAROL, by Walford Davies, found in *Songs of Praise* and other books.

203

Dear Lord and Father of mankind,
　　Forgive our foolish ways;
Reclothe us in our rightful mind;
In purer lives thy service find,
　　In deeper reverence, praise.

In simple trust like theirs who heard
　　Beside the Syrian sea
The gracious calling of the Lord,
Let us, like them, without a word
　　Rise up and follow thee.

O sabbath rest by Galilee!
　　O calm of hills above,
Where Jesus knelt to share with thee
The silence of eternity,
　　Interpreted by love!

With that deep hush subduing all
　　Our words and works that drown
The tender whisper of thy call,
As noiseless let thy blessing fall
　　As fell thy manna down.

Drop thy still dews of quietness,
　　Till all our strivings cease;
Take from our souls the strain and stress,
And let our ordered lives confess
　　The beauty of thy peace.

Breathe through the heats of our desire
　　Thy coolness and thy balm;
Let sense be dumb, let flesh retire,
Speak through the earthquake, wind, and fire,
　　O still small voice of calm!

John Greenleaf Whittier (1807–92)

These lovely verses come from a very peculiar poem called 'The Brewing of Soma', published in the *Atlantic Monthly* of Boston, Massachusetts in 1872. Soma is a plant found in north-west India, used to make an intoxicating drug that was used in religious rituals. It helped to induce a state of frenzy: and Whittier, who was a Quaker and preferred quietness in worship, saw it as a parallel to certain religious practices of which he disapproved. He had been reading about Soma in Max Müller's *The Sacred Books of the East*, and because he disliked religious services which were noisy or enthusiastic, he saw a parallel between them and the Soma-induced intoxication:

And yet the past comes round again,
And new doth old fulfil;
In sensual transports wild as vain
We brew in many a Christian fane
The heathen Soma still!

This is followed immediately by 'Dear Lord and Father of mankind', and the six verses which make up the hymn.

It is often necessary to select in this way from Whittier's longer poems, and some remarkably beautiful hymns are the result. In the present case, the lines have become greatly loved since their introduction to hymn-books by W. Garrett Horder in his *Congregational Hymns* (1884). The appeal of calm and peace is very powerful, linked as it is with a call to 'purer lives' and 'deeper reverence'. Throughout the hymn there are words which are associated with quiet: a 'deep hush' subdues all our earthly cares, the call is a 'tender whisper', and the blessing which falls is 'noiseless'. The appeal is to that within all of us which longs for quietness—the 'still dews of quietness', and peace—'the beauty of thy peace'. It is at the opposite end of the devotional spectrum from those hymns which encourage activity and energy; but everyone experiences the need for quiet meditation at some time, and this hymn encourages an almost mystical contemplation of the peace of God 'which passes all understanding'.

This hymn was first sung to a tune called REST, by Frederick C. Maker (1844–1927), written originally for a hymn by the American poet W. B. Tappan, 'There is an hour of peaceful rest'. But there is no doubt that the great popularity of this hymn is owing to its association with REPTON, by C. H. H. Parry (1848–1918). The melody was written for the words beginning 'Long since in Egypt's plenteous land' from Act I of Parry's oratorio *Judith*, first performed in 1888. Parry had a pupil and friend, George Gilbert Stocks (1877–1960), who became director of music at Repton School, and who may have suggested to Parry that it could be used as a tune for these words. It appeared in *Repton School Hymns* (1924), and (although it was too late for the first edition) in the enlarged *Songs of Praise* (1931) and the *English Hymnal* (1933). Although REST is still used in some American books, REPTON has become a firm favourite elsewhere: the repetition of the last line of each verse seems to deepen the emotion significantly, and to aid the mood of quiet contemplation which is encouraged by the words.

204 Immortal Love, forever full,
     Forever flowing free,
    Forever shared, forever whole,
     A never-ebbing sea!

    Our outward lips confess the name,
     All other names above;
    Love only knoweth whence it came
     And comprehendeth love.

    We may not climb the heavenly steeps
     To bring the Lord Christ down;
    In vain we search the lowest deeps,
     For him no depths can drown;

    But warm, sweet, tender, even yet
     A present help is he;
    And faith has still its Olivet,
     And love its Galilee.

    The healing of his seamless dress
     Is by our beds of pain;
    We touch him in life's throng and press,
     And we are whole again.

    Through him the first fond prayers are said
     Our lips of childhood frame;
    The last low whispers of our dead
     Are burdened with his name.

    Alone, O Love ineffable!
     Thy saving name is given,
    To turn aside from thee is hell,
     To walk with thee is heaven.

     John Greenleaf Whittier (1807–92)

Like Whittier's 'Dear Lord and Father of mankind' this is part of a much longer poem. It was entitled 'Our Master', written in 1866 and first published in *The Tent on the Beach* (1867): it contains verses which have become other hymns, such as 'O Lord and Master of us all'.

  Whittier's Quaker sympathies are clearly seen in this poem. He condemns what he calls 'the bigot's partial plea' and 'the zealot's ban', and continues:

    Our Friend, our Brother, and our Lord,
     What may thy service be?—
    Nor name, nor form, nor ritual word,
     But simply following thee.

The poem became well known through its inclusion in Philip Schaff's *Christ in Song* (1870), and it was brought to Britain by W. Garrett Horder for his *Congregational Hymns* (1884). Horder selected a number of verses, and successive hymn-books have followed: the text above is that of the *English Hymnal*. It represents, very clearly, the ever-present love of God, which 'our outward lips' can speak of, but which cannot be understood except by love itself. That love is seen in the life of Jesus Christ, in the Passion (signified by Olivet) and in His earlier teaching (Galilee): and this love is with us from childhood to the final days of our lives. Finally, the selection suggests that hell is the turning away from love, and heaven is to walk with love: perhaps anticipating Emily Dickinson's more enigmatic lines:

> Parting is all we know of heaven
> And all we need of hell.

This hymn, in common metre, has been fortunate in attracting some lyrical tunes, well suited to its reflective verse and to the profound sweetness of its subject-matter. The best known is probably BISHOPTHORPE, a tune first printed in the eighteenth century and sometimes attributed to Jeremiah Clarke (*c*.1670–1707). Another is STRACATHRO, by a Glasgow musician, Charles Hutcheson (1792–1860); and a beautiful modern alternative is HARESFIELD, by John Dykes Bower (1905–81).

205   To God be the glory! great things he hath done!
So loved he the world that he gave us his Son;
Who yielded his life an atonement for sin,
And opened the life gate that all may go in.
Praise the Lord! praise the Lord! Let the earth hear his voice!
Praise the Lord! praise the Lord! Let the people rejoice!
O come to the Father, through Jesus the Son:
And give him the glory! great things he hath done!

O perfect redemption, the purchase of blood!
To every believer the promise of God;
The vilest offender who truly believes
That moment from Jesus a pardon receives.
Praise the Lord! . . .

Great things he hath taught us, great things he hath done,
And great our rejoicing through Jesus the Son;
But purer, and higher, and greater will be
Our wonder, our rapture, when Jesus we see.
Praise the Lord! . . .

Frances Jane van Alstyne (1820–1915)

Frances Jane van Alstyne, sometimes known by her maiden name of Fanny Crosby, was a voluminous and prolific writer whose work became very popular in revivalist meetings and evangelical crusades. This hymn was first printed in William Howard Doane's *Songs of Devotion* (1870), and it was popularized by Ira D. Sankey and Dwight L. Moody in their meetings. It appeared in Sankey's *Sacred Songs and Solos*, where its particular rhetoric of repetition is not out of place. It is simple in its ideas, but forceful in their expression, relying on a *fortissimo* emotionalism which is entirely appropriate for certain kinds of religious gatherings.

Of the many thousands of hymns written by Fanny Crosby (she is said for many years to have fulfilled a contract with a publisher to write three hymns every week) this one and 'Blessed Assurance, Jesus is mine' are the best known. Both are still sung with immense vigour, partly because of their tunes. This one, TO GOD BE THE GLORY, was written by W. H. Doane (1832–1915) for his 1870 book. Doane, like Mrs van Alstyne, was prolific: he wrote more than two thousand tunes, often to her words.

206
    Ho, my comrades! see the signal
      Waving in the sky!
    Reinforcements now appearing,
      Victory is nigh!
    'Hold the fort, for I am coming',
      Jesus signals still;
    Wave the answer back to heaven,
      'By thy grace we will.'

    See the mighty host advancing,
      Satan leading on;
    Mighty men around us falling,
      Courage almost gone!
    'Hold the fort . . .

    See the glorious banner waving!
      Hear the trumpet blow!
    In our Leader's name we'll triumph
      Over every foe!
    'Hold the fort . . .

    Fierce and long the battle rages,
      But our help is near;
    Onward comes our great Commander,
      Cheer, my comrades, cheer!
    'Hold the fort . . .

        Philipp Bliss (1838–76)

Bliss was a musician and evangelist, who worked in Chicago, and whose hymns were used by Dwight L. Moody and Ira D. Sankey in their missionary work. This hymn held pride of place as the first hymn in *Sacred Songs and*

Solos, Sankey's famous book of gospel hymns, with the text: 'That which ye have hold fast till I come', from Revelation 2: 25. It became very popular in the revival meetings which Moody and Sankey held in Great Britain in 1873 and 1874. Astonishingly, it found a place in the refined *English Hymnal* of 1906, and was retained in 1933: its rough vigour must have appealed to the editors, who elsewhere found the Victorianism of much English hymnody distasteful.

Bliss was a great opportunist in hymn-writing, able to transpose an event into a modern parable. In the present case, the hymn derives from a battle in the American Civil War. During Sherman's campaign in Georgia, his forces were at one point outflanked by those of the Confederate General Hood, which threatened a supply base at Allatoona Pass. General Corse, holding the supply depot with less than 2,000 men, refused to surrender to a force of more than 3,000. The Union forces were driven back to a small fort on Kennesaw mountain, and were in desperate straits when they saw the signal flags: 'Hold the fort; I am coming. Sherman'.

Six years later, in 1870, a Major Whittle told the story at a Sunday school meeting at Rockford, Illinois, when Bliss was present. His hymn became so well known that on his tomb at Rome, Pennsylvania are the words 'P. P. Bliss. Author of "Hold the Fort"'.

Bliss was not only the author of the lines, but the composer of the catchy tune, known in some books as HOLD THE FORT, from the refrain, which is perhaps better known than the verses.

207   Thy kingdom come! on bended knee
     The passing ages pray;
    And faithful souls have yearned to see
     On earth that kingdom's day.

    But the slow watches of the night
     Not less to God belong;
    And for the everlasting right
     The silent stars are strong.

    And lo, already on the hills
     The flags of dawn appear;
    Gird up your loins, ye prophet souls,
     Proclaim the day is near:

    The day in whose clear shining light
     All wrong shall stand revealed,
    When justice shall be throned in might,
     And every hurt be healed;

When knowledge, hand in hand with peace,
   Shall walk the earth abroad:
The day of perfect righteousness,
   The promised day of God.

Frederick Lucian Hosmer (1840–1929)

This hymn was written in 1891 for the Commencement of the Meadville Theological School, Meadville, Pennsylvania. It was called 'The Day of God', and published in Hosmer's *The Thought of God in Hymns and Poems* (1894).

The hymn begins dramatically with a phrase from the Lord's Prayer, and continues with an expansion of that prayer. The coming of the kingdom of God is portrayed as a slow process, but one which is as inevitable as the movement of the stars. Hosmer, who was a Unitarian minister, looks forward to a world in which there will be justice, righteousness, knowledge, and peace. He sees this as being not far off: although the night watches are slow, the dawn is already beginning.

The hymn's vision of the ultimate coming of the kingdom has survived a century and more of troubled strife, and it remains a powerful expression of the belief that at some time the world will witness the coming of the promised day of God.

The usual British tune is IRISH, from a Dublin Collection of 1749; a major American book, *The Hymnal 1982*, uses ST FLAVIAN, a noble Reformation psalm tune, set to Psalm 132 in Daye's *Psalter* of 1562.

208   Where cross the crowded ways of life,
            Where sound the cries of race and clan,
         Above the noise of selfish strife,
            We hear thy voice, O Son of Man.

         In haunts of wretchedness and need,
            On shadowed thresholds dark with fears,
         From paths where hide the lures of greed,
            We catch the vision of thy tears.

         From tender childhood's helplessness,
            From woman's grief, man's burdened toil,
         From famished souls, from sorrow's stress,
            Thy heart hath never known recoil.

         The cup of water given for thee
            Still holds the freshness of thy grace;
         Yet long these multitudes to see
            The sweet compassion of thy face.

O Master, from the mountain side,
　　Make haste to heal these hearts of pain;
Among these restless throngs abide,
　　O tread the city's streets again:

Till sons of men shall learn thy love,
　　And follow where thy feet have trod;
Till glorious from thy heaven above,
　　Shall come the City of our God.

Frank Mason North (1850–1935)

This fine hymn, entitled 'A Prayer for the Multitudes', was first published in North's magazine, *The Christian City* (June 1903), and then in the American *Methodist Hymnal* of 1905. North, a Methodist minister, was corresponding secretary of the New York Church Extension and Missionary Society from 1892 to 1912, and was deeply involved in 'inner-city' work. This hymn reflects his deep concern for the problems of a big city such as New York at the turn of the century: indeed, the imagery of 'crowded ways' which 'cross' suggests the grid pattern of an American city. Within the crossings of those streets, North discerns not only the 'wretchedness and need' but also the 'restless' state of the population. In this context, the final vision of the city transformed is a glorious one, bringing the idea of the new Jerusalem (from Revelation 21) into the situation of the modern world.

It has become a commonplace among contemporary hymn-writers that more attention should be paid to the plight of the city in the modern world: it is surprising, therefore, that this hymn (which says so much that should be said, and very well) is not better known. Its language is perhaps archaic (there is a modernized text in *Rejoice and Sing*) but its sentiments are wonderfully appropriate to the modern urban condition.

The tune which is most frequently used for these words is FULDA, from the *Sacred Melodies* of William Gardiner (1769–1853), published in 1815. In some books the tune is called GARDINER, after the composer, a Leicester stocking manufacturer and enthusiastic musician. Gardiner's book consisted of tunes from the great composers, and this one was claimed to be from Beethoven; but the connection has never been satisfactorily established. Another tune is ST BARTHOLOMEW, by Henry Duncalf (d. 1762).

The Early Twentieth Century

Hymns Ancient and Modern was the pre-eminent Church of England hymn-book for the last forty years of the nineteenth century. It was used not only in Great Britain, but throughout the British Empire; and other denominations, fired by its success, revised their own books throughout the 1870s and 1880s. The result was a substantial body of accepted hymnody, common to all denominations, with additional variations: the Wesleyans included much Charles Wesley, the Congregationalists plenty of Watts.

Signs of change first appeared with Robert Bridges's *Yattendon Hymnal*, printed in Oxford between 1895 and 1899 with the most elegant typeface and layout. In its appearance, and in its contents, it was making an aesthetic statement about Church worship that was designed to contrast with the serviceable plainness of *Hymns Ancient and Modern*. The *English Hymnal*, which followed in 1906, was another challenge to *A&M*: it was edited by a forward-looking committee, which included Percy Dearmer, and its music adviser was Ralph Vaughan Williams. Vaughan Williams made use of the folk songs and English traditional melodies which were being collected at the time, and swept away much of the Victorian music of *A&M*, relegating some of it to the Appendix. He wrote magnificent tunes himself, and encouraged others to do so: he probably had more influence upon twentieth-century hymnody than any other single individual. At the same time, the *English Hymnal* also included hymns of political and social concern by members of the Christian Social Union.

Songs of Praise, the other great hymn-book of the early twentieth century, dates from 1925; but the years between had witnessed the previously unimaginable terrors of the First World War of 1914–18, and the ensuing unrest throughout Europe. *Songs of Praise* attempted to answer this by a bold selection of hymns and poems, and by being educational, non-denominational, and liberal in theology. It was very successful, especially as a book for schools, where its fresh and lively approach was greatly appreciated. An enlarged edition appeared in 1931, with hymns by writers such as Eleanor Farjeon and Jan Struther.

209

Ye watchers and ye holy ones,
Bright Seraphs, Cherubim and Thrones,
   Raise the glad strain, Alleluia!
Cry out, Dominions, Princedoms, Powers,
Virtues, Archangels, Angels' choirs,
   Alleluia!

O higher than the Cherubim,
More glorious than the Seraphim,
   Lead their praises, Alleluia!
Thou Bearer of the eternal Word,
Most gracious, magnify the Lord,
   Alleluia!

Respond, ye souls in endless rest,
Ye Patriarchs and Prophets blest,
   Alleluia, Alleluia!
Ye holy Twelve, ye Martyrs strong,
All Saints triumphant, raise the song,
   Alleluia!

O friends, in gladness let us sing,
Supernal anthems echoing,
   Alleluia, Alleluia!
To God the Father, God the Son,
And God the Spirit, Three in One,
   Alleluia!

Athelstan Riley (1858–1945)

This exuberant hymn was written for the *English Hymnal* of 1906, of which Riley, subsequently a Jersey 'seigneur' (or Lord of the Manor), was one of the editors. As a young man Riley had travelled widely in the Middle East, and had written a book about Mount Athos and its monasteries (published 1887). He was a successor to John Mason Neale in his interest in the Eastern Church, and the hymn draws upon his knowledge of early theology, especially the thinking about angels.

A treatise of the sixth century proposed a heavenly structure of threes, descending in order from the central three, the Holy Trinity. The angel choir, for example, consisted of Seraphim, Cherubim, and Thrones; Dominations, Virtues, Powers; Principalities, Archangels, Angels. This treatise was passed off as the work of Dionysius the Areopagite, who was converted by St Paul during his visit to Athens (Acts 17: 34); it is now thought to be of a later date, and the author is therefore known as the Pseudo-Dionysius, but it had a great influence on medieval ideas of heaven and on the theology of angels.

Riley beautifully fits the nine orders into verse 1, and then moves to a more demanding contemplation of the glories of the Holy Trinity, which in its threefold unity is 'Bearer of the eternal Word'. The rejoicing then spreads outwards, through Patriarchs and Prophets, to the Apostles and Martyrs, and then to all the Saints; and finally to the glad company of worshippers on earth—'O friends, . . .'. The sixfold (sometimes sevenfold) 'Alleluia' in each verse sets up a pattern of rhythmic praise; and as it engages the ear in a repeated liturgy of exaltation, so the eye can think of the orders of angels and saints, rank upon rank as they are in a Renaissance painting. When sung to the music, the words of this hymn engage the senses abundantly and joyously. It is entirely fitting for the contemplation of the Communion of Saints: so is the exotic vocabulary of 'Supernal' (that which is on high, in the heavens).

In spite of its origins in a pre-medieval theology of saints and angels, this hymn has become very popular, especially in America, where it is found in most books. This popularity is almost certainly owing to the way in which the words fit the tune. They were written for it, but it is not often that such a successful interplay of sound and meaning is obtained. The tune, LASST UNS ERFREUEN ('Let us rejoice'), is a seventeenth-century German tune from Cologne, arranged by Vaughan Williams for the *English Hymnal* (1906), where Riley's words first appeared. It was one of the great new hymns of that book.

210

Judge eternal, throned in splendour,
  Lord of lords and King of kings,
With thy living fire of judgement
  Purge this realm of bitter things;
Solace all its wide dominion
  With the healing of thy wings.

Still the weary folk are pining
  For the hour that brings release;
And the city's crowded clangour
  Cries aloud for sin to cease;
And the homesteads and the woodlands
  Plead in silence for their peace.

Crown, O God, thine own endeavour;
  Cleave our darkness with thy sword;
Feed the faithless and the hungry
  With the richness of thy word;
Cleanse the body of this nation
  Through the glory of the Lord.

Henry Scott Holland (1847–1918)

This hymn was first published in the periodical *The Commonwealth* in July 1902. Holland, who was later to become Regius Professor of Divinity at Oxford, was editor of *The Commonwealth* at the time: he also advised the compilers of the *English Hymnal* of 1906, in which this hymn first became widely known.

It is based on Isaiah 33: 22: 'For the Lord is our judge, the Lord is our lawgiver, the Lord is our king: he will save us.' It is a hymn which eloquently reflects a concern for social reform which existed in the Edwardian age before the First World War, alongside the apparent confidence of the time. Holland was a founder of the Christian Social Union, and he and his colleagues were deeply conscious of the need for better living conditions in the cities and also in the countryside (clearly articulated in verse 2). His awareness of the 'bitter things' in society leads to a prayer for justice and peace, and for the removal of that bitterness in political and public life.

Some conditions have changed since Holland wrote the hymn. This can be seen particularly in verse 3, where his original line 3 was 'Feed the faint and hungry heathen', and line 5 was 'Cleanse the body of this empire'. He was obviously well intentioned, and his hymn reflects the widely held view which fuelled missionary endeavour throughout the time of the British Empire; but the collapse of that empire, and respect for other world religions, mean that the final verse no longer has the relevance of the first two. Even so, the plea for a reformed society and a better public life is still highly necessary, and it has never been better expressed in a hymn, except perhaps in G. K. Chesterton's 'O God of earth and altar'.

The customary tune is RHUDDLAN, a Welsh melody originally written for the harp, and published in Edward Jones's *Musical Relicks of the Welsh Bards* (second edition, 1805). It appeared with these words in the *English Hymnal* (1906), and has become firmly associated with them.

211
    O God of earth and altar,
       Bow down and hear our cry;
    Our earthly rulers falter,
       Our people drift and die;
    The walls of gold entomb us,
       The swords of scorn divide,
    Take not thy thunder from us,
       But take away our pride.

    From all that terror teaches,
       From lies of tongue and pen,
    From all the easy speeches
       That comfort cruel men,
    From sale and profanation
       Of honour and the sword,
    From sleep and from damnation,
       Deliver us, good Lord!

    Tie in a living tether
       The prince and priest and thrall,
    Bind all our lives together,
       Smite us and save us all;
    In ire and exultation
       Aflame with faith, and free,
    Lift up a living nation,
       A single sword to thee.

            G. K. Chesterton (1874–1936)

This hymn has much in common with Henry Scott Holland's 'Judge eternal, throned in splendour'. Like that hymn, it was first published in Holland's monthly periodical of the Christian Social Union, *The Commonwealth*, probably in 1905. It was then included in the *English Hymnal* (1906) and in *Songs of Praise* (1925).

    Like Holland, Chesterton was concerned at the state of the country at the beginning of the last century. His hymn uses emblems of corruption to suggest the ills of society: a people who are drifting and dying, spiritually; a nation consumed by greed and pride; and (in verse 2) a world in which lies are found in the press or in speeches, cruelty and terror abound, and honour has been profaned. The result is a comprehensive indictment of the Edwardian period, that time before the First World War which seems superficially so settled and peaceful. It is clear that, for the Christian Social Union and its followers, the need for the nation to be united in the pursuit of good was urgent: the strange imagery of the final verse, with the 'living tether' tying together three parts of the State, prince, priest, and thrall, suggests the need for a common aim. Chesterton is passionately arguing for a 'living nation', consisting of those in power, the Church, and the workers, united in purpose. It is a vision which has remained relevant, and transcended time and place: the imagery is applicable to almost any advanced industrial society of the twentieth or twenty-first centuries. The hymn packs a whole sermon on Christian social thinking into three verses.

Chesterton said that he wrote the words with the tune AURELIA ('The church's one foundation') in mind, believing that it was 'the typical tune for hymns'. However, in the *English Hymnal*, Vaughan Williams set it to an English folk song tune which he called KING'S LYNN, named from one of the places where he had heard it sung. It has become the customary tune for the hymn.

212   I vow to thee, my country, all earthly things above,
    Entire and whole and perfect, the service of my love:
    The love that asks no question, the love that stands the test,
    That lays upon the altar the dearest and the best;
    The love that never falters, the love that pays the price,
    The love that makes undaunted the final sacrifice.

    And there's another country, I've heard of long ago,
    Most dear to them that love her, most great to them that know;
    We may not count her armies, we may not see her king,
    Her fortress is a faithful heart, her pride is suffering;
    And soul by soul and silently her shining bounds increase
    And her ways are ways of gentleness and all her paths are peace.

Cecil Spring-Rice (1859–1918)

This hymn was written by a career diplomat. Sir Cecil Spring-Rice worked for the Foreign Office in various posts, and may have written these lines when he was in Stockholm from 1908 to 1913. From there he went to be British Ambassador in Washington in 1913, and, although suffering from ill-health, worked tirelessly to encourage good relations between Great Britain and the USA. There were many obstacles of isolationism and prejudice to be overcome before the USA entered the First World War on 3 April 1917, and (in the words of Arthur Balfour):

he steered his course with unfailing judgement and unwearied forbearance, at a time when a single false step might have had the most serious consequences for the cause which he represented, and he might well be proud to remember that at that great moment he was ambassador to Washington . . . .

The two stanzas were sent in a letter to the American Secretary of State, W. J. Bryan, on the eve of Spring-Rice's departure from Washington on 13 January 1918. He died at Ottawa a month later, 14 February, when about to embark on the ship to take him home. As one of his contemporaries wrote:

'He gave his life for his country as surely as though he had been slain in battle.'

The sending of the verses to Bryan gave rise to the story that Spring-Rice wrote them on the night before leaving office, and with a sense of his impending death. But a poem in two stanzas, entitled 'Urbs Dei' (the City of God), written in Sweden, may have been these lines. They signify, in their stately way, an ideal of public service that is rare and honourable, while looking beyond that ideal to a world of peace and love. The use of Proverbs 3: 17 in the last line is beautifully appropriate.

The hymn became widely known through its printing in *Songs of Praise* (1925), where it was set to THAXTED, by Gustav Holst (1874–1934), taken from his orchestral suite *The Planets* (1921), where its *Andante maestoso* represents Jupiter, 'the bringer of jollity'. The use of the melody as a hymn tune, and the marrying of it to these words, were a stroke of genius, perhaps by Percy Dearmer, the editor of *Songs of Praise*.

213
    Be thou my vision, O Lord of my heart,
    Be all else but naught to me, save that thou art;
    Be thou my best thought in the day and the night,
    Both waking and sleeping, thy presence my light.

    Be thou my wisdom, be thou my true word,
    Be thou ever with me, and I with thee, Lord;
    Be thou my great Father, and I thy true son;
    Be thou in me dwelling, and I with thee one.

    Be thou my breastplate, my sword for the fight;
    Be thou my whole armour, be thou my true might;
    Be thou my soul's shelter, be thou my strong tower:
    O raise thou me heavenward, great Power of my power.

    Riches I heed not, nor man's empty praise;
    Be thou mine inheritance now and always;
    Be thou and thou only the first in my heart:
    O Sovereign of heaven, my treasure thou art.

    High King of heaven, thou heaven's bright Sun,
    O grant me its joys after victory is won;
    Great Heart of my own heart, whatever befall,
    Still be thou my vision, O Ruler of all.

        Irish, eighth century, tr. Mary Byrne (1880–1931),
           versified by Eleanor Hull (1860–1935)

This ancient and wonderful Celtic hymn is found in an Irish manuscript of the eighth century in the Library of the Royal Irish Academy. It was translated by Màiri ni Bhroin (Mary Byrne), an expert in ancient Erse, and published in *Eriù*, an Irish learned journal, in 1905. This text is from the *BBC Hymn Book* (1951).

Eleanor Hull, who was founder and honorary secretary of the Irish Text Society, published her versification in her *Poem Book of the Gael* (1912). It was used as a hymn in the Irish *Church Hymnal* (1919), set to the tune SLANE. Its poetic expression of the attributes of Christ, who is indwelling in the soul and is the 'vision' of the heart, is found in the multiple images: in verse 3 He is strength (breastplate, sword, armour, shelter, tower), and elsewhere He is riches and joy (wisdom, treasure, light, heart). At the end there is a beautiful return to the opening idea of 'vision', to sum up the sense of the wholeness of Christ and His place in the human heart.

SLANE, which comes from an Irish folk tune used for a ballad, was published in 1909. It has been modified in several books in order to accommodate the slightly irregular metre of Hull's verses (just as Hull's lines have themselves been altered to fit the music better). It is so striking that it has had two other hymns written for it, Jan Struther's 'Lord of all hopefulness' (no. 216) for the enlarged *Songs of Praise* (1931), and Jack Winslow's 'Lord of creation! to thee be all praise', published in 1961.

214
When through the whirl of wheels, and engines humming,
 Patiently powerful for the sons of men,
Peals like a trumpet promise of his coming
 Who in the clouds is pledged to come again;

When through the night the furnace fires a-flaring,
 Shooting out tongues of flame like leaping blood,
Speak to the heart of Love, alive and daring,
 Sing of the boundless energy of God;

When in the depths the patient miner striving
 Feels in his arms the vigour of the Lord,
Strikes for a kingdom and his King's arriving,
 Holding his pick more splendid than the sword;

When on the sweat of labour and its sorrow,
 Toiling in twilight flickering and dim,
Flames out the sunshine of the great to-morrow,
 When all the world looks up because of him—

Then will he come with meekness for his glory,
 God in a workman's jacket as before,
Living again the eternal gospel story,
 Sweeping the shavings from his workshop floor.

   Geoffrey Anketell Studdert-Kennedy (1883–1929)

This astonishing hymn appeared in *Songs of Praise* (1925), but never became widely known, perhaps because no good tune was ever associated with it. It anticipates, and in many ways surpasses, all those hymns written since the 1950s which endeavour to address the problems of modern industry. Since it has become a commonplace that modern hymns should be modern, and should speak to the 'real' world, it is a pity that this early attempt to address the industrial world should be neglected. It includes within its vision railways, steelworks, and coal mines, each of which is treated as a marvellous example of applied science; each also involves human energy and skill, and the miner rejoices in his strength, just as the steelworker and railwayman see the wonders of whirling wheels and tongues of flame.

These things are wonderful, but verse 4 reminds us that there is also miserable toil, miner and steelworker sweating in twilight: it is into this situation that God will come. Studdert-Kennedy sees Him as a workman, in a workman's jacket as He would have been when He was a carpenter: His job is to clean up at the end of the day, 'sweeping the shavings from his workshop floor'. The daring metaphor suggests that God, at the end of the day of our lives, will do the 'cleaning up', putting things right when they have got into a mess: and since the first four verses combine the wonders of the industrial world with the problems of working in that world, the implication is that one day God will make all things right in His workshop of the modern world.

The decline of heavy industry in the last part of the twentieth century should not prevent a revival of this hymn. It is true that today we ought to be writing about computers rather than about coal mines, but the point about industry is made so well in this hymn that it transcends the accidents of recent economic development.

The tune in *Songs of Praise* was LOMBARD STREET, an odd choice of name (with its capitalist associations) for a hymn about workers. It has never become widely known. Nor has ST OSYTH, set to these words in *The School Hymn Book of the Methodist Church* (1950). The hymn might have become famous if it had had the good fortune to be set to a tune such as Michael Baughen's LORD OF THE YEARS, written half a century after Studdert-Kennedy's words.

215   Awake, awake to love and work,
                 The lark is in the sky,
             The fields are wet with diamond dew,
             The worlds awake to cry
             Their blessings on the Lord of life,
                 As he goes meekly by.

             Come, let thy voice be one with theirs,
                 Shout with their shout of praise;
             See how the giant sun soars up,
                 Great Lord of years and days;
             So let the love of Jesus come,
                 And set thy soul ablaze.

             To give and give, and give again,
                 What God hath given thee;
             To spend thyself, nor count the cost,
                 To serve right gloriously
             The God who gave all worlds that are,
                 And all that are to be.

         Geoffrey Anketell Studdert-Kennedy (1883–1929)

This hymn is taken from a poem by Studdert-Kennedy entitled 'At a Harvest Festival', beginning 'Not here for high and holy things/ We render thanks to thee, . . .'.

It was published in *The Sorrows of God, and other Poems* (1921), and used as a hymn in the enlarged *Songs of Praise* (1931), with verse 1, line 4 printed as 'The world's awake to cry'. In the original poem, the cry 'Awake, awake' is preceded by lines which offer thanks not only for 'the common things' but for 'the silver glistering' of the stars, and 'the silent song they sing',

             Of Faith and Hope and Love undimmed,
                 Undying still through death,
             The Resurrection of the world,
                 What time there comes the breath
             Of dawn that rustles through the trees,
                 And that clear voice that saith:

             Awake, awake, to love and work . . .

The buoyancy of Studdert-Kennedy's thought, which survived his harrowing experiences as an army chaplain in the First World War (where he became famous as 'Woodbine Willie', because he gave Woodbines (cigarettes) to the soldiers), is well caught in this hymn. His enthusiasm, and his work for the Industrial Christian Fellowship, were very much in accord with the mood of *Songs of Praise*, and this hymn is as much a part of its time as 'When through the whirl of wheels'. Both speak of a hope of a new world following the Armistice of 1918, a hope which was not to be fulfilled.

The tune in *Songs of Praise* was BRUNSWICK, a tune adapted from Handel. It is now more frequently sung to SHELTERED DALE, a tune derived from a German folk song, 'Das zerbrochene Ringlein'.

216   Lord of all hopefulness, Lord of all joy,
        Whose trust, ever childlike, no cares could destroy,
        Be there at our waking, and give us, we pray,
        Your bliss in our hearts, Lord, at the break of the day.

        Lord of all eagerness, Lord of all faith,
        Whose strong hands were skilled at the plane and the lathe,
        Be there at our labours, and give us, we pray,
        Your strength in our hearts, Lord, at the noon of the day.

        Lord of all kindliness, Lord of all grace,
        Your hands swift to welcome, your arms to embrace,
        Be there at our homing, and give us, we pray,
        Your love in our hearts, Lord, at the eve of the day.

        Lord of all gentleness, Lord of all calm,
        Whose voice is contentment, whose presence is balm,
        Be there at our sleeping, and give us, we pray,
        Your peace in our hearts, Lord, at the end of the day.

                                          Jan Struther (1901–53)

This hymn is a period piece, but a fine one. It was written for the enlarged edition of *Songs of Praise* (1931), to fit the folk tune SLANE, which had been used as a hymn tune in the Irish *Church Hymnal* (1919), where it had been used for 'Be thou my vision'. In *Songs of Praise* it was given the title 'All-Day Hymn': Percy Dearmer noted in 1933 that it had rapidly become a favourite among university students. It is eminently characteristic of its age, forward-looking, non-doctrinal, non-sectarian, and concerned with the world of waking, working, homecoming, and sleeping. It was one of the first hymn texts to use the 'You' form (in the possessives).

'Jan Struther', whose real name was Joyce Torrens (later Mrs A. K. Placzek), took her pseudonym from her mother's maiden name, Anstruther, and her own initial J. She later became the author of a best-selling novel, *Mrs Miniver*, about a middle-class family just before the Second World War: one of the tunes for this hymn is named MINIVER, in recognition of this; it was written by Cyril Taylor (1907–91), and is printed in the *BBC Hymn Book* (1951).

The principal tune, for which the words were written, is SLANE, found in a collection of *Old Irish Folk Music and Songs* published in 1909, and used for 'Be thou my vision' (no. 213).

217

> Morning has broken
> Like the first morning,
> Blackbird has spoken
>   Like the first bird.
>   Praise for the singing!
>   Praise for the morning!
>   Praise for them, springing
>   Fresh from the Word!
>
> Sweet the rain's new fall
> Sunlit from heaven,
> Like the first dewfall
>   On the first grass.
>   Praise for the sweetness
>   Of the wet garden,
>   . Sprung in completeness
>   Where his feet pass.
>
> Mine is the sunlight!
> Mine is the morning
> Born of the one light
>   Eden saw play!
>   Praise with elation,
>   Praise every morning,
>   God's re-creation
>   Of the new day!

Eleanor Farjeon (1881–1965)

This morning hymn will always be associated with *Songs of Praise*. It was written for the second edition of that book (1931) at the request of Percy Dearmer, the editor. He asked Eleanor Farjeon for a poem to fit the tune BUNESSAN 'on the theme of thanksgiving for each day as it comes.' Farjeon's brilliant response to this demanding request is this three-verse text which celebrates nature in all its freshness, and sees each morning as a re-creating of the first morning in Eden. Dylan Thomas does the same thing in 'Fern Hill', and I have sometimes wondered if Farjeon's text was somewhere in his mind:

> it was all
> Shining, it was Adam and maiden,
>   The sky gathered again
> And the sun grew round that very day.
> So it must have been after the birth of the simple light
> In the first, spinning place . . .

Farjeon's springy rhythm (dactylic/trochaic) is beautifully sustained, and the poem makes a delightful and charming morning hymn. It must have been sung by generations of British children in school assemblies; it was made popular in the USA by the folk-singer Cat Stevens.

BUNESSAN, which Dearmer called 'a lovely Gaelic tune', was first published in Lachlan MacBean's *Songs and Hymns of the Gael* (1888). It was used for a Christmas hymn, 'Child in the manger', in the *Revised Church Hymnary* (1927), and later in the *Appendix* (1936) to the Irish *Church Hymnal* (1919). The Gaelic original of that hymn was written by Mary MacDonald (1789–1872), who lived on the Isle of Mull, and was born there near the village of Bunessan, where a wayside memorial to her may be seen by visitors on their way to Iona.

218

> In Christ there is no east or west,
>   In him no south or north,
> But one great fellowship of love
>   Throughout the whole wide earth.
>
> In him shall true hearts everywhere
>   Their high communion find;
> His service is the golden cord
>   Close-binding all mankind.
>
> Join hands, then, brothers of the faith,
>   Whate'er your race may be;
> Who serves my Father as a son
>   Is surely kin to me.
>
> In Christ now meet both east and west,
>   In him meet south and north,
> All Christlike souls are one in him,
>   Throughout the whole wide earth.

John Oxenham (1852–1941)

John Oxenham was one of the pen-names of William Arthur Dunkerley, a businessman who turned to writing as a full-time career: this hymn comes from his libretto for a pageant entitled *The Pageant of Darkness and Light* (1908), produced for the London Missionary Society. It was published in his book of poems, *Bees in Amber* (1913), and included as a hymn in the enlarged *Songs of Praise* (1931). It has become widely used in English-language hymn-books in many countries, although the words have frequently been altered to avoid the exclusive language. A most politically correct version will be found in *Rejoice and Sing*.

It takes Kipling's famous lines, 'Oh, East is East, and West is West, and never the twain shall meet' ('The Ballad of East and West'), published in *Barrack-Room Ballads, and Other Verses* (1892). The message that such divisions are lost in Christ is simple but effective, and very suitable for a missionary society: there is an echo of Matthew 8: 11: 'many shall come from the east and west, and shall sit down with Abraham, and Isaac, and Jacob, in the kingdom of heaven'; and perhaps also of Galatians 3: 28: 'There is neither Jew nor Greek, there is neither bond nor free, there is neither male nor female: for ye are all one in Christ Jesus.' Although it no longer carries its original message as a statement of mission, this hymn has continued to be meaningful and relevant because of the imperatives of a multiracial and multicultural society in the twenty-first century.

The hymn is sung in the USA and Canada to a fine American tune, MCKEE, named after Elmer M. McKee, rector of St George's Church, New York. It was adapted by a notable black American singer, Harry Burleigh (1866–1949), who sang in that church, from a spiritual, 'I know the angel's done changed my name'. Other tunes that have been used for it include KILMARNOCK, ST BERNARD, and ST PETER.

219   *A toi la gloire, O Ressuscité*

> Thine be the glory, risen, conquering Son,
> Endless is the victory thou o'er death hast won;
> Angels in bright raiment rolled the stone away,
> Kept the folded grave-clothes where thy body lay.
>
> *Thine be the glory, risen, conquering Son,*
> *Endless is the victory thou o'er death hast won.*
>
> Lo, Jesus meets us, risen from the tomb;
> Lovingly he greets us, scatters fear and gloom;
> Let the Church with gladness hymns of triumph sing,
> For her Lord now liveth, death hath lost its sting:
>
> *Thine be the glory . . .*
>
> No more we doubt thee, glorious Prince of Life;
> Life is nought without thee: aid us in our strife;
> Make us more than conquerors through thy deathless love;
> Bring us safe through Jordan to thy home above:
>
> *Thine be the glory . . .*

Edmond L. Budry (1854–1932),
tr. Richard B. Hoyle (1875–1939)

This hymn comes from French-speaking Switzerland, where Budry was a pastor of a Free Evangelical Church. It was written in 1884, and first published in *Chants Évangéliques* a year later. It was probably inspired by hearing a German Advent hymn sung to Handel's tune: the present hymn was written to fit the music.

It was translated into English by Richard Hoyle for the first edition of *Cantate Domino* (1924), the hymn-book of the World Student Christian Federation. The first major British hymn-book to include it was the *Methodist Hymn Book* of 1933, and it has since become very popular as an Easter hymn of celebration. It is based on the gospel accounts of the Resurrection (with a brief allusion to St Thomas and doubt in verse 3), together with St Paul's commentary on it in 1 Corinthians 15. The word 'victory' echoes verse 57: 'But thanks be to God, which giveth us the victory through our Lord Jesus Christ', and 'death hath lost its sting' in verse 2 quotes verse 55.

The tune, MACCABAEUS, which carries the words so triumphantly, was adapted from a chorus in Handel's oratorio *Joshua* (1747), which was later added to his earlier work, *Judas Maccabaeus* (1746). It was quickly transformed into a hymn tune, and appeared in Thomas Butts's *Harmonia Sacra* (*c*.1753). It is an exercise in magnificence, very appropriate for a church which is singing one of its 'hymns of triumph'.

{12}

The Mid-Twentieth Century, and the Hymn Explosion

After the excitement of *Songs of Praise* (1925, enlarged 1931) came the uneasiness of the 1930s, called by Auden 'a low dishonest decade', and the Second World War. The first important hymn-books to appear after that were *Hymns Ancient and Modern Revised* (1950) and the *BBC Hymn Book* (1951): the latter was clearly influenced by the way in which 'the wireless', as it was known, was reaching out to a new audience, often without a traditional Church affiliation. It included many new hymns and tunes, under the inspired editorship of Cyril Taylor, whose own tune, ABBOT'S LEIGH, has become one of the best known of all twentieth-century hymn tunes. It found texts by writers such as Timothy Rees, and C. A. Alington: Alington's strong and dignified hymns are among the finest of the century in the grand style.

The 1960s are sometimes thought of as a decade in which old certainties, old lifestyles, and old deferences were swept away. Certainly it was a decade of change in worship, marked especially by the publication in 1961 of the New English Bible New Testament. Timothy Dudley-Smith's 'Tell out my soul', written directly out of an encounter with this new text, heralded a new age of hymnody, full of energy and purpose, as writers sought to find new expressions for ancient truths. This new hymnody, sometimes called the 'hymn explosion', found its outlet in the many supplements which appeared during these years, most notably *100 Hymns for Today* (1969) and *More Hymns for Today* (1980); while *Hymns for Today's Church* (1982) experimented boldly with new versions of old texts.

The hymns of this final section are those of this active, experimental, energetic period: they encourage us to look forward to a twenty-first century in which hymn writing will continue to be a stimulus to worship, the freshness of the new adding to the familiarity of the old. Above all, they testify to the continuing usefulness of hymns, not only as a part of worship, but also as expressions of the deepest elements of the human spirit.

220 God of love and truth and beauty,
    Hallowed be thy name;
Fount of order, law, and duty,
    Hallowed be thy name;
As in heaven thy hosts adore thee,
And their faces veil before thee,
So on earth, Lord, we implore thee,
    Hallowed be thy name.

Lord, remove our guilty blindness,
    Hallowed be thy name;
Show thy heart of loving-kindness,
    Hallowed be thy name;
By our hearts' deep-felt contrition,
By our minds' enlightened vision,
By our wills' complete submission,
    Hallowed be thy name.

In our worship, Lord most holy,
    Hallowed be thy name;
In our work, however lowly,
    Hallowed be thy name;
In each heart's imagination,
In the church's adoration,
In the conscience of the nation,
    Hallowed be thy name.

Timothy Rees (1874–1939)

This hymn was first printed in the *Mirfield Mission Hymn Book* (1922), in the same year that Timothy Rees became warden of the Community of the Resurrection at Mirfield. It was given wider circulation when it was included in the *BBC Hymn Book* (1951). It echoes the Lord's Prayer throughout, but links it specifically to concerns in the world: 'Our father, which art in heaven' is thus expanded to include God as a God of love, truth, and beauty, and also as a God of order, law, and duty. This gives force to the idea of 'on earth as it is in heaven', which underlies this first verse. The next two verses deal with the self and the world: with the hearts, minds, and wills of the people of God, and their work and worship; and finally, with the Church and the nation. It makes a hymn that is remarkably comprehensive in its understanding of the whole self, not only the inner self of heart and mind and will, but also the self that is a member of society, a worker and worshipper.

The hymn is written in a metre that is very close to that of 'God, that madest earth and heaven'. With the singing of 'Hallowed' on one note, the hymn could be sung to AR HYD Y NOS, which may have been in Timothy Rees's mind. Fortunately, the compilers of the *BBC Hymn Book* commissioned Herbert Murrill (1909–52) to write a tune for it, CAROLYN, which has since become closely associated with it.

221
Lord of beauty, thine the splendour
Shewn in earth and sky and sea,
Burning sun and moonlight tender,
Hill and river, flower and tree:
Lest we fail our praise to render
Touch our eyes that they may see.

Lord of wisdom, whom obeying
Mighty waters ebb and flow,
While unhasting, undelaying,
Planets on their courses go:
In thy laws thyself displaying,
Teach our minds thyself to know.

Lord of life, alone sustaining
All below and all above,
Lord of love, by whose ordaining
Sun and stars sublimely move:
In our earthly spirits reigning,
Lift our hearts that we may love.

Lord of beauty, bid us own thee,
Lord of truth, our footsteps guide,
Till, as Love our hearts enthrone thee,
And, with vision purified,
Lord of all, when all have known thee,
Thou in all art glorified.

Cyril Argentine Alington (1872–1955)

This splendid hymn was written while Alington was headmaster of Eton. It appeared as 'A Hymn' in *Eton Faces*, a book of verse both light and serious, which he published on leaving Eton to become Dean of Durham in 1933.

It is a hymn which anticipates a later interest by hymn-writers such as Albert Bayly in the world of nature and of science, seeing God in the beauty of the natural world and in the laws which govern the movement of the planets. That God, who is the Lord of all science, beauty, and life, is to become the Lord of all love, who exists in the universe that He has made but also in the human heart: so that at the end, He is glorified 'in all'.

The tune which is most commonly used for this hymn is REGENT SQUARE, by Henry Smart (1813–79) (used for 'Light's abode, celestial Salem'), although in *Hymns Ancient and Modern New Standard* it was set to a tune by Basil Harwood (1859–1949) called ST AUDREY. Presumably this was not particularly successful, because *Common Praise* uses GRAFTON, a nineteenth-century French tune.

222
Good Christian men, rejoice and sing!
Now is the triumph of our King!
To all the world glad news we bring:
Alleluia!

The Lord of life is risen for aye;
Bring flowers of song to strew his way;
Let all mankind rejoice and say:
Alleluia!

Praise we in songs of victory
That Love, that Life which cannot die,
And sing with hearts uplifted high:
Alleluia!

Thy name we bless, O risen Lord,
And sing today with one accord
The life laid down, the Life restored:
Alleluia!

Cyril Argentine Alington (1872–1955)

This Easter hymn was written for the enlarged edition of *Songs of Praise* (1931), to fit the tune GELOBT SEI GOTT ('may God be beloved'). The text is now frequently altered to ' Good Christians all' in the first line, and to 'Let all the world' at the end of verse 2. It is a noble Easter hymn, emphasizing the idea of Christ as 'Lord of Life', and His Resurrection as the 'glad news' of the continuance of that life in the face of death. The beautiful line 'Bring flowers of song to strew his way' is an echo of George Herbert's 'Easter': 'I got me flowers to strew thy way'. Alington imaginatively turns them into 'flowers of song', as the Church sings its springtime joy on Easter Day.

The magnificent tune, GELOBT SEI GOTT, is sometimes known as VULPIUS, after its composer, Melchior Vulpius. It appeared in his *Ein schön geistlich Gesangbuch* (1609), and was arranged by Henry George Ley (1887–1962) for *Songs of Praise* (1925), where it was set to 'The strife is o'er, the battle done'. Ley was director of Music at Eton when Alington was Headmaster there, and it is possible that the present hymn may have come from their association.

223

Ye that know the Lord is gracious,
　Ye for whom a corner-stone
Stands, of God elect and precious,
　Laid that ye may build thereon,
See that on that sure foundation
　Ye a living temple raise,
Towers that may tell forth salvation,
　Walls that may re-echo praise.

Living stones, by God appointed
　Each to his allotted place,
Kings and priests, by God anointed,
　Shall ye not declare his grace?
Ye, a royal generation,
　Tell the tidings of your birth,
Tidings of a new creation
　To an old and weary earth.

Tell the praise of him who called you
　Out of darkness into light,
Broke the fetters that enthralled you,
　Gave you freedom, peace, and sight:
Tell the tale of sins forgiven,
　Strength renewed and hope restored,
Till the earth, in tune with heaven,
　Praise and magnify the Lord!

Cyril Argentine Alington (1872–1955)

This hymn is a sustained exercise in hymnic grandeur, a paraphrase of a passage in 1 Peter 2, but more than that. Alington here uses the eight-line stanza, broken into two halves in each verse, to set out the duty of a Christian congregation: to be a 'living temple', and to praise God for having called them out of darkness into light. So the imperatives abound: 'see that ye . . . raise'; 'tell the tidings of your [new] birth'; 'tell . . . tell'; until the earth itself, in tune with heaven (an echo of Milton) shall 'praise and magnify the Lord'.

Alington wrote the hymn for Durham Cathedral, and the lines seem to take some of their grandeur from that magnificent building. In particular, the architectural metaphor (from 1 Peter 2: 3–9), in which Christ is the cornerstone, the sure foundation on which is raised the living temple, is highly charged with the sense of a great occasion in such a place. Line-by-line, the images fit beautifully into place: the ability to place and handle such quotation, to shape it into a hymn, is reminiscent of Charles Wesley in the eighteenth century or William Chatterton Dix in the nineteenth.

There are many fine tunes for this 8.7.8.7.D metre: the one usually used for these lines is the Welsh HYFRYDOL ('good cheer'), by R. H. Prichard (1811–87), published in 1844. It makes a fine and stately setting for these words.

224

Not far beyond the sea nor high
Above the heavens, but very nigh
   Thy voice, O God, is heard.
For each new step of faith we take
Thou hast more truth and light to break
   Forth from thy holy word.

The babes in Christ thy Scriptures feed
With milk sufficient for their need,
   The nurture of the Lord.
Beneath life's burden and its heat
The fully grown find stronger meat
   In thy unfailing word.

Rooted and grounded in thy love,
With saints on earth and saints above
   We join in full accord,
To grasp the breadth, length, depth, and height,
The crucified and risen might
   Of Christ, the Incarnate Word.

Help us to press toward that mark,
And, though our vision now is dark,
   To live by what we see;
So, when we see thee face to face,
Thy truth and light our dwelling-place
   For evermore shall be.

       George Bradford Caird (1917–1984)

This hymn was written about 1945, and used in the chapel of Mansfield
College, Oxford, where Caird trained for the Congregational ministry, and
where he later became Principal. It was first published in 1962, and became
widely known after its inclusion in *100 Hymns for Today* (1969).

It is an interesting example of a hymn written 'on top of' another hymn.
The *Congregational Hymnary* of 1916, which would have been in use in
Mansfield College Chapel when Caird was a student, contained a hymn by
George Rawson (1807–89), a Congregationalist hymn-writer of some note.
Rawson's hymn, 'We limit not the truth of God', has four verses, each of
which ends with the two lines:

       The Lord hath yet more light and truth
       To break forth from his word.

This fine hymn, which is little known outside the Congregationalist tradition (and has been left out of *Rejoice and Sing*, the United Reformed Church
hymn-book of 1991), had a note drawing the reader's attention to the fact
that these words were those of Pastor John Robinson, spoken to the Pilgrim

Fathers who were about to set sail for America in the *Mayflower* in 1620. It was remembered by one of those who heard it:

He charged us before God, and His blessed angels, if God should reveal anything to us by any other instrument of His, to be as ready to receive it as any truth by his ministry; for he was very confident the Lord had more light and truth yet to break forth out of His holy word.

Caird's hymn is strong because of its ability to incorporate such phrases (and others, especially from the Bible and from Charles Wesley) into a fine and singable verse form. As a twentieth-century hymn, it is new but traditional in the best sense.

One tune used for Caird's words is CORNWALL, by Samuel Sebastian Wesley (1810–76), from *The European Psalmist* (1872). It was used in the Second Supplement (1916) to the Old Edition of *Hymns Ancient and Modern*, and has since become well known for hymns in this metre. Another tune is MANNA, by J. G. Schicht, from his *Choral-Buch* of 1819.

225   By gracious powers so wonderfully sheltered,
   And confidently waiting come what may,
  We know that God is with us night and morning
   And never fails to greet us each new day.

  Yet is this heart by its old foe tormented,
   Still evil days bring burdens hard to bear.
  O give our frightened souls the sure salvation
   For which, O Lord, you taught us to prepare.

  And when this cup you give is filled to brimming
   With bitter suffering, hard to understand,
  We take it thankfully and without trembling,
   Out of so good, and so beloved, a hand.

  Yet when again, in this same world, you give us
   The joy we had, the brightness of your sun,
  We shall remember all the days we lived through,
   And our whole life shall then be yours alone.

      Dietrich Bonhoeffer (1906–45),
      tr. Fred Pratt Green (1903–2000)

This moving poem was the last written by Dietrich Bonhoeffer from prison. He was executed by the Nazis on 9 April 1945, a month before the end of the Second World War. This poem was sent to his mother in a letter of 28 December 1944, and was printed by Eberhard Bethge in *Brief und Aufzeichnungen aus der Haft*, translated into English as *Letters and Papers from Prison* (1953).

The German text, beginning 'Von guten Mächten', was printed in a youth hymnal *Die singende Schar*, published in Berlin in 1959. In 1971, the World Council of Churches wished to use it for *Cantate Domino* (1974), and Joseph Gelineau, the Jesuit musician and translator of the psalms, wrote a tune for it. Fred Pratt Green was then asked to provide an English version for *Cantate Domino*. There is one further verse, which is usually omitted in hymn-books:

> Now, when your silence deeply spreads around us,
> O let us hear all your creation says—
> That world of sound which soundlessly invades us,
> And all your children's highest hymns of praise.

Bonhoeffer's exemplary life and his martyrdom have given this text an authority which is unique among twentieth-century hymns. It is the last poem of a man who in 1939 was on a lecture tour of America, where he was pressed to stay, but who returned to Germany to become a part of the resistance to Hitler and the Fascists, where he was arrested in April 1943.

But the hymn stands on its own, without the need of special circumstances to justify its inclusion. Its penetrating insight is apparent from the first line onwards, and the beauty of that first line is part of the evident goodness of the whole hymn: there is nothing spectacular or pretentious about these lines: they state, clearly and unequivocally, Bonheoffer's trust in God through bad times and good: his awareness of temptation in verse 2; and his hope for the future in verse 4. That he did not live to be able to 'remember all the days we lived through' gives a last tragic twist to the hymn, but does not invalidate its supreme sense of trust in God.

Joseph Gelineau's tune for the German text was called LE CÉNACLE, after the house in Geneva where the World Council of Churches' Committee for *Cantate Domino* was meeting. Fred Pratt Green's text is normally sung to INTERCESSOR, by C. H. H. Parry, written for Ada R. Greenaway's 'O word of pity' in the 1904 edition of *Hymns Ancient and Modern*.

226
O Lord of every shining constellation
  That wheels in splendour through the midnight sky;
Grant us your Spirit's true illumination
  To read the secrets of your work on high.

You, Lord, have made the atom's hidden forces,
  Your laws its mighty energies fulfil;
Teach us, to whom you give such rich resources,
  In all we use, to serve your holy will.

O Life, awaking life in cell and tissue,
  From flower to bird, from beast to brain of man;
Help us to trace, from birth to final issue,
  The sure unfolding of your age-long plan.

You, Lord, have stamped the image on your creatures,
  And, though they mar that image, love them still;
Lift up our eyes to Christ, that in his features
  We may discern the beauty of your will.

Great Lord of nature, shaping and renewing,
  You made us more than nature's sons to be;
You help us tread, with grace our souls enduing,
  The road to life and immortality.

                              Albert F. Bayly (1901–84)

This hymn dates originally from 1950. It was a brave attempt to acknowledge the scientific discoveries of the twentieth century and incorporate
them into hymnody. It was entitled 'God's age-long plan'. The present text
comes from Bayly's *Rejoice Together*, published in 1982. Part 2 of that book
is subtitled 'Hymns from the collection *Rejoice, O People* revised and up-
dated'. *Rejoice, O People* (1950) had a version of this hymn using the 'thou'
form for God, and the present version sounds more normal in using 'you' to
describe the God of science and of nature. The only other alteration (which
fits in with the title) is in verse 3, line 4, where 'age-long' supersedes 'age-
less'.

Bayly's imagery is new in one place only, in the acknowledgment of 'the
atom's hidden forces'; but his vocabulary suggests a world that is new to
hymnody, with words such as 'constellation', 'cell', and 'tissue'. The prayers
alternate between the scientific 'to read the secrets' and 'to trace . . . the sure
unfolding' (which suggest the finding of God in the cosmos and in the
created world) and the traditional 'to serve your holy will' and 'discern the
beauty of your will'. The last verse turns the idea of 'nature' neatly round
upon itself: as human beings we are, or ought to be, 'more than nature's
sons', that is governed by something greater than the laws of the survival of
the fittest.

In its short life, this hymn has had many tunes. The original tune in
Rejoice, O People was entitled HOLLINGREAVE; it was by Maurice S. Leah,

minister of Leek Congregational Church. Another, RERUM CREATOR ('Creator of [all] things') was written by John Wilson and published in *Hymns for Church and School* (1964). In *Hymns Ancient and Modern New Standard* (1983), the hymn was set to ST OSYTH, and *Common Praise* (2000) uses HESLINGTON, by Richard Shephard.

227
    Lord, you have searched and known my ways
      And understood my thought from far;
    How can I rightly sound your praise
      Or tell how great your wonders are?

    Besetting me, before, behind,
      Upon my life your hand is laid;
    Caught in the compass of your mind
      Are all the things that you have made.

    Such knowledge is too wonderful,
      Too high for me to understand—
    Enough that the Unsearchable
      Has searched my heart and held my hand.

                  Peter G. Jarvis (1925–)

This hymn was written in 1951, when the author was a student for the Methodist ministry in Birmingham. It was included in the Methodist and Ecumenical book, *Hymns and Psalms* (1983) and in *Rejoice and Sing* (1991). It is a most beautiful and unassuming rendering of Psalm 139: 1–6: 'O Lord, thou hast searched me and known me'. Even the use of the word 'compass' (wide extent) comes from the psalm, in verse 3: 'Thou compassest my path and my lying down'. What differentiates the present text from the original psalm is its unobtrusive rhythmical certainty and secure rhyming, and also the final phrase, which suggests the mind of a little child: this contrasts beautifully with the mature seriousness that has gone before, and with the adult perception of the searching of the heart.

    This is a hymn in long metre, so many tunes would fit it. The one which is used in both the hymn-books named above is WINSCOTT, by Samuel Sebastian Wesley (1810–76), one of two versions of the tune found in his book *The European Psalmist* (1872). It has a remarkable last line, suddenly swerving into the relative minor key and rising dramatically before falling back at the close. It is very suitable for Jarvis's lines.

228

I danced in the morning
When the world was begun,
And I danced in the moon
And the stars and the sun,
And I came down from heaven
And I danced on the earth,
At Bethlehem
I had my birth.
Dance, then, wherever you may be,
I am the Lord of the Dance, said he,
And I'll lead you all, wherever you may be,
And I'll lead you all in the Dance, said he.

I danced for the scribe
And the pharisee,
But they would not dance
And they wouldn't follow me.
I danced for the fishermen,
For James and John—
They came with me
And the Dance went on.
Dance, then . . .

I danced on the Sabbath
And I cured the lame;
The holy people
Said it was a shame.
They whipped and they stripped
And they hung me on high,
And they left me there
On a Cross to die.
Dance, then . . .

I danced on a Friday
When the sky turned black—
It's hard to dance
With the devil on your back.
They buried my body
And they thought I'd gone,
But I am the Dance,
And I still go on.
Dance, then . . .

They cut me down
And I leapt up high;
I am the life
That'll never, never die;
I'll live in you
If you'll live in me—

I am the Lord
Of the Dance, said he.
Dance, then, wherever you may be,
I am the Lord of the Dance, said he,
And I'll lead you all, wherever you may be,
And I'll lead you all in the Dance, said he.

Sydney Carter (1915–)

This is not a hymn, strictly speaking; but it has appeared in so many hymn-books, and is sung at so many church services, that it is now a standard part of the singing material available for worship. It became extraordinarily popular in the 1970s, and at one time it was difficult to find any broadcast service which did not include it.

It was written about 1961, and appeared in Carter's *Green Print for Song* (1963). It is a sustained metaphor of the dance as a way of life, as opposed to the stillness of death: as put into the mouth of Jesus, it becomes a daring dramatic monologue, in which he affirms life, and life more abundantly, through the image of the dance and himself as 'Lord of the Dance'. As the author himself put it, Christ 'dances the shape and pattern which is at the heart of our reality'.

The words were written to fit the very beautiful tune, usually called SHAKER TUNE, from its origins in the community of Shakers in the USA. In a manuscript of 1848, it appears as 'Shaker allegro', set to the words ''Tis the gift to be simple, 'tis the gift to be free'. It was used brilliantly as a clarinet solo by Aaron Copland (1900–90) in his *Appalachian Spring* of 1943–4, and was first used as a hymn tune in *The Cambridge Hymnal* (1967).

The Shakers, or 'Shaking Quakers', were The United Society of Believers in Christ's Second Coming, founded in Manchester in 1747 by James and Jane Wardley. The Society emigrated to America in 1774, and flourished under the leadership of Ann Lee ('Mother Ann'), whose soul was sometimes said to have entered into the composers of their dances. For the Shakers, as Carter has pointed out, 'dancing was a spiritual activity'. It was connected with another favourite word, 'Travel':

The Shakers used it in a special sense: to labour in spirit, to 'travail', if you like, to bring to birth . . . Father William, an early Shaker, is reported to have 'travelled in song' for about two hours. You could travel so hard, dancing, that you wore out the floor.

Carter's sympathy with the Shakers is evident throughout *Green Print for Song* (the title is a play on the word 'blueprint'). It allows him to use their music, and the idea of dancing, to produce a truly original and imaginative song for worship.

229
            Born in the night,
                Mary's Child,
        A long way from your home;
            Coming in need,
                Mary's Child,
        Born in a borrowed room.

            Clear shining light,
                Mary's Child,
        Your face lights up our way;
            Light of the world,
                Mary's Child,
        Dawn on our darkened day.

            Truth of our life,
                Mary's Child,
        You tell us God is good;
            Prove it is true,
                Mary's Child,
        Go to your cross of wood.

            Hope of the world,
                Mary's Child,
        You're coming soon to reign;
            King of the earth,
                Mary's Child,
        Walk in our streets again.

                Geoffrey Ainger (1925–)

This short Christmas meditation was written in 1960, when the author was a Methodist minister at Loughton in Essex. He later moved to be part of a 'team ministry' at Notting Hill in London, where the hymn was published in *Songs from Notting Hill* (1964). It was published with music consisting of a melody with guitar chording: like 'Lord of the dance' it was an example of a new kind of song for worship, but it retains a formality of rhythm and rhyme which make it a good example of a mid-twentieth-century hymn. Its delicacy of language, especially in suggesting the plight of refugees or the homeless in verse 1, is helped by the short lines: and the verses neatly celebrate Christ's life on earth, His death on the Cross, and His coming to reign.

The tune, written by Geoffrey Ainger for these words, is called MARY'S CHILD. In addition to the original guitar music, it has been adapted for keyboard accompaniment and for other instruments.

230   Tell out, my soul, the greatness of the Lord!
         Unnumbered blessings, give my spirit voice;
       Tender to me the promise of his word;
         In God my Saviour shall my heart rejoice.

       Tell out, my soul, the greatness of his name!
         Make known his might, the deeds his arm has done;
       His mercy sure, from age to age the same;
         His holy name, the Lord, the Mighty One.

       Tell out, my soul, the greatness of his might!
         Powers and dominions lay their glory by.
       Proud hearts and stubborn wills are put to flight,
         The hungry fed, the humble lifted high.

       Tell out, my soul, the glories of his word!
         Firm is his promise, and his mercy sure.
       Tell out, my soul, the greatness of the Lord
         To children's children and for evermore!

                              Timothy Dudley-Smith (1926–)

These four verses, based on the *New English Bible* translation of the Magnificat (Luke 1: 46–55), have had a profound effect on the course of contemporary hymnody. There had been other writers of contemporary hymns before this, notably Albert Bayly; but the success of this version showed hymn-writers that new but traditional hymns could be popular if they were well written and set to a suitable tune. In this case, the secret lies in the superb accommodation of the words to the line, which gives a sense of assured confidence in the writing which carries over into the singing.

The author, later to become Bishop of Thetford, notes that it was written at Blackheath, London, in May 1961, 'after reading the opening line in a review copy of the New English Bible New Testament' (see *A Collection of Hymns, 1961–1981*, subtitled 'a source-book for editors'). Its first publication in a hymn-book was in the *Anglican Hymn Book* of 1965; and it would be difficult, if not impossible, to find a major hymn-book published since then which has not included it.

In 1965 it was set to a tune called TIDINGS, by William Llewellyn, and in *Youth Praise I* (1966) to a tune written by Michael Baughen. But in *100 Hymns for Today* (1969) it was set to WOODLANDS, by Walter Greatorex (1877–1949), director of music at Gresham's School, Holt, Norfolk for twenty-five years. This robust tune, with a forceful rhythm and a dramatic high note on 'soul' in the first line, carries the words superbly.

231   Timeless love! We sing the story,
           Praise his wonders, tell his worth;
        Love more fair than heaven's glory,
           Love more firm than ancient earth!
        Tell his faithfulness abroad:
        Who is like him? Praise the Lord!

        By his faithfulness surrounded,
           North and south his hand proclaim;
        Earth and heaven formed and founded,
           Skies and seas, declare his name!
        Wind and storm obey his word:
        Who is like him? Praise the Lord!

        Truth and righteousness enthrone him,
           Just and equal are his ways;
        More than happy, those who own him,
           More than joy, their songs of praise!
        Sun and Shield and great Reward:
        Who is like him? Praise the Lord!

                   Timothy Dudley-Smith (1926–)

This is a free version of Psalm 89: 1–18, written in 1970 and published in *Psalm Praise* (1973). The phrases 'for ever' and 'to all generations' occur twice in the opening verses, and these are echoed in 'Timeless'. The author has said that ' "North and South" I take to be symbolic of the universal sway of God (as one might say "from East to West") as indicated even more widely in verse 11 with its reference to the heavens and the earth.' Verse 12 of the psalm begins 'The north and the south thou hast created them.'

'Shield' in verse 3 is from verse 18 of the psalm (Revised Version). 'Sun and Shield' come from Psalm 84: 11, and 'Shield and great Reward' are from Genesis 15: 1. These echoes of different biblical passages are important as enriching the principal idea of the psalm, which is a celebration of the mercies of God, but also His strength, justice, judgement, righteousness, and defence. The present version transforms these by adding the word 'love', as Herbert does in 'The God of love my shepherd is'. Dudley-Smith is reading the psalm with New Testament eyes, much as Isaac Watts did when he 'Christianized' the psalms in 1719.

A tune by Norman Warren (1934–) was written for this hymn in *Psalm Praise*. A more familiar tune which is sometimes used is ALL SAINTS, by William Henry Monk, used in the first edition of *Hymns Ancient and Modern* for 'Who are these like stars appearing'.

232
> In Adam we have all been one,
>   One huge rebellious man;
> We all have fled that Evening Voice
>   That sought us as we ran.
>
> We fled thee and, in losing thee,
>   We lost our brother too;
> Each singly sought and claimed his own,
>   Each man his brother slew.
>
> But thy strong love, it sought us still,
>   And sent thine only Son
> That we might hear his Shepherd's voice
>   And, hearing him, be one.
>
> O thou who, when we loved thee not,
>   Didst love and save us all,
> Thou great Good Shepherd of mankind,
>   O hear us when we call.
>
> Send us thy Spirit, teach us truth;
>   Thou Son, O set us free
> From fancied wisdom, self-sought ways,
>   To make us one in thee.
>
> Then shall our song united rise
>   To thine eternal throne,
> Where with the Father evermore
>   And Spirit thou art one.

Martin Franzmann (1907–76)

This hymn was first published in a Lutheran collection of new hymns, *A New Song* (1963), and then in a *Worship Supplement* (1969) published by the Missouri Synod of the Lutheran Church in America. It was subsequently included in the *Lutheran Book of Worship* (1978), and other books such as *More Hymns for Today* (1980) and *Hymns and Psalms* (1983).

Franzmann was a mid-Western American Lutheran, brought up in a German-speaking family and later a professor of New Testament at Concordia Seminary, St Louis. He had a particular interest in language, and chose his words very carefully: the 'huge' in verse 1 is clearly designed to emphasize the vast implications of the Fall, which is referred to in the reference to the Evening Voice and to the first murder of Abel by Cain. The hymn is a classic statement of the Fall and the Redemption, but with a call to be one with others, and with God, free from pride and 'fancied wisdom'. It is a plea for humanity rather than individualism: although we are all one in Adam, as sinners, we now find ourselves 'singly' seeking our own good; only when we are freed from 'self-sought ways' will we find a 'song united'.

The hymn is in common metre, so that it can be sung to many tunes. In *More Hymns for Today* and *Hymns and Psalms* it has been set to ST NICHOLAS, an eighteenth-century tune from Israel Holdroyd's *The Spiritual Man's Companion* (1753). Another tune which has been associated with it is ST MARY, a Welsh tune from Edmund Prys's *Llyfr y Psalmau* (1621).

233

Creator of the earth and skies,
　　To whom all truth and power belong,
Grant us your truth to make us wise;
　　Grant us your power to make us strong.

We have not known you: to the skies
　　Our monuments of folly soar;
And all our self-wrought miseries
　　Have made us trust ourselves the more.

We have not loved you: far and wide
　　The wreckage of our hatred spreads,
And evils wrought by human pride
　　Recoil on unrepentant heads.

For this, our foolish confidence,
　　Our pride of knowledge and our sin,
We come to you in penitence;
　　Your work of grace in us begin.

We long to end this worldwide strife:
　　How shall we follow in your way?
Speak to our souls the quickening word,
　　And turn our darkness into day.

Donald Wynn Hughes (1911–67)

This hymn comes from *Hymns for Church and School* (1964), although the text was subsequently amended. Its author, who was headmaster of Rydal School in North Wales, was a much-loved hymn-writer before his death following a car accident: he wrote, among other things, a new version of Jeremiah Rankin's 'God be with you till we meet again'.

This hymn is notable for its modernity, and for its plain speaking. The portrayal of the 'monuments of folly' captures the whole sense of a civilization that has built skyscrapers rather than churches; and those skyscrapers become monuments to human folly, emblems of a world of profit-making without a care for the things of the spirit. The 'self-wrought miseries' of our modern age produce a vicious circle, in which we put our trust in ourselves rather than in God, the forgotten 'creator of the earth and skies'. The conventional first verse gives way to a description of a world torn by hatred and strife: the hymn then forcefully acknowledges the problems of modern living, is penitent, and prays for grace.

It is written in long metre, so that it can be sung to a number of tunes. In *100 Hymns for Today* and *Common Praise* it is set to AGINCOURT, using a fifteenth-century tune for a modern hymn; in *Hymns and Psalms* it is set to PLAISTOW, an eighteenth-century tune; and in *Rejoice and Sing* it has TROY COURT, by Walter Stanton (1891–1978), a twentieth-century tune for a twentieth-century hymn.

234

We turn to you, O God of every nation,
  Giver of good and origin of life;
Your love is at the heart of all creation,
  Your hurt is people's pain in war and death.

We turn to you that we may be forgiven
  For crucifying Christ on earth again.
We know that we have never wholly striven
  To share with all the promise of your reign.

Free every heart from pride and self-reliance,
  Our ways of thought inspire with simple grace;
Break down among us barriers of defiance,
  Speak to the soul of all the human race.

On all who rise on earth for right relations
  We pray the light of love from hour to hour.
Grant wisdom to the leaders of the nations,
  The gift of carefulness to those in power.

Teach us, good Lord, to serve the need of others,
  Help us to give and not to count the cost.
Unite us all to live as sisters, brothers,
  Defeat our Babel with your Pentecost!

                                        Fred Kaan (1929–)

This hymn was written in 1965 for use on United Nations Sunday, when Fred Kaan was a Congregationalist minister at the Pilgrim Church in Plymouth. It was published in his *Pilgrim Praise* (1968), a collection of his hymns written during that time. It has been considerably altered since its original printing (to avoid some gender-based language, and some military imagery): the text above is that found in *Rejoice and Sing* (1991).

It is characteristic of Fred Kaan's hymnody of high purpose and social endeavour, which is sometimes reminiscent of the hymns of the Christian Social Union at the beginning of the twentieth century, such as 'Judge eternal, throned in splendour' and 'O God of earth and altar'. This hymn is a similar prayer for peace and justice, for forgiveness, and for wise government: it is lifted at the end by the contrast between human Babel (the symbol of a failure of understanding between nations) and the divine Pentecost. In that moment, as described in Acts 2: 7–11, people of all different languages could understand the disciples: it was as though the Babel failures had been broken down by the power of the Holy Spirit. The final line is therefore an apt summary of the hymn's plea for international understanding.

The tune normally used is INTERCESSOR, by C. H. H. Parry (1848–1918), which is the tune to which the hymn was first sung in 1965. It was first published in *Hymns Ancient and Modern* (1904), and has since been used for many hymns in this metre, including Bonhoeffer's 'By gracious powers'.

235

God of freedom, God of justice,
you whose love is strong as death,
you who saw the dark of prison,
you who knew the price of faith—
    touch our world of sad oppression
    with your Spirit's healing breath.

Rid the earth of torture's terror,
you whose hands were nailed to wood;
hear the cries of pain and protest,
you who shed the tears and blood—
    move in us the power of pity
    restless for the common good.

Make in us a captive conscience
quick to hear, to act, to plead;
make us truly sisters, brothers
of whatever race or creed—
    teach us to be fully human,
    open to each other's need.

Shirley Erena Murray (1931–)

This hymn is printed out of chronological order because, like the previous hymn, it was written to draw attention to the problems of the world. It dates from 1980, for a service held by Amnesty International, and was later printed in Murray's *In Every Corner, Sing* (1992). She described the hymn as 'one of my first "gap-fillers"': 'I wrote it for Amnesty International's Campaign Against Torture when I could find nothing relevant to sing at a service for Prisoners of Conscience.' As Fred Kaan's hymn prays for the work of the United Nations, so this one confronts the horrors of imprisonment and torture and lends support to the vital work of Amnesty International in drawing attention to tyranny, cruelty, and wickedness.

Shirley Erena Murray is a New Zealand hymn-writer. Her work includes a delightful Antipodean carol, sometimes called 'Upsidedown Christmas':

> Carol our Christmas, an upside down Christmas
> Snow is not falling and trees are not bare . . .

in which 'Right side up Christmas belongs to the universe'.

The present hymn was first sung to PICARDY (used for 'Let all mortal flesh keep silence'), but *In Every Corner, Sing* sets it to the tune TREDEGAR, written by Guthrie Foote for the Australian book, *Sing Alleluia*. It has also been set to RHUDDLAN (used for 'Judge eternal, throned in splendour'), which is very effective with these words.

236   We have a gospel to proclaim,
                    Good news for all throughout the earth;
              The gospel of a Saviour's name:
                    We sing his glory, tell his worth.

              Tell of his birth at Bethlehem,
                    Not in a royal house or hall,
              But in a stable, dark and dim,
                    The Word made flesh, a light for all.

              Tell of his death at Calvary:
                    Hated by those he came to save,
              In lonely suffering on the cross,
                    For all he loved his life he gave.

              Tell of that glorious Easter morn:
                    Empty the tomb, for he was free.
              He broke the power of death and hell
                    That we might share his victory.

              Tell of his reign at God's right hand,
                    By all creation glorified.
              He sends his Spirit on his church
                    To live for him, the Lamb who died.

              Now we rejoice to name him King:
                    Jesus is Lord of all the earth.
              This gospel-message we proclaim:
                    We sing his glory, tell his worth.

                          Edward J. Burns (1938–)

This hymn dates from 1968. It was written for the Chorley Deanery of the Diocese of Blackburn, Lancashire. The diocese was engaged on a 'Call to Mission', and the four meetings to expound the call dealt with the themes of verses 2 to 5: Incarnation, Crucifixion, Resurrection, Pentecost. These are given an introduction and a conclusion, to make a forceful and straight-forward modern 'proclaiming' of the gospel. It was first published in *100 Hymns for Today* in 1969, just a year after its composition.

The tune which has customarily been used is FULDA, from William Gardiner's *Sacred Melodies* (1815). This is the tune which the author had in mind when writing the words.

237
I come with joy, a child of God,
    forgiven, loved and free,
the life of Jesus to recall,
    in love laid down for me.

I come with Christians far and near
    to find, as all are fed,
the new community of love
    in Christ's communion bread.

As Christ breaks bread, and bids us share,
    each proud division ends.
The love that made us, makes us one,
    and strangers now are friends.

The Spirit of the risen Christ,
    unseen, but ever near,
is in such friendship better known,
    alive among us here.

Together met, together bound
    by all that God has done,
we'll go with joy, to give the world
    the love that makes us one.

Brian Wren (1936–)

This hymn for Holy Communion has been printed in many books, often in an earlier version beginning 'I come with joy to meet my Lord'. It was written in 1968, and the author has revised it at least twice, first to remove phrases such as 'Man's true community of love' (verse 2, line 3), and more recently to change the language of 'Lord' in the first line (see Wren's *What Language Shall I Borrow?*, 1989, subtitled 'God-Talk in Worship: a Male Response to Feminist Theology').

It is a hymn which movingly and effectively describes the processes of Holy Communion: the coming to Christ in His forgiveness; the coming together, in the partaking of the bread, becoming as one (in the witty juxta-position of 'made us, makes us'); and the going out into the world.

A tune frequently used for this hymn in Great Britain is Gordon Slater's ST BOTOLPH, a tune with a lilting and very beautiful melodic line, written in 1929 and printed in the 1931 edition of *Songs of Praise*. It was named after the parish church of Boston, Lincolnshire, where Slater was organist from 1919 to 1927. Another tune for this hymn is LAND OF REST, the American folk hymn tune collected by Annabel Morris Buchanan and published in her *Folk Hymns of America* (1938). Some American and Canadian books use DOVE OF PEACE, from a tune book called *The Southern Harmony* of 1835. This tune requires the last line to be repeated.

238

> For the fruits of his creation,
> Thanks be to God;
> For his gifts to every nation,
> Thanks be to God;
> For the ploughing, sowing, reaping,
> Silent growth while we are sleeping,
> Future needs in earth's safe-keeping,
> Thanks be to God.
>
> In the just reward of labour,
> God's will is done;
> In the help we give our neighbour,
> God's will is done;
> In our world-wide task of caring
> For the hungry and despairing,
> In the harvests we are sharing,
> God's will is done.
>
> For the harvests of his Spirit,
> Thanks be to God;
> For the good we all inherit,
> Thanks be to God;
> For the wonders that astound us,
> For the truths that still confound us,
> Most of all, that love has found us,
> Thanks be to God.
>
> Fred Pratt Green (1903–2000)

This hymn was written in 1970, and published in *The Methodist Recorder* in August of that year. It proved instantly popular, and was used by many churches for their harvest festival services in that year. It has since been adopted by many hymn-books as a fine harvest hymn for the contemporary world. In the place of the 'harvest home' sentiments of the nineteenth century, there are now references to the just reward for labour, caring for the hungry, and sharing of the earth's goods. In verse 2 there is a very appropriate suggestion of Deuteronomy 24: 19–21, with its references to the field, and the olive tree, and the vine: at the end of the harvest, there should be something left over for the stranger, the fatherless, and the widow.

The hymn was written for the tune EAST ACKLAM, by Francis Jackson (1917–), then organist of York Minster. It had been composed for the words 'God that madest earth and heaven', as an alternative to AR HYD Y NOS ('All through the night'). The power of AR HYD Y NOS was such that EAST ACKLAM was neglected until Pratt Green wrote these words for it. It is an example of the way in which, often at the suggestion of John Wilson (1905–92), who was Director of Music at Charterhouse and a tireless encourager of the best modern hymns, new words could be used by Pratt Green to revive tunes: a conspicuous example is 'When in our music, God is glorified', which brought Stanford's ENGELBERG back into use.

The hymn can, of course, be sung to AR HYD Y NOS, but the author prefers the modern tune for which the words were written.

239   When, in our music, God is glorified,
        And adoration leaves no room for pride,
        It is as though the whole creation cried:
         Alleluia!

        How often, making music, we have found
        A new dimension in the world of sound,
        As worship moved us to a more profound
         Alleluia!

        So has the Church, in liturgy and song,
        In faith and love, through centuries of wrong,
        Borne witness to the truth in every tongue:
         Alleluia!

        And did not Jesus sing a Psalm that night
        When utmost evil strove against the Light?
        Then let us sing, for whom he won the fight:
         Alleluia!

Let every instrument be tuned for praise!
Let all rejoice who have a voice to raise!
And may God give us faith to sing always:
Alleluia! Amen.

Fred Pratt Green (1903–2000)

This hymn was written in 1972 at the suggestion of John Wilson (see note to previous hymn). Wilson noted the lack of a good text to be sung to Charles Villiers Stanford's ENGELBERG, which had been written for 'For all the saints who from their labours rest' and superseded by Vaughan Williams's magnificent SINE NOMINE.

Wilson urged Pratt Green to write a text for a Festival of Praise (and it has, indeed, been sung at the Three Choirs Festival) which could be sung to Stanford's neglected tune. Pratt Green based it on Psalm 150, but included the gospel story from Mark 14: 26 in verse 4; and the language and poetic idiom are appropriately modern, especially in verse 2. In *The Hymns and Ballads of Fred Pratt Green* (1982) it was given the title (perhaps from the J. B. Priestley novel) 'Let the people sing!' It originally began 'When in man's music', which the author altered with some reluctance, believing that the strong contrast between man and God was helpful in that line.

It has since found its way into most modern hymn-books, on both sides of the Atlantic. It is usually sung to the splendid tune ENGELBERG, for which the words were written, and which includes the necessary 'Amen'. Another tune, set to these words by Ida Prins-Buttle (1908–93), is entitled MIRIAM.

240   God in his love for us lent us this planet,
Gave it a purpose in time and in space:
Small as a spark from the fire of creation,
Cradle of life and the home of our race.

Thanks be to God for its bounty and beauty,
Life that sustains us in body and mind:
Plenty for all, if we learn how to share it,
Riches undreamed of to fathom and find.

Long have our human wars ruined its harvest;
Long has earth bowed to the terror of force;
Long have we wasted what others have need of,
Poisoned the fountain of life at its source.

Earth is the Lord's: it is ours to enjoy it,
Ours, as his stewards, to farm and defend.
From its pollution, misuse and destruction,
Good Lord deliver us, world without end!

Fred Pratt Green (1903–2000)

This ecological hymn appeared in *Sixteen Hymns on the Stewardship of the Environment*, a collection of hymns organized by the Hymn Society of America in the 1970s. In that collection it had a further hard-hitting verse, not only attacking the careless but also excoriating a culture which was concerned only with profit:

> Casual despoilers, or high-priests of Mammon,
> Selling the future for present rewards,
> Careless of life and contemptuous of beauty:
> Bid them remember: the Earth is the Lord's.

The hymn has been printed in a number of modern hymn-books: it is a good example of the use of the hymn form to address an important concern, not just for the church but for the world.

Its metre is the same as that of 'Brightest and best of the sons of the morning', and it can be sung to LIEBSTER IMMANUEL, or other tunes in that metre such as QUEDLINBURG (for Neale's 'Stars of the morning, so gloriously bright'). It is most frequently set to a very suitable, easy-to-sing tune by Valerie Ruddle (1932–) appropriately entitled STEWARDSHIP, written for these words at the suggestion of the author.

241
> Give to me, Lord, a thankful heart
> and a discerning mind;
> give, as I play the Christian's part,
> the strength to finish what I start
> and act on what I find.
>
> When, in the rush of days, my will
> is habit-bound and slow
> help me to keep in vision still
> what love and power and peace can fill
> a life that trusts in you.
>
> By your divine and urgent claim
> and by your human face
> kindle our sinking hearts to flame
> and as you teach the world your name
> let it become your place.
>
> Jesus, with all your Church I long
> to see your kingdom come:
> show me your way of righting wrong
> and turning sorrow into song
> until you bring me home.

Caryl Micklem (1925–)

This attractive hymn was written to fit its lilting tune, GATESCARTH, also by Caryl Micklem. He wrote the tune about 1972 as a setting for Fred Pratt Green's hymn, 'O God of all, our Servant God'. The words were written for *New Church Praise*, the United Reformed Church supplement of 1975. The hymn has since become widely known and frequently reprinted: in *Broadcast Praise* (1981) an arrangement was made for four voices to replace the original unison version.

The hymn begins with thankfulness, but continues as a prayer for strength to 'play the Christian's part' in the drama of life: Micklem is particularly concerned with the life of the Spirit, which needs to be nourished, and which will lead eventually to the coming of the kingdom of God upon earth. The Christian's part in this process is to do the right ('righting wrong') and bring comfort ('turning sorrow into song'), before entering into that rest which is reserved for the people of God. The last line is a very touching use of the metaphor of coming home to God at the end of life.

The name of the tune, GATESCARTH, refers to a farm in the Lake District, near Buttermere, by the path (or 'gate') to the Scarth Gap.

242   Can we by searching find out God
      Or formulate his ways?
    Can numbers measure what he is
      Or words contain his praise?

    Although his being is too bright
      For human eyes to scan,
    His meaning lights our shadowed world
      Through Christ, the Son of Man.

    Our boastfulness is turned to shame,
      Our profit counts as loss,
    When earthly values stand beside
      The manger and the cross.

    We there may recognise his light,
      May kindle in its rays,
    Find there the source of penitence,
      The starting-point for praise.

    There God breaks in upon our search,
      Makes birth and death his own:
    He speaks to us in human terms
      To make his glory known.

        Elizabeth Cosnett (1936–)

This is a fine example of a modern hymn: it is written without fuss, but with a precision and economy that seem absolutely right. The vocabulary is neither ancient nor modern; the rhythms are exact; and there is no sense of straining for effect. The initial enquiry, which is from Job 11: 7, allows the answer to emerge from the contemplation of the two great pivotal moments of incarnational theology, symbolized by the manger and the Cross. It is there that we see the glory of God made known in images of birth and death.

The hymn was written in the early 1970s, and was first published in *More Hymns for Today* (1980), where it was entitled 'The Light of Christ', with the opening line 'Can man by searching find out God'. It was occasioned by a series of Bible study meetings on St Luke's Gospel, and the author has said that she hoped 'to say some things about the Incarnation which would make sense both to traditionalists and to the avant-garde.' She was clearly concerned about the difficulties of communicating the gospel in ways which would hurt neither of these groups. In a letter to the General Editor of *The Hymnal 1982 Companion*, she wrote:

I was at that time involved with a Bible study group . . . in which the question of how to interpret the stories of the birth of Jesus loomed large and caused not merely intellectual debate but real distress to individuals. I badly wanted to put into words what I myself felt to be the meaning of the incarnation for me but [in] such a way that we could all sing them together without feeling that either our faith or our intellectual integrity was being undermined.

Because it is written in common metre, this hymn can be sung to many tunes. *More Hymns for Today* used EPWORTH, by Charles Wesley the younger (1757–1834), but this was dropped in *Common Praise* in favour of a solid old favourite, ST BERNARD (used for 'All ye that seek for sure relief'). *Hymns and Psalms* uses KILMARNOCK, by Neil Dougall (1776–1862) and *Rejoice and Sing* uses a lovely twentieth-century tune, HARESFIELD, by John Dykes Bower (1905–81).

243

New songs of celebration render
  To him who has great wonders done.
Awed by his love, his foes surrender
  And fall before the mighty one.
He has made known his great salvation
  Which all his friends with joy confess:
He has revealed to every nation
  His everlasting righteousness.

Joyfully, heartily resounding,
  Let every instrument and voice
Peal out the praise of grace abounding,
  Calling the whole world to rejoice.
Trumpets and organs, set in motion
  Such sounds as make the heavens ring;
All things that live in earth and ocean,
  Make music for your mighty King.

Rivers and seas and torrents roaring,
  Honour the Lord with wild acclaim;
Mountains and stones, look up adoring
  And find a voice to praise his name.
Righteous, commanding, ever glorious,
  Praises be his that never cease;
Just is our God, whose truth victorious
  Establishes the world in peace.

Erik Routley (1917–82)

This is a paraphrase of Psalm 98, which calls upon the singer to 'sing unto the Lord a new song'. It was rendered into a French metrical version by Roger Chapal for the tune RENDEZ À DIEU, and this is Routley's translation, slightly altered (probably with his agreement). It was first published in *Cantate Domino* (1974), a book published for the World Council of Churches.

It is a fine example of an ancient hymn of praise given new life: the springy metre, with its alternating feminine rhymes, was used to fit the tune, but it has given the words a shaping that makes them seem energetic and alive.

But the chief glory of the hymn is the way in which these words are sung. The tune, RENDEZ À DIEU, was described by Archibald Jacob in *Songs of Praise Discussed* as 'in some ways, the finest of all the early psalm tunes'. It was written, probably by Louis Bourgeois, for a Reformation metrical psalm, and is found in *La Forme des Prières et Chants Ecclesiastiques*, published in Strasbourg in 1545. It has usually been used for Reginald Heber's 'Bread of the world, in mercy broken', and (as Cyril Taylor has pointed out in *Hymns for Today Discussed*) it seems to be equally adapted to strong words as to gentle ones. Certainly the words and music together make a powerful effect.

244   In praise of God meet duty and delight,
  Angels and creatures, flesh and spirit bless'd;
In praise is earth transfigured by the sound
  And sight of heaven's everlasting feast.

In praise the artist and the craftsman meet,
  Inspired, obedient, patient, practical;
In praise join instrument and voice and sound
  To make one music for the Lord of all.

The desert is refreshed by songs of praise,
  Relaxed the frown of pride, the stress of grief;
In praise forgotten all our human spite;
  In praise the burdened heart finds sure relief.

No skill of ours, no music made on earth,
  No mortal song could scale the height of heaven;
Yet stands that cross, through grace ineffable
  An instrument of praise to sinners given.

So, confident and festive, let us sing
  Of wisdom, power and mercy there made known;
The song of Moses and the Lamb is ours,
  Through Christ raised up to life in God alone.

       Erik Routley (1917–82)

This hymn was written for a Presbyterian Church in Nebraska in 1976. It has received wider circulation through its printing in *Rejoice and Sing* (1991).

It is a deliberate echo of Isaac Watts's great paraphrase of Psalm 147, 'Praise ye the Lord, 'tis good to raise', which ends its first verse:

    His nature and his works invite
    To make this duty our delight.

Routley takes Watts's skilful joining of 'duty' and 'delight' and expands it to suggest the power of worship to transfigure life. Not only do duty and delight come together: there is a meeting of artist and craftsman, earth and heaven. And if heaven is too high, the Cross stands as our ladder to it, and also as our instrument of praise. Finally, there is a meeting of Old Testament and New Testament, of wisdom/power and mercy, in the song of Moses and of the Lamb: the duty of obedience is linked to the glory of Redemption. The biblical references are deployed here with great skill 'to make one music for the Lord of all'.

There are number of tunes which would fit the metre (the same as in 'Tell out, my soul, the greatness of the Lord', so that WOODLANDS would be one). It is set in *Rejoice and Sing* to ECHTERNACH, by Caryl Micklem (1925–), a well structured and attractive tune, written for these words.

245

Hills of the North, rejoice,
   Echoing songs arise,
Hail with united voice
   Him who made earth and skies:
He comes in righteousness and love,
He brings salvation from above.

Isles of the Southern seas,
   Sing to the listening earth,
Carry on every breeze
   Hope of a world's new birth:
In Christ shall all be made anew,
His word is sure, his promise true.

Lands of the East, arise,
   He is your brightest morn,
Greet him with joyous eyes,
   Praise shall his path adorn:
The God whom you have longed to know
In Christ draws near, and calls you now.

Shores of the utmost West,
   Lands of the setting sun,
Welcome the heavenly guest
   In whom the dawn has come:
He brings a never-ending light
Who triumphed o'er our darkest night.

Shout, as you journey on,
   Songs be in every mouth,
Lo, from the North they come,
   From East and West and South:
In Jesus all shall find their rest,
In him the sons of earth be blest.

The editors of *English Praise* (1975),
based on Charles E. Oakley (1832–65)

This hymn may seem out of place among so many recently written hymns, but it is another interesting example of a twentieth-century rewriting of a nineteenth-century hymn. The text proclaims its assumptions, which are those of the 1970s as surely as the new hymns of the time.

Oakley's hymn, which was widely used in the first half of the twentieth century, was written sometime before 1865 in an age of confident missionary activity. It began quite beautifully, its nature imagery lightly sketched but crystal-clear:

> Hills of the North, rejoice;
>   River and mountain-spring,
> Hark to the advent voice;
>   Valley and lowland, sing;
> Though absent long, your Lord is nigh;
> He judgment brings and victory.

In later verses, however, the hymn referred to parts of the globe as 'wastes', and the lands of the east as being in 'the sleep of ages', while the west was (nicely rhyming) 'unvisited, unblest'. By 1975, it was thought to be too patronizing to people overseas, and the editors of *English Praise* produced a modern version.

Whether it is an improvement is open to question. It is certainly less obviously *de haut en bas*, but it still proclaims salvation to those who do not have it. It is more subtly engaged in the same message as that which is found in Oakley's hymn: now God is 'the God whom you have longed to know' (it is not clear how the compilers of *English Praise* were so sure of this). What probably makes it slightly more acceptable is that for most of the hymn (the exception seems to be in verse 3), the new light in Christ may be seen as coming to all people, including those for whom the Christian tradition has been long established. There is less distinction between 'us' and 'them'. And although the new version lacks Oakley's vivid poetic imagery, the hymn as a whole remains lively and attractive to sing.

The tune is LITTLE CORNARD, by Martin Shaw (1875–1958). It was written for these words, and it enlivens them brilliantly. The result is an unusual and interesting hymnological experience, one which makes this hymn stand out from the others.

246
    Morning glory, starlit sky,
       leaves in springtime, swallows' flight,
    autumn gales, tremendous seas,
       sounds and scents of summer night;

    soaring music, towering words,
       art's perfection, scholar's truth,
    joy supreme of human love,
       memory's treasure, grace of youth;

    open, Lord, are these, thy gifts,
       gifts of love to mind and sense;
    hidden is love's agony,
       love's endeavour, love's expense.

    Love that gives, gives ever more,
       gives with zeal, with eager hands,
    spares not, keeps not, all outpours,
       ventures all, its all expends.

    Drained is love in making full;
       bound in setting others free;
    poor in making many rich;
       weak in giving power to be.

    Therefore he who thee reveals
       hangs, O Father, on that Tree,
    helpless; and the nails and thorns
       tell of what thy love must be.

    Thou art God; no monarch thou,
       throned in easy state to reign;
    thou art God, whose arms of love
       aching, spent, the world sustain.

       William Hubert Vanstone (1923–99)

These moving and reflective verses were printed at the end of Vanstone's book, *Love's endeavour, love's expense: The response of being to the love of God*, published in 1977. The American edition (1978) was entitled *The Risk of Love*. Almost immediately it was seen as a profound meditation on the subject of human and divine love which was also capable of being used as a hymn: it appeared, slightly shortened in *More Hymns for Today* (1980), and in America it was printed in *The Hymnal 1982*. Shortened versions have appeared in other books, such as *Common Praise* (2000). The text printed above is the one approved by the copyright-holder.

In *More Hymns for Today* it was given the title 'Love's endeavour, love's expense', which drew attention to the central theme, made explicit at the end of verse 3. In contrast to the obvious and 'open' gifts of God, there is also a love which is hidden, which (in a modern rewriting of 1 Corinthians 13) 'spares not, keeps not'. That love is a reflection of the divine love: it makes others free, makes them rich, gives them power. In so doing, it allows itself to become bound, and poor, and weak: it shows us God, even as Jesus showed the love of God when He hung helpless on the Cross. Vanstone's hymn allows us to think of all those who have suffered and died for others, who become exemplars of that same love which, ultimately, sustains the world. The final verse is beautifully precise as a summary of what the hymn has been saying about the 'weakness' of love: for God exists, in this perception, not as some complacent monarch, but as the sufferer on the Cross. It is a timeless hymn about the central truths of Christianity, but it can also be seen as a twentieth-century response to the kind of suffering and self-sacrifice that many people had to endure in that century.

Several tunes have been proposed for these words, which are written in a fairly common metre, 7.7.7.7. One is SONG 13, by Orlando Gibbons (1583–1625); another is BINGHAM, by a modern composer, Dorothy Howell Sheets, used in *The Hymnal 1982*; another is EMMA, by Paul Leddington Wright, in *Rejoice and Sing*. The American *United Methodist Hymnal* uses MONKLAND (usually used for 'Let us, with a gladsome mind'), but that is probably too energetic and vigorous for these profound and meditative verses.

247

Lord Christ, we praise your sacrifice,
    your life in love so freely given.
For those who took your life away
    you prayed, that they might be forgiven;
and there, in helplessness arrayed,
God's power was perfectly displayed.

Once helpless in your mother's arms,
    dependent on her mercy then;
at last, by choice, in other hands
    you were as helpless once again;
and, at their mercy, crucified,
you claimed your victory and died.

Though helpless and rejected then
    you're now as risen Lord acclaimed;
for ever by your sacrifice
    is God's eternal love proclaimed:
the love which, dying, brings to birth
new life and hope for all the earth.

So, living Lord, prepare us now
  your willing helplessness to share;
to give ourselves in sacrifice
  to overcome the world's despair;
in love to give ourselves away
and claim your victory today.

Alan Gaunt (1935–)

This hymn deals very movingly with the theme of helplessness, which is seen as part of the process of Incarnation: that God in Christ became a helpless child, and later underwent a death on the Cross which involved a 'willing helplessness'. The prayer of forgiveness of Jesus on the Cross, 'Father, forgive them, for they know not what they do', is seen here, in a penetrating paradox, as God's power 'in helplessness arrayed'. The theme of sacrifice is profoundly explored in this hymn: it is seen as death leading to life, and as an overcoming of the world's despair by the ultimate triumph of love.

It was published in *New Hymns for Worship* (1973). Its germ was in a 'protest song' written by Gaunt in the 1960s and published in *Dunblane Praises no. 2* (1967), one of two booklets which emerged from some hymn-writing consultations between writers and composers at Dunblane in Scotland. It contained the verse:

As helpless in his mother's arms
From Bethlehem he parted,
So at the end he's crucified
As helpless as he started.

It has become Alan Gaunt's best-known hymn, published in several contemporary collections. The recommended tune is RYBURN, by Norman Cocker, used in *Rejoice and Sing*. It is set in some other books to Erik Routley's tune ABINGDON.

248 Like the murmur of the dove's song,
like the challenge of her flight,
like the vigour of the wind's rush,
like the new flame's eager might:
 come, Holy Spirit, come.

To the members of Christ's Body,
to the branches of the Vine,
to the Church in faith assembled,
to her midst as gift and sign:
 come, Holy Spirit, come.

With the healing of division,
with the ceaseless voice of prayer,
with the power to love and witness,
with the peace beyond compare:
 come, Holy Spirit, come.

Carl P. Daw, Jr. (1944–)

This hymn was written at the request of the editors of *The Hymnal* (1982) to provide new words for the tune BRIDEGROOM, by Peter Cutts. Cutts's superb tune had been composed for Emma Frances Bevan's translation of the hymn by John Tauler, 'As the bridegroom to his chosen', and used in *100 Hymns for Today* (1969).

In his commentary on the hymn in his book, *A Year of Grace* (1990), Daw notes that the verses deal in sequence with (1) how the Spirit comes, (2) to whom or where it comes, and (3) the purposes of the Spirit, or why it comes. The first verse was influenced by Louis Evely's book *A Religion for Our Time* (1968), and thinks of the dove as 'moaning' or 'murmuring' (the image in Evely's book is used for the idea of praying in distress). The second verse deals with the Spirit as a gift to the whole church as a corporate body. The third verse shows the purposes of the Spirit, to give reconciliation, prayer, and love. The unobtrusive regularity of the versification is important here, allowing the mind to concentrate on the specific imagery of each stanza.

The hymn has invariably been sung to the tune for which the words were written, BRIDEGROOM, by Peter Cutts (1937–).

249
Christ triumphant, ever reigning,
   Saviour, Master, King!
Lord of heaven, our lives sustaining,
   hear us as we sing:
   Yours the glory and the crown,
   the high renown, the eternal name!

Word incarnate, truth revealing,
   Son of Man on earth!
power and majesty concealing
   by your humble birth:
   Yours the glory and the crown,
   the high renown, the eternal name!

Suffering servant, scorned, ill-treated,
   victim crucified!
death is through the cross defeated,
   sinners justified:
   Yours the glory and the crown,
   the high renown, the eternal name!

Priestly king, enthroned for ever
   high in heaven above!
sin and death and hell shall never
   stifle hymns of love:
   Yours the glory and the crown,
   the high renown, the eternal name!

So, our hearts and voices raising
   through the ages long,
ceaslessly upon you gazing,
   this shall be our song:
   Yours the glory and the crown,
   the high renown, the eternal name!

Michael Saward (1932–)

This hymn is an exercise in compression, dealing briefly and effectively with the attributes of Christ in majesty, and referring to His Incarnation (verse 2), His Passion (verse 3), and His role as our great High Priest (verse 4). None of these is new, but the expression certainly is: the unusual rhythm of the hymn, and the tremendous opening, make it an exercise in *fortissimo* adoration. Sung with a large congregation, on the right occasion (such as Easter Day), it can have an effect of rare splendour.

It was published in *Hymns for Today's Church* (1982), of which Michael Saward was one of the editors, and it has since become widely known. It has two tunes, CHRIST TRIUMPHANT by Michael Baughen (1930–), the Bishop of Chester who was closely associated with the volume; and GUITING POWER, by John Barnard (1948–). Both settings do justice to the unusual metre and rhythm of the hymn.

250 The works of the Lord are created in wisdom;
  we view the earth's wonders and call him to mind:
 we hear what he says in the world we discover
  and God shows his glory in all that we find.

The sun every morning lights up his creation,

Not even the angels have ever been granted
  to tell the full story of nature and grace;
 but open to God is all human perception,
  the mysteries of time and the secrets of space.

The sun every morning lights up his creation,
  the moon marks the rhythm of months in their turn;
 the glittering stars are arrayed in his honour,
  adorning the years as they ceaselessly burn.

The wind is his breath and the clouds are his signal,
  the rain and the snow are the robes of his choice;
 the storm and the lightning, his watchmen and heralds,
  the crash of the thunder, the sound of his voice.

The song is unfinished; how shall we complete it,
  and where find the skill to perfect all God's praise?
 At work in all places, he cares for all peoples:
  how great is the Lord to the end of all days!

        Christopher M. Idle (1938–)

This paraphrase of Ecclesiasticus 42 and 43 (from verse 15 of chapter 42 onwards) was published in *Hymns for Today's Church* (1982). Christopher Idle was one of the editors of that book, and wrote a reasoned explanation of its linguistic practice in *Hymns in Today's Language* (1982).

The hymn recognizes the importance of human discovery, but (as in Ecclesiasticus) reminds the singer or reader that 'The Lord hath not given power to the saints to declare all his marvellous works.' The hymn's sweeping lines are very effective, allowing the hymn to be sung without too much doubt or hesitation, in spite of the problems of belief in a scientific age. The third and fourth verses, particularly, are splendidly articulate in their vision of the God of sun, moon, and stars, and of thunder and lightning (from Ecclesiasticus 43).

The final verse asks a question about the role of human beings in the praise of God. It is a question which underlies all hymnody: how can we find the skill to praise God adequately? The question remains unanswered, but the hymn, as it should, ends in the contemplation of God's greatness: as the chapter from the Apocrypha has it, 'We may speak much, and yet come short: wherefore in sum, he is all.'

In *Hymns for Today's Church*, this hymn was set to a tune by Simon Beckley (1938–) called FRIARMERE VICARAGE. It has subsequently been set to ST CATHERINE'S COURT, by Richard Strutt (1848–1927), written in 1925 for

W. H. Draper's 'In our day of thanksgiving one psalm let us offer'. It could also be sung to WAS LEBET ('O worship the Lord in the beauty of holiness').

Postscript

> All our days we will bless the Lord,
> Bless and hallow his Name adored;
> Call together to God most high,
> Drawn to him who will hear our cry;
> Ever look to him, Lord indeed,
> Friend and Father to those in need.
>
> God our refuge, our shield and sword,
> He himself is our great reward.
> In his service, with love and fear,
> Joy be theirs who in faith draw near;
> Known and cherished in all their ways,
> Life possessing and length of days.
>
> May no lies on our lips be heard,
> No dishonouring deed or word;
> Over all is the Lord above,
> Peace bestowing and steadfast love,
> Quick to answer and take our part,
> Rich in mercy to heal the heart.
>
> So delivered from hour to hour,
> Trusting God and his sovereign power,
> Uncondemned at his judgment throne,
> Victors ever by grace alone,
> We will publish his Name abroad:
> All our days we will bless the Lord.

Timothy Dudley-Smith (1926–)

This hymn was written in 1990, and published in Dudley-Smith's *A Voice of Singing* (1993). It is an appropriate conclusion to two hundred and fifty hymns, for several reasons.

First: it is based on a psalm (34), and it is a reminder of the long tradition of singing praise to God, and of the importance of the psalms as examples and sources for the long tradition of English hymnody. Indeed, an earlier version of the same psalm is Tate and Brady's 'Through all the changing scenes of life' (no. 61).

Second: it is a reminder, in its newness, of the way in which hymnody is continually being added to, often in unexpected ways. Dudley-Smith has been a great master of communicating traditional themes in ways that made them new and fresh in the late twentieth century, and (one hopes) well into the twenty-first.

Third: it is a reminder, and a spectacular one, of the importance of crafts-manship in hymnody. The use of the initial letters, and of secure rhyme, is part of a real concern for *form* which is (or should be) of great concern to all hymnologists.

Fourth: the alphabet form is not just Dudley-Smith demonstrating his skill. As he points out, Psalm 34 in the Hebrew is an acrostic, based on the initial letters of the Hebrew alphabet. So this form is an attempt to get back to something like the original experience, of a trust in God expressed in a complex and intricate form.

Fifth: the author hopes that 'something of the message of the original is conveyed in this paraphrase'. It speaks to the reader or singer of blessing the Lord, of turning to Him in need, as one who will hear our cry; of God as our great reward, and of joy in His service; of good conduct, and of mercy as well as of judgement; and finally, of grace. It would be hard to find a hymn which more comprehensively sums up the great themes that have been the concern of the preceding pages. In all of them, as in this psalm, there is the thought which drove the psalmist to write as he did, expressing the various themes of hope, and faith, and love:

> I will bless the Lord at all times: his praise shall be continually in my mouth.
> My soul shall make her boast in the Lord: the humble shall hear thereof, and be glad.
> O magnify the Lord with me, and let us exalt his name together.

Copyright Acknowledgements

Author Index

Asterisks indicate translations. In the case of joint authorship, both authors are indexed. A question mark in brackets after the hymn number indicates that the authorship is unproved.

à Kempis, St Thomas (*c*.1380–1471)   25

Abelard, Peter (1079–1142)   20

Adams, Sarah Flower (1805–48)   146

Addison, Joseph (1672–1719)   78, 79, 80

Ainger, Arthur Campbell (1841–1919)   189

Ainger, Geoffrey (1925–)   229

Alexander, Cecil Frances (1818–95)   30*, 147, 148, 149

Alford, Henry (1810–71)   161

Alington, Cyril Argentine (1872–1955)   221, 222, 223

Ambrose, St (340–97)   7(?), 8(?)

Anatolius of Constantinople, St (*c*.400–58)   5 (?)

Augustine of Hippo, St (353–430)   7(?)

Baker, Sir Henry Williams (1821–77)   6*, 157, 164, 165

Baring-Gould, Sabine (1834–1924)   167, 168, 169*

Baxter, Richard (1615–91)   52, 53, 54

Bayly, Albert F. (1901–84)   226

Bernard of Cluny, St (12th cent.)   24

Binney, Thomas (1798–1874)   138

Blake, William (1757–1827)   121

Bliss, Philipp (1838–76)   206

Bode, John Ernest (1816–74)   170

Bonar, Horatius (1808–89)   143

Bonhoeffer, Dietrich (1906–45)   225

Bourne, George Hugh (1840–1925)   185

Bowring, John (1792–1872)   136

Brady, Nicholas (1659–1726)   60, 61, 62

Bridges, Matthew (1800–94)   166

Bridges, Robert (1844–1930)   36*, 38*, 41*

Bright, William (1824–1901)   186

Brooks, Phillips (1835–93)   202

Bruce, Michael (1746–67)   119 (?)

Budry, Edmond L. (1854–1932)   219

Bunyan, John (1628–88)   55

Burkitt, Francis Crawford (1864–1935)   35*

Burns, Edward J. (1938–)   236

Byrne, Mary (1880–1931)   213*

Byrom, John (1692–1763)   85

Caird, George Bradford (1917–84)   224

Campbell, Jane Montgomery (1817–78)   162*

Campbell, Robert (1814–68)   14*, 19*

Carlyle, Thomas (1795–1881)   33*

Carter, Sydney (1915–)   228

Caswall, Edward (1814–78)   8*, 22*, 43*, 153

Chadwick, John White (1840–1904)   201

Chesterton, Gilbert Keith (1874–1936)   211

Claudius, Matthias (1740–1815)   162

Clephane, Elizabeth Cecilia (1830–69)   173

Columba, St (521–97) 31
Cosin, John (1594–1672) 17*
Cosnett, Elizabeth (1936–) 242
Cowper, William (1731–1800) 112, 113, 114
Cox, Frances Elizabeth (1812–97) 144*
Crosby, Fanny, *see* Van Alstyne
Crossman, Samuel (1624–84) 56

Daw, Carl P. Jr (1944–) 248
Dearmer, Percy (1867–1936) 10*
Dix, William Chatterton (1837–98) 159, 163
Doane, George Washington (1799–1859) 193
Doddridge, Philip (1702–51) 81, 82, 83, 84
Draper, William Henry (1855–1933) 21*
Dryden, John (1631–1701) 18*
Dudley-Smith, Timothy (1926–) 7, 230, 231, 251

Edmeston, James (1791–1867) 135
Ellerton, John (1826–93) 182, 183
Elliott, Charlotte (1789–1871) 140
Everest, Charles William (1814–77) 194

Faber, Frederick William (1814–63) 154, 155, 156
Farjeon, Eleanor (1881–1965) 217
'F.B.P.' (*c*.1580) 42
Fortunatus, Venantius (*c*.530–609) 10, 11, 12
Francis of Assisi, St (1182–1226) 21
Franzmann, Martin (1907–76) 232
Fulbert of Chartres, St (*c*.960–1028) 19

Gaunt, Alan (1935–) 247
Gellert, Christian Fürchtegott (1715–69) 144
Gerhardt, Paul (1607–76) 38, 39
Gill, William Henry (1839–1923) 192
Gillett, George Gabriel Scott (1873–1948) 12*
Grant, Sir Robert (1779–1838) 137

Green, Fred Pratt (1903–2000) 225*, 238, 239, 240
Greenwell, Dora (1821–82) 176

Hatch, Edwin (1835–89) 191
Havergal, Frances Ridley (1836–79) 174, 175
Heber, Reginald (1783–1826) 122, 123, 124, 125
Heermann, Johann (1585–1647) 36
Herbert, George (1593–1633) 47, 48, 49, 50
Holland, Henry Scott (1847–1918) 210
Holmes, Oliver Wendell (1809–94) 199
Hosmer, Frederick Lucian (1840–1929) 207
How, William Walsham (1823–97) 184
Howe, Julia Ward (1819–1910) 198
Hoyle, Richard B. (1875–1939) 219*
Hughes, Donald Wynn (1911–67) 233
Hull, Eleanor (1860–1935) 213

Idle, Christopher M. (1938–) 250
Ingemann, Bernhardt Severin (1789–1862) 169
Irons, W.J. (1812–83) 26*

Jarvis, Peter G. (1925–) 227
John of Damascus, St (*c*.675–*c*.750) 3
Johnson, Samuel (1822–82) 200

Kaan, Fred (1929–) 234
Keble, John (1792–1866) 1*, 131, 132, 133
Kelly, Thomas (1769–1855) 134
Ken, Thomas (1637–1711) 58, 59
Kethe, William (d. *c*.1594) 32
Kitchin, George William (1827–1912) 190

Lowell, James Russell (1819–91) 196
Luther, Martin (1483–1546) 33, 34
Lyra Davidica (1708) 77
Lyte, Henry Francis (1793–1847) 141, 142

MacGregor, Duncan (1854–1923) 31*

Mason, John (*c.*1645–94) 57
Matheson, George (1842–1906) 188
Maurus, Rhabanus (*c.*776–*c.*856) 17
Micklem, Caryl (1925–) 241
Milman, Henry Hart (1791–1868) 126
Milton, John (1608–74) 44, 45
Monsell, John Samuel Bewley
 (1811–75) 171, 172
Montgomery, James (1771–1854) 127,
 128, 129, 130
Moultrie, Gerard (1829–85) 2*
Murray, Shirley Erena (1931–) 235

Neale, John Mason (1818–66) 3*, 4,
 5*, 6*, 9*, 10*, 11*, 13*, 14*, 15*,
 16*, 20*, 24*, 25*, 27*, 28*
Neander, Joachim (1650–80) 40, 41
Newbolt, Michael Robert (1874–1956)
 190
Newman, John Henry (1801–90) 139,
 151, 152
Newton, John (1725–1807) 109, 110,
 111
Nicolai, Philipp (1556–1608) 35
North, Frank Mason (1850–1935) 208

Oakeley, Frederick (1802–80) 145*
Oakley, Charles (1832–65) 245
Olivers, Thomas (1725–99) 106
Oxenham, John (1852–1941) 218

Palmer, Ray (1808–87) 23*, 195
Patrick, St (*c.*386–466) 30
Perronet, Edward (*c.*1726–92) 107
Pierpoint, Folliott Sandford
 (1835–1917) 180
Placzek, A.K. *see* Struther, Jan
Plumptre, Edward Hayes (1821–91)
 187
Pott, Francis (1832–1909) 29*, 160
Prudentius, Aurelius Prudentius
 Clemens (348–*c.*413) 6

Rees, Timothy (1874–1939) 220
Riley, Athelstan (1858–1945) 209
Rinkart, Martin (1586–1649) 37
Rossetti, Christina (1830–94) 178,
 179
Routley, Erik (1917–82) 243, 244

Saward, Michael (1932–) 249
Scottish Psalter (1650) 46
Scottish Translations and Paraphrases
 (1781) 118, 119, 120
Sears, Edmund Hamilton (1810–76)
 197
Smart, Christopher (1722–71) 115
Smyttan, George Hunt (1822–70) 160
Spring-Rice, Cecil (1859–1918) 212
Steele, Anne (1717–78) 86
Stone, Samuel John (1839–1900) 181
Struther, Jan (1901–53) 216
Studdert-Kennedy, Geoffrey Anketell
 (1883–1929) 214, 215
Tate, Nahum (1652–1715) 60, 61, 62
Theodulph, St (d. 821) 16
Thomas of Celano (13th cent.) 26
Tisserand, Jean (d. 1494) 28
Toplady, Augustus Montague
 (1740–78) 108

Van Alstyne, Frances Jane (1820–1915)
 205
Vanstone, William Hubert (1923–99)
 246
Vaughan, Henry (1622–95) 51

Wade, John Francis (18th cent.)
 145(?)
Waring, Anna Laetitia (1820–1910)
 177
Watts, Isaac (1674–1748) 63, 64, 65,
 66, 67, 68, 69, 70, 71, 72, 73, 74, 75,
 76, 120
Wesley, Charles (1707–88) 87, 88, 89,
 90, 91, 92, 93, 94, 95, 96, 97, 98, 99,
 100, 101, 102, 103, 104, 105
Whiting, William (1825–78) 158
Whittier, John Greenleaf (1807–92)
 203, 204
Williams, Gwilym Owen (1913–90)
 117*
Williams, Isaac (1802–65) 150
Williams, Peter (1722–96) 116*
Williams, William (1717–91) 116, 117
Winkworth, Catherine (1827–78) 34*,
 37*, 39*, 40*
Wren, Brian (1936–) 237

Index of Composers and Arrangers

Ainger, Geoffrey 229
Antes, John 44
Armes, Philip 74, 174
Arnold, William 70
Atkins, Ivor 114
Attwood, Thomas 18

Bach, Johann Sebastian 69
Baker, Frederick George 72
Baker, Henry 133
Baring-Gould, Sabine 167
Barnard, John 249
Barthélémon, François 58
Baughen, Michael 214, 249
Beaumont, Geoffrey 37
Beckley, Simon 250
Beer, Alfred 87
Bishop, John 52
Bliss, Philipp 206
Bourgeois, Louis 32, 183, 243
Bower, John Dykes 53, 204, 242
Boyce, William 115, 151
Boyd, William 171
Bradbury, William Batchelder 140
Bridge, John Frederick 122
Brown, Arthur Henry 5, 86, 140
Buck, Percy 11
Burleigh, Harry 218

Calkin, John Baptiste 129
Campbell, Thomas 87
Carey, Henry 78
Carter, Sydney 228
Clarke, Jeremiah 63, 134, 199, 204
Cocker, Norman 247
Collignon, Charles 50
Conkey, Ithamar 136

Cooke, W. H. 172
Cooper, George 23, 176
Courteville, Raphael 193
Croft, William 54, 68, 75, 103, 137
Crüger, Johann 7, 36, 37, 45, 128
Cutts, Peter 248

Darwall, John 54
Davies, Walford 80, 188, 198, 202
Davis, Gabriel 76
De Pearsall, R.L. 173
Doane, William Howard 205
Dobbs, Jack 138
Dougall, Neil 218, 242
Duncalf, Henry 208
Dykes, John Bacchus 22, 26, 92, 114,
   120, 125, 126, 139, 143, 146, 152, 158,
   165, 169

Ebeling, J.G. 39
Elliott, James William 170
Ellor, James 107
Elvey, George Job 47, 116, 161, 166
Este, Thomas 62
Ett, Caspar 27
Evans, David 139, 180, 188, 196
Ewing, Alexander 24

Ferguson, William Harold 5, 107, 170
Filitz, Friedrich 135
Finlay, Kenneth 183
Floyd, A.E. 52
Foote, Guthrie 235

Gardiner, William 83, 123, 208, 236
Gatty, Nicholas 69
Gauntlett, Henry John 19, 66, 98,
   144, 148, 164
Gawthorn, Nathaniel 69

Gelineau, Joseph 225
Gibbons, Orlando 43, 104, 201, 246
Giornovichi, Giovanni 120
Goss, John 141, 153
Grant, David 46
Greatorex, Walter 230

Hampton, Calvin 154
Handel, George Frideric 64, 100, 215, 219
Harington, Henry 79
Harris, William H. 114, 120, 139
Harwood, Basil 47, 187, 221
Hastings, Thomas 108
Hatton, John 171
Havergal, William Henry 84, 126, 132, 175
Haweis, Thomas 81, 88, 152, 200
Haydn, Franz Josef 110, 168
Haydn, Johann Michael 82
Helder, Bartholomaeus 173
Helmore, Thomas 6, 15
Herbst, Martin 160
Hoare, Brian 165
Hodson, H.E. 9
Holdroyd, Israel 232
Holst, Gustav 178, 212
Hopkins, E.J. 53, 127, 182
Horsley, William 79, 149
Howells, Herbert 41
Hughes, John 116
Hutcheson, Charles 204

Ireland, John 56
Irons, H.S. 86, 127
Isaak, Heinrich 38

Jackson, Francis 238
Jarman, Thomas 62
Jenkins, David 177
Jones, J.D. 48
Jones, William 45, 118

Kelly, Bryan 115
King, Robert 95
Kingham, Millicent D. 189
Knapp, William 23
Knecht, Justin Heinrich 4
Kocher, Conrad 159

Lahee, Henry 65
Lampe, John Frederick 100
Lawes, Henry 52, 56
Leah, Maurice S. 226
Leoni, Meyer 106
Ley, Henry G. 115, 222
Llewellyn, William 230
Lloyd, John A. 41
Lockhart, Charles 191
Luther, Martin 33

Maker, Frederick C. 173, 203
Mann, Arthur Henry 73
Martin, George Clement 185
Mason, Lowell 88, 124, 195
Mendelssohn, Felix 90
Micklem, Caryl 241, 244
Miller, Edward 70, 112
Monk, William Henry 8, 28, 47, 91, 93, 142, 147, 157, 186, 231
Morley, H.L. 138
Morris, Reginald Owen 179
Murrill, Herbert 220

Naumann, Johann Gottlieb 71
Naylor, E.W. 93
Naylor, Kenneth 57
Nicholson, Sydney 190
Nicolai, Philipp 35
Northrop, Abraham 62

Oakeley, Herbert 23, 133
Olivers, Thomas 102
Ouseley, Frederick A.G. 79

Parry, C.H.H. 86, 98, 113, 121, 164, 203, 225, 234
Parry, Joseph 92
Peace, A.L. 188
Pettman, Edgar 179
Phillips, Thomas 88
Praetorius, Michael 13
Prichard, R.H. 101, 117, 163, 196, 223
Prins-Buttle, Ida 239
Prys, Edmund 232
Purcell, Henry 9, 101
Purday, C.H. 139

Ravenscroft, Thomas 81, 120
Reay, Samuel 99

Redhead, Richard   22, 108, 193

Redner, Lewis H.   202

Reinagle, Alexander Robert 111

Routley, Erik   47, 87, 113, 138, 146, 247

Rowlands, W.P.   101

Ruddle, Valerie   240

Sandys, William   49

Sankey, Ira D.   173

Schicht, J.G.   224

Schmidlin, Johann   76

Scholefield, Clement   183

Schulz, Johann A.P.   162

Shaw, Geoffrey   180

Shaw, Martin   47, 94, 130, 147, 169, 189, 198, 245

Sheeles, John   80

Sheets, Dorothy Howell   246

Shephard, Richard   226

Sheppard, James Hallett   34

Shrubsole, William   107

Slater, Gordon   22, 237

Smart, George Thomas   61

Smart, Henry   25, 89, 140, 141, 155, 221

Smith, Henry   199

Smith, Isaac   150

Somervell, Arthur   152

Stainer, John   1, 43, 96, 101, 136, 154

Stanford, Charles Villiers   159, 183, 184, 239

Stanley, Samuel   105

Stanton, Walter   73, 233

Stevenson, John Andrew   83

Stewart, Charles Hylton   166

Strutt, Richard   250

Sullivan, Arthur   44, 146, 168, 197

Tallis, Thomas   59, 143

Taylor, Cyril   87, 110, 115, 216

Terry, Richard Runciman   152, 166

Teschner, Melchior   16

Thalben-Ball, George   88, 122

Thiman, Eric   31, 73

Thrupp, J. F.   122

Tourjee, Lizzie S.   154

Turle, James   43, 101, 156

Vaughan Williams, Ralph   2, 12, 55, 143, 145, 151, 182, 184, 202, 209, 211

Vulpius, Melchior   29, 51, 222

Wade, John Francis   145

Wainwright, John   85

Webbe, Samuel   131, 174

Weisse, Michael   157

Werner, J.G.   89

Wesley, Charles (the younger) 242

Wesley, Samuel   66

Wesley, Samuel Sebastian   7, 95, 105, 139, 163, 181, 183, 224, 227

Williams, Aaron   10, 66

Williams, Derek   71

Williams, T.J.   196

Williams, Thomas   127

Willis, R.S.   197

Wilson, Hugh   46, 60

Wilson, John   186, 226

Witt, Christian Friedrich   96

Woodbury, Isaac Baker   130

Wright, Paul Leddington   175, 246

Zundel, John   154

Index of Hymns

A safe stronghold our God is still 33
Abide with me; fast falls the eventide
  142
Ah, Holy Jesu, how hast thou offended
  36
All creatures of our God and King 21
All glory, laud, and honour 16
All hail the power of Jesu's name 107
All my heart this night rejoices 39
All my hope on God is founded 41
All our days we will bless the Lord
  251
All people that on earth do dwell 32
All things bright and beautiful 147
Alleluia, sing to Jesus 163
Amazing grace! (how sweet the sound)
  109
And art thou come with us to dwell
  176
And can it be, that I should gain 87
And did those feet in ancient time 121
And now, O Father, mindful of the love
  186
Angels from the realms of glory 127
As pants the heart for cooling streams
  60
As with gladness men of old 159
Awake, awake, to love and work 215
Awake, my soul, and with the sun 58
Awake our souls; away our fears 64

Be thou my guardian and my guide
  150
Be thou my vision, O Lord of my heart
  213
Before the ending of the day 14

Begin, my tongue, some heavenly
  theme 63
Behold the amazing gift of love 118
Behold! the mountain of the Lord 119
Beneath the Cross of Jesus 173
Blessed City, heavenly Salem 9
Blest are the pure in heart 132
Born in the night 229
Breathe on me, breath of God 191
Brightest and best of the sons of the
  morning 122
By cool Siloam's shady rill 123
By gracious powers so wonderfully
  sheltered 225

Can we by searching find out God 242
Christ is the world's redeemer 31
Christ triumphant, ever reigning 249
Christ, whose glory fills the skies 89
Christians awake, salute the happy
  morn 85
City of God, how broad and far 200
Come, Holy Ghost, our souls inspire
  17
Come, let us join our cheerful songs
  65
Come, O thou Traveller unknown 95
Come, thou long-expected Jesus 96
Come, we that love the Lord 66
Come, ye thankful people, come 161
Creator of the earth and skies 233
Creator Spirit, by whose aid 18
Crown him with many crowns 166

Day of wrath! O day of mourning! 26
Dear Lord and Father of mankind
  203

Eternal Father, strong to save   158
Eternal Light! Eternal Light   138
Eternal ruler of the ceaseless round   201

Father of everlasting grace   99
Father of mercies, in thy word   86
Firmly I believe and truly   151
For all the saints   184
For ever with the Lord   130
For the beauty of the earth   180
For the fruits of his creation   238
Forth in thy name, O Lord, I go   104
Forty days and forty nights   160
From Greenland's icy mountains   124

Gentle Jesus, meek and mild   94
Give me the wings of faith to rise   71
Give to me, Lord, a thankful heart   241
Glorious things of thee are spoken   110
Glory be to God on high   97
Glory to thee, my God, this night   59
God in his love for us lent us this planet   240
God is the refuge of his saints   73
God is working his purpose out   189
God moves in a mysterious way   112
God of freedom, God of justice   235
God of love and truth and beauty   220
Good Christian men, rejoice and sing   222
Guide me, O thou great Jehovah   116

Hail, gladdening Light   1
Hail the day that sees him rise   91
Hail thee, Festival Day   12
Hail to the Lord's Anointed   128
Hark! a herald voice is calling   8
Hark! hark, my soul! Angelic songs are swelling   155
Hark, my soul! it is the Lord   114
Hark the glad sound! the Saviour comes   81
Hark! the herald angels sing   90
He wants not friends that hath thy love   52

Hear us, O Lord, from heaven thy dwelling-place   192
Hills of the North, rejoice   245
Ho, my comrades! see the signal   206
Holy, Holy, Holy! Lord God Almighty   125
How bright these glorious spirits shine   120
How shall I sing that majesty   57
How sweet the name of Jesus sounds   111

I bind unto myself today   30
I come with joy, a child of God   237
I danced in the morning   228
I heard the voice of Jesus say   143
I sing the almighty power of God   72
I vow to thee, my country   212
I'll praise my Maker while I've breath   76
Immortal Love, forever full   204
In Adam we have all been one   232
In Christ there is no east or west   218
In heavenly love abiding   177
In praise of God meet duty and delight   243
In the bleak mid-winter   178
In the cross of Christ I glory   136
It came upon the midnight clear   197

Jerusalem, my happy home   42
Jerusalem the golden   24
Jesu, lover of my soul   92
Jesu, thou joy of loving hearts   23
Jesus Christ is risen today   77
Jesus lives! thy terrors now   144
Jesus shall reign where'er the sun   74
Jesus, the very thought of thee   22
Judge eternal, throned in splendour   210

Just as I am, without one plea   140

King of glory, King of peace   48

Lead, kindly Light   139
Lead us, heavenly Father, lead us   135
Let all mortal flesh keep silence   2
Let all the world in every corner sing   47

Let saints on earth in concert sing   103
Let us, with a gladsome mind   44
Lift high the Cross   190
Light's abode, celestial Salem   25
Like the murmur of the dove's song
   248
Lo! He comes with clouds descending
   102
Lord Christ, we praise your sacrifice
   247
Lord, enthroned in heavenly splendour
   185
Lord, it belongs not to my care   53
Lord of all being, throned afar   199
Lord of all hopefulness, Lord of all joy
   216
Lord of beauty, thine the splendour
   221
Lord speak to me, that I may speak
   174
Lord, thy word abideth   157
Lord, you have searched and known my
   ways   227
Love came down at Christmas   179
Love Divine, all loves excelling   101

Mine eyes have seen the glory   198
Morning glory, starlit sky   246
Morning has broken   217
My faith looks up to thee   195
My God, how wonderful thou art   156
My God, I love thee; not because   43
My song is love unknown   56
My soul, there is a country   51

Nature with open volume stands   69
Nearer, my God, to thee   146
New every morning is the love   131
New songs of celebration render   244
Not far beyond the sea nor high   224
Now thank we all our God   37
Now that the daylight fills the sky   13
Now the day is over   167

O come, all ye faithful   145
O come, O come, Emmanuel   15
O for a thousand tongues to sing   88
O God of Bethel, by whose hand   82

O God of earth and altar   211
O God, our help in ages past   75
O happy band of pilgrims   4
O Jesus, I have promised   170
O little town of Bethlehem   202
O Lord of every shining constellation
   226
O love that wilt not let me go   188
O praise ye the Lord   164
O thou who camest from above   105
O what their joy and their glory must be
   20
O worship the King   137
O worship the Lord in the beauty of
   holiness   172
Of the Father's love begotten   6
Once in royal David's city   148
Once to every man and nation   196
Onward, Christian soldiers   168
Out of the depths I cry to thee   34

Praise, my soul, the King of heaven
   141
Praise to the Holiest in the height   152
Praise to the Lord! the Almighty   40
Prayer is the soul's sincere desire   129

Rejoice, the Lord is King   100
Ride on, Jesu, all-victorious   117
Ride on! ride on in majesty   126
Rock of Ages, cleft for me   108

Saviour, again to thy dear name we
   raise   182
See amid the winter's snow   153
See Israel's gentle shepherd stand   83
Sing, my tongue, the glorious battle
   10
Soldiers of Christ, arise   93
Sometimes a light surprises   113
Souls of men! why will ye scatter   154
Sun of my soul, thou Saviour dear   133

Take my life, and let it be   175
Take up thy cross, the Saviour said
   194
Teach me, my God and King   49
Tell out, my soul, the greatness of the
   Lord   230

The Church's one foundation   181
The day is past and over   5
The day of Resurrection   3
The day thou gavest, Lord, is ended
   183
The duteous day now closeth   38
The God of Abraham praise   106
The God of love my Shepherd is   50
The head that once was crowned with
   thorns   134
The King of love my Shepherd is   165
The Lord my pasture shall prepare   78
The Lord will come and not be slow
   45
The Lord's my shepherd, I'll not want
   46
The royal banners forward go   11
The spacious firmament on high   80
The strife is o'er, the battle done   29
The works of the Lord are created in
   wisdom   250
There is a green hill far away   149
There is a land of pure delight   67
Thine be the glory, risen, conquering
   Son   219
Thou art the Way: to thee alone   193
Through all the changing scenes of life
   61
Through the night of doubt and sorrow
   169
Thy hand, O God, has guided   187

Thy kingdom come! on bended knee
   207
Timeless love! we sing the story   231
To God be the glory   205
To the Name of our Salvation   27
Wake, O wake! with tidings thrilling
   35
We come with songs of blessing   7
We give immortal praise   68
We have a gospel to proclaim   236
We plough the fields, and scatter   162
We turn to you, O God of every nation
   234
When all thy mercies, O my God   79
When I survey the wondrous cross   70
When, in our music, God is glorified
   239
When through the whirl of wheels   214
Where cross the crowded ways of life
   208
Where is this stupendous stranger   115
While shepherds watched their flocks
   62
Who would true valour see   55
Ye choirs of new Jerusalem   19
Ye holy angels bright   54
Ye servants of God   98
Ye servants of the Lord   84
Ye sons and daughters of the King   28
Ye that know the Lord is gracious   223
Ye watchers and ye holy ones   209

Index of Tunes

Abbot's Leigh   110
Abends   133
Aberystwyth   92
Abingdon   87, 247
Abridge   118, 150
Addison's   80
Adeste Fideles   145
Agincourt   233
Alberta   139
All Saints   231
All Things Bright and Beautiful   147
Alleluia   163
Amazing Grace   109
Amsterdam   97
Angmering   86
Ar Hyd Y Nos   220, 238
Arden   88
Ardgowan   183
Ascension   66, 91
Augustine   47
Aurelia   7, 124, 181, 211
Austria   110
Ayrshire   129
Azmon   88

Ballerma   120
Battle Song   198
Beatitudo   120
Belgrave   79
Belmont   83, 123
Beneath the Cross of Jesus   173
Benson   189
Beulah   67
Billing   152
Bingham   246
Birling   133

Bishopthorpe   204
Blaenwern   101
Bonifacio   139
Bonn   39
Bourton   73
Breslau   194
Bridegroom   248
Bristol   81
Brunswick   215
Bryn Calfaria   185
Bunessan   217

Caersalem   116
Cameronian Midnight Hymn   52
Cannock   73
Carlisle   191
Carol   197
Carolyn   220
Castiglione   115
Chalfont Park   138
Chislehurst   91
Chorus Angelorum   152
Christ Ist Erstanden   144
Christ Triumphant   249
Christmas Carol   202
Christus Der Ist Mein Leben   51
Claudius   162
Cliff Lane   165
Clonmacnoise   30
Clonmel   113
Coburg   34
Coe Fen   57
Commandments   58
Consecration   175
Contemplation   79
Corde Natus   6

Cornwall   224
Corona (Stewart)   166
Corona (Terry)   166
Craigmillar   113
Cranham   178
Crimond   46
Croft's 136th   54, 68
Cross of Jesus   96, 154
Crucifer   190
Crüger   7, 128
Culross   43
Cwm Rhondda   116

Darwall's 148th   54
David's Harp   95
Day of Rest   170
Deirdre   30
Denbigh   195
Diadem   107
Diademata   166
Didsbury   87
Dies Irae   26
Divinum Mysterium   6
Dix   159
Dominus Regit Me   165
Dove of Peace   237
Dresden   76, 162
Dublin   83
Duke Street   171
Dundee   103
Dunstan   42

Ealing   23
East Acklam   238
Easter Hymn   77
Ebenezer   196
Echternach   244
Ein' Feste Burg   33
Elim (Hesperus)   133
Ellacombe   3, 218
Ellers   182
Eltham   69
Emma   175, 246
Engadine   115
Engelberg   184, 239
England's Lane   180
Epiphany   122
Epworth   242

Eudoxia   169
Eventide   142
Ever Faithful, Ever Sure   44
Ewing   24

Feniton Court   127
Fenwick   60
Firmament   80
Forest Green   202
Franconia   132
Freuen Wir Uns   114
Friarmere Vicarage   250
From Strength to Strength 93
Fulda   174, 208, 236

Galilee   74, 174
Gartan   30, 179
Gatescarth   241
Gelobt Sei Gott   222
Gentle Jesus   94
Gerontius   152
Glasgow   119
Gloria   173
Glory, Hallelujah   198
Gloucester   120
Gonfalon Royal   11, 176
Gopsal   100
Gräfenberg   45
Grafton   27, 221
Groeswen   41
Guiting Power   249
Gwalchmai   48

Halton Holgate   115, 151
Hampstead   188
Hanover   137
Haresfield   53, 204, 242
Harington   79
Heathlands   89
Heinlein   160
Helder   173
Helmsley   102
Herbert   47
Hereford   105
Hermitage   179
Herzliebster Jesu   36
Heslington 226
High Road   47
Hold The Fort   206

Hollingreave 226
Hollingside 92
Hominum Amator 5
Horbury 146
Horsley 149
Humility 153
Hursley 133
Hyfrydol 101, 117, 163, 196, 223

Illsley 52
Innellan 188
Innocents 94, 175
Innsbruck 38
Intercessor 225, 234
Irby 148
Iris 127
Irish 112, 207

Jericho Tune 93
Jerusalem 121
Jesmian 122
Job 70
John Brown 198
Joldwynds 183
Jubilate 113

Keats 147
Kettering 80
Kilmarnock 218, 242
King's Lynn 211
Kingsfold 143
Knecht 4

La Suissesse 155
Ladywell 107
Land Of Rest 22, 137
Lansdown 87
Lasst Uns Erfreuen 21, 209
Lasus 73
Laudate Dominum (Gauntlett) 98, 164
Laudate Dominum (Parry) 98, 164
Le Cénacle 225
Les Commandemens De Dieu 183
Leoni 106
Lewes 127
Liebster Immanuel 122, 240
Little Cornard 245
Llandinam 127

Llanfair 91
Llangloffan 113
Lobe Den Herren 40
Lombard Street 214
London 80
London New 72, 112
Lord Of The Years 214
Love Divine 101, 136
Love Incarnate 179
Love Unknown 56
Lucerna Laudoniae 180
Lucerne 76
Luckington 47
Lux Benigna 139
Lydia 88
Lyngham 62, 65, 88

Maccabaeus 219
Mckee 218
Magda 182
Manna 224
Mannheim 135
Marching 169
Marching to Zion 66
Martyrdom 46, 60, 82
Mary's Child 229
Maryton 199
Meine Hoffnung 41
Meirionydd 170
Melcombe 131, 174
Melita 158
Mendelssohn 90
Mendip 22, 67, 129
Merton 8
Metzler's Redhead 22
Michael 41
Miles Lane 107
Ministres De L'Éternel 89
Miniver 216
Miriam 239
Misericordia 140
Missionary (hymn) 124, 170
Monkland 44, 246
Monk's Gate 55
Monmouth 76
Montrose 72
Moriah 101

Morley 30
Morning Hymn 58
Mortram 85
Mount Ephraim 66
Moville 31
Moving Tent 130
Mylon 71

Narenza 84
Nativity 65
Nearer Home 130
Newcastle 138
Newington 45, 118
Newman 152
Nicaea 125
Noel 197
Noricum 180
Normanton 120
Northrop 62
Nottingham 175
Nürnberg 69
Nun Danket 37
Nun Danket All 22, 129

O Filii Et Filiae 28
O Waly Waly 70
Offertorium 7
Old 134th 84
Old 137th 57
Old Hundredth 32
Olivers 102
Olivet 195
Omni Die 154
Oriel 27
Orient 159
Ottery St Mary 115
Oxford 153

Patmos 139, 175
Peel Castle 192
Penlan 177
Pentecost 171
Petersfield 114
Petition 113
Petra 108
Picardy 2, 235
Pilgrimage 116
Pilgrims 155
Pilgrims of the Night 155

Plaistow 233
Praise My Soul 141
Proprior Deo 146
Psalm 47 56
Puer Nobis Nascitur 13, 14
Purpose 189

Quedlinburg 240

Rathbun 136
Ratisbon 89
Ravendale 186
Ravenshaw 157
Redhead No 66 193
Redhead No 76 108
Regent Square 25, 27, 141, 221
Regnator Orbis 20
Rendez à Dieu 243
Repton 203
Rerum Creator 226
Rest 203
Resurrection 100
Rhuddlan 210, 235
Richmond 81, 88, 152, 200
Ridge 66
Rochester 129
Rockingham 70
Royal Oak 147
Ryburn 247

Saffron Walden 140
Sagina 87
St Agnes 22
St Alban 168
St Albinus 144
St Anatolius 5
St Anne 75
St Asaph 120
St Audrey 221
St Austin 42
St Bartholomew 208
St Bees 114, 175
St Bernard 218, 243
St Botolph 22, 237
St Catherine's Court 250
St Christopher 173
St Clement 183
St Columba 165
St Drostane 126

St Ethelwald   93
St Flavian   207
St Francis Xavier   43
St Fulbert   19
St George's Windsor   161
St Gertrude   168
St Helen   185
St Helena   154
St Hugh   53
St James   193
St Louis   202
St Mabyn   154
St Magnus   63, 134
St Margaret   188
St Martin   34
St Mary   232
St Matthew   103
St Matthias   43
St Michael   84
St Nicholas   232
St Osmund   127
St Oswald   169
St Osyth   214, 226
St Patrick   30
St Paul (Aberdeen)   82
St Peter   111, 218
St Saviour   72
St Sepulchre   23, 176
St Stephen   45, 118
St Theodulph   16
St Thomas   10, 66
Salve Festa Dies   12
Salzburg   82
Samson   64
San Rocco   71
Sanctissimus   172
Sandon   139
Sandys   49
Savannah   114
Sebaste   1
Sennen Cove   120
Shaker Tune   228
Sheet   115
Sheltered Dale   215
Shipston   151
Shrubsole   107
Sine Nomine   184

Slane   213, 216
Soll's Sein   57
Song 1   201
Song 13   246
Song 34   104
Song 67   43, 71
Southill   42
Southwell   86
Spean   122
Stalham   42
Stamford   99
Stewardship   240
Stockport   85
Stokesay Castle 31
Stracathro   120, 204
Stroudwater   63
Stuttgart   96, 136
Surrey   78
Sussex   154

Tallis' Canon   59, 80
Te Lucis   14
Teilo Sant   138
Thaxted   212
The 113th Psalm Tune   76
The Third Tune   143
Thornbury   187
Tidings   230
To God Be the Glory   205
Ton-y-botel   196
Toplady   108
Tredegar   235
Troy Court   233
Truro   74
Tugwood   69

Uffingham   199
Unde Et Memores   186
Undique Gloria   47
University   50, 88
Urbs Coelestis   9

Veni Creator   17
Veni Creator (Attwood) 18
Veni Immanuel   15
Vermont   52
Vexilla Regis   11
Victory   29

Vision   198
Vox Dilecti   143
Vulpius   29, 222

Wachet Auf   35
Wareham   23
Was Lebet   172, 250
Wellesley   154
Westminster   43, 101, 156
Westminster Abbey   9
Whitburn   133
White Ladies Aston   114
Whitehall   52
Wigtown   129
Wilmington   146

Wilton   105
Wiltshire   46, 61
Winchester New   126
Winchester Old   62
Windermere   66
Winscott   227
Wir Pflügen   162
Wolvercote   31, 170
Woodbury   130
Woodlands   230, 244
Woodworth   140
Wrestling Jacob   95

Yn Y Glyn   196
Yorkshire   85